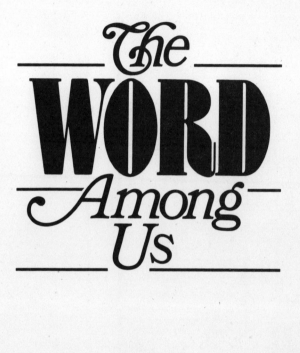

The WORD Among Us

CONTEXTUALIZING THEOLOGY FOR MISSION TODAY

Dean S. Gilliland, Editor

and the Faculty of the School of
World Mission of Fuller Theological Seminary

1989

WORD PUBLISHING

Dallas · London · Sydney · Singapore

THE WORD AMONG US

Library of Congress Cataloging-in-Publication Data

The Word among us / Dean S. Gilliland, editor.
          p.   cm.
     Bibliography: p.
     Includes index.
     ISBN 0-8499-3154-1
     1. Missions—Theory. 2. Christianity and culture. 3. Word of God
(Theology)   I. Gilliland, Dean S.
     BV2063.W59   1989
     266′.001—dc20   89-35143
                                                                      CIP

Printed in the United States of America
9 8 0 1 2 3 9 RRD 9 8 7 6 5 4 3 2 1

Contents

Foreword

"WITHOUT IT," TEVYE MUSED, "life would be as shaky as . . . as . . . as a fiddler on the roof." The *it*, for Anatevka's milkman, was tradition. For those who care about Christ's worldwide mission, the *it* is *contextualization*, a delicate enterprise if ever there was one. Like the fiddler, the evangelist and mission strategist stand on a razor's edge, aware that to fall off on either side has terrible consequences.

Fall to the right and you end in obscurantism, so attached to your conventional ways of practicing and teaching the faith that you veil its truth and power from those who are trying to see it through very different eyes. Slip to the left and you tumble into syncretism, so vulnerable to the impact of paganism in its multiplicity of forms that you compromise the uniqueness of Christ and concoct "another gospel which is not a gospel."

A delicate enterprise indeed, planting the church in unfamiliar soil. Like the fiddler's rooftop challenge, it is easier to do wrong than right. But as the fiddler knows, either because he is called or paid to, the missionary cannot be content to stand on the roof and keep her or his balance. Neither evangelists nor fiddlers are acrobats. Standing on the ridgepole, both arms extended to counter the wobbles, is not enough. There is music to be played: for the fiddler, the bittersweet bouncing rhythms of a dance in the minor key; for the evangelist, the joyful sounds of the gospel's lyrics, "Jesus saves," "Christ is Lord."

The aim of this book is to help us play Christ's music where it has not been well heard, or perhaps heard at all. This is a handbook on how to "sing the Lord's song in a strange land." It reminds us *why* we strive to clarify the message so that it will take root in new ground: the message is for all places since "the Lord God made them all." The message is for all people since God's love for all moved him to send his Son in human form to share the lot of the entire human family; the message will be heard and received differently in various parts of the world and in various eras of history since every people is shaped by a culture and will hear the Word within the customs, values, views, and language of that culture, as the Holy Spirit enables that hearing.

The *what* of contextualization comes in for attention as well. Fields like communications and Bible translation are given special scrutiny since they symbolize the bridging of cultures and underscore the complex relationships between those who send the message and those who receive it.

The *how* is represented in the sample studies of representative religions, regions, and cultures where biblical faith is gaining a foothold, as missionaries discover strategies which clear the obstacles and pave the way for solid understanding of who God is and what he has done for us in Christ. The tips and guidelines put forth here are laboratory-tested. In the past four decades, thousands of missionaries and scores of thousands of national leaders in most of the world's countries have become aware of the importance and methods of contextualization. The results of that testing, in so far as we can analyze and measure them, are recorded in this book.

Its editor and authors would never claim it to be the last word on the subject. The issues are too complex for any such cockiness, and the results are too long-term to be measured with finality this side of Christ's judgment seat. These chapters are more a start than a finish. But such a start is utterly essential if Christ's people are to make further and faster headway on the task of preaching the gospel to the ends of the earth so that the whole human family will have opportunity to hear and believe.

No word in the Christian lexicon is as fraught with difficulty, danger, and opportunity as contextualization. God's people cannot shy away from it. Even though it is problem-laden to the hilt, not to attempt it would be the faultiest strategy and worst discipleship of all. It is to sharpen our strategy and strengthen our discipleship that this book goes forth. Our prayer is that it will encourage us as Christ's heralds to become all things to all people that by all means we may win some.

David Allan Hubbard, President
Fuller Theological Seminary
Pasadena, California

Introduction

IN 1972 I WAS PRINCIPAL of the Theological College of Northern Nigeria. I had been in correspondence with Desmond Tutu, now archbishop of Capetown, about the possibility of the Theological Education Fund sponsoring one of our gifted students for study in the United States. Along with an application for scholarship he sent a modest document entitled *Ministry in Context*. The booklet set out criteria that would have to be considered before any grant would be made from the fund. The novel term caught the imagination of the faculty of our seminary in Nigeria. It seemed to challenge the much-loved word *indigenous*, which had formed mission thinking since the nineteenth century. The teaching staff at the college, as well as the students, represented a broad spectrum of African churches. As the discussion on contextualization heated up, we held faculty seminars on what it would mean for our teaching and how it could affect the life of the churches.

As useful as the principle of indigenization was, it had been locked into a segment of history that was fused with expansionism by Europe and America. Paternalism, so inevitable with colonial rule, reached into every area, including the church. In this environment the churches that were started as products of missions could develop only partially. The "overseas church" that best reproduced the "mother church" was often hailed as good mission. The "younger churches," as they were often called, had certain superficial differences with the sending church, but, in the main, they reflected the worship, thought, and polity of the missionaries who founded them. In this atmosphere of control, Christians in other cultures did not attempt much experimentation or self-analysis. The rethinking of beliefs, practices, and ethics was virtually a closed matter. Even though the gospel did not seem applicable to a host of issues and needs that touched the daily lives of people, these inadequacies were frequently overlooked. Schools and training institutions became official centers for reinforcement of the status quo. Then *Ministry in Context* and the new word *contextualization* were introduced, and mission theology has been responding to it ever since.

After fifteen years there are still questions about what contextualization is. For some, this arises from the continuing search for definition and methodology. Others wonder why "indigenous" wasn't good enough or what new elements now call for different terminology. Very early the lines were drawn on the contextualization debate. The fact that the new approach was initiated in an office related to the World Council of Churches prejudiced its acceptance by a large block of the nonconciliar churches. The heavy emphasis on justice and social development left little to be said, it seemed, for conversion and evangelism. The theology-in-context discussion followed closely the volatile 1960s which had polarized American Christianity on issues such as Vietnam and race. The early writing of James Cone (1969) added to the emotionalism that had built up around "black power." Conservatives, especially, were wary of any new theology based on social issues.

The church in Latin America had already begun to think about an appropriate theology for its own context, and the direction this theology took alarmed most evangelicals. Liberation theology was becoming known as a model that took sociopolitical issues as the "text" for theologizing. Not only were its proponents demonstrating an inadequate use of the Bible, but the methodology had a strong Marxist orientation, which was difficult for North American conservatives to accept. Before the appearance of *Ministry in Context*, Gustavo Guttiérez had already written his *Theology of Liberation* (1971) and soon afterward J. Migueuz-Bonino followed with *Doing Theology in a Revolutionary Situation* (1975). At a very early stage, both black theology and liberation theology were identified as illustrations of contextual theology. But this was only the beginning.

The decade of the 1970s brought remarkable progress in the contextualization movement. At first there was little consensus among evangelicals about the role of culture and human issues in theologizing. Yet by 1980 there was a precipitous rise in writing and discussions on both the advantages and limitations of contextualized theology. The development was not always easy to follow, because the meaning of contextualization is always open to interpretation. Naturally, scholars and missiologists introduced a lot of variety because they worked out methodologies that reflected their own assumptions as well as their respective church traditions. Many conservatives feared that the door had been opened to syncretism or that contextualization would raise cultural values to a higher level than biblical revelation. This was inevitable, perhaps, since Christian anthropologists did much of the early writing for evangelicals. Certain critics of contextualization felt that the absolute truths of the gospel were in danger of being compromised in what appeared to be a low view of revelation.

Yet the contextualization debate made serious new thinking possible, especially with regard to culture and the way in which it connects to the biblical record. As the 1970s progressed, the writing and discussion clarified directions that evangelicals should follow. A Lausanne-sponsored gathering at Willowbank (Bermuda) in 1978 took as its theme, "Gospel and Culture." The conference took seriously the role of the cultural context of the believer as well as the biblical text in defining evangelization and church development. The later 1970s also saw the rise (and demise) of the quarterly, *The Gospel in Context*. The journal's brief life demonstrated how creative and stimulating worldwide theologizing can be.

We have come a long way in a very short time. The conviction behind this volume is that contextualization, biblically based and Holy Spirit-led, is a requirement for evangelical missions today. Contextualization is incarnational. The Word which became flesh dwells among us. It clarifies for each nation or people the meaning of the confession, "Jesus is Lord." It liberates the church in every place to hear what the Spirit is saying. Contextual theology will open up the way for communication of the gospel in ways that allow the hearer to understand and accept. It gives both freedom and facility for believers to build up one another in the faith. Contextualization clarifies what the Christian witness is in sinful society and shows what obedience to the gospel requires. These are the components of a theology for mission that meets the needs of today's world.

How does the message of the gospel get into the hearts of people of all nations, and how do churches and church leaders maximize the power of the gospel touching all of life? While this is ultimately the work of the Holy Spirit, responsibility on the human side is clarified through the discipline known as *missiology*. Missiology is the multi-faceted approach to mission which embraces both theology and the behavioral sciences.

At the School of World Mission of Fuller Theological Seminary, fourteen faculty members from a variety of specializations work together with one objective: to make known the love of God in Christ Jesus and to bring the peoples of the world into discipleship under the lordship of Christ. Our commitment is to understand mission with biblical clarity, cultural sensitivity, and spiritual wholeness. The mission task is evangelization of the unreached and the development of churches that reach out again to needy people. This is also the goal of contextualization.

Thirteen of the faculty have contributed to this volume. Part One is the more theoretical section of the book, while Part Two illustrates the outworking of contextualization into a variety of areas. Part One begins with a discussion of what contextualization is and why it is the critical issue in mission today (Gilliland). The next three chapters demonstrate that contextualization is a biblical principle. In the Old Testament, God always revealed who he was in concrete ways from within the culture, utilizing human situations to make himself known (Glasser). The expansion of the gospel into the gentile world demanded new symbols for communication and careful attention to local situations while maintaining a consistent, essential gospel (Gilliland). The covenant motif encompasses all of Scripture, but contextual relevance requires that the covenant have a contemporary contextual quality as it moves through history (Van Engen). It is essential to understand that contextualization is a complex process involving the careful use of cultural forms to convey Christian meanings (Hiebert). God works at the deep levels of human receptivity, making his Word known through dynamic channels of communication (Kraft).

Part Two opens by reviewing factors of both biblical and modern contexts which impact the translation of biblical texts (Shaw). In fact, the whole area of communication and all the technical facilities available will produce results only if the whole context contributes to strategic methods (Søgaard). The discovery of leaders who are culturally authentic as well as spiritually gifted is a critical process in which the base and applicational contexts interface in determining appropriate leadership (Clinton). Approaches to development must understand the specific human situation and find solutions that are truly Christian as well as functional (Elliston). For theologizing to take place in cultural diversity, the uniqueness of people and the specialty of social groupings must be accepted and utilized (Wagner). Christian nominalism is a neglected area of mission and calls for the intense study of historical and contemporary issues that contribute to the problem (Gibbs).

The last two chapters take us into specific cultural settings. One methodology for contextualization is to highlight cultural themes or problems and deal with them in a biblical way. This is demonstrated in the Chinese setting with an ethical issue (Tan). We close our volume with the challenge of the Muslim world. When

Muslims become Christians and continue to use Muslim forms, they are, for the most part, readopting old Jewish and Christian forms of worship (Woodberry).

It is a pleasure and an honor to join our resources as a mission faculty for this momentous time in reaching out to the world for Christ and his church.

D.S.G.

PART ONE

Foundations: The Word and the World

1

Contextual Theology as Incarnational Mission

Dean S. Gilliland

WE WERE WORKING IN EVANGELISM AND MISSION ADMINISTRATION in 1968 among the Mumuye people. This is Northern Nigeria, where Islam had political control but had never won the hearts of the people. Twenty years ago changes were just beginning to come to the Mumuye. They were simple people—some would have said "primitive." Only a few were literate then, and Christianity was the new alternative to traditional ways.

Two dedicated American women set up their gospel-recording ministry about half a mile from our mission church. They had a set text which was being translated word for word in each village where they worked. After a month in one place they went on to the next. They would find a literate young person to do the transliteration into the local vernacular.

The Mumuye have no idea of punishment at death. Death is

DEAN S. GILLILAND, B.D., Th.M., Ph.D., is the editor of this volume. Professor of contextualized theology and African studies and director of crosscultural studies at Fuller Theological Seminary, he was a United Methodist missionary to Nigeria for twenty years in evangelism and pastoral training. Formerly the principal of The Theological College of Northern Nigeria, he is author of *Pauline Theology and Mission Practice* and *African Religion Meets Islam*.

passage into a different quality of life. Both the bad and the good members of the family can actually have more power after death than when they were alive. The message of the recordings carried strange information about hell. Finding no word for *hell*, the missionaries frequently referred to "the place of fire." The recordings were so novel to the ears of the Mumuye that the people began to speak of them as, "the black plates that say fire."

We are not saying that news about "the place of fire" should forever be left out of a Mumuye theology, but this initial message had no correspondence to Mumuye reality. Rather than finding a cultural theme that would also correspond to the biblical message, this piece of news only mystified the people. The theme of punishment in hell is a biblical one, but the deeper question is whether this was the place to begin. We discovered later how much better it was to use their own chief as a starting point. The traditional chief of the Mumuye is a highly symbolic and authoritative person. It is through the chief that all relationships between families are kept intact. The memorabilia of the past and all the artifacts of ancestors reside with the chief. More important for the people, it is through the chief, who is also a priest, that contact is made with the Supreme God, La. This powerful role of the chief holding together the real world and mediating on behalf of the people was the contextual case for Jesus Christ. How forcefully the plan of salvation opened up for the Mumuye people, as living themes from their own culture explained the gospel!

What is the Contextualization of Theology?

The issue at hand is the way in which the Word, as Scripture, and the Word as revealed in the truths of culture interact in determining Christian truth for a given people and place. Setting the parameters of this dialogue between the Word and the world has always been the task of theology. Theology is never a finished product, even though some traditions of theology would like to make it so. Nor are theologies completely transferrable from one time and place to another time and place. The problem of the "Word" and the "words" or the "Word and the world" is nothing new to theology.[1] The eternal universal truths are the Word, but the way in which these are understood and appropriated is the task of those who think out theologies for every time, place, and people. We are not looking at hard science after all, but we are concerned with the principles by which a church discovers its life, shares its life, and lives its life.

True theology is the attempt on the part of the church to explain and interpret the meaning of the gospel for its own life and to answer questions raised by the Christian faith, using the thought, values, and categories of truth which are authentic to that place and time.[2]

Shifts in the Theologizing Process

There is a growing emphasis on the "doing of theology" in contrast to simply learning a finished-product theology. This is in harmony with the spirit of contextualization, even though the process in classical theology may have no mission intention. A helpful example of "redoing" theology is what David Tracy calls the Revisionist Model.[3] Tracy sees this process as a much-needed correction to the basic models that would include orthodoxy, neo-orthodoxy, liberalism, and secularism. The objective of his work in revisionism is to provide a methodology for "reflection upon the meanings present in common human experience and language and upon the meanings present in the Christian fact."[4] The process calls for "symbolic reinterpretation," which means that theology must have *relevance*. This relevance is achieved by casting universal truths into a specific time and place. Revisionism advances the principle of "illumination and correction," which recognizes and uses contemporary realities. This data, in turn, determines changes in direction which the theology must take.

Tracy puts a fourth axiom in place, which he describes as "reconciliation between basic truths and existential faith." This would lead directly to the missiological objective to bring the "good news" in line with real situations in which people live. The entire approach is built around five theses, all of which are useful in the construction of contextual theologies. For example, the two sources for theology are (1) the biblical record and Christian texts and (2) common human experience and language. These sources, says Tracy, must always be under constant investigation and the results correlated in a systematic way with proposals for appropriate action.[5]

The model proposed by Tracy is philosophical and does not have a mission objective. Yet it does illustrate the significant changes taking place which point to a more flexible, more applied direction for systematic theology. Alongside this development is the growing significance of biblical theology. The Bible as source and method for theologizing is becoming much more important as Christian scholars in the Third World assume leadership. Biblical theology does not build primarily on logic but on history and the story of relationships between God and creation. "It deals with revelation as an activity or process, not primarily as a finished product." Biblical theology, as a relatively young discipline, says

Harvie Conn, "approaches the Bible not as a dogmatic handbook but as a historical book." What biblically centered theologizing means for contextualization is extremely important. It takes us away from the tendency to abstraction and theory and "underlines the dynamic character of revealed truth."[6]

The Bible is The Book with which all peoples can interact. It is a record of human experience and God's interventions. It speaks through the dynamic Spirit to the members of the body of Christ. All developing churches, including those of the Third World, can be trained to bring their own agendas to the Bible for theological reflection. And, indeed, this they must do, for many of the Third World concerns have not been dealt with in Western theological systems. "Biblical theology provides a model that, by its very nature, reminds us of the historio-contextual character of our theologizing."[7]

In a very real sense there is no theology that is not a contextual theology. The theological method takes into account the widest range of factors—religious, cultural, social, political, etc., all of which must be considered within the framework of biblical revelation. Theology clarifies what the Christian message is, in a continuing effort to understand the faith and to demonstrate obedience to Jesus Christ in all dimensions of life. We are dealing with the precious fact that transcendent reality must find expression in various human forms. This is to say, for the purpose of missions, that there must be a maximizing of the meaning of Christian truth for the particular situation in which and for which the theology is being developed.[8]

The contextualizing process requires the Spirit-led insight of the people of God and elevates the primary importance of the Word of God, rather than a "system" of theology. It requires, therefore, that the local people of faith be in a covenant relationship under the lordship of Jesus Christ. In carrying out this task they reflect upon the Word through their own thoughts and by way of their own cultural gifts in order to understand what the incarnate gospel means to them. This spiritual activity puts responsibility for thinking through Christian truth where it belongs, namely, the community of the redeemed, the body of Christ. The result is a more concrete, more fluid, perhaps even a more biblical way of interpreting the gospel than would be done by the classic philosophical process.[9]

Contextualized theology, therefore, is the dynamic reflection carried out by the particular church upon its own life in light of the Word of God and historic Christian truth. Guided by the Holy Spirit, the church continually challenges, incorporates, and transforms elements of the cultural milieu, bringing these under the lordship of Christ. As members of the body of Christ interpret the Word, using their own thoughts and employing their own cultural gifts, they are better able to understand the gospel as incarnation. [10]

CONTEXTUALIZATION IS THE APPROPRIATE
METHOD AND SPIRIT FOR MISSIONS TODAY

Our purpose is not to take the reader through the technicalities of contextualization. We have included a review of "models" as an Appendix, since they represent recent developments and show the kinds of options that are open to us. But the main reason for this chapter is to show why contextualization opens the way to evangelize every nation, as our Lord commanded, without paternalizing, dominating, or setting up foreign and dependent churches. The contextual principle begins with the moment when the first message is preached and continues through the planting, nurturing, and witness of the church. We want to consider six reasons why contextualization is the mode for the mission enterprise today and for the future.

Contextualization Guards Against the
Imperialism of Theology

Churches planted by missionary organizations can, in fact, achieve all the features of indigeneity and still never have the ownership of the members' own convictions. Once the foreign structure of the founding mission is dismantled, the church is hailed as indigenous. Usually, however, the way of thinking about the faith and the categories of Christian dogma they have learned so well remain. The churches, whether in Costa Rica or Taiwan or Uganda, not only fear but often refuse to think through the faith again for themselves. And when it occurs to a church that it should be doing this, no one knows how to go about it. Year after year goes by. The Bible is not brought to bear upon local problems, the meaning of conversion for all of life is not explored, the means for spiritual growth are not utilized nor are responsibilities taken seriously. To suggest change or discussion over issues is almost unthinkable. To do this would be to touch the status of trained leaders. Teaching institutions would be upset. An honest fear of heresy surrounds any rethinking of this kind, not because of mistrust in the Word, but because of the long arm of mission history.

In much of the mission enterprise today the foreign structures that once dominated the churches have been removed, but the substructure of absolutes, formed primarily in the West, still governs the church. The insistence on a historico-grammatical method for getting truth from the Scriptures excludes all but the few who have been trained in exegesis.[11] There is still a lot of fear in some evangelical circles that without the tools of critical exegesis the understanding of God's Word is almost impossible.

Equally strong is the fear that culture will supersede the Bible as the source for truth.[12] Yet, usually, those who say this mean their own particular interpretation of the Bible may not prevail. When the terms Bible and doctrine and theology are used somewhat interchangeably, the thought of a different theology sounds like an attempt to "change the Bible." The Bible is not a foreign book, but the imposition of a dogmatic framework for understanding the Bible is. When the Bible can only be understood once the tools of critical exegesis are in place, it becomes a closed book for most of the Christians in the world today. Or, if it can only be understood if it is explained by a foreigner or someone who has been trained in a foreign way, how can the new church claim the Book as its own? And where is our trust in the Holy Spirit to guide into all truth?

Tite Tienou, a theologian from Burkina Faso, has shown how wrong it is for those who think through the theological issues for their own people to rely on methods and sources that are foreign to the people themselves. He speaks of "mode" when he discusses how theology is carried out. The way classic evangelicalism has handled theology is in the "ideational mode." That is, certain "ideas," once in place, will lead to other ideas in logical order, etc. It is this sort of Western orderliness that the missionary feels must be passed on to others, which, if not taught, brings incredible guilt, leaving the missionary feeling that the truth has been compromised.[13] It is so deeply a part of the spiritual psyche that it is impossible to separate the way of reading and interpreting the Bible from the Bible itself. Or, as D. H. Kelsey says, "God's presence is something like understanding the basic truths about oneself and one's world. Or it is like having personally appropriated a set of concepts with such seriousness that they decisively shape one's emotions, passions, and feelings."[14]

It stands to reason that one who is proclaiming the gospel in another culture wants to hand over the experience, the full truth, without error, which has become his or her own. But it is that very spirit of domination and control which so subtly, so permanently keeps new Christians from discovering the Word of Truth in Jesus Christ for themselves in their own life and world.

Returning to Tienou, his feeling of the right for each Christian group to follow its own genius, its own gifts that God has given to build a suitable theology, is a most important issue in missiology today. In criticizing the teaching of theological topics one after the other in their philosophical order, Tienou says, "Many Third World theologians would contend that such a conception of the theological task is not only uncultural in its emphasis on logic but that it also fails to interpret the Bible properly and does not bring theology to bear on concrete life situations."[15] Rather than "ideational theology," he would prefer a "prescriptive theology," which has to do with knowing what the needs are and finding the dynamic answers in the Word of God, properly expressed, carefully applied for that particular people and place.

Jesus promised that when the Spirit comes, he will "teach you all things" (Jn. 14:26). In addition to the Bible, the truth which the Holy Spirit uses may come from a variety of sources that reveal who God is and what he is saying to his people. We can actually limit God and control other people when we say there is no truth except that which is revealed in the Bible. But even if we did confine sources of truth to the Bible alone, we then make even the discovery of biblical truth difficult, almost impossible at times. For the Bible itself was framed in history, and that special historical quality of its transmission needs to be understood and claimed by churches everywhere as God's Word for their own historical moment.[16]

To put it another way, it is in the spirit of missions today that all Christians be able to process, reflect upon, and organize biblical truth so that the Book and the truth *become their own*. This must be their right and responsibility regardless of education, class, or economic status. It was an absolute of the apostolic churches that they think for themselves and find guidance from the Spirit and the gospel they had learned.

There are, of course, principles that apply to all who are in the body, regardless of the place in time; but to deny a church the right to reflect, interpret, and apply Scripture to its own life is to withhold the essence of what it is to be "in Christ."[17] Roland Allen said boldly seventy years ago that he would rather a church falter for a time but then find itself by its own grasp of the Word, than to be propped up by an artificial system of doctrine and rules that were passed along without regard for the fact that each church must make the Word its own.[18]

Contextualization Provides for Training in the Holy Spirit

All that has just been said leads to the point that when members of the body of Christ know they have the Spirit of Christ and the "mind of Christ," they can, from the beginning, know for themselves what their belief and action ought to be. The attitude that underlies contextualization is that the grace of God in Christ meets people where they are. The fears of their own world, the limitations of their own history, the failures of their own ideas of salvation—all are subject to transformational grace. But the people themselves must exercise reliance and trust on the Holy Spirit of God to reveal to them, not to someone else, the magnitude of their problems and what the solutions are. One of the ironies of mission history is that missionaries who profess to know the most about the Holy Spirit find it very difficult to foster an environment in crosscultural situations where inexperienced Christians can really discover the Holy Spirit for themselves.

It was normative to the apostolic believers that they give themselves to the Holy Spirit for enlightenment on a host of issues. They were expected to think through their faith for themselves (Eph. 4:14; 1 Cor. 14:20; Eph. 1:17–18; 1 Cor. 2:12). It would have been impossible for the Jerusalem elders to control the gentile churches the way Western missionaries control the life of mission-planted churches today. It is with the best of intentions that the knowledgeable, usually expatriate, Christians take responsibility for the growth of the whole community. And it is this every-member approach to theologizing that is so hard to accept. It is, in effect, the members of the body asking of each other, "What has the Spirit been telling you about your new Lord and your new life?" The written text of the Bible is the supreme source of truth. Yet the Holy Spirit is an active guide in the life of every believer, and we must trust him to speak directly to the regenerated human spirit. At Pentecost God's own Spirit, nothing less, was given.[19] And it is a dependency on this totally adequate Spirit in the life of the believer that contextualization calls for.[20]

In case after case it can be shown that an "indigenous church" by the old definition will have met the criteria of what was thought to be an authentic church but still not discover the Spirit's presence in power and knowledge for itself. We have spoken of the centrality of the Bible in contextualization. It is in the comprehension of the Word by the believers that the Holy Spirit becomes a dynamic presence in the church. But comprehension of God's truth is more than mastering the techniques of biblical study. René Padilla says, "It is, rather, a wholehearted commitment to the God of truth who reveals himself through the written word and the Spirit of the living God." It follows, therefore, says Padilla, "that no true evangelical theology is possible apart from the illumination and guidance of the Holy Spirit. . . . Doing theology is not merely a scholarly but also a charismatic task."[21]

To accomplish this the church that is born in the Spirit must be nurtured by the Spirit. The Holy Spirit is the agent who brings God's truth into the minds and hearts of people. It is the Holy Spirit that enlightens the mind to comprehend and appropriate truth. If it were not for his Spirit, we would not even know that we are God's children (Rom. 8:16). Contextualization, carefully implemented, honors the Holy Spirit and opens the way for believers to confront with confidence the questions raised in their own life situations.

Contextualization Cultivates a Mission-Conscious Church

Certainly, one of the most exciting movements in mission today is the way the churches of the Third World are taking up the task of evangelization. It is not possible at this point to show how massive is the missionary force originating from many of the Asian countries, for example. Many churches in Africa are not only effectively evangelizing nearby people groups, but they have taken seriously the task of crosscultural mission work and are actively providing the training for it.[22] When we say that contextualization is mission centered, we are speaking of the incarnational aspect of the gospel, which means *the good news is for every person and must be communicated with that very person in mind.*

In reviewing the liberal models of contextualization it is clear that liberation theology, even in its more conservative forms, does not promote the spirit of evangelizing the peoples of the world. The preoccupation of liberation theology is an existential one. The text is the human predicament with the burden for salvation left in the vehicles of government and social systems. Conversion is not a change that reorients the sinful, disoriented person, but is rather a reconstruction of the environment in which people live. As good as this is, it does not motivate the church to mission because of the nature of the message. Again, there are models of contextualization of the more eclectic kind, where Christianity must take its place alongside or within another structure, such as Hinduism. It is very important, of course, that Indian Christians be involved in the dialogue between Hinduism and Christianity, for example, for in Hinduism religion and culture cannot be separated. But a philosophical synthesizing of Christianity with Hinduism, while this may be one form of contextualization, will not result in any kind of missionary spirit. The contextualization represented by this book is mission centered and will produce Christians and churches that are committed to world evangelization.

When there is total commitment to the Word of God by any church, the assumption from the beginning is that the Word is for the whole world and that people must respond, each and every group in its own context. A conference in Seoul in 1982 chose for its theme, "Theology and the Bible in Context." After expressing the fact that the Word of God is from one point of view relevant in every situation, addressed as it is to sinful persons in every culture, still

> From another point of view, the proclamation is faithful to the Word of God to the extent that it confronts men and women with God's word of judgment and grace in the concreteness of their daily lives, according to the pattern set by the incarnation. Faithfulness to the Gospel demands contextualization.[23]

The purpose of this volume is to show that contextualization, properly conceived, is absolutely basic to mission in these times. To insist on this pattern is to return to the apostolic character of the church, to become servants of Jesus Christ in taking the gospel to the ends of the earth. Some may argue that the localization of the gospel, which is inevitable in contextualization, would inhibit mission because it is predisposed to "bounded set" interests.[24] The fear would be that the local group or church would not open up, therefore, to those who are outside the home culture. But what happens is a biblical principle, "all things to all people . . . that I might win" (1 Cor. 9:19–22). A church that is contextualizing for its own life must, at the same time, rethink what it has discovered for itself so that a neighboring culture or language group will also be able to hear and respond.

The problem with the older idea of the indigenous church was that it rarely became a self-propagating church in the New Testament sense. Or it might be better to say that it was limited to mission as self-propagation and little more. That is, it could only reproduce its own life and forms in the midst of another people, and usually these were what it had already learned from Europeans and Americans. Contextualization as a motive for mission is concerned not so much with the teaching of forms or organization. Rather than self-extension as its motivation it is Word-extension—a sensitivity to the culture and needs of others so that the Word can have a lively beginning in hearts. Thankfully, some of the Third World mission organizations are already working on this.

Contextualization Fosters the Growth and Multiplication of Churches

Modern churches, in contrast, for example, to medieval state churches, are voluntary organizations. Worldwide trends toward freedom of religion are providing more citizens more freedom of choice. On the one hand, large numbers of people can choose whether to be Christian or not, and on the other hand those who do become Christian may then find that they have several options for local church membership. While most believers will never even hear, much less understand, the word "contextualization," they nevertheless intuitively find themselves attracted to adequately contextualized churches.

Undoubtedly, the most widely known church-growth principle articulated by Donald A. McGavran, father of the church growth movement, is the "homogeneous unit principle." McGavran says, "people like to become Christians without crossing racial, linguistic or class barriers."[25] The homogeneous unit principle is one of the flip sides of contextualizaion. Churches that are not contextualized seem strange to the unbelievers of that society. The gospel is rejected, not because of the scandal of the cross, but because joining it would appear as a culturally traitorous act. As McGavran has frequently said, the greatest barriers to conversion are social, not theological.[26]

Resistance-receptivity theory highlights the fact that in certain places at certain times one people group might be resistant to converting to Christianity while another might be receptive to the gospel. Biblically speaking, some harvests are ripe and some are not yet ripe. Nevertheless, research has shown that in some notable cases the apparent resistance has been caused not so much by intrinsic factors as by ineptitude in the communication of the gospel. The gospel, as presented to a given cultural community, has been so overloaded with irrelevant cultural baggage on the part of the missionaries or evangelists that it was simply not being heard by the target audience. Had the presentation of the gospel been properly contextualized, in many cases resistance would have evaporated like early morning mist.

The "people approach" to world evangelization advocated by the Lausanne Committee (and many others who are thinking in terms of effective missiological strategies) is highly dependent on contextualization. It recognizes that, if people are to be won to Christ in any considerable numbers, they must be approached with the gospel on their own terms. Forces for evangelism must be appropriate to the receptor culture as must methodologies, the focus of the message, church polities, leadership selection and training, disciplinary procedures, and worship styles. Recognizing this produces a certain enviable, ecclesiastical humility. If my church does something differently from yours, this does not necessarily mean that I am right and you are wrong. We both may well be right and equally pleasing to God.

This is especially important for the evangelization of new generations in societies open to rapid cultural change. The culture of a new generation may demand its own application of contextualization.

This was dramatized in the rise of the hippie movement in the United States during the 1960s. The hippie counterculture had alienated its followers so decisively from the traditional culture of their parents that it became virtually impossible for hippies to be won to Christ in the traditional churches. Not only didn't they like the churches, but the people in the churches didn't like the hippies. Humanly speaking, the entire hippie generation would have been lost, had not a number of intuitive contextualizers such as Chuck Smith emerged. Smith's Calvary Chapel met in a tent. The congregation sat on the floor dressed in beads and Roman sandals. Hundreds were baptized in the Pacific Ocean, and the Jesus Movement swept through the hippie culture. Currently the baby boomer generation is being effectively reached by newer movements such as John Wimber's Vineyard Christian Fellowship, characterized among other things by a new hymnology, skillfully contextualized for the new generation.

C. Peter Wagner in his chapter in this book highlights another important need for contextualization in the multiplication of churches. In a multi-ethnic society, characteristic of many modern nations, the spread of the gospel through the various subgroups by E-2 and E-3 evangelism* requires competent contextualization for optimum effectiveness.

Contextualization Promotes a Multidimensional Gospel for Multidimensional Needs

Contextualization, in contrast to indigenization, turns the attention of the members of the body of Christ to wider dimensions of their life. Almost wistfully, Christians in many of the churches started by missionary organizations have wondered why the whole of their lives has not been touched by the gospel. Power encounter, dynamic ethical behavior, human need touching the deepest levels, political involvement, ways to effect change in society, marriage and the family,

---

*E-2 and E-3 are symbols that designate evangelism to culturally similar groups and those more culturally distant.

economics and social structures—all these have literally begged for attention. But the long shadow of mission history, which did not allow for much thought or inquiry about these things, still hangs heavy over the churches. Salvation had come as primarily a balm for the soul. Bringing the gospel into the crucible of life with freedom and trust in the Spirit of Christ is an absolute for missions today.

The New Testament metaphor, "new creation," as Paul used it (*kaine ktisis*, Gal. 6:15, 2 Cor. 5:17) is what we hold out to men and women of all cultures and faiths. It is the best way to describe what happens in conversion. It is a radical, beautiful expression because it touches every part of the being of the person.

The word "creation" itself leads us back to that greatest first event when God made man and woman. It was a whole and entire being that God made. Nothing less than the remaking of the entire person is what salvation in Christ provides. The re-creation of persons on this order touches the ethical, the moral, the aesthetic, the physical, and the social. These redeemed people are in a real world; they have bodies that need to be healed, minds that must be taught, spirits that long for encouragement; they have worries about families and security. This complete being lives in a complex world, each part of which is destined to be touched by the recreating gospel. And the good news is that we have a Bible that has touched people in every known human situation.

The Lausanne Covenant did speak of evangelism as "primary" for obedience in mission. But the call was to apply the gospel in such a way that all aspects of life become reconciled. The language of the Covenant left no mistake about the wider meaning of the gospel.

> The message of salvation implies also a message of judgment upon every form of alienation, oppression and discrimination and we should not be afraid to denounce evil and injustice wherever they exist.[27]

Jesus' language at Nazareth at the commencement of his own ministry has been taken too long as spiritual metaphors. He said plainly, "'The Spirit of the Lord . . . has anointed me to preach good news to the poor, He has sent me to proclaim release to the captives and recovering of sight to the blind, to set at liberty those who are oppressed'" (Lk. 4:18). Jesus' own ministry corresponds in deed to what the psalmist declared concerning God, that along with other graces he "lifts up those who are bowed down . . . watches over the sojourners, he upholds the widow and the fatherless" (Ps. 146:8–9).

Wholeness characterized the ministry of Paul. Perhaps no word describes his theology better than the term *reconciliation*.[28] This

Pauline expression has as its germinal meaning that things are "put back into their original order." Reconciliation brings us back again to that which God intended for his creation before the fall. Paul saw the unity of "body, soul and spirit" (1 Thess. 5:23). It is into this physical, intellectual, and social makeup of the person and of the community that the power of the gospel comes. There is no turning to Christ except in the Spirit of Christ. When the Spirit of Christ is within a person the singular fruit from which all others derive is love (Gal. 5:22). Love given by the Spirit makes the conscience tender and calls Christians to see the breadth of human need leading to compassionate response to meet these needs, whatever they may be.

Harvie Conn is always the critic as well as the prophet. In his early writing on contextualization he prodded the conscience of those who fail to see that the gospel must reach into every part of life. Early in the debate Conn called for more openness on the part of evangelicals to embrace responsibility for the world as well as for people who need to be redeemed. He agreed that liberation theology can be criticized for positing the human situation as the "text" from which truth derives. But, he said, it is error on the other side when "the evangelical practice of hermeneutics remains simply one of the confrontation of the 'ancient texts' rather than also one of confrontation with the present historical reality."[29] This reality demands that the gospel be one of real issues and real needs. The deeper issue of contextualization asks, "how shall the people of God as member(s) of the Body of Christ and the fellowship of the Spirit respond meaningfully and with integrity to the Scripture, so that they may live a full-orbed kingdom lifestyle in covenant obedience with the covenant community?"[30]

"Listening to a culture," as Robert Schreiter puts it, is to be aware of the multi-faceted, changing realities that continually form the lives of people. The religious factor is only a part. Cultures are also societal, economic, political, and historical entities with each forming a critical part of what is to be "heard" in the culture. Another very special part of this sensitivity to the multi-dimensional context is to be "tuned into" change. What areas have assumed importance in the lives of the people that perhaps were not important before; what new circumstances and different concerns have evidenced themselves among the people that will lead us to the point of current need?[31] For the Word to truly become flesh for each people and place, the circumstances of the whole of life will be met as completely as when Jesus touched people in his own life and day.

Contextualization Opens the Way for
Incarnational Witness

Properly taught and modeled, contextualization takes us to the center of what God did in Christ. Reverently, we can speak of the humanization of the Son of God, the coming of God into the living context of people, himself a person. The very mind of Christ Jesus motivates and illumines what we are expected to do in mission. He "emptied himself, taking the form of a servant, being born in the likeness of men. And being found in human form he humbled himself and became obedient unto death, even death on a cross" (Phil. 2:7–8). Evangelization of the world's peoples is no longer a burden borne only by the West. As we move into the next century, it will increasingly be the new churches of the Third World that will be taking a strong initiative. These churches are Chinese, Korean, African, Philippine, Brazilian, and others who have already begun the task of training and have already placed missionary personnel in a variety of fields.[32] The traditional missionary from the West will have to fit into these new teams and be more of a motivator and trainer than ever before.

Contextualization is a principle that must be given to these young churches as they plan their missionary strategies. It is quite possible for missionaries of the so-called Third World to witness crossculturally but be as monocultural as were the missionaries who came to them in the first place. Coming from their own cultures, they can be just as unable and unwilling to seek truth in the new context or to give the freedom to believers to do so. Generally, the leaders of churches that have grown out of Western mission history understand what has hindered them from knowing this incarnational experience of Jesus Christ. At this unusual and promising moment in world evangelization there are, in summary, five reasons why contextualization is incarnational. When carried out in faithfulness to the Word and in the discipline of the Holy Spirit, it is the appropriate way to train for and "do" missions today.

Contextual Incarnation Means That the Message Will Make Sense for Each Place and People

Again, John's testimony is that "the Word . . . dwelt among *us*" (Jn. 1:14).

But this is not a generic kind of reference. The *us* refers not only to "his own," the Jews, but to each and every people, as the explicit universality of the Gospel of John declares. The context of those with whom the Word dwells is best understood through the *panta ta ethne* of Matthew 28:19. Absolute, unquestioned disclosure of God himself is what incarnation really is. The fundamental elements of the gospel, the essential biblical truths that lead to salvation by faith in Jesus Christ, must be communicated faithfully to a particular people through the means available within that culture. The message must be as clear as the human instrument is capable of making it. The important point of first-contact communication is that if the message and meaning are not a critically contextualized message, all that follows will be a distortion.[33] The consequent church will have to depend upon the outsider for its interpretation, and rather than transforming the culture from its own center it will become an exotic imitation of a church somewhere else in the world.

God demonstrates over and over through Scripture that he is concerned with specific people and is a communicator of specific messages. When we say that God is "receptor oriented," we mean that those who are meant to receive the message will determine the form which the message takes. The Incarnation is the ultimate expression of God's receptor-oriented communication. Kraft notes that God "interacts with specific people in the ways most appropriate to them concerning those topics he knows they most need. And he does it from within their life situation, from within their own context."[34] Contextualization as a discipline given to the church calls for the same sensitivity to clear communication in the human realm as God has modeled for us in his realm. We are not God; that is a given. But we are "his ambassadors," and the message of the King must be proclaimed with all the preciseness that is possible for his human messengers to bring to it.

Contextual Incarnation Elevates the Self-Perception and Self-Worth of a People

Regardless of what the particular ethnic group may be—whether an entire homogeneous nation, such as South Korea, or an extended family, such as those in Africa—cultural identity means much to people. The institutions of belonging to the group provide security and are a source of pride. The benevolent, unconscious imperialism of an earlier missionary style no longer fits today's mission. There is much of great value in the culture that receives the missionary. This must be affirmed for its own sake. But beyond this, these values and cultural themes can actually become the conduits for transmission of the good news of Jesus Christ.

Contextualization focuses on categories of truth that can be "read" from the culture and which correspond to biblical revelation. It is the essence of incarnation that the truth of God in Christ be understood by a people through the vehicle of indigenous culture. The one who witnesses, therefore, is to be a learner, a respectful inquirer of the culture. This is not something that can be done in a mechanical way. It is an attitude, an actual mode of living and interacting. Culture learning and the affirmation of people seeking to express Christ lift up their dignity and promotes a will to believe. To urge indigenous leaders, together with members of the body, to look deeply into their own world-view and traditions for communication, worship, and witness honors both God and his people. This is the attitude that must characterize mission in our day.

Contextual Incarnation Utilizes Cultural Elements That Are Consistent with the Gospel

No culture is completely good or completely bad. Most of the aspects of a culture will fit into the more neutral category. The question is how well the church exercises discernment as the members work to contextualize their practices.

For example, the primary religion of the Corinthians promoted outright immorality, and much about the Corinthian lifestyle could never be brought into the church. Yet Corinth becomes the one place where worship is dynamic, and the innovations introduced do reflect the culture and temperament of the Corinthians. The intenseness of their Christian life, bordering on the unacceptable, was the occasion for some of Paul's best teaching. Don Richardson found that his "redemptive analogy" for telling the Jesus story was already in the Sawi myth. What would appear on the surface of culture as contradictory to the gospel actually became the vehicle of truth.[35]

It takes careful study of the Word and discipline in the Spirit to know what features of the culture can be used to communicate the message and enhance the meaning of worship. Contextual theology must be thought through with these cultural values central; but certain categories of the culture will always have to be rejected.

Contextualization has the assignment to know what can be used, what will have to be rejected, and what, by God's grace, can be transformed. Paul Hiebert's chapter helps us with the problem of form and meaning in contextualization. The term "critical contextualization" calls for a careful analysis of the old beliefs and practices with the Bible close by. If this is not done, one of two consequences will result. There will be either a rigid rejection of the old beliefs, which introduces foreignness and a "double standard" in the church. Or the result will be an uncritical acceptance of traditional beliefs and practices, which usually leads to syncretism.[36] The incarnational approach to contextualization affirms the beliefs, customs, and cultural life of the people, but it demands judgment and discernment as well. Where this is being carefully carried out by the church, not only will the church itself be strengthened in the faith, but the worship and witness of the church will truly belong to the fellowship in that particular place.

Contextual Incarnation Calls for a Participatory Model of Seeking for Truth

The "experts" are those who have been trained in theology and who represent the historical churches. But the academic status given theology and the irrelevant way in which professionals carry out the theological task has had plenty of attention in the contextualization debate. The Word must "dwell among us," if it is to be incarnational. Reflection on truth is not an exercise of the trained elite alone. Rather, we use a term such as "communal hermeneutics," because "the Christian community is where the Word of God finds its home and releases its transforming power."[37] The Bible was not written for academic theological argument. Even in its most ostensible theological sections, the purpose is teaching and enablement to ministry.

Therefore, the responsibility of thinking through problems of the Christian life is one in which the trained "expert" and the local ordinary Christians are joined. The body as a whole will raise the questions because they have lived and struggled each day.[38] They will know, with the Word and the Spirit as guides, which solutions are commensurate with their own experience. The trained theologian must have sensitivity to the context, "an extraordinary capacity to listen, and an immersion in the Scriptures."[39] This will qualify him or her to join in the process of theologizing and bring the gift of historic doctrinal truth. The implication of this mutuality is the ground on which particular culture churches can know themselves, the Word, and the universal church. All of these are absolutes to the healthy, authentic church in each place. This kind of relationship over months, even years, is the environment in which contextualization can best take place. Contextual incarnation will then provide a consensus for what is required for personal and social obedience to the gospel.

Contextual Incarnation Touches All of Life

Contextualization must be understood as a principle that will characterize mission along the whole theological continuum. The first messages, the early and later discipling, the formation of the church for witness, including ethical concerns and social action—all this comes under the discipline of contextualization.

For example, the context must be taken seriously in Bible translation. The chapter by Daniel Shaw will illustrate this in a concrete way. Bible translations have everything to do with communicating the first message of the gospel in contextually appropriate ways. But the Bible is also normative for the nurture and growth of the church. Richardson's "redemptive analogies" demonstrated how forceful the myths and symbols of the culture are in bringing about conversion. What follows saving faith is that redeemed people must find ways for the gospel to become incarnational in their daily lives. The problems raised subsequent to the "turning away from old gods" (1 Thess. 1:9) must be confronted and also answered from within. It is not enough to have a relevant message leading to salvation if afterwards the Holy Spirit and the Word do not become the ground of all spiritual formation. It is equally important to face the sins of the culture and the society in which the church has been planted.

It is possible to err on either side of the continuum. The initial message may be contextualized, but the church will not develop in a theologically autonomous way, taking little responsibility to think through its own life. Or, there may be a commendable pursuit of the witness and service dimension, with a commitment to changing society and meeting human needs; but little point is made of the need for personal salvation.

For example, the resistance to contextualization by evangelicals in the early years was due in part to expressions of theology that were almost exclusively concerned with ethics and social action. We have already said that this was a major reason why the older term *indigenous* was preferred by many conservatives. The problem with the evangelical alternative was that contextual theology was aimed almost exclusively to the communication of a clear and believable gospel with conversion as the objective. Beyond this there was little attention to authentic worship or the use of indigenous forms or compatible institutions of culture in the formation of the church. The role of the church to meet human needs and to stand for truth and justice or to work for changes in society was not considered a function of contextual theology.

Contextual theology with a mission objective works for balance and integration of what could be called three dimensions of contextualization: the *evangelistic* dimension, the *nurture* dimension, and the *witness/service* dimension. Designating terms and categories of this kind is always subject to discussion, but they are given with the intention of promoting balance and wholeness to the mission witness. Each dimension interfaces with the other. It is not a case of moving from one to the other in the sense of leaving the first to begin to do the second. Yet there is something of a sequence while progress along the line to long-range contextualization also returns to inform and enrich the early stages.

Spiritual formation can only take place once the groundwork is laid in believing faith; and it is in the pursuit of witness, resulting from Christian growth, that acts of mercy and deeds of righteousness result. It could be said, therefore, that the evangelistic dimension is the *immediate range* of contextualization, the nurture dimension is the *middle range*, and the service dimension is the *long range*. The three dimensions can be illustrated as follows:

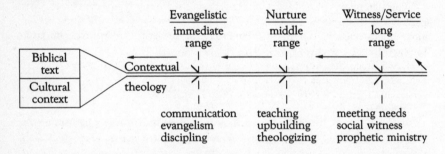

As we move through this volume, each of these areas will be dealt with. As already mentioned, there is no clear demarcation between the dimensions of contextualization. Cultural factors are as important in the nurturing of the mission church as they are in primary evangelism. It is as essential to develop leaders who are as aware of the social issues of the gospel as they are of administration and teaching. Institutions of culture and world-view insights are as important in worship as in preaching and development. Contextualization is, ultimately, a matter of attitude, translated into ministry. It calls for a humility about one's own background, a high view of people created in God's image as well as faith in the power of God to lead those who seek him. The guiding principle is to strive always for what is incarnational. The Word that is beyond culture must be expressed from within culture. Contextualization utilizes cultural factors that are compatible with the Word; it transforms what can be changed under the authority of the Word, and it confronts, even rejects, what is antithetical to the Word.

No human situation is worse or more virtuous than another as it stands before the saving power of the Word of God. Biblical studies which follow in the next three chapters will demonstrate how God always works within the limits of humankind. He must reveal himself in the particular place and in the midst of particular people. When the incarnational attitude governs all that we think and do, God is honored, and the Holy Spirit guides into all truth.

NOTES

[1] A major contribution of Karl Barth was his commitment to hear the Word within the words of the Bible. This "dialectical method," Word and world, is summed up in Barth's statement, "God is in heaven, and thou art on the earth. The relation between such a God and such a man, and the relation between such a man and such a God is for me the theme of the Bible." Barth, *The Epistle to the Romans*, trans. E. C. Hoskyns, 6th edition (London: Oxford University Press, 1933), 10.

[2] This definition opens the way for theology to serve and equip the church. The insistence that theology is a "science," using logic and reason as method, is not applicable to most of the world, and limits contextualization. Cf. Strong, *Systematic Theology* (London: Pickering and Inglis, 1965), 1–2.

[3] David Tracy, *Blessed Rage for Order* (New York: Seabury, 1979), 32ff.

[4] Ibid., 43. Tracy sees his work not as a new theology but as an articulation of criteria and method for the fundamental theological task.

[5] Ibid., 33–56.

[6] Harvie Conn, *Eternal Word and Changing Worlds* (Grand Rapids: Zondervan, 1984), 225. The book provides a much needed reevaluation of Western models of theology, especially in the world of new churches growing among the diversity of the world's people.

[7] Ibid.

[8] Schreiter's term is, "listening to a culture." His observation is that even those who are indigenous to the culture through education and influences from mission history are not dealing with the real issues. There must be careful investigation of the "sign systems" of a culture if the resultant theology is to be "imbedded in culture and take on cultural forms." Robert Schreiter, *Constructing Local Theologies* (Maryknoll: Orbis, 1985), 39–75.

[9] Supportive literature is abundant. See e.g., Charles Kraft, *Christianity in Culture* (Maryknoll N.Y.: Orbis, 1979); Conn., *Eternal Word*, esp. chapter 6; and Charles Taber, "Is There More Than One Way to Do Theology?" *Gospel in Context*, 1978, 1, no. 1 (January), 241–44.

[10] The definition emphasizes the following principles: communal hermeneutics, continuing process, transformational objective spiritual discipline, cultural relevance.

[11] See, for example, Charles Taber, "Is There More Than One Way?" 4–10.

[12] Some early critiques of contextualizaton reveal a negativism about the function of culture in the theologizing process. E.g., B. H. Kato, "The Gospel, Cultural

Context and Religious Syncretism" and B. I. Nicholls, "Theological Education and Evangelization," in *Let the Earth Hear His Voice*, ed., J. D. Douglas (Minneapolis: Worldwide Publ., 1975).

[13] Tite Tienou, "Biblical Foundations: An African Study." *Evangelical Review of Theology*, 1983, 7, no. 1 (April), 87-100.

[14] D. H. Kelsey, *The Use of Scripture in Recent Theology* (Philadelphia: Fortress, 1975), 161.

[15] Tienou, "Biblical Foundations," 91.

[16] Conn, *Eternal Word*, 220.

[17] See discussion in D. S. Gilliland, *Pauline Theology and Mission Practice* (Grand Rapids: Baker, 1983), 146-150. Also a helpful treatment by Eric Wahlstrom, *The New Life in Christ* (Philadelphia: Muhlenberg, 1940), 152: "[The Christian] can decide for himself what his course of action should be. He is 'Christ autonomous' (or) 'in Christ.'"

[18] Roland Allen, *Missionary Methods, St. Paul's or Ours?* (Grand Rapids: Eerdmans, 1972; orig. 1912).

[19] Harry Boer's book, *Pentecost and Missions* (Grand Rapids: Eerdmans, 1961), is a rich resource for the role of the Holy Spirit in the nurturing of the young church. "If we are eager to see [new Christians] gather knowledge in the Spirit, we should also be eager to see them express that knowledge they have gathered," 222.

[20] Gilliland, *Pauline Theology*, 129.

[21] C. Rene Padilla, "Biblical Foundations: A Latin American Study," *Evangelical Review of Theology*, 1983, 7, no. 1 (April), 83.

[22] Mention, for example, is made of the Nigeria Evangelical Missions Association, which is interdenominational and has a permanent organization and curriculum for training Africans in crosscultural mission work.

[23] Padilla, "Biblical Foundations," 87.

[24] A term used by Paul Hiebert to denote the ethnocentric or otherwise circumscribed experience of faith and the Christian life. See his "Conversion, Culture and Cognative Categories" in *Gospel in Context*, 1978, 1, no. 3 (July), 23-29.

[25] Donald A. McGavran, *Understanding Church Growth*, rev. ed. (Grand Rapids: Eerdmans, 1970), 223.

[26] Ibid., 215-216.

[27] *Let the Earth Hear His Voice*, 5.

[28] Ralph P. Martin, *Reconciliation, A Study of Paul's Theology* (Atlanta: John Knox, 1981).

[29] Harvie M. Conn, "Contextualization: Where Do We Begin?" *Evangelicals and Liberation* (Nutley, N.J.: Presbyterian and Reformed, 1977), 103.

[30] Ibid., 104.

[31] Schreiter, *Constructing*, 43-46.

[32] Lawrence E. Keyes, *The Heritage of Missions, A Study of Third World Missionary Societies* (Pasadena: William Carey Library, 1983).

[33] The book which deals with this and other communicational principles is Charles H. Kraft, *Communication Theory for Christian Witness* (Nashville: Abingdon, 1983).

[34] See Charles Kraft's chapter in this volume, *Contextualizing Communication*, p. 121.

[35] Don Richardson, *Peach Child* (Glendale: Regal, 1974).

[36] Paul Hiebert, "Critical Contextualization," *International Bulletin of Missionary Research*, II, no. 3 (July 1987).

[37] Padilla, "Biblical Foundations," 81.

[38] Illustrations of communal theological work, with practical results, are available from Solomon Islands, The Association, P. O. Box 556, Honiara, Solomon Islands, e.g., *Melanesian Culture and Christian Faith*, prepared by Cliff Wright.

[39] Schreiter, *Constructing*, 17.

2

Old Testament Contextualization: Revelation and Its Environment

Arthur F. Glasser

DR. SHOKI COE, A TAIWANESE THEOLOGIAN and pioneer in the development of WCC-related theological education in East Asia, and Dr. Nikos A. Nissiotis of the Greek Orthodox Church are regarded as having interjected the words *contextuality* and *contextualization* into the contemporary missiological debate. Their concern was to develop an existential approach to the task of theological reflection that would shift the focal point more directly to the contemporary context and away from what they regarded as a rigid, almost verbal loyalty to traditional and confessional statements constructed from the Bible.

They were reacting against those who regarded the redemptive gospel as so precisely defined in Scripture that harsh limits were automatically placed on any contextualization process. They argued for the need to explore the legitimate demands the gospel makes

ARTHUR F. GLASSER, C.E., B.D., S.T.M., D.D., D.Th. (candidate), dean emeritus and senior professor of theology and East Asian studies at Fuller Theological Seminary, was a missionary in Southwest China from 1946–51. He was director for CIM/OMF for fourteen years. Glasser taught at Columbia Bible College before coming to Fuller in 1976. Editor of *Missiology* from 1976–82, he is the author of *Missions in Crisis* and coauthor, with Donald McGavran, of *Contemporary Theologies of Mission*.

within any specific cultural situation by virtue of its inherent nature as wholistic—the incarnational Word of God—embracing as it does the existential totality of human need.

The call to make this shift was articulated as a change in emphasis from "indigenization" to "contextualization." The former tended in their view to be "past-oriented" because of its stress on relating the gospel to traditional cultures, which had long been erroneously regarded as rigid and static. To speak of the contextualization of the gospel seemed more appropriate since it recognized and responded to the concrete and historical situations of our day, or what they called taking into account "the process of secularity, technology, and the struggle for human justice which characterized the historical moment of nations in the Third World."[1]

Initially, when these neologisms were first popularized, many reacted quite favorably. The challenge had relevance although some expressed concern lest fascination with the newness of these terms and a preoccupation with their implications might result in an overemphasis on the context at the expense of the text itself.[2] In the years since, there has been such a broad and somewhat careless use of the term *contextualization* that it is not at all evident that missiologists today are agreed as to the precise nature of this shift from *indigenize!* to *contextualize!*[3]

Even so, many missiologists are eager to popularize the term and explore every conceivable way in which the gospel should be related to the material-spiritual world of human experience. The concern today is to go beyond the earlier vision of seeking to make sure that the gospel in every place is clothed with appropriate linguistic and cultural frames of reference. This is now judged as somewhat superficial. Whereas this urgency remains, the additional task is to ascertain the existential implications of the gospel in any given context. What is important is that the realities of dominant social concerns and ongoing cultural changes are not overlooked, and that the gospel remains free to speak prophetically to a culture from within it. *The stress today is on communication through incarnation.*

It is this pattern that we find in the Old Testament, for it is replete with evidence that God continually used a contextualizing process in his progressive self-disclosure of himself to his people. At the same time, the Old Testament calls particular attention to the abiding validity of those non-negotiables that constitute normative truths for all peoples in all situations. It warns against being so preoccupied with the changing political and social context that these abiding truths are regarded as of only secondary importance.

REVELATION AS PROCESS

The Old Testament nowhere supports the thesis that its writers "by the exercise of their minds, wrested the secrets of life and the universe from a reluctant God."[4] In contrast, the frequency with which they referred to God having laid hold of them and spoken through them leads one to assume that an essential and organic unity pervades the whole sequence, from Genesis to Malachi. Indeed, no part of this rich literature bears the impress of a writer who differed irreconcilably from the rest. Not that a flat uniformity or static unity characterizes its thirty-nine separate books. The Old Testament is complex in development and rare in repetitive material. Alan Richardson in his helpful book, *The Bible in the Age of Science* (1961), regards as "powerful and impressive" the fact that there exists "no parallel in any other language to this strange phenomenon: the whole literature of a nation for over a thousand years bearing the imprint of 'One Infallible Intelligence' slowly working out the rich organic harmony of a single developing theme."[5]

Revelation and History

One of the unique characteristics of God's disclosure of himself in the Old Testament is the unique relation between this revelation and human history. Even revelation itself has a history, for history means movement, and revelation in history must be regarded as something linear, moving toward a consummation worthy of the God of history. Hence, the Old Testament is not a collection of ethical generalizations, theological affirmations, orderly analyses of doctrines, or formal prescriptions of personal duty—all detached from the dimensions of time, culture, and situation. Its great truths are enfleshed in historical events, human experience, and prophetic exposition. Contextualization indeed!

All the writers of the Old Testament were culturally conditioned. They wrote in Hebrew and Aramaic. Although on the human level they were limited in knowledge, experience, and vocabulary, on the divine level we believe that what they wrote within this canon came not by "the impulse of man, but men moved by the Holy Spirit spoke from God" (2 Pet. 1:21 NIV). Through them "the Word of God written" came to Israel.

On the human level, they reflected the "way of life" and "total plan for living" that their particular grouping of people had developed over the years and functionally organized into a coherent whole. This had been acquired through learning (enculturation) and had the social group, rather than the individual, as its focus. Our perspective, then, is that God has not been indifferent to the issue of culture. The particular epochs in "salvation history" took place in a variety of ancient cultures. His people knew themselves as nomads (the patriarchs), slaves (the Egyptian oppression), desert wanderers (the wilderness years), a loose tribal federation (under the judges), citizens (the various monarchies), exiles (in Babylon), and finally as a minority people, ruled by a succession of gentile powers.

On the divine level, this changing historical and cultural sequence became the context in which God disclosed himself to them. The Old Testament contains the record of his "mighty acts" over more than a thousand years of history coupled with specific revelations of their meaning. All this took place in the same ancient world in which the gods of the peoples round about were likewise allegedly at work on behalf of their devotees. But here the similarity ends, because God's mighty acts consistently reflected his character—his holiness and his grace—and they were always positive, redemptive, and powerful. He never followed the pagan gods in accommodating himself to the politically powerful among their devotees, nor to any "natural" power that may have been latent within his own people. God's exercise of power was radical, for it was always conditioned on the premise that he had separated his people from the nations round about and was determined to work on their behalf—not primarily for their sake—but in order to magnify his own name among the nations. As Moses said:

> Did any people ever hear the voice of a god speaking out of the midst of the fire, as you have heard, and still live? Or has any god ever attempted to go and take a nation for himself from the midst of another nation, by trials, by signs, by wonders, and by war, by a mighty hand and an outstretched arm, and by great terrors, according to all that the Lord your God did for you in Egypt before your eyes? (Deut. 4:33, 34)

As a result, our interpretation of biblical texts is built upon the certainty that the events recorded in the Old Testament actually happened and bear particular relationship to Israel alone. God was concerned with other peoples and acted on their behalf, but not in the same revelatory sense (e.g., Amos 9:7). Martin Noth contends that the things that happened in Israel "simply never happened elsewhere."[6] This thesis is extensively developed in G. Ernest Wright's monograph *The Old Testament Against Its Environment.*[7] His contention is that "the central elements of Biblical faith are so unique and *sui generis* that they cannot have developed by any natural evolutionary process from the pagan world in which they appeared."[8]

This means that even the miracles—whether the Exodus or at Sinai, whether by Elijah or Elisha—are altogether fundamental and essential to biblical faith.[9]

Revelation and the Nature of God

The God of the Old Testament was not merely a single, all-powerful Creator, but rather the One who is the Source of all being. He did not emerge from a preexistent primordial realm of power, but is totally free from all limitations that magic and mythology forged around the gods of the non-Israelites.

God is subject to no laws or forces that transcend him. He is completely free from all mythological traits. He is not surrounded by a heavenly court of angels and demons metamorphosed from gods and goddesses whom he overcame in earlier cosmic struggles.[10] Concerning this God, Yehezkel Kaufmann has stated:

> The biblical religious idea is of a supernal God, as above every cosmic law, fate and compulsion; unborn, unbegetting, knowing no desire, independent of matter and its forces; a God who does not fight other divinities or powers of impurity; who does not sacrifice, divine, prophesy, or practice sorcery; who does not sin and needs no expiation; a God who does not celebrate festivals of his life. An unfettered divine will transcending all being—this is the mark of biblical religion and that which sets it apart from all the religions of the earth.[11]

The basic word for deity in the ancient Semitic world of the Near East was El. This was also the proper name for the supreme god of the Canaanite pantheon, and frequently appears as such in fourteenth century B.C. Ugarit religious literature. The Israelites appropriated it and gave it new meaning, in much the same way that the Jewish translators of the Old Testament into Greek (the Septuagint) later appropriated the word Theos from the Greek pantheon and transformed it (not as having shape and form as the pagans conceived god, but as pure spirit [see John 4:24]) to conform to God's unique revelation of himself. The Israelite use of El in the plural form (Elohim) but with singular meaning was not unique to Israel. Abraham identified Melchizedek's "Elohim Most High" with "the Lord" (Gen. 14:18-22). This implied a plurality of powers, of attributes, even of personhood, and did not imply a deity that was intrinsically monistic.

It has frequently been noted that it never seemed to occur to the writers of the Old Testament to make any positive estimates of the polytheistic religions of their neighbors. Actually, they were uninterested in the nature and meaning of pagan religion. Heinz R. Schlette speaks of their regard for other religions as "extremely negative"[12] and quotes in support such texts as 1 Kings 11:1-13; Jeremiah 2:26-28; 10:1-16; Isaiah 40:18-20; 44:9-20; 46:1-7. Edward R. Dewick adds that the prominent note of their witness concerning these religions is "hostility," although he qualifies this somewhat by saying there are some "notable exceptions."[13] Indeed, the gulf between the God of Israel and the gods of the nations is immense. Emil Brunner dismisses as wholly untenable the popular opinion that the biblical record of repeated acts of divine disclosure has its parallels in other religions. He contends: "The claim of the revelation (by a Revealer) possessing universal validity in the history of religion is rare. . . . No other religion knows the God who is Himself the Revealer."[14]

As a result, the Old Testament contains no serious reflection on what might be called "authentic paganism." Its writers felt no constraint to mount any polemic against the essence of polytheism or belief in other gods, much less any repudiation of the pagan myths that clustered around these gods. They merely denigrated with vehemence any thought of divinity attributed to the fetishes (idols) representing these alleged nonentities (e.g., Isa. 44:9-20).

It is only in the light of God's uniqueness that we evaluate why the Bible's sole argument advanced against pagan worship is that it is a fetishistic worship, a senseless deification of wood and stone, what anthropologists call "mana" belief. Later, in the New Testament, we find explicit reference to demonic forces associated with idol worship (1 Cor. 8:1-6; 10:19-22). In the Old Testament their presence is only implicitly inferred.

So then, the Israelites knew themselves in a world surrounded by polytheists whose views on all reality were shaped by a supposed cosmic struggle between gods and goddesses contending for the status quo, a world of order and harmony, against a world of change—the chaos and discord energized by hostile powers. In this connection G. Ernest Wright has pointed out:

> It is small wonder, therefore, that all polytheisms tend to be religions of the *status quo* and that none of them has ever produced a thoroughgoing social revolution based upon a high concept of social justice. Revolution of any sort is abhorrent to the inmost nature of such natural religion.[15]

In contrast, the Israelites were committed to God: the ethical Governor of his creation. Because he is just, righteous, and holy and because he is revealed as concerned to redeem and recreate, it is not surprising that his redemptive purpose includes the desire to make his people into an instrument for reform and social regeneration.

This concern is constantly reiterated in the Old Testament (e.g., Gen. 9:5, 6; Mic. 6:8; Jer. 22:13-16).

Wilhelm Schmidt produced six volumes (1926-1935), *Der Ursprung der Goddesidee*, to establish the thesis that monotheism, or the belief in "High Gods," can be found in the legends of many primitive peoples. At first, scholars were impressed with the vast amount of data that Schmidt had gathered to support his argument. Certainly, he had demolished once for all the evolutionary theory that there was correlation between so-called "primitive" peoples and "primitive" religion (e.g., animism).

Conservative Bible students were likewise excited. All could now contend that the existence of polytheistic and animistic religions throughout the world was the result of widespread devolution from the biblical monotheism extant at the very beginning of the human race, recorded in Genesis.

On closer examination, however, it became apparent that Schmidt's "High Gods," although characterized by a sort of solitariness, were far removed from approximating biblical monotheism in any recognizable form. It is rather unfortunate that this particular application of Schmidt's thesis has been recently revived and promoted by Don Richardson (*Eternity in Their Hearts*, 1981).[16] He uses it as a springboard for the thesis that in the culture of every people one can find redemptive analogies reflecting this primordial faith. What he unfortunately overlooks is that all alleged evidence for this one Prime Cause of all is so shrouded in mythology, so dependent on the world (rather than its Source), and so manipulatable by external forces that no common ground exists with the biblical God who is supreme over all.

Revelation and Israelite Faith

It is increasingly being recognized that the most intensive study of the changing environment and growth of Israel throughout the Old Testament period cannot account for the faith of Israel. No solid evidence points convincingly to anything approximating the evolution from a primitive animism that in time yielded to the sequence of polytheism, then henotheism, and finally ethical monotheism.[17] Indeed, ethical monotheism dominates the Old Testament from beginning to end. All attempts to buttress the myth of Israel's religious developmentalism arise from deliberately misreading the biblical literature. Critical scholars have yet to provide convincing evidence that "something in early Israel predisposed and predetermined the course of Biblical history" apart from the direct activity of God.[18] We have based these sweeping generalizations on the canonical text although we are aware of critical scholars with their speculative theories on the evolutionary development of Israel's faith.[19]

Even so, there is considerable solid evidence that on occasion the writers of the Old Testament deliberately contextualized their material. They borrowed from extant sources but reconceptualized them so radically that the primary elements of Israel's faith were always in sharpest conflict with the larger religious environment in which the Old Testament literature emerged.

Actually, when this literature was being written, a rather sophisticated level of polytheism already existed throughout the ancient Near East. Its divine gods and goddesses numbered in the thousands, and all were related either directly or indirectly to the rhythms of the nature cycle. And all reflected in varying degrees the amorality and violence that characterized the lives of their devotees.

It is widely held that the religious life of the people of Israel throughout their long history was strongly influenced by the religious myths and cultic activities of their neighbors, particularly by Baalism. Considerable syncretism resulted.

Indeed, from the conquest of Palestine onward, this Canaanite religion proved a constant temptation with its fertility festivities that encouraged drunkenness and sexual immorality. It became quite intermingled with the authentic traditions of the Patriarchs, the Exodus, and the covenants. For long and short periods even the cultic rituals associated with the tabernacle and the temple were either neglected or so poorly understood that their worship of Yahweh was offensive to him. We gain insight into this from such prophetic denunciations as Amos 5:21–27 and Isaiah 1:11–15, along with many others.

The canonical prophets regarded this syncretism as apostasy. They condemned all worship of idols, of heavenly bodies, and of other gods. They stood against the Israeli penchant for frequenting local altars and pillars, engaging in child sacrifice and religious prostitution, burning incense at "high places" to Asherim or under sacred trees. Indeed, the total, unrelieved hostility of these prophets to all forms of syncretism has its roots in the Mosaic legislation (e.g., Deut. 6:14, 15; 7:25, 26) and continued without deviation throughout the whole Old Testament period. It is significant that the very last prophet of this canon rebuked their slovenly observance of the Yahwist cult (Mal. 1:7–2:9; 3:2–4).[20] In sharpest contrast to this polytheistic world with its complex myths and philosophical speculations, the Israelis produced a religious literature that was tied neither to nature nor to mythology and constantly stood in judgment on the sins of the Israelites. This gave unique significance to every aspect of their individual and collective existence. Its central focus was on the repeated and varied interventions of God on their behalf that increasingly revealed to them his true nature.

Actually, the writers of the old Testament made no claim to a supposed religious genius that enabled them to perceive objectively the meaning of life and the purpose in their history. As a result they could rejoice times without number: "What great nation is there that has a god so near to it as the Lord our God is to us, whenever we call upon him?" (Deut. 4:7). And just as certainly, when they sinned against him and were chastened, they could confess: "The Lord is in the right, for I [we] have rebelled against his word. . . . Our fathers sinned, and are no more; and we bear their iniquities" (Lam. 1:18; 5:7).

In short, their understanding of God was not shaped by any mythology. And their understanding of themselves was that they, unlike all other of the earth's creatures, alone bore kinship to him. This did not mean that Israelites saw themselves as unique in essence and hence different from all other human beings. They believed in the unity of the human race. But they also affirmed with humility that because of God's covenant dealings with them, they alone knew the God whose image and likeness all people bore.

REVELATION AND CONTEXTUALIZATION

The most striking evidence of contextualization in the Old Testament is the manner in which God deliberately and repeatedly shaped the disclosure of himself to his people by using the widely known, ancient phenomenon of covenant. Indeed, the concept of *covenant* illuminates the structural unity and uniqueness of the Old Testament, because it was fundamental to the faith and worship of the Israelites. The prophets cannot be fully understood apart from regarding them as primarily concerned with the covenant loyalty of the people to God. In essence, they saw but one covenant: God reaching out in grace to possess a people, and his laws expressing that grace. They were burdened that one and all be taken up with nurturing this relationship, giving proper response to his saving acts and thereby deepening their fellowship with him—but always and only on his terms.

Covenant

The typical nonbiblical covenant of the late second millennium B.C. in the Near East was an agreement between two parties, clothed with such solemn and binding force that once made, a linkage of truth and life-fellowship was created not unlike the consanguine relationship within a particular clan, or between clans. Invariably the assistance of the local god or gods would be sought to protect the honor of the contracting parties. As treaty and law, these covenants were highly developed not only by the Semites of Mesopotamia, but among the non-Semitic peoples of Asia Minor long before God called Abram out of "Ur of the Chaldeans" (Gen. 11:31; 12:1). Reference should be particularly made to Hittite parity and vassal treaties, as well as those of Syria and Assyria.[21]

Each covenant arose out of a particular context and historical situation and dealt with a particular existential need. In contrast to these secular covenants, the terms that God laid down and the promises made in his covenants invariably conveyed the sense that more was to follow. God was in control of history and hence could deliberately reveal his ongoing redemptive purpose in history. Contextualization indeed!

The covenant he made with Noah was universal in scope, unconditional in validity, and everlasting in duration (Gen. 9:9–17). With Abram and his seed, God initially promised both land and descendants, and called for circumcision as its "sign and seal" (Gen. 15:4–21; 17:1–27). Although the obedience of Abraham was not made a condition, the patriarch found that a religious relationship had been thereby forged. Throughout his life he increasingly discovered that becoming "the friend of God" and enjoying his blessing and fellowship were directly related to doing his will.

At Sinai (Horeb), God called for a covenant between himself and the people he had delivered from Egyptian bondage. After recounting his acts of deliverance on their behalf, he then disclosed his desire to possess them as his peculiar treasure, to make them a kingdom of priests and a holy nation (Exod. 19:5, 6). He then revealed a series of stipulations for the continuation of their relationship with him, and upon their assent, ratified the covenant by sacrifice and the sprinkling of blood (Exod. 24:4–8). In the years that followed, this covenant was variously renewed—on the plains of Moab (Deut. 24), at Shechem (Josh. 24), with Jehoiada under Joash (2 Kgs. 11), and later by two kings of Judah: Hezekiah (2 Chr. 29:10) and Josiah (2 Kgs. 23:23).

The Sinaitic covenant was augmented by a specific covenanted promise to David that an everlasting kingdom would proceed from his lineage (2 Sam. 7:12–17; 23:5; Ps. 132:10–18; Isa. 55:3). Finally, the Old Testament contains God's promise of a "new covenant"—not so much new in essence as in the possibility of fulfillment through the inworking of the Holy Spirit (Jer. 31:31–34; 32:37–40;

Ezek. 34:23; 37:24-28). This new covenant promised that the nations will finally and fully share in this universal Davidic reign of peace in the Eschaton (Isa. 42:6; 49:8; 55:3-5; Zech. 2:11; 8:20-23; 14:16).

Through these covenants God's purpose was to assure his people of his keeping power throughout their long history and of the certainty of a redeemed Israel participating in the triumphal consummation of his redemptive purpose. No covenant was ever made without due regard for the varied historic situations in which Israel found itself. Every convenantal renewal in which the people of Israel participated was a telling reminder of their glorious ultimate future. Without this hope, a faithful remnant in their midst would never have clung to him in faith down through the troubled centuries recorded in the Old Testament, and until the first advent of Jesus Christ.

Contextualization Models: The Prophets

The prophets were masters of the contextualization process. Their messages were communicated orally or by symbolic actions devoid of all ambiguity. They spoke directly to the people in unmistakable terms. "I sat where they sat," said Ezekiel (3:15), and his ministry was a vivid demonstration of sensitivity to the context in which his hearers found themselves. We might call attention to two of the most prominent eighth-century prophets, Hosea and Amos, as illustrative of this prophetic pattern.

Hosea was a native of the northern kingdom. An astute and detailed observer of its political and religious context, he was familiar with the royal city of Samaria as well as the cultic centers at Bethel. His task was to speak from the first table of the Decalogue and reveal the anguish of Yahweh over his religiously adulterous people. While still young, just entering marriageable age, Hosea was divinely commanded to marry a harlotrous woman. This marriage issued in three children, and he gave them names that portended imminent judgment on the nation (Hos. 1:2-9).

Later, he was commanded to love a woman living in adultery with her paramour to show that Yahweh still loved his people despite their religious apostasy. By these symbolic actions and by a series of pointed messages the nation, through Hosea, learned that their worship of Baal rather than Yahweh occasioned not so much the Lord's wrath, but rather his heartbreak. These vivid and symbolic acts obviously brought Hosea into the public consciousness of the whole nation and inevitably exposed him to the hostility of its people. In other words, as James L. Mays describes this "contextualization,"

[Hosea] had to incarnate in his own personal life the word of Yahweh. That he could and did is evidence of his profound identification with his God, an identification which, if we can judge from his sayings, allowed him even to feel and experience "the emotions of Yahweh."[22]

Hosea's prophetic career (ca. 750–722 B.C.) extended from the prosperous years of Jeroboam II and concluded as the nation was sliding down the slippery slope leading to its tragic destruction by the Assyrian Shalmaneser.

During much of this same period, Amos, a prophet from Judah, also exercised his ministry in the northern kingdom. His task, unlike Hosea's, was to speak from the second table of the Decalogue. He frequently addressed the Israelites who gathered at Bethel, the most important religious center in the nation, though on occasion he proclaimed the Word of God to the women in Samaria (Amos 4:1–3), to the officials before the palace (3:9–12; 6:1–3), and to the merchant class (8:4–8). Because of the social injustice of the nation, which he exposed, Amos announced the doom that would soon come to the nation (8:2). Concerning the contextualization of his message, Mays has stated:

Amos knew the art of appropriating a variety of . . . speech-forms as the vehicle of what he had to say. His speeches display a remarkable skill at using all the devices of oral literature available in Israel's culture. He sang a funeral dirge for Israel in anticipation of its doom (5:1–2), and formulated woe-sayings as a way of marking certain kinds of action as those which lead to death (5:18; 6:1; 5:7). He used several forms that belonged to the priest to mimic and attack the cult of the nation (4:4f; 5:4, 21–24). He was especially adept at the employment of forms of speech that appear in the riddles, comparisons, and popular proverbs of folk wisdom. . . . He argued with the logic of proverbs (3:3–6) and used comparisons and riddles to make his point (2:9; 3:12; 5:2, 7, 19, 24; 6:12; 9:9).[23]

Many similar observations might be made on the other prophetic writings in the Old Testament. Again and again these men demonstrated remarkable creativity in their response to the varied mandates they received from Yahweh to stand before the people and communicate to them the Word of the living God.

Language

It needs to be kept in mind that the Old Testament was not produced in an isolated cultural and religious vacuum, but in the midst of an ancient Near East that was as much a complexity of interrelating countries as it is today. The Old Testament abounds with metaphors derived from the phenomena of nature. Sun and moon, wind and storm were referred to in the Israelite descriptions of God's will, his power, and his voice. The religious literature of Israel's neighbors also utilized verbalizations drawn from nature—but with the striking difference that the God of Israel differed from all deities in that he was portrayed as transcending both nature and history. The nature psalms (e.g., Pss. 8, 19, 65, 104) arose from within Israelite worship, because under the stimulus of his Spirit, this believing community found their eyes opened to the works of God's hands.

True, religious syncretism was widespread, as we have already seen. This has driven scholars to search for those factors, concepts, and practices in the neighboring countries that allegedly shaped both Israel's religion and her societal structure. It is not surprising that they have discovered many similarities. Sometimes the parallels are linguistic, which is inevitable because of the close relation of Semitic languages. But common language does not automatically mean that extrabiblical material has either significantly informed or shaped the biblical text. The fact remains that the writers of Scripture never introduced the least trace of polytheism into the religious literature they regarded as "the Word of God."

Social institutions were doubtless imported. We concede this. But how could this have been otherwise among a people who wanted a king "like all the nations" (1 Sam. 8:5)? "Foreign ideas of kingship contributed substantially to forming the Israelite royal tradition,"[24] but they were often in sharpest conflict with the revealed law of the King affirmed by Moses (Deut. 17:14–20).

Furthermore, the fact that Canaanite stylistic devices were introduced into early Hebrew poetry does not mean that Israelite religion contained unreconstructed elements of Canaanite religion. All this boils down to a candid recognition of the complexity of the question of foreign influences on Israel's revealed text. Concerning this Helmer Ringgren observes:

> We may ask what elements are part of a common heritage, what elements are really "imported" in the course of Israelite history, and what elements of tradition are a protest against foreign ideas. . . . It is important that foreign influence is given its right place: it should neither be flatly denied, nor be exaggerated. Above all, it should be stressed that foreign ideas were never taken over unchanged but were adapted to suit their new Israelite context. The important task of research in this area, therefore, is to assess the Israelite use of the foreign material and the reinterpretation it underwent in the framework of Yahwistic religion.[25]

When it comes to borrowing with a view to contextualization, the Old Testament provides only warnings, not encouragement. Actually, the people of God were specifically warned against adding to or turning from the truth that Yahweh had revealed to them (e.g., Deut. 4:1, 2). No other source of truth existed apart from God and his revealed will. Elijah challenged the people on Mount Carmel to be done with doublemindedness. "If Yahweh is God, go after him; if Baal, go after him" (1 Kings 18:21). By implication, Baal has nothing in common with Yahweh and must be totally eschewed. To borrow from Baal would be to court disaster.

The people often failed to obey Yahweh. Nevertheless, the Old Testament reflects an honesty in reporting this accurately, making one marvel why the Jews preserved such an incriminating record of themselves. Whereas their periods of obedience brought God much joy and their positive deeds were recorded, the Old Testament speaks quite candidly of those times when they allowed themselves to be seduced by the social and religious patterns of their polytheistic neighbors. The sinful character of Israel is not lightly regarded in the Old Testament (e.g., Deut. 9:6, 24; Isa. 1:4; Jer. 6:30). Their faithful God could not but point out that no concord can possibly exist between his people and those who did not acknowledge his name— especially in matters pertaining to truth (Isa. 52:11). Hence, any contextualization process was perilous to the issue of divine truth.

True vs. False Prophets

Again and again in Israel's history there were those who contended for what seemed to be the authentic demands of the context. But their arguments invariably turned out to be syncretistic snares, and abhorrent to God. Consider the experience of Jeremiah—a true prophet of Yahweh. His contextualized ministry had the note of God about it. But had we been his contemporaries, we would have been hard-pressed to be absolutely certain he was an authentic spokesperson for God—one whose message represented the essential demands of the gospel in the context of that day. Jeremiah's unvarying message was that Judah's leaders and people had to heed God's *no!* —the call to repentance—before they could expect to hear God's *yes!* and know themselves as continuing in the sequence of his "salvation history." In contrast, the false prophets ignored this sequence.

How then could the people distinguish the false from the true in those closing days before the Babylonian captivity when "prophetic word was hurled in the teeth of prophetic word, and prophet called prophet a liar"[26]? The false prophets did not have a message totally

unrelated to the context—as they understood it. They spoke of peace
and of Yahweh. They spoke of his covenant with David that to them
guaranteed the perpetual security of Jerusalem, David's city. They
proclaimed to the people the impossibility of Yahweh not being able
to turn back the menacing armies of the Babylonians. Had he not
overcome the threatening Assyrians a century before (Isa. 36–37)?

But they were wrong, dead wrong, and their best efforts at contextualization were utterly destructive. Jeremiah called for spiritual
repentance, but the false prophets spoke of political realism, of alliances with powerful neighbors, of the legitimate will of the people
to resist the enemy. Jeremiah preached the truth that had been revealed by God—particularly the abiding validity of the conditions
God had attached to the Sinaitic covenant made with the nation
hundreds of years before. He spoke of the faithfulness of God and
pointed with conviction to the certainty of God's ultimate triumph
in history. The false prophets saw only the immediate present and
shouted down all efforts to confront the issue of truth. All which
makes painfully clear the reason why evangelical Christians cannot
endorse much that passes today for contextualization. Unless disciplined effort is made to submit to the whole Word of God contained
in the whole of Scripture, distortions of truth and deviations from
its central concerns will inevitably follow. Without this, what many
herald as insightful contextualizing of theology and praxis will be
finally revealed as wide of the mark.

When it comes to discerning correctly the dominant signifi-
cances of any particular historical context, all of us do well to avoid
dogmatism. That God is constantly at work in secular history, none
will deny, but there is an inscrutability about his self-disclosure that
is in sharp contrast with the vividness of his witness in the Scriptures, and particularly in Jesus Christ.

The writers of the Old Testament had a special calling from
God as well as special insight from him that enabled them to discern
the acts of God in secular history. Marc Spindler of the International
Association for Mission Studies ended his survey of contemporary
approaches to biblical reflection on mission with the reminder that
history is not only the theatre of "godly" developments but also
the place of evil. As a result he felt he had to posit the mystery of
God's alleged witness in human history after Auschwitz, Hiroshima,
and Sharpeville, and concluded with an observation by H. D. Beeby:

> The prophets can only witness to the mighty acts of God in history
> because they have stood in the council of God and been told, so to
> speak, whose side God is on in a particular struggle and what precisely

he is doing in his world. Without such "revealed" information the so-called discerning of God's activity in the world seems to be the peculiar prerogative of the false prophets.[27]

Wisdom Literature—Partly Borrowed?

Only in Israel's wisdom literature do we find the contextualization process carried to the point where an occasional item of Canaanite poetry was edited and then incorporated into the Old Testament canon. When this happened, a bridge was thereby erected to other peoples that demonstrated the commonality of human experience. This follows because the patterns of life and the rules of conduct to which individuals and peoples adhere are derived from their past experiences. This "wisdom" enables them to come to terms with their environment and with one another. They thereby discern good from evil, truth from error, virtue from vice, and duty from self-indulgence. More, this wisdom underscores the importance of industry over laziness, prudence over presumption, honesty over all forms of deception, and the pattern of adhering to the sort of values that have positive long-range validity rather than pursuing the attractions of the moment.

Within the canonical Scriptures of ancient Israel, several books (Job, some of the Psalms, Proverbs, and Ecclesiastes) were devoted to "wisdom." They do not deal with the ongoing of Yahweh's purpose in history, but with the basic issues of life which together give order and system to human existence in this world.

> This experiential knowledge is not only a very complex entity, but also a very vulnerable one. It renders man an invaluable service in enabling him to function in his sphere of life other than as a complete stranger and puts him in the position of understanding [it], at least to a certain extent, as an ordered system.[28]

Whereas this ordered system of moral maxims is strengthened by the experiences of individuals and nations, it is terribly threatened by each and every contrary experience for which the system's wisdom has no explanation. Hence, although the tendency within any society is to resist change and preserve its accepted norms, there are times when revision and addition are necessary. But making such changes is never easy; it is always traumatic.

Israel gathered into literary form her experiential knowledge, generally in the form of sentence-type proverbs, and these precepts often were similar to those of her neighbors. Scholars have argued that on occasion certain Israelite psalms conceivably could have been derived from Canaanite psalmody (e.g., 19 and 104). But when the original Canaanite psalms are not available, this becomes mere conjecture. Parts of Proverbs 22–24 are likely an abridged edition of the Egyptian "Teaching of Amenemope," but this is "not at all astonishing in view of the international character of the wisdom literature."[29] To use such literature would be to underscore to the Israelites the universality of this type of mental activity, and would confirm their understanding of the unity of the human race.

However, Israel's growing deposit of wisdom literature contained perspectives that went beyond those of her neighbors. She traced this beyond human discernment and linguistic ingenuity to Yahweh himself and to his moral governance of people: "The fear of the Lord, that is wisdom; and to depart from evil is understanding" (Job 28:28). Wisdom is derived from God and should be attributed to God alone (Job 12:13; Prov. 3:19, 20; 8:22–31; Isa. 31:2). Wisdom is one, whether worldly or divine. Worldly wisdom is less elevated than divine wisdom, differing in degree rather than in kind. Whereas Israel would grant that victories were achieved through heeding good counsel (Prov. 24:6), yet she was quick to recognize that any and all victories were ultimately attributable to Yahweh alone (Prov. 21:31).

The highest point in Israel's reflection on wisdom is Proverbs 1–9. Here one encounters the "sudden personification" of wisdom and its direct equation with deity. Wisdom "cries in the streets" (1:20–33) and happy people "hear her" (3:13). More, she was the first component in the drama of creation (8:22–26) and became God's "Assistant" in its subsequent development (8:27–31).[30]

We grant that the Wisdom Literature does not directly concern itself with the ongoing redemptive purpose of God, even though some might argue that Job intimated otherwise when he said: "The fear of the Lord, that is wisdom; and to depart from evil is understanding" (28:28). But missionaries have on occasion used these Old Testament books to prepare the way for the gospel.

For example, Ecclesiastes was written "to convince men of the uselessness of any world view which does not rise above the horizon of man himself."[31] Its author experiments with all the possible options open to the one who regards personal happiness as the highest good. The total frustration experienced as a result of these efforts at self-deification brings the author to the conclusion that one should fear God, remain within the guidelines of the Torah (the cultural mandate and the Sinaitic code), and prepare for the Day of Judgment (12:11–14). But this is manifestly unsatisfactory since it does not provide answers to all the primary questions concerning one's existence, life's meaning, and the implications of physical death. In this silence we confront the incompleteness of the Old Testament revelation.

Conclusion

How does the Old Testament's long historical sequence of revelation and response, progressive addition and enlarged interpretation fit into the contextualization debate in our day? Quite simply, this sequence is an indication of something inherent in the self-disclosure of God. All valid contextualization is but a reflection of the incarnation principle which came to fullness when "the Word became flesh" and dwelt among the people of God (John 1:14). Down through Old Testament history God again and again met with his people where they were (in context!) and moved his purpose forward through intimate interaction with them in their varied existential situations.

In a very real sense, there was only one covenant he made with them, and it provided him with the vehicle for dispensing his grace and fulfilling his promises. All his prophets from Moses onward were intensely loyal to the witness of their predecessors; and the new truths they revealed brought changes in worship forms, heightened ethical imperatives and enlargement of theological understanding, but no radical discontinuity. God's truth remained free from contradiction because there is only one God.[32]

NOTES

[1] TEF Staff: *Ministry in Context* (London: Theological Education Fund, 1972).

[2] Dr. Shoki Coe's chapter in *Asian Christian Theology*, ed., Douglas J. Elwood, "Contextualization as the Way Toward Reform," (Philadelphia: Westminster, 1976), 48-55, contains illuminating insight into the historical emergence of this term.

[3] For a detailed and comprehensive discussion of this range of understanding and the problems it has created consult the following excellent articles: "The Problem of Contextualization" by Krikor Haleblian (*Missiology*, XI, 1 [January 1982], 95-111), and "Models of Contextual Theology" by Stephen Bevans (*Missiology*, XIII, 2 [April 1985], 185-202).

[4] Harold H. Rowley, "The Antiquity of Israelite Monotheism," *The Expository Times* 61 (1949-1950): 333-38.

[5] Alan Richardson, *The Bible in the Age of Science* (London: SCM Press, 1961), 71-72.

[6] Martin Noth, *The History of Israel*, trans. by Stanley Godman (New York: Harper and Row, 1958), 2-3.

[7] G. Ernest Wright, *The Old Testament Against Its Environment* (London: SCM Press, 1968).

[8] Ibid., 7.

[9] What God did and said in Old Testament times is absolutely determinative in shaping our understanding of the manner in which he invariably discloses himself. The hinge of history between the particularity of his dealings with Israel and with the Church is the Christ Event wherein by one great act of revelation and redemption God made certain the final eschatological triumph of his kingdom in history.

[10] Psalm 82 is one of the very few Old Testament passages that is allegedly syncretistic. It portrays God in the midst of a hierarchical gathering of the national gods of the nations. Taken at face value it is an ironic depiction of God condemning these gods for aiding and abetting the world's wickedness and injustice. Because of the searching judgment of God, they are condemned to death like mere mortals. The obvious lesson is that only when God judges the nations and utterly obliterates their false gods will justice come to earth.

[11] Yehezkel Kaufmann, The Religion of Israel, trans. and abridged by Moshe Greenberg (Chicago: University of Chicago Press, 1960), 121.

[12] Heinz R. Schlette, Towards a Theology of Religions (New York: Herder and Herder, 1966), 25.

[13] Edward C. Dewick, The Christian Attitude to Other Religions (Cambridge: Cambridge University Press, 1953), 63.

[14] H. Emil Brunner, Revelation and Reason: The Christian Doctrine of Faith and Knowledge, trans. by Olive Myon (Philadelphia: Westminster, 1946), 235-36.

[15] Wright, The Old Testament, 45.

[16] Don Richardson, Eternity in Their Hearts (Ventura, Calif.: Regal Books, 1981).

[17] See Rowley, 333-38.

[18] Wright, The Old Testament, 15.

[19] During the last two centuries much scholarly activity has focused on tracing the allegedly lengthy process of collecting and editing the text of the Old Testament from the original autographs that eventuated in the canonical text we have today. In the late nineteenth century a documentary hypothesis was conceived to explain the reason for parallel narratives, slightly different traditions, and troublesome discrepancies (e.g., concerning Israel's feasts, Levites vs. priests, etc.). This hypothesis was shaped by the presumption of an evolutionary development of Israel's understanding of God. Today scholars are far less agreed as to the validity of this "source criticism" and the highly conjectural and problematic theories it has generated. We base our interpretations of the Old Testament on the final result of whatever long process took place by the inspired authors and editors God used to produce the canonical text. For supporting scholarly authority consult Brevard S. Childs, Introduction to the Old Testament as Scripture (Philadelphia: Westminster, 1979), 46-83, 112-35; Gordon J. Wenham, "The Religion of the Patriarchs," in Essays on the Patriarchal Narratives by Alan R. Millard and Donald J. Wiseman, eds. (Winona Lake, In: Eisenbrauns, 1980), 157-85; William Sanford LaSor, David A. Hubbard, and Frederic W. Bush, Old Testament Survey (Grand Rapids: Eerdmans, 1987), 54-75; etc.

[20] For a detailed description of the syncretism that the prophets spoke against, consult Walter J. Harrelson, "Prophecy and Syncretism," Andover Newton Quarterly, 4, no. 4 (March 1964), 6-19; Frank E. Eaken, Jr., "Yahwism and Realism Before the Exile," Journal of Biblical Literature, 84 (1965), 407-14; Donald E. Gowan, "Prophets, Deuteronomy, and the Syncretistic Cult in Israel," in John C. Rylaarsdam, Transitions in Biblical Scholarship (Chicago: University of Chicago Press, 1968), 93-112.

[21] Striking formal similarities between ancient treaties of the late second millennium B.C. and certain biblical passages are found in Treaty and Covenant by Dennis

J. McCarthy (Rome: Biblical Institute Press, 1978). It is significant that these similarities are in sharpest contrast to the later covenants of the first millennium B.C., the period in which critical scholars attempt to establish the late evolution of Israelite religion. See also Kenneth A. Kitchen, *Ancient Orient and Old Testament* (Chicago: InterVarsity Press, 1969), 99.

[22] James L. Mays, *Hosea. A Commentary* (Philadelphia: Westminster, 1969), 3.

[23] James L. Mays, *Amos. A Commentary* (Philadelphia: Westminster, 1969), 5-6.

[24] Helmer Ringgren, "The Impact of the Ancient Near East on Israelite Tradition," in *Tradition and Theology in the Old Testament*, Douglas A. Knight, ed. (Philadelphia: Fortress, 1977), 36.

[25] Ibid., 45.

[26] John Bright, *Covenant and Promise* (Philadelphia: Westminster, 1976), 181.

[27] H. D. Beeby, "Comments on Marc Spindler's 'Visa for Witness,'" in *Mission Studies*, vol. IV-1, 1987, 65-68, quoted by Marc Spindler, "Witness Under Cross-Examination," *Mission Studies*, vol. IV-2, 1987, 67-73.

[28] Gerhard Von Rad, *Wisdom in Israel* (Nashville: Abingdon, 1972), 3.

[29] Ringgren, "The Impact", 40.

[30] Roland K. Harrison, *Introduction to the Old Testament* (Grand Rapids: Eerdmans, 1969), 1008.

[31] Gleason Archer, *A Survey of Old Testament Introduction* (Chicago: Moody, 1964), 459.

[32] In preparing this chapter I was stimulated by an article by Millard C. Lind, "Refocusing Theological Education to Mission: The Old Testament and Contextualization," *Missiology*, X, 2 (April 1982), 141-60. However, I have not used any of his material because his presuppositions on the formation of the Old Testament involve concessions to source criticism that I find difficult to accept. However, I cite this study for those who are concerned to grasp the breadth of scholarly reflection on contextualization in our day. See also the articles by Stephen Reid, "The Book of Exodus: A Laboratory for Hermeneutics" and by Edesio Sanchez-Centina, "Hermeneutics and Context: The Exodus," in *Conflict and Context*, Marc Lau Branson and C. Rene Padilla, eds. (Grand Rapids: Eerdmans, 1986), 155-70.

3

New Testament Contextualization: Continuity and Particularity in Paul's Theology

Dean S. Gilliland

THE GOOD NEWS FOR ALL PEOPLE EVERYWHERE is that the Word *became* flesh (Jn. 1:14). Speaking contextually, the Word must *become* flesh again and again in each locale and for every people. Saying this is never to suggest that there is some Savior other than Jesus Christ or a different incarnation from that of the Scriptures. Yet there must be a connection of that absolute incarnational Word with human life today.

When we speak of mission, we are saying that what God did once and for all in Jesus Christ must become Life in every human situation. This is partly what Paul had in mind when he wrote, "complete what is lacking in Christ's afflictions for the sake of his body, that is the church" (Col. 1:24). It is never easy to take the good news across cultural barriers. There must be adjustments of message and variety in the way the message is presented. Thankfully, this spontaneous process began as preaching of the gospel broke out of Jerusalem.

No systematic or all-encompassing theology resulted from the missionary preaching of the apostles or from the epistles of Paul. There was no formal theologizing as we speak of it today. The beginnings of the ordering of truth happened almost unconsciously as a by-product of the apostolic mission. We speak of the result, therefore, as a diversity of theological emphases, rather than a completed theology. Specific themes or perspectives on central truths fit the local Christian setting, whether Corinth, Thessalonica, or Rome. To recognize these multi-faceted views of foundational truth is to discover contextualization in the New Testament.[1]

The living Word of God must become *real* in every cultural setting. When Jesus came, he "dwelt among *us*" (Jn. 1:14). He didn't live in some bland way with people in general and certainly not as an alien to anyone. It is this precise, incarnational presence of the Word that must be carefully understood as we look at the post-Pentecost church. The "us" among whom he dwells is a particular people and place. In looking back we can say that contextualization was an intrinsic mission principle in the New Testament. This was because *witnessing* dominated the purpose of apostolic theology, and the result was a variety of subjects and expressions. What a rich coloration of words, ideas, and emphases! The object was to *hold forth the Word of life* (Phil. 2:16) in a way that ordinary people would know why and how they should turn to this new Lord Jesus Christ.

Theologians today, whose first concern is mission, find their task is really no different from that of the first apostles. The central truths are absolute, while communication and application fit local needs and questions. This does not mean that we make Jesus over to fit every situation or need as it arises. It does mean, however, that while firmly anchored to the Christ of apostolic witness, there must be an immediacy about the gospel. There must be a recognizable identity for Jesus and clarity about what he taught, so that persons in this place and time can say, "My Savior and *my* Lord!"

THE SHIFT FROM JERUSALEM TO ANTIOCH

The fledgling church could well have died in Jerusalem but for two reasons. One is that Judaism already had cultural links with the gentile world. Then, there was the catalyst, Saul of Tarsus, who broke the hold on a Jerusalem-style Christianity. Internal forces in Judaism were in severe tension, pulling inward and pushing outward. It was the arch-conservative spirit of the Judaizers that held sway in Jerusalem. Judaizers fiercely resisted every form of what they regarded as antinomianism. The thought that the Lord's Supper would be a simultaneous communal rite for Jew and gentile was even more offensive.[2] Most Christian Jews took the new movement to be a renewal within Judaism. They would have abhorred the idea of being included in any religion that gave gentiles full privilege with them.

For these reasons and because of its ethnic diversity and unorthodox worship style, the upstart Antioch church threatened the status quo at Jerusalem. To make matters worse, it attracted people in great numbers. The removal of circumcision as a requirement for the gentiles must have increased Jewish fears that The Way would soon be overrun with gentile travelers.

In contrast to the innovative ambiance of the Antioch congregation, Jerusalem was the Orthodox Establishment Church. It had been almost impossible for Christians there to accept the fact that Cornelius might have equal rights with the circumcised.[3] Naturally, Jerusalem elders felt the need to "check out" the Antioch church, and in doing so they seem to have affected the Jewish Christians at Antioch in a negative way. Paul later says that the "inspection" caused Jewish believers in Antioch to stop eating with the gentiles (Gal. 2:12). The general effect was seen as an effort by Jerusalem traditionalists to bring the Antioch church into line with Jewish forms and practice.

The Hellenists were on the other side, pulling away from centered Judaism. While keeping their Jewish identity, the Hellenists had an openness to the non-Jewish world. The crisis that arose in Jerusalem churches over administration and community (Acts 6) was the opening for a more liberal stance toward gentiles. Greek-speaking Jews, such as those close to Stephen, saw the insurmountable barrier that circumcision placed on any non-Jew who desired to follow Jesus. It was these same Hellenists who very early showed true missionary fervor with the result that several Samaritans were converted through Hellenistic witness (see Acts 8:12). This development, along with the "Antiochan experiment," was more than most Jerusalem-based Christians could tolerate. Fortunately, by God's design, the Antioch model prevailed, and this innovative spirit guaranteed that the gospel would go to the gentiles.

The differences between Jerusalem Christians and the congregation at Antioch are extremely important. What took place at Antioch points to *a spirit of contextualization* in the new Syrian church.[4] Basic evidence of this spirit is startling growth, spontaneity, and excitement about worship. Growth is inevitable where there is proper contextualization. Contextualization calls for a high level of participation by the members and the freedom to develop appropriate worship forms. Most important was that Antioch showed a sensitivity to "body life."[5] This means there was a recognition of diversity within the congregation while working for oneness under Christ's rule and teaching.

It is understandable why Antiochans were the first to call Jesus' followers "Christians." They may have coined the term disrespectfully, yet it proves that something was very different about this group. No one took them for a sect of the Jews. This religious community was authentic. It had linkage to Jerusalem as well as elements which suited this cosmopolitan city and people. Here were the components of a contextual church. Contextualization builds churches that have continuity with history and tradition while breaking new ground. Unfamiliar experiences and attention to contextual problems do introduce an element of discontinuity. But discontinuity need not be syncretism or heresy, as the Hellenist churches proved. It was this recombination of traditional ways with local expression that made faith in Jesus real for the mixed congregation at Antioch.

Transitional Terminology

The ministry of Paul provides us with the clearest of case studies for contextualization in the New Testament. This is because we not only have immediate access to Paul through his epistles, but we have the record of Luke as well. It is important to be aware of certain problems when attempting to relate Luke's writings with those of Paul.[6]

But when all the evidence is in, Acts is an indispensable narrative for studying ways in which the gospel interacted with a variety of ethnic and religious situations from Antioch to Rome. Both Acts and the Epistles illustrate how Paul constantly searched for language that best suited the questions raised in each place. He found expressions that conveyed truth with the highest degree of local impact. He had no quarrel with Jewish terms when he was addressing issues that related to Jews, and he did not arbitrarily reject the language of the Torah, for he was always a Jew. But his loyalty to traditional expression was never the final guide. What determined Paul's terminology was the particularity of the context. He took the freedom to use one term here and another there, even when discussing similar topics.

Ralph Martin has made a strong case for *katallasso* (reconcile) and *katallage* (reconciliation) as the metaphor that unifies Paul's thinking with respect to the work of Christ. Clearly, this is a word that fits the gentile world.[7] The Greek world-view called for a resolution of tensions between people and their gods. But the term would have related poorly to the Jews. The more acceptable way to speak of the mediating work of Christ for the Jews would be the use of *hilaskesthai* (to propitiate or make expiation for). But Paul never uses *hilaskesthai*. The writer of the Hebrews uses it once (2:17); otherwise, it is not found in the New Testament. The surprising thing about *katallasso* is that it was always used in secular ways, never in a theological way. For example, in diplomatic exchanges it translates as, "exchange of hostility for friendship." Paul seizes on this "worldly" term and makes it into a beautiful picture of the way Jews and gentiles come to God through the ministry and death of Christ. The new meaning that Paul gives is that God has taken the initiative; God wants to be reconciled with his people. The conduct that humans have always shown for each other is now applied to God. With Paul's choice of *kattallassein* God truly comes to the level of ordinary people.[8]

On occasion Paul is not afraid to use phraseology that was familiar to the mystery cults. It could be somewhat disconcerting, even today, to admit that Paul went into the local religions to find ways to teach Christ. But this is surely part of the reason why God chose him as the apostle to the gentiles. In Romans 15:16 he speaks of himself as a "minister" of Jesus Christ (*leitourgon*). The gift from the Philippian church (4:18) is a "libation" (*thysia*) and a "sacrifice" (*leitourgia*). Paul introduces another popular, even secular word when he describes "spiritual worship" as *latreian* (Rom. 12:1). This is but a sampling. The purpose is obvious. Paul transforms expressions that had always been associated with rituals of gentile cultic practice to construct a fitting new language about the love of Christ for people and of people for each other.[9] This is dynamic communication.

J. Christiaan Beker shows how secular language is turned around by Paul to express what God does in the everyday life of the believer and what Christ's example means for the new lifestyle.[10] It is reasonable to expect that new converts might not understand that following Jesus calls for a break from their traditional cultic forms. The use of this idiomatic language intensifies what it means to separate from the old idols to the true and living God (1 Thess. 1:9). The way in which Paul selected his terminology to get his message across is, in itself, illuminating evidence for contextual thinking on his part. Through the guidance of the Holy Spirit, Paul introduced expressions that were formative in an early christology. Paul saw the incarnation somewhat differently than John. Just as the idea of *logos* in

Johannine thought would meet a different need at a later time, the kenosis-thinking of Paul was uniquely his. Paul saw Jesus' sacrifice as already beginning in eternity.[11] What Jesus had already given up in order to live as a mortal man, even before his death, amazed and humbled Paul (Phil. 2:5-11). The Greeks knew nothing of this among the gods of their pantheon.

Paul was "doing theology" when he explained Jesus' coming as kenosis. This was, of course, revelational theology. Paul's choice of this term was to form a fundamental Christian concept. Its place in canonical Scripture makes it normative for Christianity. Subsequent theologizing of the church would never be of the same magnitude. But Paul's relentless search for relevance under the guidance of the Holy Spirit, his openness to new, even controversial, symbols is the point at issue.[12] It is erroneous theologizing to make the precise terms of Paul absolute to all cultures, without reenacting or even appreciating the process that produced his theology.[13]

THE BIPOLAR THEOLOGY OF PAUL

The work of Paul is a masterful case of contextualization. The principle is simple to state but intricate and complex to apply. Paul communicated central truths of the gospel in a variety of ways, depending on the particular situation. In achieving this, two components were in constant interaction. First, to use the term of J. C. Beker, the "coherent center" was always in place. This refers to the fundamental themes of the gospel or what is sometimes called the "core doctrine." The second factor, deriving from the first, was the interpretation given the central message for a particular people and place. At first, this may sound like steps into any basic course on hermeneutics. But it is more than this; the reciprocity between these two components is the most notable aspect of Paul's theology. It is also the aspect that nearly all scholars of Paul fail to grasp.

Beker has taken a clear position on Pauline theology which rests on this bipolar foundation. Beker's terms to describe these two dimensions are "coherence" and "contingency."[14] His major work of 1980, Paul the Apostle, The Triumph of God in Life and Thought, is basically an explication of coherent center and local contingencies. It is the dialectic between these two components that forms Paul's theology. This principle was not taught to Paul, except as God's Spirit taught him. Careful attention to the center, knowing what it is and what it is not, and equal sensitivity to the local situation is the hermeneutical key to the apostle's thought.

We shall speak in more detail about these two principles and how they are demonstrated in Paul's epistles. But first we must be sure about the missionary nature of the Epistles. Commitment to relevance is what makes the theology of Paul so hard to organize. The compelling nature of his apostolic mission was clarity and specific application. We have seen this in the terminology he used. He had no doctrine, as such, which he took from place to place and for which he could demand universal acceptance. There was no dogmatic listing of beliefs that were binding on all places and peoples. Seemingly conflicting statements do come up in Paul's letters if we line them up one against the other. We shall illustrate this with the way he treats the Second Coming. But hard logic and consistency is not what is expected in missionary theology; rather, one looks for a timely, intelligible presentation of the good news.[15]

We have referred to Paul's use of terms and symbols that opened up new ways to speak of Christ's work. Considering their source, taken at face value, most of these expressions would not qualify for a place in sacred theology. They were tainted with the profanity of the world. But we can now look back on Paul's methodology to see that this was not a search for novel expressions. He demonstrated that the gospel will be a living faith only as it takes seriously the concrete values and dynamic issues raised by each culture. In general, the Jews balked at a reframing of the order and terminology. They would rather have encapsulated the gospel, because they feared loss of ownership and tradition. They had an abhorrence of what might become syncretism, should the gentiles be given too much liberty. Yet if this liberating gospel had become imprisoned within Jewish belief and practice, the result would have been a Jewish brand of syncretism. This, in fact, almost happened. Paul had to fight Judaistic distortions through his correspondence on at least two occasions.[16]

So Paul does not give a closed message. There are no "monstrous repetitions" of Pauline doctrine "to which intellectual assent must be given." The good news is something that Jesus died to give the world. Paul, therefore, cannot demand that people accept what is alien to them or what they do not understand. This search for an entrée into particular contexts does not mean that Paul accommodated the gospel to "whatever the market would buy." It was not "an incoherent display of incidental, opportunistic and compromising thoughts that vary from situation to situation."[17] It was a deep commitment to proclaim the Christ whom he, Paul, had discovered through revelation and experience. His was to form the message for each audience without compromise to its lifegiving content or reduction to a wooden dogma. We shall now look at the *continuous word* (or the center of the message) and then turn to the *particular word* (or situational focus).

The Continuous Word

It is important to contextualization that fixed points guide the process. A theology in context is not something that is constructed carte blanche in each situation. Paul was formed in Judaism and never separated from the assumptions of his own indigenous world-view or his religion.[18] Finding the center of Paul's gospel is a fascinating exercise. Any attempt to reduce the apostle's Christianity to one or two simple phrases is almost impossible. Interpretations of Paul have always reflected the orientation of the scholar who is doing the work. As a result, the apostle has been presented in a variety of ways. He is described as the "doctrinal Paul," the "cultic Paul," and the "mystic Paul."[19]

All of these insights make a legitimate contribution, but none by itself does justice to the complexity of the theology of Paul. He cannot be pinned down. Reductionism is out of the question, because the most prominent characteristic of Paul's theology is its *local relevance*. The array of ideas that describe how Paul handled the source religion (Judaism) together with the new revelation (Jesus Christ) shows how difficult it is for scholars to agree on the "normative Paul." Keck describes the unifying elements of Paul's theology as "motifs." Whitely prefers "fundamental doctrines," while Sanders speaks of "coherent patterns." Käsemann sees the *mitte*, or center, as "the faith," while Schweitzer says the *mitte* is "eschatological mysticism."[20] Dahl speaks of the emphasis on the "risen Lord" as the main theme, and Bruce sees the "quintessence" of Paul coming from the book of Ephesians.[21]

The center is surely there and must be identified, but we do not read Paul's correspondence as finished theological documents. Marcion made this error when he focused on the order and unity of Paul. He devised a way of reading the Epistles so as to keep Paul "pure." To do this he gave a higher order to certain of the Epistles which confirmed what he, Marcion, wanted Paul to say. Hence, Galatians and Romans became the "canon within the canon."[22]

We can grant the good intentions of Marcion in a confused, heretically inclined environment. Yet a disservice was done, for in his preoccupation with unity, Marcion overlooked Paul's sensitivity to context, which was the missionary nature of his theology. Contextualization declares that truth, however absolute, cannot be abstracted from the particularity of the context. We can speak of the underlying truth principles of Paul, but we cannot say that he "emptied out a ready-made system into the diversity of historical situations."[23]

What, then, do we say about the center of Paul's gospel? I shall speak of this center as the "continuous word," which is the foundational message that brings continuity into all that he preached and wrote. Clearly, Paul's teachings can never be separated from his personal background. Alongside the personal dimension there is a truth-field which reflects the deep-level assumptions held by Paul and his audiences. Most of what Paul wrote and preached reveals a consensus around this symbolic center. Then there is, of course, the content, the facts of the message that are drawn from personal experience and revelation.

The *continuous word* of Paul, therefore, can be understood as having three dimensions, each bringing important insights for understanding his constant message as he moved from place to place. We identify these as the *personal* dimension, the *symbolic* dimension, and the *content* dimension. I make these distinctions with an awareness of the missiological bias of our writing. But it is Paul the missionary that needs to be rediscovered among the countless volumes written about Paul the theologian.

The Personal Dimension

Before anything else, Paul was a Jew. For all his innovations, Paul could never abandon the convictions of his Jewish background. Paul's roots in Jewish thought are the strongest element in the continuity of his gospel, and in this dimension he is most clearly linked with Jesus. The liberal movement of a generation ago tried to separate Jesus from Paul.[24] F. F. Bruce always worked to keep Paul and Jesus within a common tradition while allowing for their differences in "upbringing, education, environment, and temperament."[25] No one interpreted Jesus more faithfully than Paul. Both were loyal to the religious culture into which they were born. Yet both Paul and Jesus shocked the guardians of Israel's law in a variety of ways, and both made mortal enemies of the priestly establishment at Jerusalem.

So, the continuous word of Paul draws deeply from the well of Judaism and Jesus. The changes he introduced, when compared to Jesus' teaching, center on their perspectives of history and shadings of truth derived from personal experience.[26] But in the understanding of the Old Testament there is massive continuity.

Paul's preaching is characterized by the conviction that Jesus is the Christ of Israel, and Ridderbos notes that Paul "can only be understood against the background of the history of the revelation which the Old Testament describes."[27] Paul's loyalty to a messianic interpretation of the Old Testament is a most formative influence out of his personal background. Christ is the center of Paul's message, because there is no other way to understand the Old Testament. The rock in the wilderness out of which Israel received water was Christ (1 Cor. 10:4). The promise to Abraham is spoken to Christ (Gal. 3:16). God's grace in the Old Testament cannot be explained apart from Christ (Rom. 4:6). In fact, the entire revelation of God is bound up in Christ (Rom. 10:15–18).

The personal dimension carries with it all the unique gifts of ministry with which Paul was endowed. But the redemptive purpose of God, manifest through Israel and the messianic role of Jesus, keeps the thought of Paul anchored in the Old Testament.

The Symbolic Dimension

Along with this personal feature we refer next to the pervasive influence of the apocalyptic on Paul's theology. The consistent references he makes to end time, the universal cosmic expectation, and the Parousia in general reveal a thought paradigm that was widespread in Paul's day. Scholars like Ernst Käsemann demonstrate in an impressive way that apocalyptic is "the mother of Christian theology."[28] Paul's frequent apocalyptic references are central to his theology, because they organize his thinking around a salvation process that will consummate in the absolute reign of God.

Paul's apparent dualism between "this world and . . . the next" (Eph. 1:21 TEV) borrowed heavily on the Jewish hope of an absolute end time that would usher in the new age. J. C. Beker has made a unique contribution to an understanding of Paul's theology by focusing on the "apocalyptic core," as he calls it.[29] Truth gathered from both tradition and revelation are cast into a consensus that this age is passing and there is real hope in the age to come.[30]

Because the apocalyptic motif was so widespread in Paul's day, it is taken up as a theme without need for explanation. Apocalyptic can almost be equated with world-view, as a pervasive assumption of context within which Paul's thinking developed. Apocalyptic as a symbol of the times has numerous facets. Koch shows six subthemes of apocalyptic, all of which are reflected in the theology of Paul. Besides a dualism between the old and the new and the imminent end of the world there is a pervasive sense that "beyond the catastrophe a new salvation arises, paradisal in character and destined for the faithful remnant."[31]

In his other writings Beker is so conscious of the apocalyptic that he sets it out as the very "center" itself. References to "apocalyptic" persist from the earliest letter (1 Thessalonians) to the latest (Philippians); and his conclusion is that, "Apocalyptic is not a peripheral curiosity for Paul but the central . . . focus of his thought."[32] Rather than being taken as theme in the sense of basic message, apocalyptic should be identified as symbolic framework into which the central message fits. While Paul reflects preconversion ideas with his use of apocalyptic, God leads Paul to take these assumptions directly into account, because they are held almost universally.[33] Timothy Carriker, using the Beker thesis, shows that, "apocalypticism is a significant formative characteristic of Paul's conceptual framework (background or world-view) and as such influences his contextualization of major theological themes . . . but does not, itself, constitute the center of his message."[34]

The Content Dimension

The continuous word of Paul's gospel, shaped by his personal Jewish history and set into apocalyptic symbolism, is a Word based on incontrovertible facts. This truth crosses all cultural and ethnic situations. Even so, an irreducible statement of this gospel cannot be fully contained in a single expression. The center is contained within all the information Paul received concerning Jesus Christ both by revelation and experience. It can only be described by a combination of terms and symbols. This is because the objective content and universal claims of the gospel compelled Paul to give an intelligible, specific presentation for each need and situation. It bears restating that reciprocity between the continuous word and the particular word is the hallmark of Paul's contextual theology.

The continuous word is not complicated, though it could be defined in different ways. One pragmatic test for separating out the "essence" of the word would be to analyze the preaching and teaching of the apostles as recorded in Acts and in the Epistles. The themes that occur in every case or with the greatest frequency would lead us to the center of the message. Immediately the phrase "in Christ" must be reckoned with. Including cognates, "in Christ" occurs some seventy-two times in Paul's writings. Only 2 Thessalonians does not mention some form of this expression. "In Christ" is more than a metaphor of Pauline mysticism which might easily be stripped of its salvific meaning. It is the way Paul communicates the intimate relationship God has initiated between the believer and the risen Lord.[35] Paul never speaks of being "in Jesus," for it is not the historical person Jesus who is the Word; it is the resurrected, ever-living Christ.[36]

This leads to a second pervasive emphasis. This Jesus Christ is *alive*. The resurrection is a supracultural, divine event that all people must hear about whether Jew or gentile. In the resurrection is contained all the teaching on the death of Christ. The core of the Pauline *kerygma* (e.g., Acts 13:28–34; 1 Cor. 15:3–5) is that Christ "*died*, that he was *buried*, that he was *raised*, and that he *appeared*." Bruce notes that the facts touching Jesus' death and resurrection are always primary in importance. The need for corroborative evidence was essential because the resurrection was so extraordinary.[37] Such first-hand evidence was considered legal testimony in Roman courts, so it had special importance for the gentiles. But it was the resurrection which gave Christ the right to lordship and to Paul his calling and apostleship. It is not surprising that there are more references to the resurrection in apostolic preaching than to the death of Christ and the cross of Christ. Because this Christ is alive, the human spirit will also be made alive and will be joined with Christ in a totally new relationship (Eph. 2:1; 2 Cor. 5:17; Gal. 2:20).

The content of Paul's continuous word is grounded in his own phenomenal conversion experience. His conversion has to be understood in the context of his call to the gentile world.[38] The call is not conversion but rather is the witness to his conversion and is dependent upon conversion. Unless the "call" is supported by the reality of his changed life, the commissioning makes little sense.[39] It was the resurrected Jesus who addressed him. The core of the Pauline message is here in his conversion and call. This is knowledge communicated both by revelation and experience at the deepest personal level.

> Is not, after all, Paul's conversion experience the secret behind his theological thinking, thus making his thought rooted in his conversion experience and inexplicable apart from it? . . . Does not the passionate character of Paul's theological language point to its origin and source in his dramatic conversion experience?[40]

The basic content of the continuous word, given concrete proof by his conversion and call, is that the risen Christ gives *new life*. Salvation through Christ is the *new way*. The old order has given way to the new. Salvation results in a completely new life. The strongest and most convincing appeals Paul made were those in which he compared the old order with the new.[41] His own conversion and the thought that comes from it is primary data. It was this transition from the old order to the new that fit so well the apocalyptic framework.

The Particular Word

In turning to the particular word, the gospel is cast into the specific locale and moment. The particularity of Paul's gospel helps explain why one theme comes up in certain epistles but not in others. It also helps us understand why the emphasis on one theme is different in one place from another.[42] The Word must connect to the world, and it is in the contingencies of truly human situations that this connection takes place. "Particularity and occasionality do not constitute a contamination of Paul's 'pure thought'; rather they serve to make the truth of the gospel the effective Word of God."[43]

Our case study returns us to the central symbol of apocalyptic in order to see how teaching on the Parousia differed in Thessalonica and Corinth. While the underlying theme of Christ's return is firmly in place in both cases, the questions arising and the peculiarities of understanding in each case are tied to separate contexts.[44]

As a methodology for seeing the particular word, it is helpful to proceed along four lines of questioning. These questions ought to be raised when doing theology in any contemporary mission situation where believers should be thinking through their faith for themselves.

What is the general background?
What are the presenting problems?
What theological questions arise?
What appropriate directions should the theology take?

The Second Coming in Thessalonian Context

The Thessalonian correspondence gives an intimate picture of the earliest of Paul's writings. Among other insights into Paul's primary teaching at Thessalonica[45] the most distressing problem comes from unclarity about the return of Jesus Christ (1 Thess. 4:13-5:11). Our purpose is to analyze briefly the contextual issues that guided Paul in writing as he did to the Thessalonians. Then, by looking at the same theme in First Corinthians we shall see differences in the teaching because of a situational focus of needs presented by the two contexts.[46]

The Background

There are considerable differences among the scholars regarding the social and political situation when the gospel first came to the city of Thessalonica.[47] The majority of Thessalonian believers were probably non-Jewish. It would also seem that the believers came from the ordinary working class, since Paul makes direct reference to the need for continuing work and earning daily wages (1 Thess. 2:9–12).

The Thessalonian religious situation had an apocalyptic quality. The major cult, the cult of the temple of Roma, stood for a coming new era, a victorious and prosperous age that was about to dawn under a powerful ruler. The hope for such a day was expressed by such terms as "lord" and "son of God."[48] So pervasive was the belief in what was going to happen that, on one hand, Paul's word about Jesus would have had an immediate audience. But, on the other hand, leaders in cultic society would have seen Paul as disruptive to the system, as an upstart competitor.

Among the plethora of subcults the most popular was dedicated to Cabirus. It carried the tradition of "a martyred hero" who was "murdered by his brothers," "buried with symbols of royal power," and "expected to return to help lowly individuals."[49] The myth is strikingly similar to Paul's message about Jesus. The Cabirus cult had originally been open to all classes, but by Paul's time it had developed into a religion for the wealthy and politically powerful. So, the working classes who were in need of "a savior" readily accepted the new Lord, Jesus Christ.

The Presenting Problem

Probably not long after Paul left, the Christians went through some kind of crisis which Paul described as *thlipsis* (1 Thess. 1:6; 3:3, 7). The "affliction" was related to their conversion, it seems, and, in light of Acts 17, it could have come as a direct aftermath of what Paul went through when he was there. It is quite possible that the outbreak was so severe that some Christians were actually martyred. Short of suffering martyrdom, the stress and anxiety of natural death brought a variety of questions to the surface. The thought of being separated from dead loved ones upon Jesus' return was a fearful prospect. It could have been that Paul had not given them teaching to cover this situation perhaps because he had to leave so unexpectedly that he couldn't finish all he had planned.

Theological Questions

Now answers had to be given on two critical points: (1) What is the state of those who have died and the relative advantage or disadvantage of those who remain alive? (2) When will the day of the Lord occur?[50] It is very possible that the Thessalonians understood that the body was to be "translated" rather than "transformed," and to be translated bodily one would have to be alive. So, what of those who had already passed on? Initially all had expected the return of Christ while they were all yet alive, but now the state of those loved ones who had died was very uncertain.[51]

The Contextual Answer

Paul seems to argue that the good news concerning hope for their dead is something that the Thessalonians had not known before (1 Thess. 4:13). In summary, the resurrection of Christians who had already died would take place as the first event signaling the Lord's return. So those who had died and those who are still alive have equal privilege. Those who are alive shall "not precede those who have fallen asleep" (1 Thess. 4:13–18). The second question which has to do with the timing of the Second Coming turns into an exhortation on preparedness. The real issue is not when Jesus will return but that Christians be always ready! (1 Thess. 5:1–11).

It is important to note that in building his teaching concerning the time of the Parousia Paul uses local expressions. These metaphors are unique to his Thessalonian correspondence. There are several examples, but the most notable is "thief in the night" (1 Thess. 5:2). A phrase of this kind would have immediate impact. A second set of idioms is "sons of light" and "sons of the day," which he uses in a variety of ways to make his case for preparedness.

In conclusion, therefore, this section of primary revelational theology is developed from within the context. It does not cover all that is to be taught concerning the Parousia but deals with two points that needed attention in a particular place. Another quite different situation existed in Corinth where the same theme required a different kind of theological answer.

The Second Coming in Corinthian Context

The Background

The backdrop to the eschatological problems in the Corinthian Church is a complicated cross-weave between social and economic tension, religious plurality, and ethnic diversity. To summarize in a few words the Corinth that Paul knew is presumptuous. Factors that bear on both death and resurrection must be understood as developing quite naturally out of the chaotic make-up of this city. The seaport attracted all sorts of people. Jews were well represented and worshiping in the synagogues. The popular religion of Aphrodite was sensual and debased. To "live like Corinthians" was an epithet that stood for a loose, immoral lifestyle. Corinth was the center for business, sports, arts, and open individualism. In this environment, little place was found for deeply spiritual things. Based on its reputation alone, Paul might not have chosen to preach in Corinth, but such a strategic center could not be ignored.

As for the church, it was begun in great difficulties. There was such strong Jewish opposition at first that Paul moved his activities to the home of a man called Justus (Acts 18). As in Thessalonica, it would seem that most of the converts were from the lower classes (1 Cor. 1:26ff.). However, several of the Christians did come from the ranks of eminent people (Rom. 16:23). It is important to see the heterogeneity of the church and the tendency to excesses on both the liberal and conservative sides. The carnality of Corinthian ritual caused a counter movement which disdained the body and material things. This created a problem on one hand, while radical independence and exhibitionism was also a source of trouble on the other.[52]

The Presenting Problem

This unusual situation had the effect of producing both the finest and the worst models of apostolic Christianity. The revolt against the flesh and the world resulted in extreme forms of spirituality.[53] On the other side, it was here that the church encountered its grossest case of immorality (1 Cor. 5:1–5). In the median expression of Christianity were demonstrations of the *charismata* which had to be brought into spiritual order, and innovations in worship that testify to a dynamic experience of Christ (see 1 Cor. 14).

Behind the misinterpretation of the resurrection were some extremists who felt they had special status and had reached a state of completeness. We meet this group in 1 Corinthians 4:8, where Paul writes:

> Already you are filled! Already you have become rich! Without us you have become kings! And would that you did reign, so that we might share the rule with you!

With this ironic language Paul addressed a group of super spiritual people (*pneumatikoi*), or those who claimed some sort of finished perfection (*teleoi*). Paul referred to the confusion raised by this group in his long resurrection passage, chapter 15. The problem they had created can be described as "over-realized eschatology." Some scholars have taken the position that it was this "group of fanatical believers who relied heavily on Christian sacraments to give them power and guarantee their salvation."[54] The problem this group raised for the church was that they believed the resurrection had already taken place. Their Christian baptism had endowed them with the "spiritual knowledge" that, indeed, the resurrection had already taken place.

This was the Corinthian version of those in Timothy's care who believed the same thing (2 Tim. 2:18).

A second problem arose from the supposed spirituality of the resurrectionists. They had disdain for the weaker "unspiritual" members of the church. It was easy, in any case, for the congregation at Corinth to become fragmented because of the class society; this theological heresy brought further rift between the pneumatikoi and those whom they considered weak and without knowledge.

Theological Questions

The specific theological issue that all of this raised is summed up in 1 Corinthians 15:12: "Now if Christ is preached as raised from the dead, how can some of you say that there is no resurrection of the dead?"

Considering the context, incredible Corinth, it is not surprising that believers had taken positions on opposite ends of the resurrection issue. Some were saying they had already passed through the resurrection. This was also the group that denied the reality of death (having already been resurrected). The other side denied any kind of resurrection. For them, when death came, which indeed must happen, that was the end. These questions naturally were attached to other subissues, but Paul sets up his argument in 1 Corinthians 15:20–27 to meet the distortions of both groups.

The Contextual Answer

Paul's theologizing is done in a thoroughly contextual way. One can see that according to Paul's Jewish heritage, resurrection was an end-time event. Death is a fact that cannot be disregarded or wished away. And since death precedes the end, only those who are alive at the time of Jesus' return will escape it. Paul stresses "the presence of death in order to counter the Corinthian emphasis on the presence of the resurrection. . . . Death is the last enemy and will, in fact, continue to rage until the very end."[55]

For his Jewish audience in particular, Paul introduces Psalm 8 and Psalm 109 (1 Cor. 15:25, 26). The Corinthian tendency to gnosticism and false spirituality had caused them to misread the order of cosmic events. Christ's role is to subdue all things and finally bring them into subjection under God. Only when Christ, yet in the future, "ends" that conquest with the destruction of death will God himself be all in all.

The contextual answer, then, is twofold. The Christian's resurrection is in the future, and death is real. There has been no resurrection, nor will there be until a time known only to God. Before this happens, Christ must subdue all things and bring them under God's rule. Christ's own resurrection does inaugurate the reign of the Messiah, but it is the future application of the resurrection that is needed for Corinth, so Paul emphasizes this. In summary, "all persons must continue to suffer death. . . . Christians will be victorious, but only in view of the end which is yet to come."[56]

The way in which continuity and particularity interact is, therefore, not exceptional but is normative for the formation of the apostolic gospel. Paul's epistles cannot be understood if they are abstracted from the local setting and recast into a set order or bound together by propositions. The Epistles must be understood as the "fleshing-out" of the Word for people in their particular worlds as much as they are universal statements of crosscultural truth.

ABRAHAM'S FAITH AS A CONTINUOUS AND PARTICULAR THEME

It would be a valuable study, were there space to do so, to look in detail at the Abraham theme in both Galatians and Romans. I conclude by suggesting how the continuity-particularity principle is reflected. The theme of saving faith clearly underlies the argument in both epistles, but the purpose and function of the Abraham motif is much different in Galatians than in Romans.

Galatians

The way Abraham is introduced into Galatians is as a metaphor of truth in the fight against a devastating heresy among mainly gentile Christians (cf. Galatians 3-5). The Judaizers had begun perverting the gospel by working out a recombination on the themes of Abraham, the Torah, circumcision, and Christ. This was unallowable syncretism. People of faith could not look to the law for salvation. The law was a curse and was antithetical to the liberating message of Christ. Isaac, the son of the free woman, was the symbolic center (Gal. 4:21-31). Abraham must be identified with the new freedom in Jesus Christ. Abraham stood for faith, not works; for freedom, not slavery. The mission message of Galatians is that Abraham was given a promise that embraced the nations—the gentiles (Gal. 3:8-9). No one, Jew or gentile, could ever go back to the law. The continuous issue was faith. The particular issue was that a heresy had arisen which cut out the heart of the gospel.

Romans

The Abraham motif (cf. Romans 4, 9) conveys a different meaning because, again, it is constructed to meet a particular need. While Galatians connected Abraham to the hopelessness of the law, in Romans the focus of Abraham is on the new body of Christ, made up of both Jews and gentiles. The church at Rome is a mixed church, rather than a predominantly gentile church. In this epistle the relationship of people who have been redeemed by Christ to each other is central. The "core" gospel is that the conversion of the gentiles as well as the Jews is a fulfillment of Judaism rather than a betrayal.

In Rome, gentile Christians demonstrate openly what Abraham's call meant to "the nations" (Gn. 12:1-3). It is "not the children of the flesh who are the children of God, but the children of the promise are reckoned as descendants" (Rom. 9:8). Paul's dialogue with the Jews in chapters 9-11 meant as much to new gentile Christians who were in doubt about their place in the church as it did to the Jews. The conflict between Jewish and gentile Christians at Rome gave Paul the opportunity to "address the church about the fundamental role of Israel in salvation history in the framework of the universality of God's grace in Christ for all people."[57]

The gospel graciously broke out of Jerusalem into Antioch and the gentile world. This meant that if the non-Jewish world were to be included in the body of those who accept the lordship of Christ, there would have to be a change in the forms and symbols of communication. Paul's call to the gentiles was a call to contextualize the gospel. It demanded faithfulness to the central Word of truth and openness to the uniqueness of each situation. The apocalyptic theme in 1 Thessalonians and 1 Corinthians demonstrates the principle of continuity and particularity. We have only suggested what Galatians and Romans illustrate with respect to Abraham.

The intention of this chapter has been to emphasize the contextual methodology of Paul. The apocalyptic and Abraham themes are but illustrations of the way in which the whole of the apostolic gospel was presented. The central message of Jesus was carefully retained while, as the Spirit directed, this message was given incarnational expression. Paul worked in a variety of local situations with no text other than the Old Testament. In theologizing today, as we move from culture to culture, we have the Scriptures. Revelational truth is the foundation on which particular theologies are constructed. We must know the Word, and we must know the culture.

The hermeneutic of the culture will guide us in appropriating the Word, while at the same time the irrevocable truth of the Word will judge and transform the culture.

NOTES

[1] A principle recognized by D. von Allman in his article, "The Birth of Theology," *International Review of Missions* (Jan. 25 1975, 253):37. "The prime quality required of a theologian is careful attention to the living expression of the Church's faith" with a sharp eye for cultural issues that make for relevance as well as those that tend toward heresy. Throughout this study a careful distinction needs to be made, however, between revelational or primary theology and subsequent theologizing done by the church.

[2] One of the best sources for the Jewish problems is Schuyler Brown, *The Origins of Christianity: A Historical Introduction to the New Testament* (New York: Oxford University Press, 1984).

[3] Ref. "contention," (Acts 1:2) and Peter's sermon that followed.

[4] The heterogeneous make-up of the church, ministry of laity, openness of worship, and readiness to commission Saul and Barnabas are unique qualities.

[5] Ibid.

[6] E.g., the Epistles are not a source for Acts. But the Epistles confirm the historical structure of Acts, and the narratives of Acts make it possible to weave together fragmentary information found in the Epistles. See the helpful discussion in Donald Guthrie, *New Testament Introduction: Gospels and Acts* (London: Tyndale, 1968), 322.

[7] See chapter 5 especially and Martin's critique of Ernst Käsemann, *Reconciliation: A Study of Paul's Theology* (Atlanta: John Knox, 1981), 71.

[8] See Cilliers Breytenbach, "Reconciliation: Shifts in Christian Soteriology" in *Reconciliation and Reconstruction* (Pretoria: University of South Africa, 1986), 1.

[9] See Nikolaus Walter, "Christusglaube und Heidnische Religiositat in Paulinischen Gemeinden," *New Testament Studies* 25 (1979):422.

[10] J. Christiaan Beker, *Paul the Apostle: The Triumph of God in Life and Thought* (Philadelphia: Fortress, 1980).

[11] William Barclay, *The Mind of St. Paul* (New York: Harper and Row, 1975). Discussion on "incarnation," 60.

[12] For example, his contextual uses of such terms as justification, liberation, and reconciliation. See Dean Gilliland, *Pauline Theology and Mission Practice* (Grand Rapids: Baker, 1983), 99.

[13] Daniel von Allman's sequence: missionaries, translators, poets, and theologians, "The Birth of Theology."

[14] Beker, "The Character of Paul's Thought," *Paul*, 11.

[15] The problem of "harmonizing" Paul is insoluble only if we see his statements as propositions rather than divergent pictures. Paul is a coherent rather than systematic thinker. Beker speaks of his "timely and intelligible kerygma." Ibid., 9.

[16] The burdens of his polemic in Galatians (Jewish) and in Colossians (a local heresy).

[17] Beker, *Paul*, 11.

[18] See Gilliland, *Pauline Theology*, 20.

[19] "Doctrinal Paul," as in F. C. Baur, *Paul the Apostle of Jesus Christ*, second edition, 2 vols. (London: Williams and Norgato, 1876). "Cultic Paul" as in W. Heitmuller,

"Zum Problem Paulus und Jesus," *Zeitschrift fur die neutestamentliche Wissenschaft*, 13, 1912, 320. "Mystic Paul" as in Adolf Deissmann, *Paul: A Study in Social and Religious History*, second edition (London: Hodder and Stoughton, 1926).

[20] Leander E. Keck, *Paul and His Letters*, Proclamation Commentaries (Philadelphia: Fortress, 1979), 65; Denys H. Whitely, *The Theology of St. Paul* (Philadelphia: Fortress, 1964), 45; E. P. Sanders, *Paul and Palestinian Judaism* (Philadelphia: Fortress, 1977), 123, 518; Ernst Käsemann in "The Righteousness of God," *New Testament Questions of Today* (Philadelphia: Fortress, 1969), 168; A. Schweitzer, *The Mysticism of Paul* (New York: H. Holt and Co., 1931).

[21] Nils A. Dahl, "Review of Sanders, *Paul and Palestinian Judaism*" in *Religious Studies Review* 4 (1978):153; F. F. Bruce, *Paul, Apostle of the Heart Set Free* (Devon: Paternoster, 1977), 424.

[22] Beker notes the words of Franz Overbeck, "In the Second Century, noboby understood Paul except Marcion, who misunderstood him," *Paul*, 30.

[23] Beker, *Paul*, 31.

[24] The liberal interpretation of *religionsgeschichtliche* school of interpretation was treated by Herman Ridderbos in *Paul and Jesus* (Grand Rapids: Baker, 1958), 3.

[25] F. F. Bruce, *Paul and Jesus* (Grand Rapids: Baker, 1974), 16.

[26] Ibid., 22.

[27] Ridderbos, *Paul and Jesus*, 59.

[28] Käsemann, "On the Subject of Primitive Christian Apocalyptic" in *New Testament Questions of Today* (Philadelphia: Fortress, 1969), 108.

[29] Beker, *Paul*, 16.

[30] See Philipp Vielhauer, "Introduction to Apocalypses and Related Subjects," *New Testament Apocrypha*. ed., W. Schneemelcher, 2 vols. (Philadelphia: Westminster, 1963-65), 2:581.

[31] Klaus Koch, *The Rediscovery of the Apocalyptic*, Studies in Biblical Theology (London: SCM Press, 1972).

[32] Beker, *Paul*, 144.

[33] Beker now seems to have modified his earlier position which claimed that apocalyptic is, in fact, the center. In a 1986 article he uses the term "master symbol" to describe apocalyptic. See J. C. Beker, "The Method of Recasting Pauline Theology," *Society of Biblical Literature* (1986) seminar papers, 596.

[34] Timothy Carriker, "A Review of J. Christiaan Beker's Thesis in Light of 1 Thessalonians 4:13-5:11 and 1 Corinthians 15:20-28," an unpublished Ph.D. seminar paper done at Fuller Theological Seminary, March 1987.

[35] See Gilliland, *Pauline Theology*, 146, esp. footnotes 51 and 53, on views by C. von Weizsacker and A. Diessmann.

[36] Barclay, *The Mind*, 122.

[37] Bruce, *Paul and Jesus*, 49.

[38] Gilliland, *Pauline Theology*, 29.

[39] Krister Stendahl, *Paul Among Jews and Gentiles* (Philadelphia: Fortress, 1981), 177. See a critique of Stendahl's position by R. Martin, *Reconciliation*, 24-31.

[40] Beker, *Paul*, 7.

[41] Summary of texts in Gilliland, *Pauline Theology*, 24.

[42] The work of Robert Schreiter in the area of "semiotics"—the discovery of "signs" or themes from cultures for construction of theologies—has opened up much helpful debate in this area. *Constructing Local Theologies* (Maryknoll, N.Y.: Orbis, 1985).

[43] Beker, *Paul*, 24.

[44] For much of what follows I am indebted to Timothy Carriker, who has done careful exegetical work in an unpublished paper. See footnote 34.

[45] The apostolic gospel, an early statement of Paul's teaching, is summed up by Roland Allen in *Missionary Methods: St. Paul's or Ours?* (Grand Rapids: Eerdmans, 1972, sixth ed.), 68.

[46] It needs to be emphasized that while our theologizing must follow the bipolar models of Paul, it is not our intention to place revelational theology on the same plane as subsequent theologizing done by the church. See footnote 1.

[47] See the valuable discussion in K. D. Donfried, "The Cults of Thessalonica and the Thessalonian Correspondence," *New Testament Studies* 31 (1985):336-56.

[48] Donfried, *New Testament Studies*, 342ff.

[49] Robert Jewett, *The Thessalonian Correspondence, Pauline Rhetoric and Millenarian Piety* (Phildelphia: Fortress, 1986), 128ff.

[50] Carriker, "A Review," 17.

[51] For discussion on "transformation" vs. "translation" in the Thessalonian context see J. Gillman, "Signals of Transformation in 1 Thessalonians 4:13-18," *Catholic Biblical Quarterly* 47 (1985):263-81.

[52] See Leon Morris' article on "First Epistle to the Corinthians" in *ISBE*, 1 (rev.), G. W. Bromiley, ed. (Grand Rapids: Eerdmans, 1979), 775ff.

[53] The case of abstinence from sexual intercourse in marriage as a revolt against the immorality of prevailing traditional custom is one interpretation of 1 Corinthians 7:36-38.

[54] Carriker, "A Review," footnote 50, p. 32.

[55] Ibid., 45.

[56] Ibid., 52.

[57] Beker, *Paul*, 92.

4

The New Covenant:
Knowing God in Context

Charles Van Engen

PAUL AND DOROTHY MEYERINK have been translating the Bible for the Tzeltal people of southern Mexico. Some years ago I sat in Paul's living room discussing a major translation problem he was facing. With obvious frustration Paul explained his problem:

> The Tzeltals have no word for king, and no concept of kingship. They have the concepts of the head of a clan, the president of a municipality, and a large ranch-owner. But none of those accurately reflect the biblical idea of the kingdom of God. How can the Tzeltal people come to know God as their Lord who reigns in heaven and earth, without a concept of a king?

As Paul and I talked, it became clear that we were dealing with something much deeper than "dynamic equivalence" communication. Paul's question was a fundamental one of epistemology, that is, about knowing God in context. But Paul and I realized that the

CHARLES VAN ENGEN, M.Div., Th.M., Ph.D., assistant professor of the theology of mission at Fuller Theological Seminary, was raised in Mexico where his parents served as missionaries of the Reformed Church in America. He trained Spanish-speaking pastors for twelve years. Van Engen studied missiology at the Free University of Amsterdam and taught at Western Theological Seminary, before coming to Fuller. His books are The Growth of the True Church and Hijos del Pacto.

problem was ours as well. How could Westerners whose mathematics teaches that one does not equal three conceive of a trinitarian God? How could North Americans steeped in materialism think about God as a "spirit"? How could two very individualistic missionaries comprehend the "body" image of Paul's ecclesiology?

Paul and I were at the bedrock of the problem of contextualization—a problem much deeper than the communication of the gospel by Christians to non-Christians. Contextualization is most fundamentally a problem of knowing God within the limitations of culturally specific human contexts. God's self-disclosure in the midst of human cultures is like a square peg in a round hole, the dialectical mystery, at once revelatory and hidden, whereby we come to know God and to understand that we do not fully know God. The first question, then, in contextualization is not the communication of the gospel so much as the understanding of the gospel, the knowledge of God in context.

THE MYSTERY OF REVEALED HIDDENNESS

The apostle Paul referred to God's hidden self-disclosure both in terms of the created order, and in relation to God's special revelation in Jesus Christ. (Cf. Romans 1:20 and 11:33–34.) Revealed hiddenness—this is the paradox of divine self-disclosure in human consciousness and the most difficult part of contextualization theory.

Karl Barth spoke of the role of faith in our knowing God's hidden self-disclosure:

> It is in faith, and therefore in the fulfillment of the knowledge of God, that we can understand the fact that we know, view and conceive God, not as a work of our nature, not as a performance on the basis of our own capacity, but only as a miraculous work of the divine good-pleasure, so that, knowing God, we necessarily know His hiddenness. . . . With this assertion we confess that, knowing God, we do not comprehend how we come to know Him, that we do not ascribe to our cognition as such the capacity of this knowledge, but that we can only trace it back to God. It is God alone, and God's revelation and faith in it, which will drive and compel us to this avowal.[1]

In other words, the very fact that we know God through *faith* should tell us that we do not know all there is to know about God. In fact, we only "see in a mirror dimly" (1 Cor. 13:12). Texts like Psalm 139:6; Job 36:26; Acts 14:16, 17; Rom. 11:25; 12:33–36; 1 Cor. 2:7; Eph. 3:3; Col. 1:15, 26; 1 Tim. 1:17; 3:16; and Rev. 10:7, emphasize the "mystery" and "unknowability" of God. Many theologians have affirmed this basic characteristic of God's revelation.[2] So the first "contextualization" of the gospel involves the mystery of God's self-revelation in human cultures.

THE MYSTERY OF REVELATION IN MULTIPLE CONTEXTS

But there is a second and more complex sense of the misfit of the gospel in human cultures.[3] This greater mismatch is a result of the Christian missionary movement.

As the gospel crossed cultural barriers over several centuries the faith assertions of Christendom did not seem to fit the new cultures encountered by the gospel. So a progression of attempted solutions were suggested, with an accompanying succession of words like, *persuasion, Christianization, compulsion, accommodation, adaptation, fulfillment, syncretism, indigenization, transformation,* and *dialogue.*[4]

The latest word, "contextualization," involves some difficult theological issues like incarnation, revelation, truth, divine-human interaction, and the shape of corporate religious experience. Contextualization takes seriously the difference between gospel and culture, and accepts the fact that "the gospel always stands in divine judgement on human culture."[5]

RESPONSES TO THE MYSTERY: MODELS OF CONTEXTUALIZATION

Contextualization theory has generated a number of models for explaining how the gospel may take shape in various cultural contexts. Krikor Haleblian,[6] Stephen Bevans,[7] and David Hesselgrave[8] have each suggested models by which contextualization theory may be synthesized. These have been examined more fully elsewhere in this volume.[9] For the purposes of this essay, we could distinguish four major models of "contextualization," based on their primary purposes: communication,[10] cultural relevance,[11] socio-economic change,[12] and inter-faith dialogue.

Louis Luzbetak summarized the first three of these models.

One cannot deny that considerable progress has been made in contextual methodology in recent years. The most common form of contextualization, that of the liberation theologians, has begun to temper its rhetoric, refine its concepts, and more clearly and explicitly indicate its methodology. . . . Some form of translation seems necessary particularly in beginning a local church—and here Kraft provides many useful insights. On the other hand, once the seed is sown, the new plant must be watered and cultivated so that it might grow and thrive—and here Schreiter provides us with an invaluable tool, a triple dialectic between the Gospel, the Church, and the local culture. In a word, contextualization is by no means a kind of missiological fad but a definite direction of great and lasting promise.[13]

More recently a fourth model arose out of the phenomenology of experiential faith and the common search for the holy, as inter-faith dialogue spilled over into "contextualization." Here the Christian faith was viewed as one of the world's religions standing beside other world religions. In cultures where Islam, Hinduism, Buddhism, and other religions found their acceptance, Christians were to compare their experiences of "faith" with those of people of other faiths. In an increasingly pluralistic world many sought, rightly, to demonstrate their acceptance of radically diverse cultural forms. But the growing awareness of cultural diversity sometimes contributed to the acceptance of religious relativity as well.[14]

Maybe it is time for the contextualization debate to move further in the process of understanding the gospel in culture. Might there not be another major model from which to understand the task of contextualization?[15] The remainder of this essay will explore the biblical theology of *covenant* as a possible model for knowing God in multiple cultural contexts.

The need to consider a new model of contextualization springs from an awareness of the new reality of the world church. It is an acknowledged fact that the "center of gravity" of the world church has shifted to Asia, Africa, and Latin America. This fact has called us to a reorientation of mission not only in numerical, strategic, and organizational terms, but also in relation to doing contextual theology. We now have Christians from a multitude of cultures reading the Scriptures, reflecting on God's revelation, and seeking to know God in their own context. James Scherer recently observed that,

> While the matter of cultural adaptation or inculturation is happily a virtual non-issue, further research is necessary to clarify how the understanding of the gospel is affected by receptor cultures, not merely in the linguistic transmission of the gospel message but in the actual understanding of the gospel and its appropriation within a given culture. We need to study more about how the gospel is understood in diverse cultural contexts, thereby increasing our understanding of the richness of God's revelation.[16]

On the opposite side of the coin, some Westerners, like Lesslie Newbigin, are beginning to call for a radical reexamination of biblical faith without all of the layers of Western cultural assumptions that cloud Western understanding of God, the gospel, Jesus Christ, and Christian faith. There is a growing realization that all theologies are local theologies.[17] Maybe it is time to look again at the matter of the "square peg in a round hole"—but now from the standpoint of knowing God in context.

THE NEW COVENANT, A BIBLICAL MODEL FOR KNOWING GOD IN CONTEXT

We are back to our original question—how do we come to know the mystery of a hidden God revealed in multiple contexts? Nowhere is this mystery more poignantly expressed than in the conceptual framework of a biblical theology of the covenant. We will not deal here with the extensive and complicated aspects of biblical theology of the covenant. Nor are we looking at "covenantal theology" as it was developed in the Reformed tradition over a couple of centuries after the Protestant Reformation. Rather, we are interested in using the newer methods of exegesis which examine the text as it has been received, viewing it as a narrative articulation of the theological perspectives of the people of God throughout the centuries. Our major concern is the covenantal perspective as a possible model for knowing God's hidden revelation in diverse contexts.

Harvie Conn is among those who have called for a covenantal perspective as a new theological center for a contextual hermeneutic.[18]

> Emerging from the debate (surrounding evangelical hermeneutics) is an evangelical call to see theology as the discipled (not simply disciplined) reflection/action of "knowing God . . . ."
>
> This process may be called contextual hermeneutic, the covenant conscientization of the whole people of God to the hermeneutical obligations of the gospel in their culture . . . .
>
> The core of this contextual hermeneutic is the recovery of the covenant dimension of doing theology—a dimension modelled most beautifully by John Calvin's expository method, of *theologia pietatis* . . . .[19]

The Historical Development of the Covenant

The covenant refers to the actions of God in history which reveal the eternal God's hiddenness in relationship with his people through time and space. But this presents a real problem, as Martin Noth has explained.

In the biblical witness we deal with a revelation of God which has occurred within history while, after all, God cannot be limited to history and time.[20]

To soften the dialectic between God's eternality and humanity's temporalness, Noth speaks of Israel's continual, "re-presentation," the constant reenactment, and reparticipation of the people of God in both past and future events where God had broken into history in relationship with God's people.

> As in all history, so this history is especially involved in the tension between the course of time and the presence of God which is not bound by time, between the "mediateness" and the "immediateness" of God, of which Karl Barth speaks in discussing God's unending creations. "Re-presentation" is founded on this—that God and his action are always present, while man in his inevitable temporality cannot grasp this present-ness except by "re-presenting" the action of God over and over again in his worship.[21]

The Covenant: Same Meaning, Many Forms

In the covenant we find a historically conditioned (or better, a historically contextualized) relationship between an eternally present God and a temporally specific humanity. The historicity of the covenantal forms also means a tremendous variety of cultural, political, and social contexts in which the covenant may be found. Thus in the covenant we have essentially the same relationship at all times and in all places, and yet one which takes on radically different forms in each time and place. Referring to this relationship as "the covenant of grace," Herman Bavinck emphasized its eternal sameness.

> The covenant of grace is everywhere and at all times one in essence, but always manifests itself in new forms and goes through differing dispensations. . . . God remains the first and the last in all the dispensations of the covenant of grace, whether of Noah, Abraham, Israel, or the New Testament church. Promise, gift, grace, are and remain the content of it. . . . The one great, all-inclusive promise of the covenant of grace is: "I will be your God, and the God of thy people." A single straight line runs from the mother-promise of Gen. 3:15 to the apostolic blessing of 2 Cor. 13:13. . . . It is always the same Gospel (Rom. 1:2 & Gal. 3:8), the same Christ (John 14:6 & Acts 4:12), the same faith (Acts 15:11 & Rom. 4:11), and always confers the same benefits of forgiveness and eternal life (Acts 10:43 & Rom. 4:3).[22]

Old Testament scholars like Norman Gottwald,[23] Lucien Cerfaux,[24] and Gerhard von Rad[25] have emphasized the continuity of the covenant concept throughout Israel's history. Although we may not subsume the great diversity of scriptural perspectives as tightly within the covenant concept as W. Eichrodt did,[26] it is almost impossible to understand the continuity and meaning of God's revelation to humanity apart from the concept of the covenant. In its most fundamental and essential meaning, the covenant could be stated, "I will be your God, and you shall be my people."[27] This timeless relationship was expressed in various epochs in strikingly similar structural forms.

1. There is a recitation of God's mighty acts.
2. The Word of God spells out the covenantal relationship.
3. Promises are associated with the covenantal relationship.
4. Worship and sacrifice are carried out by the people.
5. YHWH gives a physical sign or symbol of the covenant.[28]

Grace, revelation, law, cultic practice, communal self-identity, corporate response, and the meaning and goal of YHWH's acts in history are all incorporated and given meaning in this covenantal relationship. As John Kromminga said it, quoting from W. van der Merwe, "The covenant is to be understood as that relationship between God and creature, ordained in eternity, instituted in history and directed to consummation."[29]

And yet we are all aware of the radically distinct contexts in which this timeless relationship has been expressed. This incredible diversity can be illustrated by summarizing the covenant in at least six contextual manifestations.

1. Adam: the covenant and the ultimate victory over evil (Gn. 3:9–21)
2. Noah: the covenant and the preservation of all living things (Gn. 6:17–22; 9:1–17)
3. Abraham: the covenant and the election of Abraham's seed for the sake of the nations (Gn. 12, 15, 17. We must also include here the "re-presentation" of that covenantal relationship in both an inherited and a personal way with Isaac—Gn. 26:3–5; and with Jacob—Gn. 28:13–15.)
4. Moses: the covenant and the law, a nation formed (Ex. 2:24; 19:4–6; 20:1–17; 24:1–10; 25:10–22; 31:16–17; 32; 34:1–10; 40:18–38; Lv. 26:6–12; Dt. 9:15; Num. 14. In Ex. 32 and Nm. 14, God offers to make from Moses "a great nation," each time specifically in reference to promises made earlier to Abraham. With Joshua, the covenant is related to the possession of the promised land, but intimately connected with Moses and the Exodus. Cf. Dt. 29:1–29; 30:1–20; Jos. 5; 24.)

5. David: the covenant and the Davidic reign—a kingdom (1 Chr. 16:15-17; 17:1-27; parallels in 2 Sm. 7:1-29; 23:5; 2 Kgs. 1-12; Pss. 89:34-37; 105:8; 111:5; 106:45; Is. 42:6; 55:3; 59:21.)
6. Jesus Christ: the covenant and the Holy Spirit, redemption wrought once-for-all, the church, the kingdom come and coming (Is. 54:10; 55:3; Jer. 4:3-4; 31:31; 32:36-40; Ez. 34:24; Mt. 3:11, 16; 26:28; Mk. 14:24; Lk. 22:20; Acts 3:25-26; Rom. 11:27; 1 Cor. 11:25; 2 Cor. 3:6; Gal. 3:6; Heb. 7:22; 8:6, 8; 9:15, 19-20; 10:12, 24, 29; 13:20-21)[30]

The Covenant: Same Meaning, Fuller Knowledge

Thus on the one hand, we see the continuity of the covenantal relationship of God with his children at all times and in all contexts. But there is also something wonderfully progressive about this history that forces us to accept the fact of the incompleteness of that which Adam, Noah, or Abraham, or Moses, or David knew of God's nature and revealed will. Precisely because we see the "continuity" of progressive revelation, we also see the deeper, fuller, and more complete self-revelation of God down through history. This seems to be the intention of the writer of Hebrews when he says,

In the past God spoke to our forefathers through the prophets at many times and in various ways, but in these last days he has spoken to us by his Son, whom he appointed heir of all things, and through whom he made the universe. (Heb. 1:1-2 NIV)

Whether it was an understanding of God's nature, God's redemptive activity, God's providential care of the world, God's love for all the nations, or God's ultimate plan for the whole of creation—in each manifestation of the covenant there was something more deeply revealed, something more fully understood. Here is the crux of the matter. Within a fundamental sameness of the relationship, each subsequent historical-cultural-political context revealed something more concerning God's nature and relationship with his people.

The Covenant: a Series of Hermeneutical Circles

One way we may comprehend the dialectic is by viewing covenantal revelation as a series of "hermeneutical circles." The concept of the "hermeneutical circle" is not new, but has received a renewed emphasis in the praxeological theology of Latin American theologians of liberation.[31] The methodology is also proving helpful to many who are not from Latin America. Recently David Bosch, for example, highlighted the dynamic character of this methodology.

The issue as to whether we should use the Bible deductively or inductively is really, therefore, a nonissue. We are, whether we like it or not, and whether we know it or not, involved in a two-way interpretative process. This "hermeneutical circle" ought not to be a vicious circle, but one in which a dynamic and creative dialogue takes place between "text" and "context." Without the context the text remains ambiguous and misleading. . . . These facts (of indigenization in church history) should not upset us unduly. If we take the incarnation seriously, vastly different forms of indigenization and contextualization are to be expected and applauded. As a matter of fact, the Bible itself is an example of contextualization.[32]

From the standpoint of the knowledge of God, the covenant gives us an opportunity to understand how the "hermeneutical circle" served in each context to reveal something deeper and fuller about God's nature. Paul referred to this as "the mystery made known to me by revelation" in Ephesians 3. He spoke of,

the mystery of Christ, which was not made known to men in other generations as it has now been revealed by the Spirit of God's holy apostles and prophets. This mystery is that through the gospel the Gentiles are heirs together with Israel, members together of one body, and sharers together in the promise of Christ Jesus. . . . this grace was given to me: to preach to the Gentiles the unsearchable riches of Christ, and to make plain to everyone the administration of this mystery (oikonomia tou mysteriou), which for ages past was kept hidden in God, who created all things.

(Eph. 3:4–9 NIV)

What could have been more "discontinuous," more "mysterious," for Paul than the salvation of the gentiles? And it is precisely in radically new historical contexts (through Jesus Christ, after Pentecost, in the church, and propelled by the gospel's spread throughout the gentile world) that Paul saw God's revelatory purposes taking on deeper and fuller meaning.

(God's) intent was that now, through the church, the manifold wisdom of God should be made known to the rulers and authorities in the heavenly realms, according to his eternal purpose which he accomplished in Christ Jesus our Lord.   (Eph. 3:10–11 NIV)

We could represent the various historically contextualized manifestations of the covenant as a "hermeneutical spiral" whereby over time the eternal God becomes progressively more completely known to God's people.

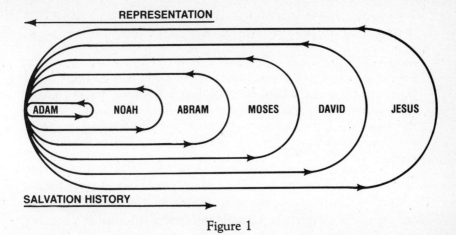

Figure 1

God's self-revelation never really gets beyond the most basic issue of God's triumph over evil (Adam), and God's election of a people
for service as a blessing to all the nations (Abram) (see 1 Peter 2).
God's law is never abrogated, nor are the promises of David's eternal
reign ever annulled. And yet in each new context something deeper
and fuller is revealed. Paul exemplified this discontinuous continuity
when he spoke of the fact that as in Adam all died, so in Christ, all
will be made alive (Rom. 5:12–21).

The Revelational Contextualization of the Covenant

Once we have seen God's covenantal revelation as a continuous
progression through time, we need to go back and look at it contextually. Not only is there an increased deepening and fullness across
time, but in each context where the covenant is manifested, it is
shaped precisely for that particular context.

The Covenant as Historical Contextualization

Consider the first humans, created in God's image, living in
perfection in Eden, with the possibility of disobeying their creator.
The particular contextual question has to do with their continued
obedience and the possibility of evil entering the world. With their
fall, the question becomes even more urgent—will evil triumph over
God's good? The covenantal formula in Genesis 3:15 clearly speaks
to this issue, though the promise is darkened by the result of Adam
and Eve's sin, with dire consequences for them and their children.

In the case of Noah the context deals with the increasing sinfulness of humanity chronicled in Genesis 4–6. Such was the distance of the created ones from their creator that God,

> was grieved that he had made man on the earth, and his heart was filled with pain. So the Lord said, "I will wipe mankind, whom I have created, from the face of the earth—men and animals, and creatures that move along the ground, and birds of the air—for I am grieved that I have made them."   (Gn. 6:6-7 NIV)

Here the contextual question has to do with the continued existence of all living things, including humanity whose sin has tainted all creation. God's revelation in this context contains all the basic elements of the covenantal formula (recitation, command, promises, worship/sacrifice, and a sign), and conveys a specific knowledge of God in a particular context.

The contextualization of God's covenantal revelation can be described in similar terms in relation to Moses, David, and Jesus Christ. The particularity of each context contributed to something deeper and fuller being known about God's hiddenness, precisely because the context called forth a degree and content of revelation hitherto unknown.

The Covenant Becomes the "New Covenant"

The combination of the particularity of God's revelatory action in specific contexts over time, coupled with the universality of the covenantal relationship, seems to be the background of the biblical theology of the "new covenant," articulated in the prophets and later in the New Testament. This development of the covenant idea is linked to the Septuagint.

> (In the Septuagint) the covenant of Yahweh with the patriarchs, Moses, David and the people became freely given ordinances, or dispositions of the sovereign will of God, which declare both His demands and His saving purposes. And in Jer. 31:31ff, to mention the instance which is most important from the NT standpoint, and which represents both the climax and end of the OT idea of the covenant, the concept *kaine diatheke* allows us to conceive of the religion of the age of salvation, to which the gaze of the prophet is directed, only as the free gift of God, as the declaration of His saving will, as the revelation of grace, in relation to which Israel can only be a recipient. "Disposition," "declaration of the divine will," "the divine will self-revealed in history and establishing religion"—this is the religious concept of the *diatheke* in the LXX, and it represents a significant development of the Hebrew term even while preserving its essential content.[33]

As we move from the perspectives of Isaiah and Jeremiah through the intertestamental period into the age of the New Testament, we see an intricate interweaving of two concepts of the covenant: *kainos* and *neos*. And precisely in the interconnection of these two concepts we may find an approach to epistemological contextualization that both preserves the continuity of God's revelation and deepens the knowledge of God's hiddenness as revealed in each new context.

The "Neos" Covenant and Discontinuity

Of the two most common words for "new" since the classical period, namely, *neos* and *kainos*, the former signifies "what was not there before," "what has only just arisen or appeared," the latter, "what is new and distinctive" as compared with other things. *Neos* is new in time and origin, i.e., young, with a suggestion of immaturity or of lack of respect for the old. *Kainos* is what is new in nature, different from the usual, impressive, better than the old, superior in value or attraction. . . .[34]

Neos represents the idea of radical discontinuity which we normally associate with the English concept of "new." But it is quite rare in the New Testament. (Cf. Mt. 9:17; Lk. 5:39; 1 Cor. 5:7; Eph. 4:23; Col. 3:10; and Heb. 12:24.)[35] In each case the emphasis is on a complete break with the past, something totally disjunctive in kind from that which went before. Only in Hebrews 12:24 is the term used specifically concerning the covenant.

In the New Testament there is in fact a radical break between the "law and the prophets" and the complete, unique revelation of God in Jesus Christ. Paul emphasizes this radical discontinuity when he speaks of the "covenant" in legal terms like a marriage pact between two parties which then is cancelled upon the death of one party (Rom. 6:1-7:6). The same disjunction is emphasized by Paul in 2 Cor. 3:6-18, contrasting the former (written) covenant with the new one (of the Spirit).[36]

Earl Ellis spoke of this discontinuity in terms of the "typological" use which the New Testament writers made of the Old Testament, marking the consummation of the "Old" covenant in Jesus Christ.

New Testament typology is thoroughly christological in its focus. Jesus is the "prophet like Moses" (Acts 3:22ff) who in his passion brings the old covenant to its proper goal and end (Rom. 10:4; Heb. 10:9ff) and establishes a new covenant (Lk. 22:20, 29). As the messianic "son of David," i.e. "son of God," he is the recipient of the promises, titles and ascriptions given to the Davidic kings.

Because the new covenant consummated by Jesus' death is the occasion of the new creation initiated by his resurrection, covenant typology may be combined with creation typology: as the "eschatological Adam" and the "Son of Man," i.e. "Son of Adam," Jesus stands at the head of a new order of creation that may be compared and contrasted with the present one.[37]

The uniqueness of the Christ-event has a two-pronged significance for contextualization. In terms of the past it affirms the radically different nature of the "new" age inaugurated in Jesus Christ, the age of the Spirit, the church, grace through faith, and a "circumcision of the heart." But this discontinuity also impacts the future. The sequence of Adam, Noah, Abraham, Moses, David, Jesus Christ in fact stops with Jesus Christ, for there is nothing more to be fulfilled, or added, or completed. In terms of the contextualization of the gospel we may never go beyond the Christ-event, we may never add to it "another gospel" (in Paul's terminology), or take away from it the completeness found in Jesus Christ. To do so is anathema (Rv. 22:18–19). This forces us to look again at the covenant.

The "Kainos" Covenant and Continuity

The predominant idea of "new" in the New Testament is represented by *kainos*, and speaks of continuity in the midst of change. (See Mark 16:17; Luke 22:20; John 13:34; Rom. 6:4; 1 Cor. 11:25; 2 Cor. 3:6; 5:17; Gal. 6:15; Eph. 4:24; Heb. 8:8; 9:15; 2 Pet. 3:13; 1 Jn. 2:8; Rev. 2:17; 3:12; 21:1.)[38]

Jesus developed this concept in the context of his farewell speech.[39] In reference to the coming of a radically different age, Jesus issued a "new" (*kainos*) commandment: to love (Jn. 13:34). But this was not really new. The disciples of Jesus understood *agape* as simply an enrichment of that love which had been enjoined upon the people of God from very early times. Love for neighbor "is found already in the Old Testament (Lev. 19:18; Prov. 20:22; 24:29). In fact, love for God and for neighbor is the summary of the law (Mark 12:29)."[40] C. H. Dodd, in reference to John's teaching on love, pointed to the matter of continuity.

The entire process of man's salvation is set in motion by the love of God for the world (Jn. 3:16). The love of God is expressed in action by the Son whom He sent. The Father loves the Son, and the Son responds in obedience (3:35; 5:19–20). That is why the words and deeds of Jesus are the words and deeds of the Father (14:11, 24). Hence it is with the eternal love of God that Christ loves His own and loves them to the end (13:1).[41]

But Jesus called it a *kainos* commandment. "The command-ment is new," says C. K. Barrett, "in that it corresponds to the command that regulates the relation between Jesus and the Father (Jn. 10:18; 12:49ff; 15:10); the love of the disciples for one another is not merely edifying, it reveals the Father and the Son."[42] This is the revolutionary factor being injected by Jesus. "His followers are to reproduce, in their mutual love, the love which the Father showed in sending the Son, the love which the Son showed in laying down his life."[43]

This ancient command to love is now given to those followers who will live "between the times," after Jesus' going and before Jesus' coming again. It is the same concept as that found in Deu-teronomy, but now fuller, deeper, and more significantly revelatory of God's nature and will than ever before. It is a *kainos* command-ment giving living expression to the *kainos* covenant, sealed in Jesus' shed blood, and signified in the cup of communion (Lk. 22:20; 1 Cor. 11:25).

It is always the same covenant, but one that faces ever-new con-texts. David Bosch has called attention to what Andrew Walls has referred to as "the pilgrim principle."

> Andrew Walls, therefore, correctly adds to the need for recognizing the "indigenizing" principle the equally necessary "pilgrim" principle. "Along with the indigenizing principle which makes his faith a place to feel at home, the Christian inherits the pilgrim principle, which whispers to him that he has no abiding city and warns him that to be faithful to Christ will put him out of step with his society; for that society never existed, in East and West, ancient time or modern, which could absorb the word of Christ painlessly into its system. . . .
>
> A real danger exists, therefore, of overcontextualizing the gospel, of letting it become subservient to a group's interests and ideological predilections. This is certainly no imaginary fear in the case of third world Christianity. But neither is it for us.[44]

The "pilgrim principle" means that although in each con-text something deeper and fuller is revealed, yet that is only in relation and in continuity with what has gone before. Senior and Stuhlmueller emphasized this with regard to the "new" covenant in Hebrews.[45] Richard de Ridder pointed to the impact of this "new" covenant concept on our understanding of Great Commission in Matthew 28:18-20.[46]

This constantly deepening perspective of the "new covenant" in pilgrim continuity with the old might be represented as a series of contexts labeled Adam, Noah, Abram, Moses, David, and Jesus, as shown in Figure 2.

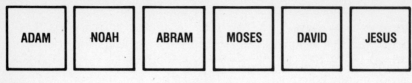

Figure 2

The covenantal revelation of God in each context would then be shown by the smaller boxes, labeled 1^c, 2^c, 3^c, 4^c, 5^c, and 6^c.

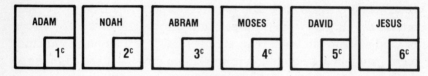

Figure 3

In southern Mexico we drank water from deep wells. However, each dry season those wells would have to be deepened by several meters. The covenant seems to be like a well. Each manifestation deepens the reception of the revelation. It is always the same well and the same water, but over time there is more water, clearer and colder, and running in much more quickly because the revelation draws from an increasingly more accessible source.

We could represent the relationship of the *kainos* covenant to earlier contexts by using a quasimathematical formula. This relationship is not additive or cumulative, but rather consists of a deepening understanding and a greater fulfillment of that which was always there.

What appears below the line qualifies and gives meaning to what is above the line. That which is above the line is revelation given at a particular time in a specific context and is a function, an extension, a deepening and fulfillment, of what appears below the line. The "Special Revelation" is, therefore, the totality of God's revealed hiddenness in the fullness of time, completed in Jesus Christ, "in these last days," as Hebrews 1:2 says it.

$$\frac{6c}{1c \,/\, 2c \,/\, 3c \,/\, 4c \,/\, 5c} = \text{(Special Revelation)}$$

Figure 4

THE NEW COVENANT, A MODEL OF
CONTEXTUALIZATION TODAY

Now we can return to our original problem. The "square peg" of God's revelation does not fit well within the "round holes" of today's cultures either. Clearly, if in each culture we force the gospel to take on radically different content in the sense of *neos*, we are being unfaithful to the continuity of God's revelation in Jesus Christ.[47] On the other hand, to force the "round holes" of our world cultures to configure themselves to a specific understanding of the gospel will violate the uniqueness and richness of the contexts in which God wishes to be known.[48] And yet God can only be known in the here-and-now of our historically and culturally conditioned existence. As Roger Haight has said,

> All knowledge of God is knowledge that is mediated through the world. There is no immediate knowledge of God precisely because God is transcendent and other than the world while all human knowledge, like freedom itself, is bound to and mediated through the world. Even what appears to be "direct" experience or knowledge of God is really a mediated immediacy because it cannot be had apart from the existence of human freedom in the world and its determination by the world and society. . . . Revelation has always been considered by Christians as the word of God. But that word of God must "appear" in human consciousness to be heard.[49]

In the midst of such a complex dialectic, it seems that the concept of the *kainos* covenant holds the most fruitful possibility for a gospel that is both revelationally continual and contextually relevant.

New Suggestions for Old Problems

A *kainos* understanding of covenantal revelation may help us avoid some of the common pitfalls faced by contextualization. It may get us beyond what Paul Hiebert has called "uncritical contextualization,"[50] and move us to recognize that questions of truth are legitimate concerns when there is a potential for syncretism or religious relativity. And it affirms Harvie Conn's emphasis that a covenantal dimension is foundational for perceiving divine truth as our response in word and deed to God's faithfulness.[51]

The *kainos* covenant will provide a continuity with the history of revelation that protects the church in all contexts from syncretism. As Saphir Athyal,[52] Gleason Archer,[53] and Bruce Nicholls[54] have rightly pointed out, syncretistic mixing of God's truth with human falsehood has been one of the major dangers of contextualization. The *kainos* understanding of the covenant creates a major touchstone whereby God's revelation in each culture, though contextually relevant, can be revelationally consistent with that which has previously been known about God. In Charles Taber's words,

> As converts together study and obey the Scriptures, and as their testimony begins to penetrate the broader context, it is indeed the aim of contextualization to promote the transformation of human beings and their societies, cultures, and structures, not in the image of a western church or society, but into a locally appropriate, locally revolutionary representation of the Kingdom of God in embryo, as a sign of the Kingdom yet to come.[55]

It is in the *kainos* sense that Harvie Conn can say, "Every command of Christ through the Scripture is also de facto a command to contextualize."[56] This method of contextualization derives from what Conn earlier called, "covenant witness."

> In terms of hermeneutic, this divine pattern of covenant speaking forbids us from isolating covenant witness from covenant life. It does not permit a split between thought and action, truth and practice. Covenant witness affirms the divine word given and calls the creature to covenant life before the Creator in the world of history and its cultures. Unconditional submission to covenant remains the responsibility of covenant man in context.[57]

New Contributions in Changing Contexts

In other words, the *kainos* covenant involves a continuity with a basic "core" of biblical revelation that is dynamically and contextually relevant to the multiple contexts of today's world. In the midst of cultural diversity, the people of God are guided by the never-changing covenant of God, "I will be your God, and you shall be my people—now, in a totally new context." However, this also means that the *kainos* covenant takes on deeper and fuller, and sometimes quite unexpected, content that was not there before. This calls for theologians in each culture to accept a most difficult task, as Daniel von Allman has outlined.

> It will be seen that the prime quality required of a theologian is careful attention to the living expression of the Church's faith, coupled with a sharp eye for detecting in that expression of the faith both where the promising efforts are to be found and where its fatal tendencies and "heretical inclinations" might be.[58]

Charles Taber suggests that the "criteria for theology" in this endeavor would include being, "biblical, transcendent, Christological, prophetic, dialogical (with the community and the world), open-ended, and subject to the Holy Spirit."[59]

There is a sense, therefore, in which *kainos* covenantal contextualization would not allow us to speak of "theologies." If by "theology" we mean the knowledge of God in *context*, we would do better to speak of God's self-revelation in the culturally conditioned here-and-now through a covenantal relationship with his people. However, if by "theology" we mean the knowledge of God in context, we must also allow the revelation of God's self-disclosure in each new context to influence all other understandings, all other "theology" arising in other times and cultures.

Clearly we are dependent on the Holy Spirit here. During his farewell discourse, Jesus emphasized the didactic role of the "Spirit of truth." "The Counselor, the Holy Spirit, whom the Father will send in my name, will teach you all things, and will remind you of everything I have said to you" (Jn. 14:17, 26 NIV). Again, there is clear unity of the truth; it is the truth of Jesus Christ, and it will not be a *neos* truth. It will be a *kainos* truth, which is both continuous with previous revelation and discontinuous in its radical contextualization.

New Methodology for an Unchanging Gospel

So down through the history of the church, beginning in Acts, we find a development of the knowledge of God, resembling what we saw earlier. We can see the work of the Holy Spirit in the church throughout the church's history, developing a deeper understanding of all previous knowledge of God. We could, for example, represent the early Jewish-Christian community as "M," and subsequent contexts (Greek, Roman, Eastern Orthodox, Medieval European Synthesis, Protestant Reformation, the Industrial Revolution) as "N," "O," "P," "Q," "R," and "S," respectively. The covenantal self-disclosure of God in each of these contexts could then be represented by M^c, N^c, O^c, P^c, Q^c, R^c, and S^c, as follows in Figure 5.

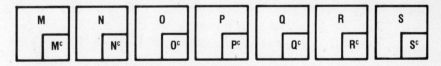

Figure 5

These various contexts, however, are not independent of each other. Over time, each is related to the others in a "hermeneutical spiral," as can be seen in Figure 6.[60]

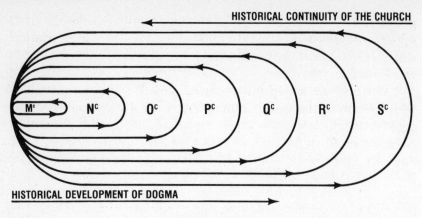

Figure 6

But it is also important to see the relationship of this spiral to the previous one, as seen in the covenant formula by which we depicted the *kainos* perspective (Figure 4, on page 88). The knowledge of God in ever-changing contexts throughout the history of the church must at once recognize the closure of the canon of Scripture, and the ever-new inspiration, guidance, and teaching of the Holy Spirit. We might picture this relationship with the following formula:

$$\frac{\text{Jesus Christ} \subset}{\text{Adam} \subset /\text{Noah} \subset /\text{Abram} \subset /\text{Moses} \subset /\text{David} \subset} = \frac{M \subset / N \subset / O \subset / P \subset / Q \subset / R \subset / S \subset}{(\text{Special Revelation})}$$

Figure 7

What appears above the right-hand line is a function, an extension, a deepening and fulfillment, a greater understanding, of that which was revealed in "special revelation," which in turn is the completed but not fully comprehended revelation of God from Adam to Jesus Christ (below the left-hand line). Notice that this understanding of *kainos* contextualization down through history is not a cumulative affair. We do not stack up new opinions in an endless addition of theological thought. Nor are we dealing with knowledge of God that is essentially different from, or in contradiction to, or in substitution of, what has gone before (that would be subtraction). What we have here is more like a picture, taken by a Polaroid camera, which needs time and light to be developed. The picture is already recorded, but to see it takes time and study. Each context is understood with reference to (divided by) all other revelation which has gone before. Here we are able to preserve the uniqueness of God's self-disclosure in a particular context and affirm its *kainos* relationship to God's self-disclosure of the same covenantal relationship in early contexts.

But now we are in the twentieth century, in a new situation with relation to the world church, and we deal with a multitude of contexts in which we struggle to know God. We could represent the covenantal knowledge of God in the contexts of Asia, Africa, Latin America, North America, Western Europe, and Eastern Europe by I^c, II^c, III^c, IV^c, V^c, VI^c, as in Figure 8:

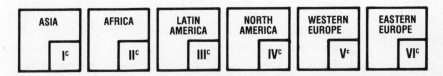

Figure 8

The *kainos* knowledge of God in context, then, would be related to all that has gone before by means of the following formula:

$$\frac{\dfrac{\text{Jesus Christ}\,c}{\text{Adam}\,c\,/\text{Noah}\,c\,/\text{Abram}\,c\,/\text{Moses}\,c\,/\text{David}\,c}}{} = \frac{\dfrac{I\!c\,/\,II\!c\,/\,III\!c\,/\,IV\!c\,/\,V\!c\,/\,VI\!c}{M\!c\,/\,N\!c\,/\,O\!c\,/\,P\!c\,/\,Q\!c\,/\,R\!c\,/\,S\!c}}{\text{(Special Revelation)}}$$

Figure 9

We need to avoid theologically "reinventing the wheel" in each context. Our present contextual theology is neither an addition to, nor a subtraction from, historical theology. Rather, it is divided by (as a function of) what has gone before. But historical theology has itself developed as a reflection upon, a deepened understanding of, and an extension of God's unique covenantal self-revelation in Scripture, fulfilled in Jesus Christ.

Thus, we must also affirm the special nature of God's self-disclosure in each new context. There is something unique and in that sense "discontinuous" about the radically different cultures, languages, and peoples that form the new contexts of God's covenantal self-revelation. The top level of the formula (Figure 9) allows us to ask new questions, develop deeper understanding, and gather surprising new insights which are especially and uniquely relevant to those contexts. But notice that the entire world church is at the same level, and each context is related to the others not by a "+" sign, but by a dividing line, meaning that we are also accountable one to the other in learning from each other God's nature and will for all of God's people. A good example of this methodology is P. J. Robinson's missiological treatment of the Belhar Confession, where "knowing God" in the South African context calls the entire world church to ask *kainos* new questions about themselves, their faith, their Scriptures, and their obedience to God.[61]

CONCLUSION: GOD'S NEW COVENANT IN NEW CONTEXTS

Paul Meyerink and I began to discover that his translation of the Scriptures involved a difficult exercise in contextualization precisely because of the mystery of God's hidden self-disclosure in diverse human cultures. And yet we found hope in the covenantal model which Scripture affords for knowing God in context. The "square peg" of God's self-disclosure does not fit well in the "round holes" of a multitude of human contexts. Yet by God's Spirit his nature and will are in fact revealed to—and through faith perceived by—human consciousness. And this mystery drew Paul and me closer to the Tzeltal Christians who were struggling with the same contextual questions as we were.

Together, the Tzeltal Christians and Paul and I discovered that in spite of cultural diversity, we needed to

Make every effort to keep the unity of the Spirit through the bond of peace. [For] there is one body and one Spirit . . . one Lord, one faith, one baptism, one God and Father of all, who is over all and through all and in all.   (Eph. 4:3-6 NIV)

Maybe all together, as one church, we can come to know God in context through the model of covenantal revelation. Based on a *kainos* perspective of the covenant, we may be able to enter a new era of contextualization. In this new age of the world church, the *kainos* covenant may open the way for us to know God's revealed hiddenness. As Morris Inch stated in *Doing Theology Across Cultures*,

God's revelation lies at the heart of our theological endeavor. There are not, strictly speaking, many truths, but one truth viewed from differing perspectives. Christianity is not capable of radical reinterpretation: rather, it is one faith communicated to all (humanity). Ignoring the common heritage in the Christian fellowship is as grievous an error as failing to appreciate its rich diversity.[62]

As the gospel continues to take root in new cultures, and God's people grow in their covenantal relationship to God in those contexts, a broader, fuller, and deeper understanding of God's revelation will be given to the world church. In the end we may come to appreciate what Augustine of Hippo (A.D. 354–430), in his conflict with the Donatists, affirmed: that the truth is that which everyone, everywhere always has believed about the gospel.[63]

NOTES

[1] Karl Barth, *Church Dogmatics*, vol. II, 1 (Edinburgh: T & T Clark, 1957), 184. Barth devotes an entire paragraph (par. 27) of this volume to the discussion of the knowledge of God. Barth divides this in two parts: the *terminus a quo* (from which our knowledge proceeds by the grace of God's self-revelation to us) and the *terminus ad quem* (to which our knowledge conduces us to faith in the hidden God). Ibid., 179–254. It is important to compare this section of Barth's *Dogmatics* with vols. I, 2, par. 17; IV, 1, 483ff.; and IV, 3, 135–65.

[2] See, e.g., Louis Berkhof, *Reformed Dogmatics* (Grand Rapids: Eerdmans, 1932), part 1, sec. 1, chap. 2; G. C. Berkouwer, *General Revelation* (Grand Rapids: Eerdmans, 1955), 285ff.; Emil Brunner, *The Christian Doctrine of God* (Philadelphia: Westminster, 1949), 117–36; and Hendrikus Berkhof, *Christian Faith* (Grand Rapids: Eerdmans, 1979), 41–56, 61ff.

[3] Richard Niebuhr highlighted this matter in his famous book, *Christ and Culture* (New York: Harper, 1951).

[4] Each of these words represents a particular approach to relating the gospel to a new culture. Each also demonstrates a particular understanding of God's self-disclosure in the midst of human cultures and the ability or inability of those cultures to "know" God in the context of their own cultural forms.

[5] Paul Hiebert, "The Gospel and Culture," in *The Gospel and Islam: A 1978 Compendium*, ed. Don McCurry (Monrovia, Calif.: MARC, 1979), 63.

[6] Cf. Krikor Haleblian, "The Problem of Contextualization," *Missiology* 10 (January 1983): 95–111. See also K. Haleblian, "Evaluation of Existing Models of Contextualization" in *Contextualization and French Structuralism: A Method to Delineate the Deep Structure of the Gospel* (Ph.D. diss., Fuller Theological Seminary, School of World Mission [1982], 34–50). Cf. Dean S. Gilliland and Evertt W. Huffard, "The Word Became Flesh:" *A Reader in Contextualization* (Pasadena, Calif.: Fuller Theological Seminary, n.d.), 84–90. Haleblian is primarily referring to Charles Kraft, *Christianity in Culture: A Study in Dynamic Biblical Theologizing in Cross-Cultural Perspective* (New York: Orbis, 1979) and Robert Schreiter, *Constructing Local Theologies* (New York: Orbis, 1985).

[7] Stephen Bevans, "Models of Contextual Theology," *Missiology* 13 (April 1985): 185–202.

[8] David Hesselgrave, "Contextualization and Revelational Epistemology," in *Hermeneutics, Inerrancy and the Bible*, ed. Earl D. Radmacher and Robert D. Preus (Grand Rapids: Zondervan, 1984), 694. Hesselgrave went on to discuss at length four "epistemic pre-understandings" or models of "revelational epistemology": the

"demythologization" of Rudolf Bultmann and Paul Tillich, the "dynamic equivalence" of Charles Kraft, the "providential preservation" of Edward Hills and the "relational centers" of Bruce Nicholls.

[9] An excellent review of the literature involving the various models within the incarnational approach may be found in Harvie Conn, "Contextualization: Where Do We Go from Here?" in *Evangelicals and Liberation*, ed. Carl E. Armerding (Nutley, N.J.: Presbyterian and Reformed, 1977), 90–119. A handy compilation of some of the early writings by Wonderly, Smalley, Luzbetak, Mayers, Nida, Loewen, Kraft, et. al. may be found in William Smalley, ed., *Readings in Missionary Anthropology II* (Pasadena, Calif.: WCL, 1978).

[10] Cf. David Hesselgrave, *Today's Choices for Tomorrow's Mission: An Evangelical Perspective on Trends and Issues in Missions* (Grand Rapids: Zondervan, 1988), 161. Note also the predominance of communication theory, communicational language, and linguistic/translation issues in the Willowbank Report and the accompanying papers in Robert T. Coote and John R. W. Stott, eds., *Down to Earth: Studies in Christianity and Culture* (Grand Rapids: Eerdmans, 1980).

Further background may be found in Eugene Nida, *Message and Mission: The Communication of the Christian Faith* (New York: Harper and Bros., 1960), 33–61; Don McCurry, "Cross-Cultural Models of Muslim Evangelism," *Missiology* 4 (July 1976): 268–69; and Bruce Nicholls, "Theological Education and Evangelization" in *Let the Earth Hear His Voice*, ed. J. D. Douglas (Minneapolis: Worldwide, 1975), 634–45.

The Lausanne movement also defined contextualization in strongly communicational terms (see Douglas, ibid., 1226–27). Bruce Fleming distinguished between the "supracultural," "transcultural," and "cultural" aspects of the gospel contextualization in *The Contextualization of Theology* (Pasadena, Calif.: WCL, 1980), 73. Cf. also James O. Buswell, "Contextualization: Theory, Tradition and Method" in *Theology and Mission* ed. David Hesselgrave (Grand Rapids: Baker, 1978), 87–111. See also Louis Luzbetak, "Signs of Progress in Contextual Methodology," *Verbum* 22:39–57. (Reproduced also in Gilliland and Huffard, *The Word Became Flesh*.)

[11] Cf. also Schreiter, *Constructing Local Theologies*. The broad range of theological positions possible within this cultural relevance model was brought out by Bong Rin Ro, who spoke of four types of contextualization in Asia: "syncretism, accommodation, situation theology and biblically-oriented Asian theology." See Bong Rin Ro, "Contextualization: Asian Theology," in *The Bible and Theology in Asian Contexts: An Evangelical Perspective on Asian Theology*, ed. Bong Rin Ro and Ruth Eshenaur (Taiwan: Asia Theological Association, 1984), 63–77.

[12] Latin American liberation theology is a good example of this model of contextualization, spelling out the relevance of the gospel primarily in socio-political and economic terms.

[13] Luzbetak, "Signs of Progress," 53.

[14] Some years ago, W. A. Visser t'Hooft warned us about the danger of too closely linking cultural diversity with religious pluralism. See his *No Other Name* (London: SCM Press, 1963), 85–86. His subsequent discussion (pp. 96–103) of "Christian Universalism" in the volume is very helpful at this point. The relativizing of faith as a companion to the diversity of cultures is an idea with a long history.

In our century, this perspective received its major impetus from William Hocking and the Laymen's Foreign Missions Enquiry entitled, *Rethinking Missions*. More recently, W. Cantwell Smith, Paul Knitter, John Cobb, John Hick, and Raimundo Panniker are among those following a similar path, although seeking major refinements and redefinitions to the thinking of the 1930s. The recent use of the word *ecumenical* in World Council of Churches circles to mean Muslims, Hindus, Christians, and Buddhists worshiping together, each in their own way, is another example of religious relativity. Cf. Stephen Neill, *A History of Christian Missions* (New York: Penguin, 1964), 455–56; David Bosch, *Witness to the World* (London: Marshall, Morgan and Scott, 1980), 161–64; and Gerald H. Anderson, "American Protestants in Pursuit of Mission: 1886–1986," *International Bulletin of Missionary Research* 12 (July 1988): 106–108. See also Paul Knitter, *No Other Name? A Critical Survey of Christian Attitude toward the World Religions* (New York: Orbis, 1985); and John Hick and Paul Knitter, eds., *The Myth of Christian Uniqueness: Toward a Pluralistic Theology of Religions* (New York: Orbis, 1987).

In a review of the latter work, Carl Braaten states, "The essence of this pluralistic theology is not as new as these authors imagine. None of the leading ideas—relativism, mystery, justice—as the core of the religious enterprise is new," *International Bulletin of Missionary Research* 12 (July 1988): 136. An enlightening discussion of this matter can be found in the *Journal of Ecumenical Studies* 24 (Winter 1987). Cf. J. Verkuyl, "Contra de Twee Kernthesen van Knitter's Theologia Religionum," *Wereld en Zending* 2 (1986): 113–20.

[15] Harvie Conn first alluded to this concept in "Contextualization: A New Dimension for Cross-Cultural Hermeneutic," *Evangelical Missions Quarterly* 14 (January 1978): 39–46. He further refined these observations in *Eternal Word and Changing Worlds* (Grand Rapids: Zondervan, 1984), 211–60.

[16] James Scherer, *Gospel, Church and Kingdom: Comparative Studies in World Mission Theology* (Minneapolis: Augsburg, 1987), 239–40.

[17] See, e.g., Lesslie Newbigin, *Foolishness to the Greeks: The Gospel and Western Culture* (Grand Rapids: Eerdmans, 1986). Ten years earlier Jacob Loewen had called attention to the "blindness (of the crosscultural missionary) to the problems produced by the missionary's own culture." Cf. Loewen, "Evangelism and Culture" in *The New Face of Evangelicalism*, ed. René Padilla (Downers Grove, Ill.: InterVarsity Press, 1976), 181.

[18] Cf. Conn, "Contextualization: A New Dimension," 39–46; Arthur Glasser, "Help from an Unexpected Quarter or, The Old Testament and Contextualization," *Missiology* 7 (October 1979): 403–409; Gleason Archer, "Contextualization: Some Implications from Life and Witness in the Old Testament" in *New Horizons in World Mission: Evangelicals and the Christian Mission in the 1980s*, ed. David Hesselgrave (Grand Rapids: Baker, 1979), 199–216; and Millard Lind, "Refocusing Theological Education to Mission: The Old Testament and Contextualization," *Missiology* 10 (April 1982): 141–60.

[19] Conn, "Contextualization: A New Dimension," 43. See also H. Conn, *Eternal Word and Changing Worlds*, 229–34. Cf. also Donald Hohensee, "Models of Contextualization" in *Rundi World View and Contextualization of the Gospel* (D. Miss. dissertation, Fuller Theological Seminary, School of World Mission, 1980), 131–45.

[20] Martin Noth, "The Re-Presentation of the Old Testament Proclamation" in *Essays on Old Testament Hermeneutics*, ed. Claus Westermann (Richmond: John Knox, 1960), 77.

[21] Ibid., 83–85. Noth quotes here from Karl Barth, *Kirchliche Dogmatik*, vol. 3:1, (1945), 83.

[22] Herman Bavinck, *Our Reasonable Faith: A Survey of Christian Doctrine* (Grand Rapids: Eerdmans, 1956), 274–76. More recently, Fred Klooster presented a similar perspective in "The Biblical Method of Salvation: A Case for Continuity" in

Continuity and Discontinuity: Perspectives on the Relationship Between the Old and New Testaments, ed. John S. Feinberg (Westchester: Crossway, 1988), 150.

[23] Norman Gottwald, *The Tribes of Yahweh: A Sociology of the Religion of Liberated Israel, 1250-1050 B.C.* (Maryknoll, N.Y.: Orbis, 1979), 95. Gottwald points to Exodus 19:3-8; 24:1-11; 34:2-28; Deuteronomy 26:16-19; and Joshua 24 as examples of "theophanic and covenant" texts which were "included as sources for premonarchic Israel because they contain reflections of how the relations between Yahweh and Israel were conceived in early times." Cf. ibid., 57. See also N. Gottwald, *A Light to the Nations: An Introduction to the Old Testament* (New York: Harper and Row, 1959), 102ff.; and James D. Newsome, Jr., *The Hebrew Prophets* (Atlanta: John Knox, 1984), 40 ff., 57ff., 120-23ff., 210.

[24] L. Cerfaux, *The Church in the Theology of St. Paul* (New York: Herder and Herder, 1984), 31-32. Cf. also Jakob Jocz, *The Covenant* (Grand Rapids: Eerdmans, 1968), 283. Fred Klooster calls the covenant "basically an oath-bound promissory relation." Cf. Klooster, op. cit., 149. See also David L. Watson, "Salt to the World: An Ecclesiology of Liberation," in Mark Branson and R. René Padilla, *Conflict and Context: Hermeneutics in the Americas* (Grand Rapids: Eerdmans, 1986), 121-24.

[25] Gerhad von Rad, *Old Testament Theology*, vol. 1 (New York: Harper and Row, 1962), 129-33. Von Rad points to Deuteronomy 26:5ff. as an example of the "historical summaries" which articulate this unified covenantal perspective. Cf. Dale Patrick, "The Kingdom of God in the Old Testament" in *The Kingdom of God in 20th-Century Interpretation* (Peabody, Mass.: Hendrickson, 1987), 67-79.

[26] See Walther Eichrodt, *Theology of the Old Testament* (London: SCM Press, 1967).

[27] Compare, e.g., Gn. 17; Ex. 19, 24, 29, 34; Lv. 26; Jos. 24; 1 Sm. 12; 2 Sm. 23:5; Ps. 89; Jer. 31; 2 Cor. 6; and Rv. 21. Cf. Wolfgang Roth and Rosemary Reuther, *The Liberating Bond* (New York: Friendship, 1978), 2-3; Jakob Jocz, *The Covenant*, 23-31; and Lucien Cerfaux, 31-32. I have dealt with the universal significance of Israel's covenantal theology in C. Van Engen, *The Growth of the True Church* (Amsterdam: Rodopi, 1981), 116-60. (See the accompanying footnotes in this latter volume for bibliographical support.) See also *diatheke* in G. Kittel, *TDNT*, vol. 2 (Grand Rapids: Eerdmans), 106-34; and John Bright, *A History of Israel* (Philadelphia: Westminster, 1959), 128-60, 356-59, and 440-42; and Henrikus Berkhof, *Christian Faith: An Introduction to the Study of Faith* (Grand Rapids: Eerdmans, 1979), 229-30, 339-40, 423-26.

[28] For the details concerning these forms, cf. my *The Growth of the True Church*, 123-24. Also cf. John H. Hayes, *An Introduction to Old Testament Study* (Nashville: Abingdon, 1979), 195-97; 303ff.

[29] James Dekker, "The 8th Reformed Missions Consultation: Covenant in Search of Mission," *RES Mission Bulletin* 5 (March 1985):1.

[30] Cf. Carlos Van Engen, *Hijos del Pacto: Perdon, Conversion y Mision en el Bautismo* (Grand Rapids: TELL, 1985), 41-51. See also *NIV Study Bible* (Grand Rapids: Zondervan, 1985), 19. Cf. G. Ernest Wright, *The Old Testament Against Its Environment* (London: SCM, 1950), 54ff.; and H. H. Rowley, *The Missionary Nature of the Old Testament* (London: Kingsgate, 1955), chaps. 2-4.

[31] Cf., e.g., Juan Luis Segundo, *The Liberation of Theology* (Maryknoll, N.Y.: Orbis, 1976), 8; and José Miguez Bonino, *Doing Theology in a Revolutionary Situation* (Philadelphia: Fortress, 1975).

[32] David Bosch, "An Emerging Paradigm for Mission," *Missiology* 11 (October 1983): 493, 496.

[33] Kittel, *TDNT*, vol. 2, 127.

[34] Ibid., vol. 3, 447.

[35] There are other texts where the term means "young" or "younger." Those do not relate to this discussion.

[36] Cf. Kittel, vol. 4, 896–901.

[37] E. Earle Ellis, *Prophecy and Hermeneutics in Early Christianity* (Grand Rapids: Eerdmans, 1978), 166–67. Cf. also Norman Gottwald, *A Light to the Nations*, 370ff.; and Geerhardus Vos, 23–26; A. A. van Ruler, *The Christian Church and the Old Testament* (Grand Rapids: Eerdmans, 1971), 75ff.

[38] Cf. Kittel, vol. 2, 130–32; vol. 3, 447–54.

[39] Cf. Berkhof, *Christian Faith*, 302–303.

[40] Cf. *New Testament Commentary*, vol. 2, (Grand Rapids: Baker, 1954), 253; and C. K. Barrett, *The Gospel According to St. John* (Philadelphia: Westminster, 1955), 451.

[41] C. H. Dodd, *The Interpretation of the Fourth Gospel* (Cambridge: Cambridge University Press, 1953), 405.

[42] Ibid., 452.

[43] Ibid., 405.

[44] David Bosch, "An Emerging Paradigm for Mission," 501. Bosch is quoting from Andrew Walls, "The Gospel as the Prisoner and Liberator of Culture," *Faith and Thought*, 108:1–2, 45.

[45] Cf. Donald Senior and Carroll Stuhlmueller, *The Biblical Foundations of Mission* (Maryknoll, N.Y.: Orbis, 1983), 20–21.

[46] R. de Ridder, *Discipling the Nations*, (Grand Rapids: Eerdmans, 1971), 176–79.

[47] David Hesselgrave issued a recent warning against such "aberrant contextualization" in *Today's Choice for Tomorrow's Mission* (Grand Rapids: Zondervan, 1988), 153–58.

[48] Cf. Jacob Loewen, "Which God Do Missionaries Preach?" *Missiology* 14 (January 1986):3–19. See also Harold Netland, "Toward Contextualized Apologetics," *Missiology* 16 (July 1988):289–303.

[49] Roger Haight, *An Alternative Vision: An Interpretation of Liberation Theology* (New York: Paulist, 1985), 8–9, 56. John V. Taylor has highlighted the effects in Africa of missionary teaching about a transcendent God who is not in the here-and-now of African experience in *The Primal Vision: Christian Presence and African Religion* (London: SCM Press, 1963), 75–84.

[50] Cf. Paul Hiebert, "Critical Contextualization," 108.

[51] Harvie Conn, *Eternal Word and Changing Worlds* (Grand Rapids: Zondervan, 1984), 210.

[52] Saphir Athyal, "The Uniqueness and Universality of Christ," in *The New Face of Evangelicalism*, ed. René Padilla (Downer's Grove, Ill.: InterVarsity Press, 1976), 51–66.

[53] Cf. Archer, "Contextualization: Some Implications for Life and Witness," 202.

[54] Cf. Bruce Nicholls, "Towards a Theology of Gospel and Culture," in *Down to Earth*, 49–62.

[55] Charles Taber, "Contextualization, Indigenization and/or Transformation," in *The Gospel and Islam: A 1978 Compendium*, 150.

[56] Harvie Conn, "Contextualization: Where Do We Go from Here?" in *Evangelicals and Liberation* (Nutley, N.J.: Presbyterian and Reformed, 1977), 44.

[57] Conn, "Contextualization: A New Dimension for Cross-Cultural Hermeneutic," 43.

[58] Daniel von Allman, "The Birth of Theology," in *Readings in Dynamic Indigeneity*, eds. Kraft and Wisely (Pasadena: WCL, 1979), 335. Reprinted from *IRM* 64 (January 1975):37–55.

[59] Charles Taber, "The Limits of Indigenization in Theology" in Kraft and Wisely, 388–97.

[60] The concept of the "hermeneutical circle" as it works out to a "hermeneutical spiral" of deepening understanding has been mentioned by René Padilla, "Hermeneutics and Culture: A Theological Perspective" in *Down to Earth*, 76. This was reprinted from Padilla, *Mission Between the Times* (Grand Rapids: Eerdmans, 1985), 83ff. Edward Schillebeeckx has worked with the idea as well. Cf., e.g., *Edward Schillebeeckx: The Schillebeeckx Reader* (New York: Crossroad, 1987), 104ff.

[61] P. J. Robinson, "The 1982 Belhar Confession in Missionary Perspective" in *A Moment of Truth*, eds. G. D. Cloete and D. J. Smit (Grand Rapids: Eerdmans, 1984), 42ff. The growing number of church confessions being elaborated by churches around the world constitute a very positive sign that the *kainos* type of contextualization is beginning to find a place.

[62] (Grand Rapids: Baker, 1982), 16.

[63] Cf. J. Pelikan, *The Christian Tradition*, vol. 1 (Chicago: University of Chicago Press, 1971), 293ff.; H. Bettenson, *The Latter Christian Fathers* (London: Oxford University Press, 1970), 240ff.; and P. Schaff, *Nicene and Post-Nicene Fathers*, vol. 1 (Grand Rapids: Eerdmans, 1974), 391ff.

5

Form and Meaning in the Contextualization of the Gospel

Paul G. Hiebert

TWO QUESTIONS FACE EVERY CROSSCULTURAL MISSIONARY. First, what shall we do with the existing cultural practices, particularly those related to the people's religion? How should we respond to veneration of ancestors, witchcraft, magical charms, idol worship, and human sacrifice? Second, how can we best express the gospel in the new culture? Can we use the people's words for God when these are deeply tied to their existing religious beliefs, or should we introduce foreign terms which they do not understand? Can we reinterpret their marriage and funeral customs to convey a Christian message, or will the message itself become captive of their old beliefs?

Central to the debates in missions that have surrounded these questions is the relationship of form and meaning.[1] To understand these debates, we will look briefly at a history of missionary responses in the past century, and then at the nature of symbols in human cultures.

PAUL G. HIEBERT, M.A., M.A., Ph.D., professor of anthropology and South Asian studies, was born and raised in India. He served there as a missionary for seven years with The Mennonite Brethren. He taught anthropology at Kansas State University and the University of Washington and was Fulbright Scholar at Osmania University, India. He is the author of various books, among them *Konduru: A South Indian Village* and *Anthropological Insights for Missionaries*.

FORM AND MEANING IN MISSION HISTORY

The history of the modern mission movement coincided with the histories of Western colonialism and modern science. It is important, therefore, that we understand the relationship between meanings and forms within the context of colonialism and science, and the recent changes that have taken place within them.

Era of Positivism: Meaning and Form Equated

The first missionaries in the modern mission movement, such as Ziegenbalg, Plutschau, Carey, and Judson, went as guests to the lands in which they served. As guests they had a high appreciation of the cultures around them. They adopted local dress and lifestyles, translated the Scriptures into local languages, and used local worship forms in the churches. The techno-economic differences between the East and West were not great, and the missionaries found much to admire in the courts of India and Burma.

By the midnineteenth century, however, European colonial expansion had established a dominance of the West. With this grew a sense of cultural superiority that affected not only rulers and traders, but missionaries from the West as well.

The nineteenth century was also characterized by the emergence of positivism as the dominant epistemology underlying Western thought. In positivism, human knowledge—particularly scientific knowledge—was seen as true in an absolute sense.[2] By means of careful observation the human mind could perceive reality as it is. Scientific theories, properly proved, were, therefore, facts. The atomic theory of matter and evolution were not our human understandings of reality—they were part of reality itself. Form and meaning became one. Truth could be stated in formulas and logical propositions.

Such an epistemology required precise symbols and words to express truth. Consequently, a great deal of effort was made to develop mathematics and a scientific language that did not have the "fuzziness" and ambiguities of ordinary symbols.[3] In these technical languages, meaning and form are closely tied. Precise meanings require precise words, or the meanings are lost.

The obvious (at least to those in the West) superiority of science led scientists and other Western people to reject other systems of belief as "prelogical," "animistic," "primitive," and "superstitious." In the confrontation of science and these systems, these systems had to go. It was assumed that in time they would be replaced by scientific thinking.

Colonialism, positivism, and the explosion of science had a profound effect on Western missions. Missionaries were products of their time, and it should not surprise us that they came increasingly to equate Christianity with Western civilization.

Many missionaries also thought in positivist terms. For them, forms and meanings were essentially one. They believed that the Scriptures had to be translated literally and the gospel expressed in precise words and symbols or the meanings would be lost. There was a widespread fear that the use of native symbol forms would introduce "pagan" meanings that would lead to syncretism. Consequently, the use of local symbol systems was widely rejected. Native architectural forms, melodies, drums, marriage and funeral rites, and art forms were suspect. Conversion involved not only following Christ, but also adopting Western cultural forms.

To avoid syncretism, Western forms were often introduced to convey Christian meanings. Western tunes, ritual forms, instruments, and words were used in the hope of preserving Christian meanings. The result was a foreign gospel which, in the eyes of the native peoples, answered Western questions and was tied to Western cultural ways.

There were attempts to counter this equation of Christianity with the West, the most notable of which was the call by Venn and Anderson for the "Three Selves." Young churches in new lands should be self-supporting, self-governing, and self-propagating. But this was more a call for an indigenous church than a contextualized gospel. The emphasis was on social relationships between sending and receiving churches, not on the cultural symbols in which the gospel was expressed. There was some discussion of adopting indigenous architectural styles and dress forms for the clergy. But in Bible translation, theological writings, and rituals, forms and meanings were still seen as essentially one.

Pragmatism: The Divorce of Form from Meaning

The twentieth century has seen a rapid decline in colonialism. Men and women in Western colonies, trained in modern schools, led nationalist movements that challenged Western rule. In a remarkably few decades colonial empires collapsed and "colonialism," which once was uttered in pride, became a pejorative label.

Positivism and its equation of form and meaning were also under heavy attack. Anthropologists had shown us that people in different cultures see the world in different ways, and that systems of knowledge had to be understood within their cultural contexts. Sociologists and psychologists made us aware of the subjective dimension of human knowledge, including science. Philosophers of science called positivism into question. But the linguists, who separated meaning from form, made the greatest immediate impact on missions and the debates regarding contextualization.

Linguists studying the structure of human languages became aware of the profound ways in which these languages shape the way people see the world.[4] They pointed to markedly different meanings that are associated with certain objects, such as trees, rocks, and even humans, in different cultures, and to similar meanings that are often associated with very different forms. Many linguists argued that no universal set of symbols underlies all human thought; not only do different languages have different words for the same thing, but also those words have different connotations in the cultural contexts within which they are found. Forms and meanings could no longer be treated as one.

The impact of these linguistic insights on Bible translation was far-reaching. Translators began to realize that literal translations not only lost but also distorted much of the meaning of particular passages. Some words—such as *mountain, lamb, snow,* or *plow*—cannot be translated in many languages because these concepts do not exist in them. Many other words—such as *God, sin, sacrifice,* and *ancestor*—have such different meanings in different cultures that they are almost unusable in Bible translations.

Out of these insights emerged an emphasis on dynamic equivalent translations.[5] In these the translator sought to convey in another language the *meanings* found in a particular text even though this required a change in the *forms* found in the passage. For example, if Papua New Guinea highlanders had no sheep and sacrificed pigs in the same way the Israelites in the Old Testament offered sheep, then it might be best to translate "sheep" as "pigs" in the highlanders' Bibles. At least, then they would understand the importance of sacrifice in the Old Testament. If the translator were to use the Hebrew or English word for sheep, or coin a new word, the non-Christians would have no understanding of these texts at all.

The concept of "contextualization" expanded this emphasis on translating meaning, not form, to all areas of mission activity. It said, wherever possible, local forms should be used to convey the gospel. In communication, it is good to employ drama, bardic narratives, traditional story-telling forms, native melodies, and dance if these are more meaningful to the people than preaching and translated Western hymns. Local marriage and funeral ceremonies, ancestor veneration rites, and important festivals should be modified to convey Christian meanings. In theology, the thought patterns within the culture, which are familiar to the people, should be used to express biblical truths.

Behind this divorce of form and meaning lay an epistemological shift from positivism to instrumentalism. Instrumentalists argue that we cannot know whether human knowledge is ever true, because it is subjective. We only know whether it is useful or not. The result is relativism—all systems of explanation have their own internal integrity and we cannot say that one is better than another. The result is also pragmatism—we should assess ideas in terms of their usefulness in helping us solve problems.

In instrumentalism, form and meaning are divorced. Because knowledge is seen as subjective, what is important is preserving meanings in the mind, and meanings are not attached to external forms and realities. We can, therefore, use *any* forms so long as inner meanings are understood (some would say "discovered").

This separation of meaning from form and its expression in dynamic equivalence translation and contextualization are important steps in our understanding of the mission process. We are freed from a rigid formalism that tied Christianity to Western ways and hindered the crosscultural communication of the gospel. Young Christians in other cultures were also freed to study and interpret the Scriptures in their own settings. But the divorce of meaning from form poses another set of dangers which we must examine.

A Too Simple View of Culture

First, the separation of form and meaning is based on a too simple view of culture. In this view, language is the basis of culture, and all other areas of culture can be understood by analogy to linguistics. But culture is more than language. It is made up of many symbol systems, such as rituals, gestures, life styles, and technology. In these, as we will see later, the relationships between form and meaning are often complex. Moreover, even in language the linkage between form and meaning is not always arbitrary.[6]

If we divorce meaning from form and reduce culture to purely mental processes—to ideas, feelings, and values, we reinforce the Neoplatonic dualism between mind and matter, ideas and behavior, that has plagued Western thought. Thought categories become arbitrary creations of the mind, and cultures become isolated islands of meaning between which there can be no real communication. People in other cultures will interpret what we say in terms of their own cultural categories, and there is no way to test whether their ideas correspond with ours or not.

Furthermore, if we separate meaning and form we are in danger of reducing Christianity to a set of beliefs to which people must mentally subscribe. There need be no change in behavior, no change in culture, no change in life. Cultural forms and systems become essentially value free. But humans are sinners, and capable of creating social systems and symbols that are oppressive and evil. Not all cultural practices can be used to communicate the message of the gospel.

An Asocial Perspective of Symbols

In the second place, a total separation of meaning and form tends to be asocial. It does not take seriously enough the fact that symbols are created and controlled by social groups and whole societies. As individuals and minority groups we may create our own symbols and words to express our faith in our own circles. When we try to reinterpret symbols used by the dominant society, however, we are in danger of being misunderstood and ultimately of being captured by its definitions of reality.

One of the greatest powers a society has is to impose its views of reality upon people. It does so by enculturating its young and acculturating those who join it. Ultimately, this definition of reality begins by controlling the definitions of key words. When we call people to become Christians, we call them to accept a new definition of reality, and, therefore, new definitions of key concepts. The result is a struggle to control the meanings of important words.

In primal societies with local tribal religions, the coming of a universalist religion, particularly when it is backed by political dominance, generally leads to quick victories. Christianity, Islam, and Hinduism soon impose their definitions of reality on tribal peoples. In old civilizations, however, the struggle to control the meanings of words is often difficult. For example, in South India the Christians use *devudu* for God, but Christians constitute only some 5 percent of the people in most regions. The Hindus who dominate the culture and make up over 75 percent of the people also use the word, but with Hindu connotations. In such a setting it is difficult for the Christian community to maintain a biblical understanding of God. In the long run the church is in danger of accepting the Hindu world-view of the dominant society around it.

The belief that we as individuals can freely redefine old and create new symbols reflects our Western individualism. In much of the world, however, it is the group and its leaders who define the key cultural symbols, and enforce the dominant beliefs.

The radical separation of form and meaning is asocial in another sense. It overlooks the extensive debate regarding "natural symbols." Mary Douglas and others hold that there are universal human symbols found in most societies arising out of our common human experiences. For example, she argues that the human body as an organic system is an analogy all people use in understanding reality.[7] Similarly, with few exceptions, going up spatially is seen as moving in the direction of the gods and the sacred. Temples and shrines are commonly placed on the tops of hills. Steps lead up into churches and mosques. Likewise, the birth process is widely used as an analogy for other transitions in human life, such as initiation ceremonies, admission into closed societies, and even death. Sexual union is widely used as an analogy for joinings of many types, including union with God.

An Ahistorical View of Symbols

Third, to separate meaning and form is to ignore history. Words and other symbols have histories of previously established linkages between form and meaning. Without such historical continuity, it would be impossible for people to pass on their culture from one generation to the next or to preserve the gospel over time.

We are not free to arbitrarily link meanings and forms. To do so is to destroy the people's history and culture. Moreover, it is to forget that people who become Christians gain a second history—the history of Christianity. Among their new spiritual ancestors are Abraham, Moses, Jesus, Paul, Aquinas, Calvin, Luther, and many others.

A Modern Bias

The separation of meaning from form reflects a modern, individualistic view of human experience. As Mary Douglas points out, people in tribal and peasant societies do not view symbols in that way.[8] For them, form and meaning are intricately related in important symbols, particularly religious symbols. To say a word of curse is indeed to curse. To perform the rain dance is not a way of asking the gods to send rain; it is to create rain. The rituals are thought to cause things to happen. Symbols, in fact, are seen as performative.

A problem arises when modern missionaries use traditional ritual forms and give them new meanings, or change established practices in churches in non-Western societies, or introduce dynamic equivalent translations that are easily changed. In the eyes of many non-Western

Christians, they are denying the sacred nature of the gospel, for sacredness rests, in part, in tight linkages between form and meaning.

Relativism and Pragmatism

The greatest danger in separating meaning from form is the relativism and pragmatism this introduces. Relativism undermines our concern for the truth of the gospel. Pragmatism turns our attention from the cosmic history of creation-fall-redemption to solving the immediate problems of our everyday life.

Critical Realism: Form and Meaning Re-Wedded

Faced with the corrosive effects of pragmatism and relativism, there is a growing movement in the sciences to find an epistemological foundation that affirms truth but does so with humility, not arrogance; that affirms objectivity but allows for the subjective dimension in human knowledge.[9]

On the international scene there are attempts to move beyond an anticolonialism which is still tied to the old colonial agendas in order to find new ways of building global relationships between nations whose independence and autonomy is not in question. In missions, too, there is a growing concern that cultural relativism and pragmatism have undermined the Christian message. Missions must search for new epistemological foundations that enable missionaries to proclaim the gospel boldly and without compromise, but in love and humility.

In all these fields there are many who are moving toward what Barbour calls a "critical realist epistemology."[10] In this epistemology, knowledge is in human minds, so there is a subjective dimension to it. But this knowledge corresponds to the realities of the external world, so that it has an objective, truthful dimension to it. This correspondence between inner and outer worlds is not that of a photograph, but that of a map, blueprint, or model. In other words, the correspondence is complex and varied. At some points a map must correspond exactly with reality, or the map is useless. At other points, a map reveals hidden realities. For example, a political map colors one country green and another yellow. This does not mean that these countries are physically these colors. Rather, it means that one territory belongs to one country, and the other to another. Finally, on a map some points are arbitrary. A country may be colored blue or green or yellow without destroying the truthfulness of the map. The only requirement is that the whole country be colored the same color.

In critical realism we as Christians affirm the absolutes of God, the universe he created, and history. The last includes the events of history and God's involvement in them. On the other hand, we recognize that *our understanding* of those absolutes is partial. This does not mean those understandings are totally subjective and relative, but that they should be growing. We see "through a glass, darkly," but we do see. We see enough to live in a real world, and, through divine revelation, we see the path to salvation and fellowship with God.

In critical realism, however, form and meaning are related in complex ways, depending upon the nature of the symbol. In some, the linkage is arbitrary, and forms can readily be changed in order to preserve a given meaning. In others, the two are equated. To change the form is to change the meaning. In most, however, the relationship is more complex.

Given this epistemological foundation, the missionary is not against contextualization, as was the case in positivism. In positivism missionaries equated form and meaning and assumed that the introduction of the former automatically led to an understanding of the latter. The missionary, however, also rejects an uncritical contextualization in which forms are changed readily in order to preserve subjective meanings. Rather, we pursue a critical contextualization realizing that meaning and form are related in complex ways, and that the gospel has both objective and subjective dimensions to it. This, however, requires that we examine more carefully the varied nature of the symbols we use to communicate the gospel in other cultures.

Form and Meaning in Symbols

If we cannot equate meanings and forms nor totally separate them, where does this leave us with regard to contextualization? Here, recent insights in semiotics are helpful. The fact is that in any culture the relationship between meanings and forms varies according to the nature of the symbol. In some the relationship is arbitrary, so forms can readily be changed in order to preserve meanings. In other symbols the relationship is more complex, ranging from loose to tight linkages. To change the forms in these inevitably changes the meanings in some way. In still other symbols, meaning and form are essentially one. To change the form is to change the meaning. In contextualization, therefore, we need to examine the nature of symbols in the Scriptures and church, and the nature of symbols in the society into which these are being contextualized. Here symbolic anthropology provides us with useful insights.[11]

Meaning and Form Arbitrarily Linked

It is easiest for those of us from the West to begin by looking at symbols in which the link between form and meaning is arbitrary and loose. A simple example is giving names to our children. Young parents in the West spend hours looking for the "right name," but in the end the choice is theirs. A creative few make up new names, but most are limited by social convention (certain names are girls' names, and others are boys' names), and by history (names that have been used in that culture in the past).

Similarly, the link between form and meaning in ordinary words used in everyday discursive speech is essentially arbitrary. In English, we look at a tree and say "tree." We could have said "chetu," or "preta," or even "dog." There is no essential sound pattern in the word *tree* that links it to the objects we call trees. Once we have agreed in our community to call this object a tree, however, the linkage becomes one of social and historical, not private, definition. It is then passed down from generation to generation. In other words, the link is no longer arbitrary. I may try to change it, but my efforts are meaningless if I cannot get the community to accept the changes.

This social nature of symbols explains why subgroups in a society seek to control or change the definitions of words. For example, the black community in the United States made a conscious effort to change the meaning of "black." Now, women are pressing for inclusive language. In both cases there has been considerable resistance by whites and males. *The ability to control the definitions of words that the people use is one of the greatest powers dominant groups in a society have, for in controlling definitions, they control the way the people see reality.*

Discursive language is the basis of most of our verbal communication. We use it to talk about the ordinary, everyday things of life—things we can see and experience directly. We change it easily as new words are coined to represent new realities we observe or create (Coriolis, calculator, satellite) and concepts we need (paradigm, world-view).

In contemporary missions, discursive symbols present a number of theoretical problems, but we readily translate the Scriptures into local languages using the words and sounds of the local society.

We realize there will always be some slippage, particularly in the connotations associated with different words. This means we must work hard to make certain that the meaning of a passage is preserved as accurately as possible in the new language. In order to do this, we readily change the forms. "Tree" becomes *chetu* in Telugu, and "woman" becomes *stree*. We no longer argue, as did the church leaders in the Middle Ages, that people should not translate Scripture because this distorts its meaning and destroys its truthfulness and trustworthiness.

Similarly, as missionaries we are to identify with the lifestyles of the people we serve as far as our consciences and psychological capabilities allow. We should dress as the people dress, eat their foods, and live in their kinds of houses, for in so doing we build trust and communicate to the people our love and acceptance of them.

Meanings and Forms Loosely Linked

In many symbols the links between form and meaning are arbitrary. In others, however, the links vary along a continuum ranging from loose ties based on similarities and analogies, to more direct ties based on direct connections, and to symbols in which form and meaning are one.

Among "loosely connected" symbols, form and meaning are often linked to each other on the basis of similarities and analogies. Humans live on the same earth and many of their experiences are the same. They see the sun, moon, and stars. They see animals and plants. It should not surprise us then that certain "natural symbols" have wide cultural distributions, such as the association of light with life, up with sacred, darkness with evil, and so on.[12] Humans also have similar bodies. Normally they have one head, two arms, and two feet. They are born, eat, reproduce, and die. These common experiences serve as the basis of widespread biological symbols. Finally, all humans create culture. All eat food and drink water. Most use fire, shelters, and simple technologies. These, too, provide humans with ready symbols and analogies for thinking about their lives.

Universal Symbols

In the 1930s, Edward Sapir and Benjamin Whorf sought to show that different cultures classify natural phenomena in different ways, and that, in essence, their classifications are essentially arbitrary.[13] Each society creates categories according to its own internal perceptions of reality.

Recent studies have shown, however, that the categories cultures create to describe the external material world are not totally arbitrary. Brent Berlin and Paul Kay demonstrated that there is a clear progression in basic color categories, both within and between cultures, as the number of these categories increases from four to eight.[14] In other words, color categories are not totally cultural creations. They also reflect the order in nature and the biological processes of perception. Sahlins notes "the unexpected findings challenge such basic doctrines as the arbitrary nature of the sign or, even more fundamental, the *sui generis* character of culture."[15]

Hunn has shown that there is widespread cultural agreement with regard to the basic categories for birds and other animals.[16] Miller has done the same with the plant world.[17] In other words, many symbols dealing with the natural world do reflect basic differences found in nature itself.

It is not enough, however, to simply show that all cultures agree that black and white are different, and that "cows" are not a kind of "bird" and differ from "horses." Most symbols have secondary connotations. Are any of these widespread or universal?

Natural Symbols

The human body itself provides many basic symbols that have multiple uses. Douglas argues that "the organic system provides an analogy of the social system which, other things being equal, is used in the same way and understood in the same way all over the world."[18] For example, the head, arms, breasts, legs, and life itself provide metaphors that people in most cultures use to think about their worlds. Blood is generally associated with red and life; and excreta with defilement and impurity.

Eliade, in his extensive survey of religions, notes the common triad of land-fertility-female that is found in most agricultural societies.[19] Similarly, male is commonly associated with battle and violence. Sexual union is commonly used as an analogy of union with God, death, or end and/or exit; birth is an analogy for beginnings, fertility, and newness, and the birth channel, as gates and thresholds.

Hallpike makes a strong case that long hair is a symbol of being in some way outside society, and that cutting of hair symbolizes reentering society or living under a particular disciplinary regime in society.[20]

Nature provides us with other natural symbols. There is an almost universal association of "up" with "sacred." Temples and shrines, as we have noted, are generally built so that people have to climb steps or hills to reach them. "Down" and worlds under the ground are usually seen as dangerous or evil. Eliade analyzes the meanings of sky (symbol of transcendence), water (symbol of both death and rebirth), sacred space, mountains, and cosmic trees or poles (*axis mundi*) reaching to heaven in religions around the world.[21]

A case can be made that children in most cultures learn adult roles by imitating them. Thus a girl may play "mother" by behaving as she observes real mothers behave.

Cultural Symbols

Another category of symbols in which meaning and form are indirectly linked has to do with human cultures and technology. Lévi-Strauss argues that most cultures equate the cooking of food with being human (not animal) and civilized.[22] Mauss shows that gift exchanges are widely used in establishing human relationships.[23] Transvestites in many cultures wear the clothes of the opposite sex as a sign of their lifestyle.

On another level, Marshall McLuhan shows how the products of technology, such as books, cars, and radios, serve as symbols that shape the society.[24] In other words, the forms these media take have their own messages apart from the formal messages they convey. For example, the introduction of the clock radically altered life in Europe.

Meanings and Forms Tightly Linked

In some symbols, meaning and form are linked more closely than those we have considered so far. The closeness of these ties makes such symbols, and those we will consider next, more stable. They often provide the skeleton on which the rest of a culture is hung. As Peter Berger points out, "[t]he cultural imperative of stability and the inherent character of culture as *unstable* together posit the fundamental problem of man's world building activity."[25] In the past, many of these symbols were religious. Now that religious symbols have lost their character as overarching, stable symbols in many modern societies, we must find integration elsewhere.

Expressive Symbols

In symbols expressing emotions, the experience itself is a central part of the message. A child's cry, an adult's laughter, an injured person's groans, an angry person's gestures—all of these may be culturally shaped or masked, but the basic patterns are widely distributed. To eat together is to relate. To bow or prostrate one's self before another is widely understood to mean subservience.

Dance and music are another case. Here the rhythms, melodies, and styles are themselves much of the message. For example, the loudness and beat of heavy metal rock music conveys a feeling of rebellion that is reinforced by words. Firth has noted a very wide association between percussion sounds, such as firecrackers, drum beats, and gun shots with the summoning of and dealing with spirits.[26]

The taking of drugs offers yet another case. Here the means produces the message—the ecstatic experience, the higher vision of reality. Similarly, meditation and self-torture are closely tied to the experiences they are expected to generate.

Ritual Symbols

The ties between meaning and form in rituals and sacred symbols vary a great deal from society to society. Douglas notes that one of the characteristics of modernity is the divorce of form and meaning.[27] Thus, a modern Christian says, "I go to church in order to worship." In other words, going to church is not itself part of worship, but brings one to a place where worship (often perceived as an inner personal experience) occurs. On the other hand, in most traditional societies meaning and form in rituals and sacred symbols are essentially one. A Christian in these societies would say, "In going to church I am worshiping." The very acts of washing, dressing in special clothes, and going to the church are themselves part of worship—a testimony to the world of one's faith.

The same debate continues in the church regarding the Lord's Supper. Catholics and other high-church Christians see the bread and the wine as more than loose symbols of the body and blood of Christ. After the consecration it in fact "becomes the body and blood of Christ" in some mysterious way that ordinary language and thought cannot express. The forms, particularly after consecration, do in fact become the message, the means by which grace is administered to the repentant sinner.

In traditional societies many ritual symbols are of this nature. For example, among the Shilluk the kings are believed to descend from Nyikang, a leader of the Shilluk in the heroic age. The investiture of a new king is a lengthy ritual in which, among other things, the king-elect sits on the royal stool which is the locus of divine and kingly power. The stool does not just represent this power—it is believed to contain it.[28] Along the same line, idols are often seen not only as reminders of the gods or even as abodes in which the gods live, but as the gods themselves.

The same close equation of form and meaning is found in contagious and imitative magic intended for evil. In the former, the form must be from the person against whom the magic is performed—a lock of hair, a finger nail, a piece of clothing, or a footprint. In the latter, the form must replicate the person in some basic way. A doll is molded and given the name of the person. Then what is done to the doll is believed to occur to the person. The same tie is seen in other forms of magic. In magical chants every sound must be correct, or the chant is ineffective. In amulets, the shape itself has magical power.

The location of sacred sites is often essential to their meaning. The tombs of saints or kings mark the site of the body. The sacred tree or pole is the *axis mundi* where earth breaks through into heaven. The same is true of sacred land. Palestine is not just any land for Jews and Muslims. To offer them free land in another part of the world would not meet their demands.

Forms Equated with Meanings

There are a few symbols in which form and meaning cannot be separated. To change one is to change the other.

Historical Symbols

Specific historical facts are tied to specific times and places. To alter these is to introduce error. For example, God came to earth in the form of a man, living in Palestine some two thousand years ago. He lived, died, and rose again, and by these actions he both completed and communicated to us his salvation. He was named Jesus and we as Christians are called to name that name (2 Tim. 2:19; 1 Jn. 4:2).

It is helpful here to note the distinction between art and history. The religious artist is seeking to communicate a deeper spiritual message, not a historically accurate picture of events. Thus, a noted Korean artist painted a series of pictures on the life of Christ in which Christ is depicted as a Korean teacher with a black hat (in traditional Korea all teachers wore such hats). The houses and clothes are Korean in style. If the artist were to claim this as historical fact, his drawings would be false. But he has tried to depict the deeper truth that Christ identified himself with humanity, all humanity, in his life and death.

Performative Symbols

Some symbols, generally religious or legal, not only communicate. They perform a change. For example, when a judge says to a defendant, "I find you guilty," he is not just communicating information. By his pronouncement he transforms a person innocent before the law into a criminal. In other words, he changes that person's status in the society. The person becomes another kind of person. Similarly, when a king issued an edict, it in fact became law.

Similarly, for Christians, when a minister says, "I pronounce you husband and wife," he or she changes the bride and groom into a married couple in the eyes of the state and society. In Catholic and other high churches with sacramental views of marriage, the pronouncement goes further. It not only changes the couple's social status and calls on God to bear witness to this, but also changes the divine order of things recorded in heaven. In both these cases of law and ritual the form the symbols take is essential to their meaning.

Boundary Symbols

A case might be made that in boundary symbols form and meaning are essentially one. Fences and rocks marking fields, lines marking lanes in roads or volleyball courts, and temple walls not only show where boundaries are; they create those boundaries.

IMPLICATIONS FOR CONTEXTUALIZATION

What implications does all this have for contextualization?

First, it is clear that contextualization is more complicated than we have thought. On the one hand, we need to avoid the anticontextual approach that characterized many earlier missionaries with positivist epistemologies. They often sought to avoid syncretism by introducing new symbols. The result was often nominalism. The gospel remained foreign. It did not take root at the core of people's lives. They were right, however, in their deep commitment to the truth and its preservation.

On the other hand, we need to avoid the reductionism of an uncritical contextual approach characteristic of instrumentalism and its divorce of form and meaning. In our eagerness to make the gospel understood by the people, we readily use and reshape the symbols of the culture. We are in danger, however, of reducing meaning to subjective understanding, whether of senders or receptors. With no objective dimension to it, we are left with pragmatism and relativism.

The only measures we have of successful communication are people's positive responses. There is no way to test whether the receptor's understanding of the message corresponds in any way with that of the senders.

What we need is a more comprehensive model that takes into account the variety of symbols. We need to examine carefully the nature of the symbols in the gospel—in Scripture, rituals, and Christian life—in order to determine the extent to which they can be changed to fit another culture.[29] We need also to examine the nature of the symbols in the new culture we want to use to convey the biblical message. Some of these can be used because their meaning corresponds in some essential ways with symbols in the gospel. Others cannot be used because they are too closely tied to non-Christian meanings. For example, the use of aqua blue in Indian dramas signifies the Hindu god Krishna. It would be almost impossible to use that color on the face of an actor in a Christian drama without drawing in Hindu mythology.

This view of symbols is rooted in a critical realist epistemology that focuses on the search for truth and affirms that it can be known, but that recognizes both the subjective and objective nature of human knowledge. Meaning is located in people and shapes them. It is also located in an objective world which enables people to test the correspondence between their understandings. Communication is measured, therefore, not in what the sender sends, nor what the receptor receives, but in the correspondence between what the sender sends and the receptor receives.

Second, we must examine how the nature of the missionary task affects contextualization. The Bible translator seeks to make the Scripture known in a new language. His or her responsibility is to remain true to the original text. Consequently, he or she must "provide the closest natural equivalent of the source-language message, so that it too may be employed effectively by receptor-language expositors in their task of transposition."[30] Preachers, on the other hand, seek to apply the biblical message in the local context. Their task, therefore, is to draw as much as possible upon the local culture's experiences and idioms in order to make the implications of the message clear.

Third, we need to guard lest the people misunderstand the nature of the symbols we use in communicating the gospel. We need to make clear in teaching and preaching what is history and what is poetry or allegory or culturally determined styles. In particular, we must guard lest Scripture passages be taken to be magical formulae to acquire supernatural power or to harm a rival. In this process of "critical contextualization" we need church leaders and missionaries working together to contextualize the gospel in a new cultural setting.[31] They need a thorough knowledge of the symbols of Scripture and church history, and of the receptor culture and its symbol systems.

We need to be aware, too, that national leaders and missionaries are influenced by their own cultures in the way they see symbols. Leaders in traditional societies often do not separate meaning and form in religious symbols while missionaries from modern societies do. The result is misunderstanding. Modern missionaries readily change Christian symbols in order to make them more meaningful. National leaders see such changes in the traditional symbols of the church as destroying the gospel itself.

Finally, it is important that we see contextualization as a long process, not an instant achievement. For first generation converts their old religious symbols are too closely tied to pagan religious beliefs to be used in expressing Christianity. For instance, it was the early African converts as much as the missionaries who rejected the use of drums used in spirit worship rites. On the other hand, the traditional ties between form and meaning in native symbols are weakened among second- and third-generation Christians in the culture. It is possible, therefore, for them to reexamine the old forms and use them in new ways in the church with less of a danger of syncretism. Thus, the early church rejected Greek sculpture which was generally religious, but the later church turned it into art and put it into museums.

Contextualization is, indeed, no simple task. It is important, therefore, that we seek to understand it more fully. Moreover, contextualization is not a once-for-all task. It is an ongoing process by which Christians seek to live as God's people in communities in a fallen world. It is important, therefore, that we institute procedures whereby the church as a community of believers seeks to understand God's Word to it and through it to the world in which it lives.

NOTES

[1] For some key discussions on the subject, see Eugene Nida, *Message and Mission* (New York: Harper and Row, 1960); Charles Kraft, *Christianity in Culture* (Maryknoll N.Y.: Orbis Books, 1979); and Eugene Nida and William Reyburn, *Meaning Across Cultures* (Maryknoll N.Y.: Orbis, 1981).

[2] For a more extended discussion of various epistemological positions and the current epistemological shifts taking place in the sciences and theology, see Paul G. Hiebert, "Epistemological Foundations for Science and Theology," *TSF Bulletin* 8

(March–April 1985), 5–10; and "The Missiological Implications of an Epistemological Shift," TSF Bulletin 8 (May–June 1985), 6–11.

[3] See R. Carnap, Meaning and Necessity (Chicago: University of Chicago Press, 1950).

[4] Much of the discussion has centered around the Sapir-Whorf hypothesis. See Edward Sapir, Selected Writings of Edward Sapir in Language, Culture and Personality (Berkeley: University of California Press, 1949), and Benjamin Whorf, Language, Thought, and Reality (New York: John Wiley and Sons, 1956).

[5] Nida, Message, and Kraft, Christianity and Culture.

[6] The broad study of symbol systems, including language, has led to the theoretical field known as semiotics.

[7] Mary Douglas, Natural Symbols (New York: Vintage, 1973), 12.

[8] Ibid., see especially chapters 3 and 6.

[9] In anthropology this is reflected in the rejection of cultural relativism that has dominated anthropological thought since the late 1970s. For an analysis of this, see G. W. Stocking, Jr., "Afterword: A View from the Center," Ethnos 47 (1982): 172–86; and Clifford Geertz, "Distinguished Lecture: Anti Anti-Relativism," American Anthropologist 86 (June 1984):263–78. In the philosophy of science, this is reflected in books by Larry Laudan, Progress and Its Problems (Berkeley: University of California Press, 1977); and Jarred Leplin, ed., Scientific Realism (Berkeley: University of California Press, 1984).

[10] See Eugene Nida and William Reyburn, op. cit., for an excellent discussion of how an awareness of literary genre and level of symbols is essential in Bible translation.

[11] See Janet Dolgin, David Kemnitzer, and David Schneider, eds., Symbolic Anthropology (New York: Columbia University Press, 1977); and Clifford Geertz, ed., Myth, Symbol and Culture (New York: W. W. Norton, 1971).

[12] See Mary Douglas, Purity and Danger (London: Routledge and Kegan Paul, 1966); and Raymond Firth, Symbols: Public and Private (Ithaca, N.Y.: Cornell University Press, 1973).

[13] See Sapir, Selected Writings, and Whorf, Language.

[14] The original analysis appeared in Brent Berlin and Paul Kay, Basic Color Terms: Their Universality and Evolution (Berkeley: University of California Press, 1969). There has been a great deal of discussion of their findings in journal literature since, but essentially their thesis has withstood critical analysis.

[15] Marshall Sahlins, "Colors and Cultures," Symbolic Anthropology, Janet Dolgin et. al., eds. (New York: Columbia University Press, 1977), 166.

[16] Eugene Hunn, "Utilitarian Factor in Folk Biological Classification," American Anthropologist 84 (December 1982): 830–47.

[17] Jay Miller, "Matters of the (thoughtful) Heart: Focality or Overlap," Journal of Anthropological Research 38 (Fall 1982): 274–87.

[18] Douglas, Purity, 12.

[19] Mircea Eliade, The Sacred and the Profane (New York: Harcourt, Brace, Jovanovich, 1959).

[20] C. R. Hallpike, "Social Hair," Man 4 (1969): 256–64.

[21] Eliade, The Sacred.

[22] Claude Lévi-Strauss, The Raw and the Cooked (New York: Harper and Row, 1969).

[23] Marcel Mauss, The Gift (London: Cohen and West, 1954).

[24] Marshall McLuhan, Understanding Media: The Extensions of Man (New York: McGraw-Hill, 1964).

[25] Peter Berger, *The Sacred Canopy* (New York: Doubleday, 1967), 6.

[26] Raymond Firth, *Symbols: Public and Private* (Ithaca, N.Y.: Cornell University Press, 1973).

[27] Douglas, *Purity*, chapter 3.

[28] E. E. Evans-Prichard, *Essays in Social Anthropology* (London: Faber, 1962), 66–86.

[29] Eugene Nida and William Reyburn pioneered a reevaluation of the relationship between form and meaning in *Meaning Across Culture.*

[30] Nida and Reyburn, *Meaning*, 32.

[31] For a more detailed discussion of critical contextualization and some steps in the process see Paul G. Hiebert, "Critical Contextualization," *International Bulletin* 11 (July 1987): 104–12.

6

Contextualizing Communication
Charles H. Kraft

IT'S ANY SUNDAY MORNING in almost any church in the world. The procedure is virtually identical no matter what country, no matter what language the meeting is conducted in. The meeting starts with an introductory word followed by prayer, followed by a song consisting of words in the national language wedded more or less appropriately to a Western tune. After that come the reading of some passage of Scripture, another prayer, other songs, an offering, and an intellectual discourse, presented in monologue fashion concerning some topic suggested by the Scripture reading. A benediction or another prayer follows the sermon and people go home with little carry-over of what they have heard and done into their daily lives.

In the remote area of northeastern Nigeria where I served as a missionary, one frequent response to such church meetings was the question, "Why does the Christian God not respect our old men?" I was told that any meeting in which the older men who led the village were not allowed to speak first was considered an insult to them and to the village as a whole.

CHARLES H. KRAFT, B.D., Ph.D., professor of anthropology and intercultural communication at Fuller Theological Seminary, has served as a missionary to Nigeria with the Brethren Church. He taught at Michigan State University and the University of California, Los Angeles, before coming to Fuller in 1969. Among his numerous writings are *Christianity in Culture* and *Christianity With Power*.

I was also made aware of the fact that Western hymn tunes gave the impression that God endorsed Western music and condemned their traditional music. Furthermore, speaking intellectually rather than practically or pictorially in the sermons gave the impression that only those who went to Western schools and learned to think like white men would be able to understand what these messages were about and, therefore, be acceptable to God. And speaking about a God who used to do wonderful things but who is apparently powerless to do such things in the present provided very little reason for following Christ. People, therefore, found the primary attraction of Christianity to be in the things offered by Western culture, not in the things spoken of in the Bible.

But Africa is not the only place we can speak of. J. B. Phillips says an experience he had with a group of British youth during the Second World War helped propel him into doing a contextualized translation of the New Testament. In response to their experience of Christianity couched in antique language, antique buildings, antique forms of worship, and often led by antique people, these youth assumed that God was "an old gentleman who lived in the past and was rather bewildered by modern progress."[1] Many in the Western world would concur with these youth concerning such an impression of Christianity. They would say that it stems from the pervasive out-of-dateness and irrelevance that are by-products of the vehicles used to communicate Christian messages.

These few things are but the tip of the iceberg when we begin to consider the widespread impression that Christianity is irrelevant to the real lives of peoples. Who would ever guess from the way Christianity is presented that God is our contemporary?[2] Yet, in Jesus, God's desire to be understood as relevant and important to contemporary human life led him to so contextualize himself as a human being that he was not even recognized by most of the people of his day. He looked too human.

For the Incarnation is the ultimate contextualization of the Christian message, since with messages aimed at affecting life, "the person who communicates the . . . message is not only the vehicle of the message, but the major component of the message."[3] If such a message is not contextualized in human life, then, it ceases to be true to what God intended, and the message, as presented, becomes to some extent heretical.

This kind of contextualization, taught by Jesus through demonstration, was carried on by his disciples and articulated by Paul in 1 Corinthians 9:19–22. Our task as contemporary disciples of Jesus is, then, to live our lives in a way that is "dynamically equivalent"[4] to those of Jesus' first disciples. Yet our theological curricula, ostensibly designed to teach us to minister as Jesus and his first followers ministered, tend to ignore this dimension rather completely.

COMMUNICATION AS A VALID THEOLOGICAL TOPIC

Our God is a communicating God. His desire to communicate with his creatures is obvious from the very beginnings of human existence. He no sooner had created humans than he began to talk to them (Gn. 1:28–30). He who spoke the universe into being chose to speak to the highest of his created beings. For reasons I cannot claim to understand, he seems to have an incurable love affair with humans. And he works hard to communicate his concern.

In communicating to humans, then, he chooses to express himself in ways human beings can understand and respond to. His concern is to be understood, so he chooses ways that will be intelligible at our end of the process. Though his thoughts and ways are high above ours (Isa. 55:8, 9), he chooses to limit himself to human vehicles when he relates to us.

This being true, it is unfortunate that communication is not more firmly established as a legitimate theological specialization.[5] For example, dealing with the deity of Christ is considered a "must" in every theological curriculum. But Jesus' favorite name for himself did not focus on his deity but on his humanity. He regularly referred to himself as "Son of Man," a designation intended to assert his relationship with humans.

If we see Jesus as a kind of bridge between God and humans, it is significant that Jesus so frequently emphasized the relationships at the human end of that bridge. For at this end the name of the game is communication. And, apart from his carrying out the plan of salvation, it was the communication of God's messages to humans to which he devoted his ministry. To neglect the communicational aspects of the activity of the triune God is, therefore, to miss a major part of what he did and said.

It is, therefore, highly appropriate in any treatment of the contextualization of biblical Christianity to address the contextualization of the communication of that message initiated by God for the sake of his errant creatures. At least three principles can be observed as basic to God's communicative activity:[6]

Our God Is a Relational God

God's communicational aim is not simply to inform. He desires a relationship with his creatures. They may philosophize about him or about that relationship. But that philosophizing or theologizing is merely a by-product, never to be confused with his true aim: to relate and interact with humans.

And this relating is a living thing. He does not treat his people as "faceless." They are treated as genuinely alive within their contexts and it is the concern of a living, life-giving God to relate "life to life" with them. This is why mere words can only point to, never contain, the Christian message. This message is a "life" or "person" message and can only be adequately conveyed in and through life. That life and the relationship that feeds it can be spoken about; but it can only really be portrayed incarnationally—in human flesh.

It is theologically significant, therefore, that the medium must be life, not simply words. Words can convey information (e.g., a news broadcast). But only life can convey relationship. The fact that God is relational and the message incarnational must inform all of our efforts to communicate it to others.[7]

Our God Is Self-Revealing

No one can coerce God into communicating. He communicates of his own free will. Furthermore, he is not passive. He chooses to reach out to make himself known to his creatures. Even though as humans we have continually distanced ourselves from him through rebellion, God has chosen to seek to make contact with us.

This pattern is first displayed in the Garden of Eden (Gn. 3). Adam had disobeyed God and, therefore, forfeited his right to God's favor. At that point, God could legitimately have called off the whole experiment. But the very evening of their disobedience we find God walking in the garden calling out to the man, "Where are you?" (Gn. 3:9).

As with Adam, so with us—God himself takes the initiative in the communication process. It is theologically noteworthy that he neither neglects us nor waits for us to seek him. As Jesus said, his purpose in coming is "to seek and to save the lost" (Lk. 19:10). God speaks; God acts. And in so doing he opens up the communicational channels by means of which we can be aware of and respond to him.

Our God Wants To Be Understood

He does nothing simply to perform or show off and is not content if people merely think well of him or admire him. Impressive church buildings, flowery language, and majestic music do not adequately represent his true nature. For he is in the business of communicating, not impressing.

As with any good communicator, he wants people to interpret what he says and does in such a way that they get his point and respond to it. For this to happen, he enters the frame of reference of those he seeks to reach, employing their languages, their cultures, their ways of life—and ultimately in Jesus—even human form to get his messages across.

Any theology of the Incarnation should, therefore, deal with the implications of such an approach to communication,[8] for it both informs us concerning the nature of God and provides us with an inspired model for our own efforts to serve him.

God's way of working for relating, revealing, and being understood is to contextualize his messages within the language, culture, and thought forms of the people he seeks to reach.

THE CONTEXTUAL NATURE OF GOD'S COMMUNICATIONAL ACTIVITY

In seeking insight into the nature of God's communication, we look to the Bible as the source of basic understandings and to our experience for confirmation and reinforcement of what we find there. Though all interpretation is strongly influenced by experience, the inspired biblical record of certain of the past experiences of certain of the people of God is normative. We turn to the Bible, then, to measure and regulate even our own experiences.

When Paul speaks of living like a Jew to win Jews, like a gentile to win gentiles, and like the weak in faith to win the weak in faith (1 Cor. 9:20–22), he is making a statement concerning God's approach to communication. He presents God as a contextualizer, one who adapts his approach to the context of those he seeks to reach. We should not assume that the fact that God's message is the same for all peoples requires a single, simple approach to getting it across.

Rather, God practices what I have called "communicational love."[9] His orientation is to do whatever is necessary to put the receptor at ease, at whatever expense to himself. This means that:

1. *God chooses human media* as those he will use to reach humans.[10] The rules of human communication require that people who wish to interact understandably must function within the same frame of reference. To interact, they will need to make use of symbols (such as words and gestures) to which they will attach agreed-upon meanings.[11] The frame of reference will define how the meanings are to be attached to the symbols used. In human experience, the primary frames of reference are cultural and, beyond culture, "human commonality" (see point 3 below).

Presumably, God could have required that humans interact with him in his own frame of reference. If this were the case, we would have to learn a special divine language and culture in order to relate to him. Though these would undoubtedly be more precise than human languages and cultures can be, the effort required to learn them would be enormous. And only after they were learned could any meaningful communication between Creator and creature take place.

Though human cultural vehicles (including language) are pitifully inadequate and imprecise as media for conveying God's messages, he has chosen to humble himself to use them. At all points in the Scriptures we see God's revelation in human life and thought. Indeed, this is true to such an extent that the greatest challenge for an exegete is to disentangle God's eternal truths from the cultural trappings (especially the world-view assumptions and values) in terms of which they are presented.[12]

By way of contrast, it is often the human practice to require those of another language and culture to adapt to the frame of reference of the communicator. The latter has the power, as it were, to require people to move his or her way if they are to understand and relate. Note, for example, how often highly schooled persons (including preachers) require that those who listen to them understand their language and adapt to their customs as preconditions to relating to them. Preachers and those who have attended church for a long time are often so used to using the jargon of the theology classroom and of antique Bible translations that they are seldom understood by new converts.

God, however, is not like that. He speaks the language of the people he seeks to reach—even disrespected languages such as Galilean Aramaic (Jesus' language) and koine (common people's) Greek. And he uses even cultural practices such as those of the pagan society of which Abraham was a part and those of the pagan Greeks of the first century. He chooses to adapt to his receptors rather than requiring them to adapt to him. He chooses to risk the impreciseness of the receptors' vehicles of communication in order to put the receptors at ease. This is communicational love. It is also communicational contextualization.

2. *God chooses to appeal to needs felt by humans at a level deeper than culture.* Though he uses the cultural context as the medium of his interaction with us concerning our felt needs, the most important of these needs lie deeper. So he contexts his messages even beyond the context of culture, in the deepest needs and longings of the human heart.[13]

Among these are the needs for forgiveness from sin, freedom from satanic oppression, and the security that can only come from a relationship with God. This is a kind of contextualization not ordinarily in view—into the depths of human need that cannot be satisfied through socio-cultural structuring and relationships. Though the scriptural message is presented in cultural terms, it concerns these deeper needs.

People come into the world insecure, powerless, and to some extent, at the mercy of suprahuman powers. Feelings of inadequacy in the face of such a condition, then, plague us and cause us to cry out for assistance. Though human relationships and structures cushion the impact of such feelings to some extent, most people still seek more power and security for the living of life. A contextually oriented God chooses to address these subjects in terms intelligible at the deepest personal level.

Through offering covenantal relationships to humans, he addresses the security need. By means of such relationships he offers protection from evil spiritual forces and the assurance of favor with the Creator and Sustainer of the universe. He offers release from sin and freedom from bondage to any of Satan's schemes, such as poverty, captivity, blindness, or oppression (Lk. 4:18). He thus speaks contextually to the deepest felt needs of his creatures.

3. *God's preferred method of contextualization is incarnation.* He comes to where we are as persons in a way that is maximally within our context and intelligible to us—through other persons. He has from the beginning of human existence usually chosen this incarnational approach to reaching people. In Jesus, then, he produced the supreme example of incarnation. Since this is where people are, such an approach is contextually appropriate.

We may, therefore, call him "receptor-oriented." That is, like the best of human communicators, he makes it his primary concern to focus on the results of his communicational efforts at the receiving end. He will, then, do whatever is necessary to bring the receivers of the message to the point where they understand and respond to it. And this means incarnating the message in human flesh within the trappings of human contexts in order to reach those whose lives are lived within such limitations.

Both his message and his method remain the same from generation to generation.[14] The method is, however, to adapt the specifics of the message in such a way that the receptors understand it. He adapts his presentation to the context[15] and, beyond that, to the felt needs of those he seeks to reach. Thus, each receptor is approached on his or her own terms.

Within the human context, then, our God does not simply generalize concerning the topics he treats. His concern is specific both to the persons and to their needs. He interacts with specific people in the ways most appropriate to them concerning those topics he knows they most need. And he does it from within their life situations, from within their contexts.

4. *Our God does not depend simply on words to get his messages across.* His primary medium is life. He demonstrates in and through life what he recommends for life. His letters are in flesh (2 Cor. 3:2, 3). In Jesus and through those who obey him, he uses his power to show his love, especially to the powerless and others victimized by satanic and human misuse of power.

What I have called "word messages"[16] simply convey information about their subject matter. They do not require a relationship to be effective. Nor does the acceptance of them necessarily require a life change. News broadcasts and answers to requests for information can be rendered in word messages. When one asks, "How much are 2 and 2?" a simple word answer suffices.

Words alone are not sufficient to adequately convey most of God's messages, however. What he offers needs to be lived by the communicator to be truly intelligible. For he offers a "person or life message," from the source of life, through the life of the communicator aimed to effect a life-change in the receptor. God's messages, therefore, require incarnation, a living out that may be spoken of in words but never limited to mere words. It moves from person to person via life rubbing against life to produce in the receptor a higher quality of life.

Love must be demonstrated if it is to be understood. So must righteousness, truth, faithfulness, acceptance, forgiveness, and all the rest of the treasures of Christianity. Jesus said, "I *am* the Way, the Truth and the Life," (Jn. 14:6 NIV). None of these comes via words alone. They are personal, relational, and life-related both in their expression and in their communication. God, therefore, contextualizes them in the lives of his people for all to see and respond to.

5. All of this implies that *God is also in favor of contextually appropriate extending media.* That is, though the basic medium of person messages is the human being himself, God is in favor of using appropriate secondary vehicles such as music, storytelling, public presentation (various kinds), poetry, ritual, dance, and the like.[17] He stands, however, against the imposition by a more powerful group on a less powerful group of their own vehicles as if only those vehicles were especially endorsed by him.

He would, therefore, stand against the contextual inappropriateness of the usual practice of imposing Western music,[18] ritual, and lecture forms on non-Western peoples as if these forms were sacred and to be adopted by everyone. God's method would be to see traditional cultural forms used to express a people's relationship with him and to communicate his messages to others.

INTERFERENCE IN GOD'S COMMUNICATIONAL PROCESS

1. God's communicational process is, of course, interfered with at every point due to the Fall. Human sin of all types and especially our rebellion against God's sovereignty in our lives interfere at both the receptor's end and in the lives of God's human communicators. Satan, furthermore, does his best to confuse things at both ends of the process.

Whenever there is sin in the lives of God's people, God's process is interfered with. Likewise, when we turn to merely human means to attempt to accomplish spiritual ends (Gal. 3:3). When, for example, we fail to wage God's battles in prayer, both the communicators' and the receptors' ends of the process are affected adversely. Satan cannot be defeated by merely human means. Nor can those who have not properly dealt with their sinfulness provide adequate channels for God's messages.

2. In addition, God's plan for contextualized witness is often rendered inoperable by those of his people who for one reason or another are perceived by the receptors as failing to live his messages. We are called to contextualize God's messages by living in such a way that his witness comes across accurately through our lives, whether or not we also speak for him. Often, however, quite unconsciously we are perceived as living for someone or something other than the Lord we claim to serve.

As humans, we will be observed by others. Our lives thus become witnesses to something. If our lives are lived in foreign, noncontextualized ways, they become witnesses to foreignness.[19] Or our behavior may easily be misinterpreted to be witnessing to something we never intended. We may, for example, be interpreted as greedy or arrogant or as misusing power when we are simply living according to our normal cultural patterns.

3. Interference comes from attempts to reduce the life message to a word or a ritual message. Much church communication consists simply of words and/or religious rituals concerning God and his objectives. But God never intended to introduce another religion. He came to bring life (Jn. 10:10), to contextualize a relationship

between humans and himself in the very fabric of human existence. But humans often reduce his plan to mere religious rhetoric and ritual, thus frustrating God's communicational intent.[20]

4. We often go about communicating without spiritual power. We imitate the Galatians whom Paul accused of starting by God's Spirit but then turning to human means (Gal. 3:3). Jesus told his followers to wait until they received the power of the Holy Spirit before they set out to witness (Acts 1:4, 8), because God's messages are not adequately portrayed without the demonstrations of spiritual power that always accompanied the words of Jesus and his apostles and that he promised would accompany his followers (Jn. 14:12).[21] Nor are those messages as appealing as they should be to the majority of human receptors for whom the quest for greater spiritual power is primary in life.

In Jesus, God was contextualized as a God of great authority and power who always uses his power to express God's love to victims and his judgment to the victimizers. Any gospel without that power used in that way is not the true gospel of Jesus Christ.

The wedding of spiritual salvation to material and secular power that characterizes so much of western Christianity is problematic in that, though it appears to be contextually relevant to certain segments of Western societies, in reality it is only true to part of God's revelation. Those segments of Christianity that use God's power for purposes other than to show his love are, however, equally to be questioned. For, though their use of spiritual power may be perceived as relevant, its use in a way God did not intend distorts his message.

5. The misuse of human prestige and power in the communication of God's messages is frequently an evidence of human interference in God's plan for contextualization of his messages. Those in power frequently impose on those not in power their own cultural forms, as if they were ordained by God to be used by all peoples everywhere. This is the problem behind the controversy dealt with in Acts 15.[22] The Jewish Christians assumed that God wanted gentile converts to adopt Hebrew culture.

Westerners frequently err in this regard also. Whether consciously or unconsciously, they often expect that God wants them to ignore the receptors' communicational vehicles and introduce such Western practices as reading, Western music, monologue preaching, church buildings, and even rationalistic theology and school-based training. Such vehicles were little used, if at all, throughout the Bible; instead, whatever vehicles were appropriate to the receptors were used.

Biblical peoples seemed to share with most of the peoples of the Two-Thirds World* the recognition that oral communication is far more relevant than written;[23] indigenous music is far more appropriate than Western; apprenticeship-type training is far more effective than school-based learning;[24] and discussion is far more sure than monologue,[25] if one wants to get a point across. Jesus also seemed to know that working personally and in depth with a few leaders is more effective than trying to work more or less impersonally with groups of more than twelve.

Again, God is receptor-oriented in desiring that the primary vehicles of communication be those of the receptors, not those of the witnesses who bring the message. I doubt that he is totally against some use of reading and classrooms. But the wholesale introduction of these vehicles while almost totally ignoring most of the indigenous vehicles is surely against his will, especially since it contributes to the impression that he wants receptor peoples dominated by Western methods and techniques.

6. God's plan to contextualize his messages in every sociocultural context is often thwarted through what may be termed "overcontextualization" to the sociocultural assumptions and values of the receiving society. God seeks to adapt his messages, but not to have them "captured" by the world-view of the receptors. Thus, we see throughout the Scriptures a judging of the values and assumptions of biblical peoples even while their cultural vehicles are being used by God.

The Jews had overcontextualized in their assumption that Yahweh belonged to them alone. And when Jews became Christians, many of them refused to allow gentiles to come to Christ without also converting to Hebrew culture (Acts 15:1). These who overcontextualized in Hebrew culture but fought contextualization in gentile cultures were soundly condemned by Paul (Gal. 1:6–2:21). This problem is, of course, tied to the question of power. Those with the power to admit or to keep others out of organizations supposedly endorsed by God tend to set their standards according to their own cultural norms rather than according to the intent of God.

In our day, this has been a major problem with Western Christianity. On the basis of our cultural prestige and power, we, too, have imported into other cultural contexts Christian messages already overcontextualized in our own. Western Christianity, unfortunately, exhibits a high degree of overcontextualization to a series of quite

---

*Two-Thirds World is used in preference to the rather condescending term "Third World."

unscriptural Western cultural assumptions and values—such as individualism, rationalism, secularism, and materialism.[26]

When such Christianity is exported to societies with worldviews differing greatly from Western world-views, the misimpression is often given that God intends that all peoples everywhere accept Western brands of Christianity. Both the receptors and, frequently, those Westerners who carry God's messages often conclude that Western Christianity is the epitome of what God intended. Those in power, who earn their living in Christian ministry especially, often fail to notice the vast difference between God's ideals as expressed in the Bible and the Christianity forged in the West.[27]

The God who, in the Scriptures, is seen as seeking to contextualize in Jewish ways for Jews and in Greek ways for Greeks (1 Cor. 9:20-21) is often seen as One who demands conversion to Western cultural forms as part of the price of a relationship with him. The cultural prestige and power of the West is frequently employed (often quite unconsciously) to propagate the heresy that God is not a contextualizer but, rather, One who seeks to impose Western cultural vehicles as the only adequate containers for Christianity. Biblical teaching on contextualization is thus obscured as we make the same mistake the Judaizers made in the first century.

7. But overcontextualization can happen even within societies that are virtually powerless to impose their understandings on other peoples. Through conversion followed by a lack of guidance into scriptural understandings of what Christianity ought to be, people can "nativize" their new allegiance. That is, they can accommodate it to all kinds of assumptions and values that should be judged and abandoned.[28] This form of overcontextualization can be just as dangerous and can interfere just as much in God's communicational process as the overcontextualization of the Christianity of the powerful.

Nativization (often called *syncretism*) has occurred when, for example, the founder of a Christian movement is identified with the Third Person of the Trinity.[29] It is also apparent when allegiance to pagan gods and spirits is continued, though they may now be called by different (supposedly Christian) names,[30] or when mushrooms or other hallucinogens become a crucial part of Christian worship,[31] or when God is understood as bound to obey our wishes whenever we use the proper words or rituals.

In any of these seven ways and, probably, in many others, the contextualizing essence of God's communicational strategy can be hindered and messages communicated that distort his very nature. He seeks to communicate his love and concern in ways that will be maximally understandable and relevant to the receptors. Human efforts, however, often obscure his intent and convey a distorted picture of who he is.

LEARNING TO CONTEXTUALIZE

If contextualization is God's method, then, we need to learn how to carry out our efforts on his behalf by employing his method. Toward that end, I have attempted to identify some of the ways in which God contextualizes. We then looked at the kinds of interference that contribute to the frequent differences between our efforts and what God seems to intend.

I believe we can assert that God's ultimate intent in this area, as in many others, is shown in the life and ministry of Jesus.[32] We should, therefore, pattern our communicative activity after his. To that end, the following points are offered:

1. Preliminary to any attempt to communicate, we need to be sure we are both presenting the correct message and employing the correct method. Jesus demonstrated that *working under the authority of and in dependence upon God is the starting point for both message and method.* In coming to earth, Jesus became a distinct being from God the Father. He refused, however, to work separately from the Father. Rather, he practiced an intimate, childlike dependence on the Father, stating, "'the Son can do nothing on his own; he does only what he sees his Father doing'" (Jn. 5:19 TEV), and "'I can do nothing on my own authority . . . I am not trying to do what I want, but only what he who sent me wants'" (Jn. 5:30 TEV).

Whatever we do, then, needs to spring from the same kind of dependence on God. It is not enough to connect well with the receptors of our messages. We must connect tightly with the proper Source of all we seek to do. So, establishing and maintaining our intimacy with and dependence upon God in the same ways Jesus did is our first order of business.

As Jesus regularly withdrew to be with the Father (Lk. 5:16), so should we. During these times, I doubt that Jesus did as much talking as he did listening. He cultivated intimacy and the ability to hear what the Father was saying. He then said only what the Father had instructed him to say (Jn. 8:26, 28) and did only what he saw the Father doing (Jn. 5:19). We need to cultivate the same kind of intimacy and to develop the same spiritual sharpness of hearing and seeing, if we are to do his works in his way.[33]

2. *As Jesus became Emmanuel, "God with humans," so must we become genuinely human to those we seek to reach.* The incarnational method is the supreme biblical method. And all that we do and teach

needs to be biblical if we are to avoid communicating the wrong things. We need to live the Bible morally, spiritually, and communicationally. But such living out of the Bible needs to be in terms intelligible to our receptors. This requires a contextually interpretable lifestyle. That is, how we live our lives in the receptor context needs to be enough in their style for them to interpret it as consonant with biblical principles.[34]

Our spirituality must also be contextually interpretable. That is, what we do both in private and in public to express our relationship with God needs to make sense to them in terms of the only world they know. Often their standards for spirituality are higher, or at least different than ours. The privacy and lack of ritual and public expression of our spirituality, then, though considered adequate by us, often makes our Christianity seem very secular to them.[35]

3. *A focus on living—especially spiritually meaningful living— according to their criteria provides the kind of witness at the deep personal level that God desires.* Beyond the cultural differences, people everywhere seek relationships, love, and enough power to handle life needs. God offers relationship through his own people within human contexts. If we are to serve him, we need to be present and intelligible within the life contexts of those he seeks to reach. This provides the basis for all person-level communication.

The love people seek can then be expressed by Christians, as long as it is done in their ways rather than according to foreign patterns. Western impersonal generosity, for example, seldom is understood as loving in person-to-person societies. Such relationship and love, then, provide the channel through which the power of God for guided human living is provided. People seek enough power to enable them to persevere in the face of both normal and abnormal challenges to their survival. Christians are often best understood in non-Western contexts when offering the spiritual power we have been authorized to use (Lk. 9:1, 2).

CONCLUSION

If, then, we are to learn how to communicate God's messages in God's way, we need to take account of at least the following points highlighted earlier:

1. Those at the receiving end of God's communicational activity are very important to him. He seeks to relate to them, reach out to redeem them, and to be understood by them. Those we seek to reach should be equally important to us. We should, therefore, imitate God's approach to them.

2. God seeks to employ appropriate sociocultural vehicles to reach those receptors. Those vehicles are the ones familiar to the receptors. God is, therefore, a contextualizer. We should, then, confidently imitate his approach.

3. God's appeal, however, is not to the concerns that lie closest to the surface of culture but to the deeply felt human needs that lie at the deepest levels of human life. Recognizing this, we should be concerned to learn to use cultural vehicles to get beyond purely cultural concerns.

4. God's messages need to be conveyed through life, not simply through words. Only life is an adequate conveyor of messages directed to the deepest levels of human experience. This kind of communication can be contextualized only through persons who live in other people's contexts as incarnationally as possible.

5. God's messages are to be accompanied by the works of God. God does not simply talk. He demonstrates. Thus he *shows* who he is and what the benefits of a relationship with him involve.

6. The messages communicated should be biblical, not merely the overcontextualized versions of God's messages in the forms of Western or any other culture. There should be no contrast in people's minds between what the Bible teaches and what those teach who claim to represent the God of the Bible.

7. The vehicles used should be contextually relevant, not simply imported from a more prestigious or powerful source. God can make use of whatever is present within the receiving society. He endorses no vehicles as the proper ones for all contexts.

NOTES

[1] J. B. Phillips, *Plain Christianity* (New York: Macmillan, 1954), 65.

[2] Phillips was one of the most articulate early advocates in the traditional church world for what we are now calling contextualization. In each of his books (many based on talks broadcast over the radio) he contends for a perception of God and Christianity as relevant, contemporary, and meaningful to moderns. A similar movement was going on within missionary thinking, with Eugene Nida and others associated with the American Bible Society leading the way. It is interesting that much of the impetus for the contextualization movement has come from those involved in Bible translation (e.g., Phillips, Nida, Smalley, Reyburn, Loewen, Taber, Kraft).

[3] Charles H. Kraft, *Communication Theory for Christian Witness* (Nashville: Abingdon, 1983), 62.

[4] The term "dynamic equivalence" was developed by Eugene Nida to designate an approach to Bible translation that gives primary attention to "the degree to which the receptors of the message in the receptor language respond to it in substantially the same manner as [did] the receptors in the source language" (Eugene A. Nida and

Charles R. Taber, *The Theory and Practice of Bible Translation* [Leiden: Brill, 1969], 69. The best Bible translations in English (e.g., Good News Bible, Phillips) and in many other languages are produced in accordance with this theory. In *Christianity in Culture* (Maryknoll N.Y.: Orbis, 1979) I have expanded the use of this concept to speak of a "dynamically equivalent" Christianity in which churches, theologizing, conversion, cultural transformation, and other aspects of our understandings and expressions of the gospel messages approximate the understandings and expressions of those messages recommended in the Scriptures. Though the term *contextualization* is more widely used, my preference would be to describe a truly biblical contemporary expression of Christianity as dynamically equivalent to what the Scriptures indicate to be God's desire.

[5] Unfortunately, there seem to be very few attempts to deal with a theology of communication. Robert Webber (*God Still Speaks* [Nashville: Nelson, 1980]), Charles Kraft (*Christianity in Culture, Communicating the Gospel God's Way* [Pasadena: William Carey Library, 1979], *Communication Theory for Christian Witness* [Nashville: Abingdon, 1983]), and an unpublished dissertation by Knud Jorgensen ("The Role and Function of the Media in the Mission of the Church" [Ann Arbor: University Microfilms, 1986]) are among the works that at least partly tackle the subject.

[6] See *Christianity in Culture, Communicating the Gospel*, and *Communication Theory*, as well as Eugene A. Nida (*Message and Mission* [Pasadena: William Carey Library, 1960]) and David J. Hesselgrave (*Communicating Christ Cross-Culturally* [Grand Rapids: Zondervan, 1978]) for further elaboration of these points.

[7] See Kraft, *Communication Theory*, for more on this subject.

[8] See Nida, *Message and Mission*.

[9] Kraft, *Christianity in Culture*, 23.

[10] See Jorgensen, *The Role and Function*, for an excellent treatment of the church as God's primary medium of communication.

[11] As communication theorist Berlo asserts in a classic statement concerning the relationship of meaning to people, messages, and symbols, "meanings are in people . . . not in messages. . . . The elements and structure of a language . . . are only symbols. . . . Meanings are not transmittable. . . . Only messages are transmittable, and meanings are not in the message, they are in the message-users" (David K. Berlo, *The Process of Communication* [New York: Holt, Rinehart and Winston, 1960], 175). See also John C. Condon, *Semantics and Communication*, 2 ed. (New York: Macmillan, 1975) and Paul G. Hiebert, *Anthropological Insights for Missionaries* (Grand Rapids: Baker, 1985) on symbols and meanings.

[12] See Kraft, *Christianity With Power* (Ann Arbor: Vine Books, 1989), for more on this.

[13] The fact that in dealing with humans we need to deal with both the cultural and the deeper personal level argues for an approach to witness that combines the insights of anthropology with those of theology, as I have attempted to do in *Christianity in Culture*. Theological training seeks to enable people to deal with the deeper needs of humans but often without the ability to get at them through understanding the more visible, culturally defined felt needs in which anthropologists specialize.

[14] See Kraft, *Christianity in Culture*, 194-97, 227-35.

[15] See Edward T. Hall, *Beyond Culture* (New York: Doubleday, 1976) and Kraft, *Communication Theory*, op. cit., for important understandings concerning the use people make of their contexts in the ways they construct meaning.

[16] Kraft, *Communication Theory*, 58-63.

[17] See Herbert V. Klem, *Oral Communication of the Scripture* (Pasadena: William Carey Library, 1982) for a particularly good presentation of both contemporary and scriptural bases for using indigenous methods of communication. Viggo Sogaard, *Everything You Need to Know for a Cassette Ministry* (Minneapolis: Bethany Fellowship, 1975) and *Applying Christian Communication* (Ann Arbor: University Microfilms, 1986), and Hans-Rudi Weber, *The Communication of the Gospel to Illiterates* (London: SCM Press, 1957) are also useful.

[18] For insight into contextualized communication of Christianity through music, see Roberta King, *Readings in Christian Music Communication* (M.A. thesis, Fuller Theological Seminary, School of World Mission, 1982) and her forthcoming Ph.D. dissertation.

[19] Illustrations of foreignness in approaches to the communication of the Christian message abound in books such as William A. Smalley, ed., *Readings in Missionary Anthropology* (Pasadena: William Carey Library, 1974); *Readings in Missionary Anthropology II* (Pasadena: William Carey Library, 1978); Eugene Nida, *Customs and Cultures* (Pasadena: William Carey Library, 1954); Jacob Loewen, *Cultures and Human Values* (Pasadena: William Carey Library, 1975); and Louis Luzbetak, *The Church and Cultures* (Pasadena: William Carey Library, 1963, 1975). Reading in such sources can greatly help the reader who is tempted to feel that the problem is not as serious as we seem to think it is.

[20] See Kraft, *Communication Theory*, Edward T. Hall, *Beyond Culture*, and John C. Condon, *Semantics*, for treatments of different levels of language usage.

[21] The contemporary movement, sometimes termed the "third wave" of the Holy Spirit, is an attempt to contextualize the use of the power Jesus has given his followers within an evangelical context. See John Wimber, *Power Evangelism* (New York: Harper, 1986); *Power Healing* (New York: Harper, 1987); C. Peter Wagner, *How to Have a Healing Ministry Without Making Your Church Sick* (Ventura, Calif.: Regal, 1988); Donald Williams, *Signs, Wonders and the Kingdom of God* (Ann Arbor: Vine, Servant Publications, 1989); and Charles H. Kraft, *Christianity With Power* (Ann Arbor: Vine, Servant Publications, 1989) for examples.

[22] See Kraft, *Christianity in Culture.*

[23] See Klem, *Oral Communication*, Jack Goody, *Literacy in Traditional Societies* (London: Cambridge, 1968), and Weber, *Communication.*

[24] This was recognized as long ago as A. B. Bruce, *The Training of the Twelve*, fifth ed. (Edinburgh: T & T Clark, 1898), but it is seldom taken seriously in theological circles even today.

[25] See Kraft, *Communicating the Gospel*, and *Communication Theory.*

[26] See Kraft, *Christianity With Power.*

[27] J. B. Phillips, in order to point up this difference, re-phrased the Beatitudes as believed by contemporary Westerners to extoll the "pushers" "for they get on in the world," the hard-boiled for they don't let life hurt them, those who complain for they get their way, the blasé for they don't need to worry over their sins, the slave drivers "for they get results," the knowledgeable for "they know their way around," and the troublemakers "for they make people take notice of them" (*Plain Christianity* [London: Epworth, 1954], 19). Each Western "beatitude" is nearly the opposite of what Jesus recommended, yet the extent to which these have been incorporated into Western Christianity is frightening.

[28] Three articles by Alan R. Tippett in Tetsunao Yamamori and Charles R. Taber, eds., *Christopaganism or Indigenous Christianity?* (Pasadena: William Carey Library, 1975) are especially helpful in understanding the problems of syncretism.

[29] See James E. Bertsche, "Kimbanguism: A Challenge to Missionary Statesmanship," in *Practical Anthropology* (1966), 13, reprinted in Smalley, *Readings II*, 373–93.

[30] See William Madsen, *Christo-Paganism: A Study of Mexican Religious Syncretism* (New Orleans: Middle American Research Institute, 1957) and William L. Wonderly, "Pagan and Indian Concepts in a Mexican Indian Culture," in *Practical Anthropology* (1958), 5, reprinted in Smalley, *Readings*, 1974, 229–34.

[31] See Eunice Pike and Florence Cowan, "Mushroom Ritual Versus Christianity," in *Practical Anthropology* 6 (1959), 145–50, reprinted in Smalley, *Readings*, 1974, 52–57.

[32] See Kraft, *Communicating the Gospel*, and *Communication Theory*.

[33] See the focus on intimacy with God as the source of Jesus' and our authority in Kraft, *Christianity With Power*, and Wimber, *Power Evangelism*, and *Power Healing*.

[34] See articles by Reyburn in Smalley, *Readings II*, op. cit., and Loewen, *Culture*, op. cit., for excellent treatments of human identification in the receptors' context as the best we can do in aiming at incarnation.

[35] This is often true in societies such as those of India. John Thannickal, *Ashram: A Communicating Community* (Ann Arbor: University Microfilms, 1975) gives helpful insight from an Indian point of view.

PART TWO
Ministry: Transformation Through the Word

7

The Context of Text:
Transculturation and
Bible Translation
R. Daniel Shaw

"WITHOUT CONTEXT, THE CODE IS INCOMPLETE since it encompasses only part of the message."[1] This is true of both language and culture. An understanding of the context into which God originally communicated his holy Word illuminates a perspective quite different from that of our day. It is this understanding of the language and culture in which the source message was communicated that is essential if Bible translators are to communicate the same message to modern receptors.

The new context does much to alter the "code." It forces communication that will allow the new audience to understand the meaning of the message. Thus, the form of the original code and the new receptor code are different (the Word enters different contexts). The meaning, however, is the same and, hopefully, the response will

R. DANIEL SHAW, B.A., M.A., Ph.D., associate professor of translation and oceanic studies at Fuller Theological Seminary, served with Wycliffe Bible Translators/ Summer Institute of Linguistics (SIL) in Papua New Guinea for twelve years. Presently an anthropology consultant with SIL, he is the author of *Transculturation: the Cultural Factor in Translation and Other Communication Tasks* and *Kandiya: Samo Ceremonialism and Interpersonal Relationships.*

impact the lives of the men and women who hear the Word and become doers of it, i.e., they build a local church based on that Word.

Lengthy is the list of cases where these principles were not applied. One example will suffice to make my point. In the Toaripi region of Papua New Guinea, an inappropriate interpretation of vernacular Scripture touched off a cargo movement. In a vision a man was told to read the entire New Testament, but to focus especially on Matthew 6:4 and John chapter 12. Shortly after, while sitting in the cemetery, he began to teach the people to keep their villages clean, fence burial grounds, respect the dead, and stop quarreling and stealing. While commendable, this teaching showed little relationship to the passages in focus. When challenged, the prophet for this graveyard cult countered that he was simply following God's bidding which "merely reinforced and made clear what was already set out in the Bible."[2] This was a culturally appropriate response that was inappropriate to the Scripture upon which it was based. The translation apparently did not communicate enough of the original cultural context to clarify the setting for the Toaripi villagers. How people understand God's Word relates directly to how they perceive and interpret the biblical context, culturally, linguistically, and theologically.

Translators have traditionally emphasized linguistic understanding. The study of biblical languages and modern receptor languages has long been a hallmark of the worldwide translation effort. But what about the cultural implications assumed by the original audience? How do cultural issues impact translators who, in turn, must communicate in such a way that the source context is taken seriously while the receptor context is not ignored?

My purpose here is to establish the need to take culture seriously. In order to avoid the predicament described for the Toaripi, translators must be serious about both the linguistic and cultural contexts of Scripture. They must then seek to communicate, using all the richness of the receptor language and culture to present the same message. This task is both an exegetical and hermeneutical process; both the source and the receptor must be considered. Bible translators must bring the skills of the theologian and exegete together with that of the anthropologist and linguist to ensure understanding and effective communication of truth. Translators must "decode" Scripture to understand the nature of the entire sociolinguistic context and then "recode" in the new context so receptors understand. In a word, they must *transculturate*.[3]

KEY CONCEPTS

Transculturation

Successful translation of Scripture requires that translators understand the impact upon the message itself of the context in which a message was communicated.

- To what kind of cultures did the biblical writers communicate?
- How do these contexts compare to cultures evident in the world today?
- What consequence does the translator's culture have on the transfer process from source to receptor?

These are some of the questions that the *transculturation* concept seeks to handle. Transculturation is to the cultural and nonverbal aspects of communication what translation is to verbal and literary forms. The application of anthropological principles to communicating source contexts into receptor contexts allows for a presentation of the message to people in very different times and places.[4]

Translators, then, need to consider the cultural conditions influencing the way the message had to be structured to ensure that the original recipients understood it. This requires a careful consideration of the economic, ideological, social, and political issues of the original context. Were these people living at a basic subsistence level of a kinship society in which everyone knew each other, as in Abraham's time?[5] Was there a hierarchy based on prestige and social or religious order that influenced behavior as developed during the time of the kings?[6] Or, perhaps the recipients were living in a commercial context that demanded interaction based primarily on exchange of money or goods and increasing individualism as reflected in the cities of the Roman Empire to whom Paul ministered.[7] Regardless of the context, the principles of transculturation apply. Translators need to understand how God intended to be heard, and appropriate that knowledge to an appreciation of the intended meaning. Such an understanding can assist when communicating the same message to modern receptors.

If modern receptors have a cultural context similar to the original audience they will quite likely understand much of what was intended, once implied information and the context of communication is clear.

If, on the other hand, the context is very different, considerable study and presentation of supplementary information is necessary in order to appreciate what God was saying and why.[8] Hence, many translators from the so-called "West" need a course in anthropology. They need to be aware of the specific application of anthropology to the translation process in order to transculturate between the original text and modern peoples who need to grasp the meaning originally intended.[9]

This is exegesis: "to inquire what was the meaning intended by the original authors."[10] The process should include a linguistic and textual understanding as well as cultural analysis of the entire context in which the message was communicated. How did the context structure the text? This understanding will be of great assistance when transferring the meaning into a context in which it has never before been presented.[11] Figure 10 outlines this concept. This brings the whole issue of fidelity into focus. Beekman and others[12] point out the need to recognize that fidelity is a two-way street; translators must be faithful both to the source and the receptor.

Source Meaning	Translator Understanding	Receptor Communication
Exegete source context including the forms and meanings used to effect response.	Understand original meaning with respect to the translator's context and the receptor situation. Appreciate source response and anticipate receptor reaction.	Communicate/translate source meaning using receptor cultural and linguistic forms that effect a life-changing response.

←――――――― THE TRANSLATION CONTEXT ―――――――→

The entire process is necessary for Transculturation

(Taken from Shaw 1988:223.)

Figure 10   The Process of Transculturation

If the equation is unbalanced, the product cannot be correct. Faithfulness to the source, on one hand, requires the closest possible equivalence. Faithfulness to the receptor, on the other, demands naturalness such that the people do not recognize the material as translation at all. Exegetically correct while at the same time communicationally natural is the emphasis of fidelity and transculturation.

Surface Structure - Deep Structure

To appreciate the meaning of a text requires an understanding of both the linguistic and cultural structures that contribute to that meaning. The surface structure is two-dimensional. It is the forms or codes (words, sentences, paragraphs, and discourse types) that serve to convey the verbal communication. It is also the cultural elements (behavior patterns, material culture, religious beliefs) that ensure the message is clear. These are all manifestations of language and culture—anything that can be viewed and described by an outsider is, by definition, part of the surface structure.

The deep structure, on the other hand, holds the meaning of those surface manifestations. Linguistic and cultural forms must be analyzed in order to ascertain their meaning for those who use them. Often this meaning cannot be explicated but is central to a people's assumptions and values.[13]

The surface-deep structure contrast relates meaning to behavioral patterns within a specific socio-linguistic system. It establishes what people need to know in order to talk and act right. As surface structure can be analyzed in terms of its grammatical or cultural elements, so deep structure is also organized based on the commonality of relationships that have meaning in any human context.[14] Deep structure is more universal to all cultures, which manifest it in a myriad of culture-specific ways. Therefore, if translators can implement a methodology for ascertaining the deep-structure meaning of the source text, they can transfer that meaning to the surface-structure forms necessary to communicate in any receptor context.[15] Figure 11 depicts this process for translators.

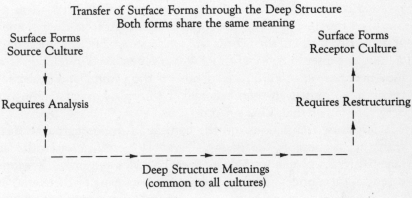

Transfer of Surface Forms through the Deep Structure
Both forms share the same meaning

Surface Forms   Surface Forms
Source Culture   Receptor Culture

Requires Analysis   Requires Restructuring

Deep Structure Meanings
(common to all cultures)

(Adapted from Nida and Taber, 1982:33.)

Figure 11

Literal vs. Idiomatic Translation

Translations range from very literal to unduly free.[16] This range of types basically divides into two kinds of translation, literal and idiomatic. Literal translation is an equivalence based on surface forms.

A completely literal translation is only intelligible when the two languages share many structural features. An interlinear text is a good example of a very literal translation; it helps the reader follow the original structure. There may still be considerable misunderstanding, however, because of the tendency to use equivalent words rather than equivalent ideas. An idiomatic translation, on the other hand, is based on meanings: the deep structure. Forms with equivalent meanings in the receptor are substituted whenever necessary to communicate the intended meaning of the source.

Literal translations do not take culture into account. The cultural meaning of the source is seldom communicated to the receptor, perhaps because translators do not understand the meaning themselves. In fact, literal translations are much easier to produce because an equivalence of meaning is not the focus. The translator simply works through a word-for-word translation that can go quite quickly; but the transfer of meaning may be minimal.

Such translations often produce misunderstanding because of the wide variety of interpretation and diversity of opinion about the meaning of the text. A quick look at the history of problems associated with literal translations demonstrates this. Receptors can read their own meaning into them; they are open to interpretations that are not part of the intended meaning.

Because literal translations are essentially "culture free" with respect to the receptor context, people are free to interpret them as they like. People will always approach information from their frames of reference. When the words are understood but the meanings are not, the intentionality of those words is perceived in relation to a focal perspective, and interpretive error is the natural (and expected) result. The translation then becomes the people's understanding of Scripture rather than God's Word.

Idiomatic translations, on the contrary, force receptors to deal with the meaning of the passage. Personal identification with the material forces people to evaluate their lifestyles and make decisions based on their understanding of what God is saying to them.

Translators often fail to realize that literal translation is not translation at all, because meaning is largely ignored. While not advocating "unduly free" translations, the focus should be on *communication*. There should be a balance between historical and cultural fidelity to the source on one hand, and license in the use of receptor forms on the other. This is why the transfer of deep-structure concepts is so much more important than surface-level codes. The receptor must be able to grasp the intent and meaning of the source. That meaning, however, can only be relevant as it is communicated within the receptor context: the language and culture of which people are a part. It is essential that a translation communicate in the same style that people communicate. We should attempt to produce translations that utilize local styles and thus are recognizable to the people who use them.[17]

TRANSLATION PRINCIPLES AND CULTURAL FACTORS

With these key concepts in mind, I turn to their application to translation principles, principles that account for linguistic and textual issues as well as a careful consideration of cultural matters. All this makes a difference when transferring the original context to a new and different one.

Implied Information

As the biblical authors made the Word available, there was much they assumed along with their audience. This body of common knowledge allowed them to allude to background information that everybody knew. Further, it allowed them to compress their speech in order to remove unnecessary grammatical redundancy, and focus their communication. In this way recipients would not be bored with unnecessary details.

Much of the communication within a given context depends upon various types of implied information, much of it cultural in nature. People in a particular context assume a great deal about what is correct behavior. Their world-view dictates a preconceived notion of what to expect. Hence, they are able to concentrate on the concepts, logic, argument, or story that requires their attention rather than on cultural details that are assumed. Where cultural assumptions are shattered by uncultural behavior, attention is quickly diverted to those matters regardless of the intended message.

For translators, the focus on what is important creates a significant problem. What biblical authors viewed as important may be different from what receptors now consider important. Implied information is very much a surface problem. When a message was originally encoded to reflect the surface structure of the source, the cultural factors that impinged on the message were taken seriously by the communicator. And the audience understood the message and acted upon it. When translators communicate this same message to modern receptors, the only way to ensure that it is not taken as strange or irrelevant is to focus on the meaning of the message—not the original forms.

However, because of cultural variance and time and space distinctions, the implications for today's receptors are different from those of the original audience. Unless these issues are taken seriously, the meaning will be skewed. The unfortunate, even tragic, result is demonstrated by incidents like the Toaripi graveyard cult.

The critical question for translators, then, is when and how to make implied information explicit, and vice versa.[18] Beekman and Callow[19] present some guidelines. Implicit material may be expressed explicitly when (1) "required by the receptor grammar," (2) "required by fidelity to the meaning," i.e., when fidelity to the original demands explication in order to avoid "zero" or "wrong" meaning, and (3) it is "required by dynamic fidelity," i.e., when fidelity to the receptor demands structural or stylistic changes to ensure correct communication. Thus, "to correct wrong meaning that distorts the message of Scripture, the use of implicit information is always justified."[20]

I would like to add another guideline to deal specifically with cultural information: *implied information relevant to the source-cultural context but not to the receptor, must be made explicit.* Whenever it is culturally necessary to provide information in order to maintain fidelity, either to the source or the receptor, translators must do so.[21] This assumes that translators are aware of the cultural context of both the source and receptor and are able to ensure sufficient understanding in order to avoid miscommunication that may distort divine truth. It is imperative that translators be adequately aware of the total translation context in order to communicate the message effectively.

For example, in Luke 10:12, Jesus condemns the towns that may reject his messengers by saying that "God will show more mercy to Sodom" (TEV). The phrase shows that God will be more lenient on foreigners than on the Jews who knew so much about God. It also suggests that the people of Sodom may be more inclined to repentance than the Jews of Jesus' day. These ideas, both implied but well understood by the people to whom Jesus was speaking, may need to be explicated for modern receptors. The focus must be on the receptors and their understanding. Implied information is necessary to the extent that it provides understanding of what the original audience assumed.

Translators, however, dare not use this principle to shift the focus of the message; they must not sidetrack the receptors. The inclusion of implied information is legitimate only to maintain faithfulness to the message and ensure understanding. Implied information must be explicated when receptors can misinterpret if the assumed knowledge that was part of the source context is not part of the receptor context. Culture is such a pervasive part of these concerns that without an understanding and application of it, translators are severely handicapped.

Figures of Speech

Figures of speech are a constant translation problem because they are so language- and culture-specific. They intentionally use surface forms that convey meaning beyond their normal usage. Figurative meaning is based on association that is in some way inferred or derived from the larger context. Again, culture plays an obvious role. Clinton has helpfully organized figures of speech into broad classes based on their function in the text: figures of comparison, figures of substitution, figures of restatement, and figures of apparent deception.[22]

Clinton's steps to "capture" a figure help to explicate its meaning. (1) Recognize the author's intended meaning. (2) Replace the figurative language with nonfigurative. (3) Restate the figure with another or similar meaning or in a manner that reflects both the meaning and emphases of the figure in its context.[23]

Context is the critical word here. By that is meant all the linguistic and cultural assumptions necessary to make up the totality of both the source and receptor environment. All languages reflect figurative usage, but the figures are specific to the context of people's experience; cultural meaning is reflected in speech forms. Translation lies not so much "in the linguistic code but in the context, which carries varying proportions of the meaning."[24]

Assumptions about the qualities of items in a figure originate within the cultural base and must be communicated through the translation.

For example, Jesus told his disciples to go "tell that fox" (Herod), what he was doing (Lk. 13:32). What did he wish to communicate? What qualities did Herod share with a fox that would have triggered such a comparison? He may have been implying one or more of several qualities: cleverness, slyness, stealth, and/or a predatory nature.

However, to the Cuicatecox of Mexico, the comparison indicated Herod was a homosexual. The Zapotecs of Villa Alta thought it meant that he cried a lot, and the Otomi were sure Jesus had called Herod a chicken thief.[25] To the Maxakali of Brazil, Jesus was calling Herod a redhead; and to the Samo of Papua New Guinea, who had never seen a fox, it meant nothing at all. It is not sufficient for translators to use their own cultural assumptions about qualities being compared in figurative usage. They need to research the assumptions of the source as well as those of the receptor with respect to the qualities of each metaphor or simile.

For figures of substitution, the figurative sense of words is based on association with the primary meaning of a lexical item. When the apostle Paul refers to Christ as the "head of the church" (Eph. 1:22; 4:15; Col. 1:18), the analogy of the church as Christ's body was obvious to Greek speakers and transfers well to English usage. However, speakers of many languages may consider this synecdoche degrading. How can the Lord be viewed as a mere body part? Each culture has acceptable associations that are viewed as relevant, and when unacceptable associations are introduced, the value of God's Word may be considerably reduced. Again the meaning of cultural attributes, features, and associations is necessary to effectively communicate the intended meaning of the author.

Figures of restatement abound with cultural information unique to the context in which they are used. Idioms are highly language- and culture-specific and can never be translated literally without total loss of original meaning. Euphemism alerts translators to taboo subjects or topics of embarrassment: body functions, death, spirits, and many more.

The Jews avoided using God's name; and Matthew, accommodating them, speaks of the "kingdom of heaven" and refers to Christ as the "Son of Man." Luke, on the other hand, eliminates the euphemistic expressions when communicating primarily to gentiles, using "kingdom of God" and "Son of God" to express the same ideas. Both authors desire to communicate the meaning clearly to their audiences. To do so, one must use euphemism in order not to offend, while the other must be more direct in order to remain clear. Such examples from Scripture give insight to the way the Holy Spirit is aware of and utilizes cultural factors for more effective communication.

Figures of apparent deception are only "deceptive" from an outsider's perspective. From the perspective of those who use them, these figures do not deceive, but rather provide style and a variety of communication. While clarifying in one context, their transfer to another setting may be cause for confusion and miscommunication.

The rhetorical question, for example, is a favorite style of the apostle Paul. The Greek language allowed its use in a way not entirely unfamiliar to speakers of English. For the Samo, however, rhetorical questions are restricted almost entirely to ridicule. Therefore, unless ridicule was the intention of a particular Pauline passage, I had to rephrase it for the Samo. This required using a positive statement that more correctly conveyed Paul's intended meaning. If receptors are unable to supply the missing or implied information, or the extended senses assumed in the source text, then translators have failed to communicate an author's intended meaning and, therefore, have not really translated the text.

Other Structural Problems

Many other problems—such as pronominal referents, genitives, passives, quotations, order, and, of course, key terms—lurk in the source text materials. While these issues have been covered in detail with respect to their linguistic qualities, little focus has been given to the cultural context from which these difficulties emerge. Attention must be given to the culture which spawns their usage on the one hand and their transfer and appropriation on the other. Many forms vary their meaning with the context. It is crucial to match the proper forms with the intended meaning if that meaning is going to communicate. Some brief examples will suffice.

Key Terms

When choosing key terms, translators must have an adequate understanding of an author's intentions, the components of meaning of those terms, and their range of meaning with respect to other words. They should ask: What did the term mean in its original setting? A Greek or Hebrew lexicon, a range of usage both in Scripture and secular literature of the day, and a history of its etymology are all helpful to an understanding of the semantic content of a term.

The cultural implications must be added to this research. What were the connotational meanings and emotive responses to the term? How did it influence people's behavior? The emotion and awe surrounding the Hebrew use of the Tetragrammaton is a case in point. The Greeks lost much of this awe with the use of *Theos* adapted from their pantheon. The emotive content was different as indicated in the way Matthew and Luke refer to *YHWH* and *Theos* respectively. This meaning changes again when placed into the cosmology of modern receptor cultures.

The relationships implied by a particular term must fit into people's expectations. For example, when depicting the relationship between God and human beings, Scripture writers often use the father-child dyad. In some matrilineal societies of Melanesia, however, the relationship between a man and his mother's brother or (in some cases) a woman and her father's sister is more appropriate. Using a term for God that communicates the kind of relationship that will result in an awareness of concern and care rather than revulsion is critical for understanding in any culture. To call Christians "children of God" may well communicate relationships that would be detrimental to the church rather than building believers in the faith.

Key terms are critical for communicating meaning vital to the message of the source text. It is essential, to the extent possible, to focus on those meanings and discover forms that most effectively communicate them while generating emotions and cultural responses that demonstrate they have been understood.[26]

Pronouns

Pronouns have language-specific usage, but generally serve to keep things and people, relationships and actions in focus. If the author of a source text uses a pronoun in a manner which may confuse the referents, for example, by extending the primary usage in a particular way, the translator must clarify that usage and ascertain the author's intent before transferring it to the new context.[27] Ultimately, pronouns, like all other lexical units, must be translated in such a way that the receptors understand what the source intended. Where culture plays a role in this complex of associations, it must be understood and utilized for maximum communication.

Order

The way a text is ordered, details presented, and logic structured has a prominent impact upon effective communication. Order not only affects a time sequence but relates to logic which, by its very nature, is dictated by the genius of a language and culture. In the translation process, translators need to recognize the likelihood that the receptor does not follow the same logic of sequencing as the source. In such situations, if the original order is maintained, the message will not communicate.

If people are to understand the message, it must be communicated with respect for their frame of reference which, by its very nature, is closely tied to cultural expectations and presuppositions that determine the way they perceive and understand reality.

Reality, however, is relative to a particular context. Thus a "biblical relativism," to borrow a phrase from Nida,[28] is essential for meaningful translation. We must not be afraid to restructure the text in the surface forms of the receptor language, for that is the only way to communicate the meaning intended by the author who himself was forced to structure messages, using the style and perspective of a specific language and culture.[29] Restructuring, of course, makes verse numbering in a printed edition difficult; of central importance, however, is how a translation communicates, not how verse numbers are printed.

Quotations

The use of oral forms of literature throughout Old Testament times results in a style of communication well known to many modern pre- or semiliterate peoples. By New Testament times, Greek writing style was more rigorous but still quite loose by modern academic standards. References to Old Testament passages were quite vague: "it is written . . ." or "God says . . . ," with no indication of where the quote originated.

Such use of background information may suggest audience familiarity with Scripture, leaving the citation implied so as not to insult their intelligence. Regardless of the rationale, the cultural context of the source communication was apparently understood and the communication was effective. Modern oral cultures are more likely to appreciate the use of background material (including quotes) to validate an argument. The form such validation takes, however, is often cultural in nature and implies the context in which it was used.

Nonverbal Aspects

Hall makes clear that nonverbal communication is culturally relative and critical to communication. It also has a significant effect on the translation process. Sperber and Wilson[30] make a similar point when discussing relevance theory.

Scripture abounds with culturally specific gestures and contextual associations that convey whole complexes of meaning. In every culture, certain actions are symbolic, and it remains for translators to determine what that symbolism is and communicate it through appropriate gestures or meanings recognizable to the receptors.

When a phrase such as "wagging their heads" (Mt. 27:39 and Mk. 15:29) is used, it may have a variety of meaning that is quite distinct from that assumed in the original context. At the every least, an adjustment indicating the nature of the implied information is necessary, e.g., "they wagged their heads in ridicule." We must exercise caution to avoid obscenities when translating symbolic action. Appropriate gestures in one context are often inappropriate in others. The meaning must be the focus.[31]

Languages around the world abound in paralinguistic forms. For example, onomatopoeia and idiophones provide, in oral communication, a way to vocalize sounds appropriate to the context. These sounds convey emotion and add color. Add to this proverbs, poetry, plays on words, audience participation, and musical forms, and the richness available to a translator is extended far beyond the text itself. These were manifestations which the psalmist and other Old Testament writers knew well.

Tonal languages lend themselves to musical interplay that makes the distinction between oral and musical communication a fine, often irrelevant line. Oral communicators in many cultures around the world today are skilled orators who know that their communication is far more than a matter of words, much less words on cold, noninteractive paper.[32] Failure to use these paralinguistic forms in dramatic stories, such as the fall of Jericho, results in an unnatural, uninteresting, artificial recitation of facts that portray little feeling. Translations must feel right, to communicate emotively.

The communication styles that are so much a part of people's lives should become part of the translation in order for it to make sense. These styles give the gospel a quality that people can take seriously. When the local mythology presents a moral that is considered relevant, then Scripture must demonstrate applicability to the same points.[33] When the proverbs a people use every day communicate the necessity for smooth interpersonal relationships, the translated Scriptures must communicate this just as dynamically.

For Scripture to be considered meaningful and worthy of attention, it must do so in forms people consider relevant. Translations need to communicate in such a way that they earn credibility in order to warrant people's attention. The truth of the gospel must be clear! It should be presented in such a way that people consider it more powerful, more complete than their own wisdom tradition. Translators who overlook these styles may find people have little interest in their translations. Every effort should be made to remove translation from the "stimulus-poor" category in contexts where "the expectations concerning the use of communicational stimuli are high."[34]

Translators need to carefully choose a style of communication that will speak to all within the receptor language group and not just to the educated few (who may be products of their interaction with industrial nations). Translations should adopt communication styles common to the receptors as authors did for the original audience. Then people can identify with the message because the communication is not foreign.

IDIOMATIC TRANSLATIONS

Once particular translation problems have been identified, analyzed, and captured, linguistically and culturally, they are ready for translation. Unfortunately, most translators at this point ask "what is the best way to translate this?" The more appropriate question is "how might the author have written/said this if the receptor language were the language of communication?" Such a question implies a series of related questions:

- What is the most accurate and natural way to communicate these ideas in order to maximize receptor comprehension?
- How does the receptor use the semantic and cultural features expressed in the source?
- When are they appropriate?
- What are the surface-structure manifestations of deep-structure meaning?

If, indeed, the author intended to be understood, then translators must communicate in a way that receptors receive the same message.

Meeting people's cultural expectations within the translation process may revolutionize the whole concept of translation and the communication of the gospel in general. Western translators ministering out of a primarily industrial culture base have considered translation as part of a literary tradition; they have strongly encouraged recipients to learn to read. Such a focus implies that nonreaders are unable to understand God's Word.

An elaborate educational system established by many missions in the nineteenth century became the basis of modern education in nations around the world. These schools became monuments to the Western emphasis on writing skills and reading Scripture. Research now indicates the great importance people place on *their own* traditions and communication styles.[35] Therefore, rather than insisting that people adapt external emphases and styles, the focus needs to shift to adapting Scripture within communicational emphases that more closely reflect kinship or peasant styles.[36] We should attempt to know and use the richness of those traditions to transmit and transculturate biblical concerns within the receptor's communicational framework.

The poetry of the Bible should read like poetry, not like a dull prose account. Similarly, the letters of Paul should reflect something of the freshness of a general letter, and not sound like a theological dissertation.[37] Just as the original audience received the message within a specific context in styles unique to them, so modern receptors should have the privilege of receiving the message in their contexts and making decisions accordingly.

As national translators come into prominence, they should be encouraged to explore these possibilities. Experimentation with traditional forms (oral, musical, dance, and drama) helps communicate to the receptors that God understands them and desires to become incarnationally real. God communicated in this way among the Jews, and Jesus himself was the ultimate example of transculturation. The message of the Bible must not be viewed as presenting a strange religion developed by people speaking strange tongues and living in far-off places long ago. Rather, it should communicate in ways that enable people to appreciate its relevance and respond in life-changing ways. The message should communicate in such a way that it becomes part of the context in which it is presented, viewed as important and necessitating a response.

CONCLUSION

People act out their lives in real circumstances. The Scriptures must come to people in forms that are as real as their own lives. As Scripture was for the original audience, so it must become for modern receptors. Individuals depicted in a translation must not only talk right; they must also act right to be believable. As the Scriptures function in a dynamic way within a cultural context, the people will have a model to follow when they apply its meaning to their lives. Christians must be able to act out their salvation if it is to have any meaning. Similarly, the actors in the biblical case studies should be viewed as real people.

This is not to say that all cultural activities different from those of the receptors can be glossed over or changed to "fit" the context. Rather, they must be communicated in such a way that the receptors view them as valid though different, happening in another time and place. History cannot be ignored nor passed over lightly. Biblical peoples did things differently from modern people, especially if the latter come from industrial cultures.[38] Those actions, however, must be believable and the implied information encased within them communicated in a way that receptors understand the deeper message—why those accounts were included in Scripture.

Ignoring cultural issues and their impact upon exegesis and established principles of translation will dramatically affect the relevance of Scripture. Exegesis is essential to a correct understanding and appreciation of the source message and context, the totality of meaning communicated through the Word. The application of anthropological principles to traditional translation principles allows for a transculturation of a message within the context of very different times and places. Translation principles provide a mechanism for transfer, while cultural considerations provide the medium for emotive and nonverbal appreciation of information. This allows modern receptors to respond to the same Word which the original receptors understood.

While misinterpretation has long been a translator's occupational hazard, heresy based on scriptural texts that are inappropriately translated can be greatly reduced if the *context of the text* is taken seriously. Once Scripture is in people's hands, we want them to apply Scripture to their context, make it theirs, and provide a foundation for the growth of the church. But relevance must be based on truth, not someone's misinterpretation. Without an application of cultural principles to the translation process we are only half translating. We must make the biblical context real so receptors can appropriate the reality of the message for themselves. We must transculturate. We must contextualize.

NOTES

[1] Edward T. Hall, *The Silent Language* (New York: Doubleday, 1959), 86.

[2] Dawn Ryan, "Christianity, Cargo Cults, and Politics Among the Toaripi of Papua," *Oceania* 40 (1969), 114.

[3] For a detailed discussion of this concept, how to do it, and what it means to the entire translation process as manifested by the modern translation explosion taking place in the world today, see Shaw's recent book, *Transculturation: The Cultural Factor in Translation and Other Communication Tasks* (Pasadena: William Carey Library, 1988).

[4] Ibid.

[5] Wheeler Robinson, *Corporate Personality in Ancient Israel* (Philadelphia: Fortress, 1980).

[6] Hans W. Wolff, *Anthropology of the Old Testament* (Philadelphia: Fortress, 1981).

[7] Wayne A. Meeks, *The First Urban Christians: The Social World of the Apostle Paul* (New Haven: Yale University Press, 1983).

[8] An example of this is when members of an industrial culture attempt to understand the culture reflected in the Pentateuch. It is no accident that most translators from industrial societies start by translating the New Testament—they identify with the context of Paul's letters and his cogent arguments.

[9] Cf. R. Daniel Shaw, "The Translation Context," *Translation Review* 23 (1987): 25–29, Special Theory Issue. Translators interacting with people living in kinship or peasant-type cultures may find them more attuned to the cultural implications of Scripture than they may be themselves. Culturally, the gap between industrial

cultures and the Scriptures (particularly the Old Testament) is considerable. Translators, then, may be able to learn much about the meaning God originally intended
from those for whom they translate.

[10] Ralph Martin, "Approaches to New Testament Exegesis," Howard Marshall,
ed., New Testament Interpretation (Exeter: Paternoster, 1977), 220.

[11] Bernhard Frank, ("Reculturing, or the Kimono Won't Go in Oshkosh," Translation Review 26 (1988):27–28, has recently drawn attention to this concept in translating French poetry. He calls for a "reculturing" of the text in order to remove
"oddity" and restore meaning to a new audience (Frank, 1988, 27). Catholic theologians use the term "inculturation" to express a similar concept: a focus from within
a culture that "animates, directs and unifies . . . transforming and remaking it so
as to bring about 'a new creation'" (Pedro Arrupe, "Letter to the Whole Society on
Inculturation," Studies in the International Apostolate of the Jesuits VII [1977]: 1–2).
This, however, moves us from the process of communicating to the product of
effective communication which comes very close to contextualization.

[12] John Beekman, John Callow, and Michael Kopesec, The Semantic Structure of
Written Communication (Dallas: Summer Institute of Linguistics, 1981), 33ff.

[13] This is not in any sense another form of sensus plenior, a meaning not intended
by an author but considered central to God's communication and understood by
later audiences as a "developing revelation" of the text (Martin 1977, 224).

[14] Joseph Casagrande and Kenneth Hale, "Semantic Relationships in Papago Folk
Definitions," in D. Hymes and W. E. Bittle, eds., Studies in Southwestern Ethnolinguistics (The Hague: Mouton, 1967), 165–96.

[15] The surface-deep structure distinction should not be confused with the etic-
emic concept. The latter is concerned with understanding linguistic and cultural
data from different perspectives (outside a culture or within a culture respectively).
Etic issues relate to general concepts upon which human cultures are based, while
emic concerns focus on the structure of a particular context (Pike, 1967, 37–41).
This is quite different from understanding the meaning of various cultural concerns
and noting their implications to behavioral patterns within a linguistic/cultural system. For a more expanded description see Shaw 1988, op. cit., 26–28.

[16] John Beekman and John Callow, Translating the Word of God (Grand Rapids:
Zondervan, 1974), 21ff. Also see Mildred Larson, Meaning-Based Translation: A Guide
to Cross-Language Equivalence (Lanham, Md.: University of America Press, 1984),
15ff.

[17] Beekman and Callow, Translating, 34.

[18] It also happens that explicit sometimes needs to be made implicit. See Larson,
op. cit.

[19] Beekman and Callow, Translating, 57ff.

[20] Ibid., 59.

[21] Shaw, Transculturation, 210.

[22] J. Robert Clinton, Interpreting the Scriptures: Figures and Idioms (Pasadena:
Barnabas Resources, 1977), 14.

[23] Ibid., 12.

[24] Edward T. Hall, Beyond Culture (New York: Doubleday, 1976), 86.

[25] Beekman and Callow, Translating, 138.

[26] Transfer of meaning is focal in determining key terms even if the emotive content is not the same. YHWH vs Theos is a good example. Therefore, teaching must
make up the difference. Translation, church planting, and discipling should all work
together for the spiritual development of believers (Matt. 28:19, 20 and 2 Tim. 3:16).

[27] St. Paul's well-known use of first person plural to mean first person singular is a good example of such semantic skewing.

[28] Eugene Nida, *Customs and Cultures* (New York: Harper and Row, 1954), 52.

[29] Cf. Charles H. Kraft, *Christianity in Culture* (Maryknoll N.Y.: Orbis, 1979), 116ff.

[30] Daniel Sperber and Dierdre Wilson, *Relevance: Communication and Cognition* (Cambridge: Harvard University Press, 1986), 46ff.

[31] The contrast between interactive, oral communication, and the same message in a literary format is considerable. The message remains the same, but the communicative value is entirely different. Thus oral and written style are very different forms. Therefore, written translations and translation on cassette tape should not be the same.

[32] Roberta King, "Say It With a Song," *Impact* 44 (1987): 10–11.

[33] Shaw, "The Structure of Myth and Bible Translation, *Practical Anthropology* 19 (1972): 129–32.

[34] Herbert Klem, *Oral Communication of the Scripture: Insights from African Oral Art* (Pasadena: William Carey Library, 1982), 145.

[35] Viggo Sogaard, *Audio Scriptures* (New York: United Bible Society, 1988).

[36] Euan Fry, "An Oral Approach to Translation," *The Bible Translator* 30 (1979): 214–17.

[37] Eugene Nida and Charles Taber, *The Theory and Practice of Translation* (Leiden: E. J. Brill, 1982), 25.

[38] Cf. Shaw, *Transculturation*, 149ff.

8

Dimensions of Approach to Contextual Communication

Viggo Sogaard

COMMUNICATION IS CENTRAL TO ALL PHASES OF MISSION. It is impossible to conceive of evangelism without seriously considering communication. The Christian religion itself is a religion of communication with a communicator God. The Bible is a narrative of revelation, the communication of God to mankind: through creation, through the prophets, through "his mighty acts," through his Son Jesus Christ, through the Holy Spirit, and through his people, the church. Indeed, communication is rooted in the very nature of God. The challenge of the unreached and the challenge to make contextual missionary efforts effective lead us directly into a study of communication principles.

For an excellent model of true contextualized communication, we can turn to the Scriptures and learn from our Master himself. The incarnation must be the ideal we strive for. Incarnation begins with a concern for making the message clearly understood in each specific context. For such communication to happen we must take the

VIGGO B. SOGAARD, M.A., Ph.D., assistant professor of communication at Fuller Theological Seminary, is also a media consultant for United Bible Societies. He served as a missionary to Thailand from the Danish Covenant Church and has been a communications consultant to World Vision and other organizations. He is senior associate for the Lausanne Movement and author of *Cassette Ministry* and *Applying Christian Communication*.

cultural context seriously, and the audience in particular. Listening to their needs and their cries is the starting point of true and effective Christian communication.

In light of this, it is a strange fact and a tragedy that across the decades theology has created such a distance between itself and the science of human communication. We often find a general ignorance of communication principles among Christian leaders, even among many of those who are deeply engaged in evangelism and the use of media. An ignorance of communication principles will also cripple our dealing with biblical content that is so pervaded with God's commitment to effective communication. It would be helpful if we could discuss theological perspectives of communication, but our primary concern is the effective communication of theological content to people in their social and cultural contexts.

PROBLEMS AND POSSIBILITIES

Unfortunately, the development of communication theory has, primarily, taken place within disciplines other than theology. Many of our insights are gained from sociology, persuasion studies, marketing research, public relations, and advertising. Developments in communication theory from a Christian perspective lag seriously behind.

Negative attitudes to the topic of communication come from two different streams in the Christian church. In some evangelical circles, a negative attitude persists with regard to the topic of communication theory in general[1]; and in the so-called ecumenical groups, there is quite a negative attitude toward the use of media in particular.[2] There are, of course, a number of reasons for such skepticism, even though most are caused by misunderstanding. On the one hand, we see the misuse of media and the extravagance of some television evangelists, resulting in public disgrace; and on the other hand, many communication books are too theoretical for ordinary practitioners. Evangelism suffers because of poor thinking about communication. Breakdown in effective, contextualized communication will lead to ineffective ministries. A blockage is created, and people are not given a real opportunity to respond to the gospel of our Lord.

We are suffering from *program orientation* that keeps us concentrating on *our* agendas rather than focusing our attention on the needs of the listener, the reader, or the viewer. Only when focusing on the needs of the audience will we be able to design effective programs that are truly contextual in nature. We also have problems with *media orientation*. We tend to select the medium before we define the problems and establish objectives and goals. This often leads to a strained use of a medium, forcing media to accomplish tasks for which they are really not well suited. Thirdly, evangelism suffers because of the widespread use of *Western productions*, rather than developing local productions and media that are understood and appreciated by audiences in specific contexts. The export of Western media products by Christian organizations has serious negative implications for the development of the local church in other parts of the world.

In spite of these and other problems, tremendous opportunities do exist. The theories and principles have been developed and resources are available. If we let our minds do some "possibility thinking," our eyes will be opened to avenues for world mission that have been largely untouched or unexplored. In the area of media use, it is not a question of *if* but *how*. From a mission strategy perspective, it is too costly not to use media, and from a stewardship perspective too costly to misuse media. We cannot let ill-conceived assumptions and outdated approaches hinder effective outreach. Millions of people still need to have the gospel communicated to them in meaningful, concrete ways.

A word on *effectiveness*. By that term I am not primarily concerned with numbers. We need to see effectiveness from the perspective of God and the Christian communicator, as well as from the perspective of the receptor (the audience). For *God*, effectiveness is measured from the perspective of eternity, with the goal of creating true and harmonious relationships. Finally, God is more concerned with our obedience and faithfulness within that broader context than with short-range "evangelistic results." But, for the Christian communicator, effectiveness will be seen in light of the commission given to us to go and make disciples of all nations. We are called to use our talents, skills, and gifts, and to witness by word and deed. Effectiveness will be seen in the fruits of our labor. The receptors will judge effectiveness in terms of how their needs are met and how joy and fullness of life in fellowship with God and other human beings is experienced.

As we approach the topic of contextual applications of communication principles, it is important for us to have certain guidelines. The following ten dimensions together form an approach that will help us be biblical and effective in a Christian sense. The various dimensions can serve as a grid on which we test our communication programs and products.[3]

1. The Commission-Dimension

"What am I here for?" might serve as a good daily reminder, or as an inscription on the studio wall, a question to answer during sessions of praise and intercession. We so easily lose sight of the reason for our mission: to do the will of Christ. The challenge of Jesus in John 20:21, "*as* the Father has sent me, *so* I send you," has implications far beyond our human understanding. Jesus was sent on his mission by the Father to communicate who God is in a worldly context. People could look at Jesus and see the Father. They could listen to him, and hear the Father. They could watch him at work, and see the work of the Father (Jn. 14:6).

In that same way, Jesus is sending us, his church, to communicate him, his words, and his deeds to the whole world. Our communication is, therefore, not based on some idealistic or political ambition, but on the clear call from Christ to proclaim the gospel to all people. The moment we lose this perspective or forget the primary purpose of our Christian communication, we will be ineffective.

In his stirring article, "Who's Converting Whom?" Chuck Fromm points out that many Christians enter the arena of the performing arts and media to utilize the stage as a platform of ministry.[4] But, sadly, because they lack the background and the ongoing counsel of church leaders, a number of them become "converted" to the media and the demands of the media. They become "stars," and results are measured by records sold and the level of personal publicity, rather than how much God is praised. The same general problems face the missionary in crosscultural situations. Rather than a ministry that facilitates Christian communication, our ministry becomes an end in itself, and all our strength is spent on keeping our particular project going.

The mission belongs to Christ. It is his mission, and we are the agents of it. This also means that through prayer and study of his Word, we seek his constant guidance in making plans and carrying out our tasks. The real challenge of the world and contextualized communication is, therefore, the challenge of Christ who is the Lord of the mission; the incarnation of Christ is the method, and the cross is the price. We then can see the millions who do not know him and the peace of his kingdom, and be compelled to be involved with Christ at whatever cost to ourselves.

This is the perspective with which the Christian communicator must enter the world of communication and media. Within the context of a given situation, he or she will carry out the service according to standards for behavior, excellence, and success that are often at odds with the world's standards.

2. The Spirit-Dimension

Any adequate Christian communication theory for contextual applications will need to account for the fact that all spiritual growth depends on the Holy Spirit (Jn. 6:44; Tim. 3:5-7). It is a matter of letting God be God. In order to keep this perspective, it is important to realize that Christian communication is influenced by certain constant factors and certain variable factors. These not only set it apart but also make it superior to other forms of communication. Contextual communication operates in the context of variable factors, but it does so on the basis of a set of constant factors. A clear grasp of these constant factors will guide us in Christian application even in the midst of seemingly confused contextual factors.[5]

Constant factors are fundamental aspects that never change. Some of these will be:

(1) The presence and activity of the powers of darkness.
(2) The fallen nature of human beings.
(3) The revelation of God.
(4) The work of the Holy Spirit.
(5) Faith.
(6) The Scriptures.
(7) The goal of disciple-making.

(1) *The presence and activity of the powers of darkness* (Eph. 2:1-2; 2 Cor. 4:4). As long as we live in this age, our task of communicating the Word of God will meet with hostility and obstruction from the powers of evil. The evil one will blind the minds of people who do not believe, and will construct other roadblocks to hinder our ministry.

(2) *The fallen nature of human beings* (Rom. 3:10-11). The fallen human race is in rebellion against God. Since understanding is a primary purpose of communication, we cannot expect the unsaved person to comprehend much of the things of God without the help of someone in whom the Spirit of Christ abides. God uses the human communication process with all its limitations to bring people to Christ. This is accomplished by the Holy Spirit, which serves to encourage and humble the Christian communicator.

(3) *The revelation of God* is evident all through Scriptures (Ps. 19:1-4; Jn. 1:14; Heb. 1:1-3a). Throughout the ages God has communicated himself to mankind through nature, conscience, and history, as well as through special revelation. As Christian communicators we must remember that we are entering into a ministry that has been the concern of God through the ages.

(4) *The work of the Holy Spirit* is a constant factor that sets Christian communication apart (1 Cor. 2:1–16). Missionary work must be a spiritual work, and ultimately, all results will depend on the Holy Spirit. In the task of proclaiming the gospel, the Spirit utilizes the church and its members as his agents. The obvious implication for the development of communication strategies is to commit ourselves through prayer to the guidance of the Spirit. We can then anticipate the mighty work of the Spirit in conviction and healing, and the creation of true wholeness.

(5) *Faith* (Jn. 3:16). Christianity is a religion of faith, and Christian communication must be carried out in faith. Through the eyes of faith we behold God; and without faith, no spiritual work can be done. Salvation is received by faith, the Christian life is lived in and by faith, and the gospel is extended to all mankind in faith. It is a faith that is confident of God's intervention.

(6) *The Scriptures* are the essential context and content of all aspects of evangelism (2 Tim. 3:14–17; Rev. 22:18). God has provided us with a uniform message, and this message centers on Christ. It is the good news of the kingdom of God for all.

(7) *The goal of disciple-making* is also a constant, and it must always be given high priority in our communication applications (Mt. 28:18–20). We are not just communicating for the purpose of dialogue or to show our presence, but in order to make disciples for Jesus Christ.

These constant factors form the basis on which the Christian communicator can enter the "real world" of contextual communication—a world made up of factors that change from context to context. We are often unprepared for a contextual response and may be tempted to turn specific alternatives into constants, or construct a predetermined response or program for all situations.

In our submission to God and dedication to his work we should expect God to manifest himself in ways we could never even dream of. In light of this, the term *strategy* takes on new dimensions and meaning, and strategic planning becomes a work of faith. Or, stated differently, strategy development is a planning process in which we attempt to align our thinking and plans with God's plans.[5] Under his guidance, exciting plans can be developed for contextualized communication of the gospel.

3. The Person-Dimension

The final and complete communication of God to mankind was in the form of a human body: the incarnation of Jesus Christ.

Similarly, the Christian communicator needs both to realize what it is to a specific human being and learn how to communicate like a human being.[6] Our contextual applications must, consequently, find their roots in the lives of people rather than in impersonal organizations or media.

The commission given by Jesus was a person-based commission: "You are witnesses of these things. . . ." People may look at church as a collective group, but they need to experience church as individual people. Jesus gave us the example of becoming a real human being, participating in our affairs. From secular communication research we also see that effects are closely related to "person involvement." In Jesus, the message and the medium become one.

What gives communication its character is, therefore, not only the message but the messenger. The way Jesus used parables illuminates this person-centered communication. Parables are created out of the everyday life of the people in the audience, that is, meaning is created within the context of the listeners. In parables, members of the audience become players; as such, each one discovers new truths and principles. The need in Christian communication is not for preconceived answers or prepackaged stories and programs, but life involvement on behalf of the communicator with the people among whom he or she is sent to communicate Christ.

Since the effects are so related to the communicator, we also need to study the ways and possibilities for communicating personalness by a given medium. The answer will be found in the development of integrated strategies that allow the media to enhance the ministry of the local church; the medium, in turn, is personalized by the local Christians.

We learned in Thailand of the importance of the personal use of cassette tapes in evangelism. There, the life and testimony of the Christian who plays the tape is most important. Only then will the non-Christian listen. The taped program must enhance this interpersonal communication with relevant content, voices, and formats. The tape does not work by itself, but only in unison with the person who uses it.

This may look like a paradox: at the same time we attract attention to a credible source we must also be so transparent that Jesus is the one who is seen and praised. Perhaps the answer lies in this analogy: the Christian communicator has to be like a clear window pane through which others see Jesus and through which his light reaches them, and not like a stained-glass window that blocks the view and draws attention to itself.[7]

4. The Church-Dimension

The church as an organized body of believers is God's primary agent for world evangelization. It alone has the mandate to be a servant to all people, with a priestly, missionary, and evangelistic vocation. The church is permanent, and it alone can provide permanent structures for the effective use of media and process-oriented communication. For example, free literature does not seem to be effective when given out at random, but it can be very effective if church members distribute the material to family and friends. The local church can make media messages effective, but it can also create barriers. If we broadcast to a certain town and the local churches are involved in internal squabbling, it is unlikely that anyone will believe our radio message of hope, reconciliation, and peace.

The local church as a body of believers within a given context should also function as the center for our strategies and communicational activities. This also implies that the decision power concerning media employment and program design cannot rest exclusively with parachurch organizations. Sometimes we may even need to delay the use of mass media until such a time as local churches are ready to do their part in the ministry. Otherwise, our expressed devotion to contextual principles will remain only a theory. The local church, using and feeling ownership of the media, produces the results; outside agencies function as true servants in helping with productions.

We can, with gratitude, note the development of significant church-based strategies in various countries. In Kenya, Cinema Leo has developed a training system for local church leaders. When their movie vans come to a community, the local church has ownership of the program, gives the welcome, and prays with those who seek conversion. The local Christians can, in this way, utilize more advanced approaches in a local, contextualized situation. Film showing will be delayed until training has taken place and a local church is ready.

Many personal evangelism training programs have been conducted for "individuals," that is, whether the individual concerned is a church member or not. More recent programs have focused on individuals as members of a local church, with the church being the center of strategy. The person-to-person program developed jointly in England by the Bible society, Scripture Union, and Campus Crusade for Christ is a striking example of such a church-based approach to personal evangelism. It makes sense of contextualization in the local context with its many subcultures.

We could also mention Robert Schuller's Southern California-based television approach. In this well-thought-out strategy, Schuller uses television to draw people into his church. He is extending the Sunday morning service through the television channel—that is, the morning service serves like a television program with the congregation functioning as a studio audience. Schuller has given the main audience (in homes with television) the priority. But his strategy does require that the church congregation accept this approach. Others who have tried to broadcast a regular church service have often failed because the "program" did not fit the medium and the audience.[8]

5. The Receptor-Dimension

Good contextualized communication is, in essence, an understanding of the audience and its context, and an adaptation of the message to fit the needs of people in that context. This is nothing new. If we are to follow the example of Jesus in our approach to communication, we will always start with the receptor and his or her needs.[9] Let us look at two examples as found in John's Gospel.

In John 3, the receptor was a highly educated man, a philosopher, a man with status, someone who would be embarrassed if seen talking alone with Jesus. Jesus showed his acceptance and empathy by sacrificing his sleep to meet with Nicodemus at night when no one would see them. The very language Jesus used shows respect for Nicodemus and an understanding of his needs and context. Jesus aptly entered into that frame of reference and from there led Nicodemus into new discoveries.

In the following chapter, the audience is a very different person: a Samaritan woman who would be treated by the Jews almost as a nonperson, an outcast. The Jews would not even talk to this woman. What did Jesus do? He spoke to her, treated her as a real person, lifted her self-esteem. He used language that she would use and that would not intimidate her. Again, we see him entering into the frame of reference of the receptor, and from within that context he led her also to new insights about herself and her life. This receptor orientation of Jesus is an outstanding example of contextual communication.

We can summarize a receptor-oriented approach by four questions:

(1) *Who* is my listener?
(2) *Where* is my listener?
(3) *What* are the *needs* of my listener?
(4) *How* can I meet the needs of my listener?

These questions may sound easy and simple, but they are extremely profound. A lot of work and dedication, as well as a new orientation, are required to carry them out in practice. There is no shortcut if we want to be contextualized and relevant in our approach. The starting point is an analysis of the context and needs of the audience. Then begins a search for appropriate communication channels, followed by the development of programs that will meet these needs and guide the listener into a true understanding of who Jesus is.

Such an approach may challenge the traditional evangelical approach to evangelism and mission, but it is important that we see the audience in a total perspective. The dichotomy between evangelism and social work does not fit and is completely unrealistic if the total needs of the receptors are to be met. The dynamics of the approach of Jesus must permeate our approaches, as in a Christlike manner we meet people in their total spiritual, mental, and physical needs. We will put our insights from theology, psychology, sociology, and ecology into one approach. This, in turn, has significant implications for our use of media.

Breakthrough, an evangelistic magazine in Hong Kong, set out to meet the needs of teenagers in the fourteen- to seventeen-year-old group. Its pages provide a wholesome response to their needs, and point to the ultimate answer in Christ. In creating the magazine, the intent was to sell it to this group, rather than give it away. This policy placed demands on the editorial staff, who had to produce a magazine that would sell. The need for relevant, up-to-date information was a priority, especially as the audience is one that is in constant change and is influenced by new forms of behavior, dress styles, and interests. One way in which the creators achieved their objective was to appoint a group of twelve people who had as their one task to discover the topics high school students discuss during break time. The result is a high-quality magazine that sells on the newsstands and which has led the organization into numerous other related ministries, including a telephone counseling program for young people. A few other magazines, like *Step* in Africa, have followed suit, as has a magazine for people living in the Middle East.

Some years ago the Franciscans produced a series of excellent television spots in their facilities in downtown Los Angeles. During twenty-second or one-minute spots they were able to capture attention through a pertinent, human interest topic, give a punch line that would not be forgotten, and then tie it in with another program or outreach from a local church. The Mennonites have done similar things through short programs on "drive-time" radio.

6. The Goal-Dimension

Christ stated clearly his commission: "Go and make disciples." The Christian communicator is, therefore, not just communicating for the sake of communication or for the purpose of highlighting a "Christian viewpoint" on a specific topic. There is always that ultimate goal of reaching other people with the gospel in such a way that they will want to listen, understand, follow, and commit themselves to be disciples of Jesus Christ.

Jesus communicated for a response.[10] A basic dimension of God's communicational activity is that he seeks to elicit a response from his listener. This response is not manipulated or conditioned, but is a true, conscious, and voluntary response. Jesus first cultivated this kind of free, human response to his message. Then, little by little, he "filled in the blanks," resulting in a kind of total educational process. He came to seek and to save. As agents of God-communication we will do the same, seeking to help people respond within their present cultural and social contexts. The mass media, for example, will serve the listener and heighten his or her dignity by providing facts on which he or she can base a sound judgment. To say it another way, we will provide stimuli for thinking, rather than forcing decisions.

For our planning, we need a series of subgoals, or a matrix of subgoals that will point toward the ultimate goal. Consequently, for each program and each use of communication media, a clear subgoal must be established. For the definition of such subgoals, a clear understanding of the needs and context of a given audience is needed. This spells serious problems for prepackaged approaches to communication, for they cannot define relevant subgoals.

Goal orientation raises questions concerning the measurement of missionary/evangelistic activities. The traditional way has been to describe activities such as the number of radio programs, the number of tracts distributed or meetings conducted. We have rarely asked questions about actual effects. But activities and effects are not the same. We know of churches with many—often, too many—activities, but with seemingly no effect. Goal-oriented communication will challenge us and guide us into defining the purpose of our mission and evaluating how far we actually reach our goals.

During an analysis of the needs in Thailand, we discovered that when local Christians were witnessing to neighbors, they often ran into difficult questions. The local Christians were often unschooled rural people who did not know how to answer or even if there was an answer. The result was ridicule, which, in turn, caused the cessation of personal evangelism.

A number of these questions that non-Christians raised were gathered, which became the topics for two audio cassettes which had the specific goal of helping the local Christians answer the questions. As a result, the Christians could be brave enough to enter into a dialogue. The cassettes were used extensively, with remarkable results. Numerous testimonies told how they helped "passive" Christians become active in evangelism. The identification of a specific need helped define the goals and apply communication principles in a specific context.

7. The Process-Dimension

Seen from a production and technical perspective, communication is a process. It is also adaptive, in that it seeks to relate to the needs of the audience. The audience, in turn, lives through a decision process that spans from initial exposure and awareness to full understanding and, hopefully, acceptance. During this process the needs of the audience will change; the communicator must adapt methods and programs to meet such needs. In each situation, there is both a history and a context; and together, these provide the parameters within which we seek to elicit cognitive, affective, and behavioral changes.

The communication process that is involved could be likened to a 16 mm movie. We see it as a living, moving process, but it is in reality a sequence of individual "still" pictures. In the same way, each program, each encounter provides a picture that together with many other pictures forms an ongoing process. We need to relate this principle to contextual communication of the gospel.

Growth is a process, and the corresponding communication process must start at the present position of the audience. We may often be tempted to look away from the hard or so-called unresponsive fields and turn to the more obviously responsive areas. But before turning away, we should seek to discover the reasons for "unresponsiveness." What are the barriers and how did they get there? Have we really taken time to understand them? Do we try to communicate in a language they do not understand? Have we failed to "incarnate" the message in life and blood? Have we actually constructed barriers that turn people away from the churches? Are we starting the process in the wrong place?

Disciple-making is a process. When a person accepts Christ as Lord and Savior, it is only one step in a long series of steps.[11] In that pilgrimage to Christ and his church there are steps of affective changes (attitude change) and steps of cognitive changes (new knowledge). In order to visualize that process, we use conceptual models. Models are not reality, but they help us understand reality. They are not finite or exclusive, but they serve as frames of reference.

Some people do not even have an awareness of a living, personal God; others have some knowledge, and yet others have received ample knowledge about Christ. The vertical axis of the model (Figure 12) is the cognitive dimension and indicates the level of knowledge.[12] This increase in knowledge will be illustrated as an upward move and should be an ongoing process. There is no fixed conversion point on this scale, as decisions for Christ can, theoretically, take place at any stage of the cognitive process. In practice, we often see people accepting Christ at a very low level of biblical knowledge. Such a situation demands heavy emphasis on cognitive input in the form of Bible study to nurture further growth and facilitate permanent results.

A person may have a certain level of knowledge but at the same time be very negative or directly hostile to the gospel. Others are just passive. Some are prejudiced by misunderstandings or by historical events. The second dimension of our model indicates this affective

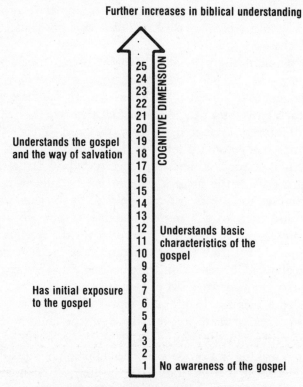

Figure 12   The Cognitive Dimension of the
Two-dimensional Strategy Model

dimension, how one feels about the message presented. This could be called a person's attitude toward Christ and his church. If there are negative attitudes, there will most likely be negative response. Conversion is probably based more on feelings than on a cognitive process, even though a decision is usually based on a cognitive foundation.

The resulting model is a matrix on which strategy can be developed. Through research we are able to discover a person's or a people group's position on the model, and we can discover the latitude of acceptance or rejection for a given position. Within that latitude a person is receptive, and, consequently, our communication strategy must take its starting point there. The journey toward spiritual maturity becomes a journey from where one is presently toward the upper right hand corner of the model (Figure 14). Most likely this will not be a straight line. It may fluctuate between cognitive and affective changes. Or both may take place at the same time.

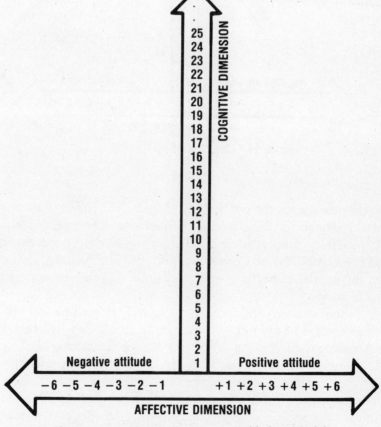

Figure 13   Affective Dimension Added to Model

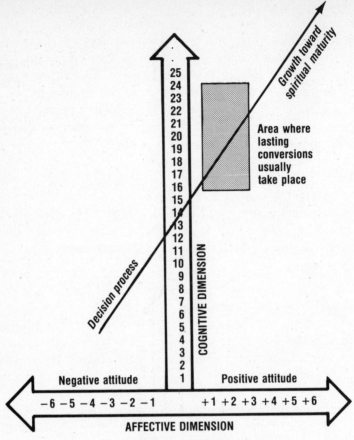

Figure 14   Concept of Spiritual Progress

For each step, the application of media will differ. We can give certain guidelines for the use of media at different sections of the model, primarily based on the general needs of the audience and the capabilities of a given medium. But the final decision concerning media applications and media mix will depend on contextual factors.

Often, missions and local churches have limited ministry to the middle section of the model. This may be due to the lack of a comprehensive strategy, but it is also due to the limitations of their research measurements. Often they have measured only conversions, baptisms, or church membership; such indicators relate to the middle section of the model. Consequently, the desire to measure effectiveness and show results has forced many to concentrate strategy development on areas where they can readily measure.

The development of a comprehensive, integrated strategy is like planning a highway from the present position of the person or group to spiritual maturity. Such a highway will consist of different methods, approaches, and media applications. Each ministry or program becomes a section of the highway and must therefore be closely integrated.

As an illustration, we could mention the earlier work of the Christian Arts and Communications Service (CACS) in Madras, India. They have been engaged in evangelism through traditional Indian dances. The Hindu audience knows very little about the gospel and is basically negative toward the gospel; but presenting the gospel in Indian dress and Indian dances caused it to be perceived as Indian. While the cognitive content of the dances was limited, a change of attitude followed.

CACS also produced radio programs that provided biblical content and further understanding. The actual contact ministry was based on local church outreach. And in order to assist the churches in this ministry, CACS produced a number of cassette tapes. The actual nurture of new Christians was seen as the responsibility of the churches. So we have here an example of a parachurch group with limited scope of ministry linked with local churches in order to provide a comprehensive program, built on process understanding (Figure 15).

Another example could be taken from the ministry to a group of young people in Denmark. The group has a fair understanding of the gospel, but is rather negative toward the church and its message. A church has established a youth club, which is a contact ministry. There is no preaching, but as the leaders spend time with the youth who come there, a Christian testimony is established and a relationship of trust is formed. This should provide a basis for affective changes from negative toward a neutral position. The leader of the club conducts a Bible study in his home, and interested youth are invited to attend. Here, basic Bible teaching is given to provide growth in knowledge. The nearby church has occasional youth rallies, and interested young people from the club can be brought along. Such evangelistic rallies will provide a definite challenge to accept Christ. Those who are converted will then be channeled into the discipling programs of the church (Figure 16).

The planning of such an integrated ministry was enhanced by the use of the process model. It helped the church to understand the need for a long-term strategy, and that the workers should not expect results in the form of conversions from each aspect of the ministry.

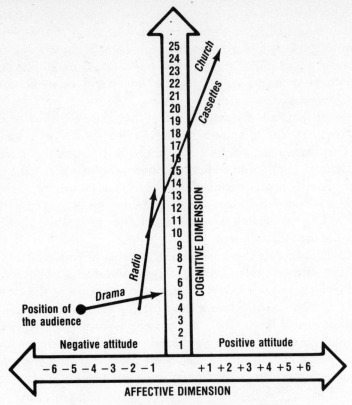

Figure 15   The Ministry of Christian Arts
and Communications Service in Madras

Any model or scale of the spiritual decision process will be incomplete. Even if we could construct multidimensional scalings, they would be insufficient in depicting the spiritual life of human beings. We may, therefore, be in disagreement as to which dimensions should be depicted on a model. The work of the Spirit was earlier explained as a constant factor. That unseen dimension is basic to all our ministry, but it cannot be depicted on graphs or scales. The Spirit, like wind, blows where he wills, and we know that all spiritual growth depends on the inner work of the Holy Spirit. We cannot, humanly speaking, cause that growth, but we can by our witness and concern make the move more likely.

8. The Research-Dimension

Contextualization without research is impossible. We cannot contextualize without good information about the people and their context, and such knowledge can only be obtained through some kinds of

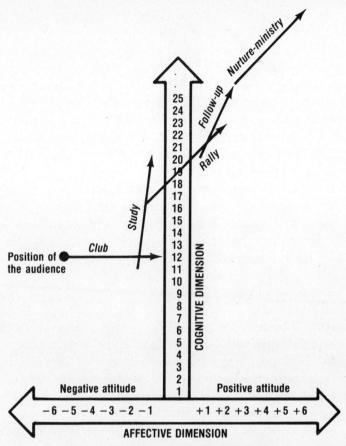

Figure 16   Integration of Youth Ministry

formal or informal research. For any receptor-oriented approach, for the setting of goals, and for intelligent and effective planning processes, we need good information; and for the sake of being accountable in the ministry, we need tools that measure effectiveness.

Research principles and methodologies are available to us, but, unfortunately, research is not always readily acceptable to Christian leaders. The term itself may be rejected due to theological reasons. We often hear, "only God can truly evaluate the effectiveness of ministry." We do not disagree with this, but research must be seen as a valuable and indispensable tool of effective and accountable ministries. Actually, it is a nonthreatening daily phenomenon that we all engage in as we seek information from or about each other. We desire to be accountable and good stewards, so we should have no problem with viewing research as a legitimate tool of communication. We need a good *information system* that will provide data on all steps in the communication process, with a primary concern to limit management errors.

In addition to the basic tools of observation and measurement, a media researcher must have a conceptual framework by which he or she transforms information and data into generalizations that can be used in strategy applications. But research methodologies also need to be contextualized. For example, the way a questionnaire is constructed will depend significantly on the given cultural and social context. Western approaches to research are not all readily acceptable in other parts of the world.

In Christian communication, marketing research is the primary source for methodology and technique. For other areas of communication research we need to learn from the insights of anthropological research, particularly the analysis of a people's world-view, their daily lives, their felt needs, and everyday concerns.

9. The Integration-Dimension

Mission is the function of one body with many members. We are all created differently, with varying talents and gifts that must be used in a wide, cooperative effort for maximum results. Similarly, no one medium or approach is capable of meeting the needs demanded by a comprehensive strategy. As already mentioned, the strengths and weaknesses of each medium and method vary and are strongly influenced by the society and context for which the strategy is developed.

The two-dimensional model presented earlier can give us a framework for developing a comprehensive and integrated strategy. The circular strategy development model created by Edward Dayton (see Figure 17) can be of tremendous help as it guides us through brainstorming sessions and forces us to ask questions.[13] In answering such questions we will inevitably arrive at an integrated approach.

The first step is always a clear statement of mission or purpose. We often find that the purpose or mission statement of a Christian organization is either so vague or so broad that it is of little help. An inclusive statement may be broken down into specific objectives to make strategy development easier.

In India, World Vision has developed an interesting and effective integrated cassette ministry. The general purpose has been to enhance both its traditional community development work and the evangelistic work. Stated differently, the goal is to develop a ministry that will achieve wholistic effects. The answer was found in an integrated and comprehensive communications program. As most of the people concerned are nonreaders, the obvious tool to use was the audio cassette.

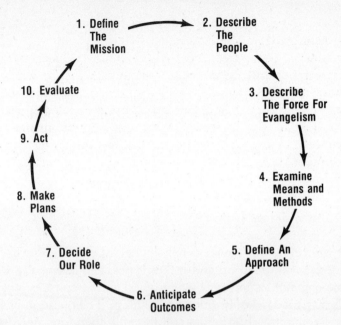

Figure 17   Circular Planning Model
(Dayton and Fraser 1980:43)

And the results were remarkable. One project manager expressed with amazement, "Since we introduced the cassettes we have seen more results of our work in seven months than we earlier saw in five years."[14]

It took almost a year to develop the first tape, as it involved quite extensive research and testing to arrive at the right topics and appropriate format and voices, and to develop the distribution system. Also, local people were brought into the planning and production so that the issues raised and the answers given would be truly contextualized. After initial and outstanding results were seen, the project quickly expanded to other projects and languages. In each case, the local churches are involved as well as the project staff. In some projects the whole communications program is church-based, and it is the church that coordinates and uses the cassettes. Volunteers play the cassettes in the communities. Having the project church-based and integrated into the local communities assures the continuation of the actual community development project.

As an urban example, Eagles Evangelism in Singapore has developed a special program for reaching young executives with the gospel.[15] After careful research of the context of the executives and their use of (and lack of) time, an integrated strategy was developed. The focal point is a banquet at a major hotel. Follow-through is achieved by the way the programs are announced. A Christian working in a company will reserve a (Chinese) table with ten seats, two for him and his spouse and the rest for four colleagues and their spouses. There will already be a certain level of familiarity among all members at the table. Good food is served, and then an outstanding program with music, media presentations, and preaching is provided by the Eagles. Follow-up is provided by the person who invited his or her friends, but the Eagles assist in this by providing each person with a package of materials as well as invitations to an Eagles rendezvous. Introduction to local churches will come naturally.

10. The Intercultural-Dimension

As human beings, we are totally immersed in our culture.[16] This both limits communication and makes it possible. Essentially, we use the same communication symbols in our different cultures, but such symbols may have radically different meanings. The question of meaning when communicating across cultures will, therefore, need special attention. We need to study how communication takes place across cultural boundaries, or rather how one can enter a new cultural context and communicate accurately within that new culture. To do this we need a high view of culture in which we do not see it as anti-Christian but something given by God. As expressed by the leader of the national Balinese church, Wayan Mastra, "Bali is my body, Christ is my life." The gospel must be clothed in the local culture as it penetrates that culture with the true life of Christ and then, from within that same culture, it unfolds to new tunes and new instruments.

Media tools and media systems are used differently by different cultures and societies, each one giving meaning both to the medium itself and to interpretation of its messages.

For example, television takes on new dimensions when used in the United States with heavy emphasis on commercial utilization, in Sweden with its emphasis on cultural and educational use, in Israel with its special concern for national development, or in the Soviet Union with its concern for political control.[17] Seen from a Christian communications perspective, all attempts should be made to produce within cultural contexts. We must be intercultural, rather than imposing foreign productions on an indigenous society. Let us imitate Jesus, who became like us, spoke like us, lived like us, acted like us, in order to present the message of the kingdom of God to us in a form we could understand.

An intercultural understanding will automatically lead us into investigating local and traditional music, art forms, and media. This is not to say that we will be limited to folk media, but it does mean that such media will be involved. It will also mean, for example, that we will not impose a seven-tone musical scale on a people who traditionally sing in a five-tone scale.

A number of people have demonstrated that folk media can be used effectively in evangelism. A group in Thailand always attracts huge crowds with the Thai traditional forms for dance and drama. If well integrated with the local churches and other ministries, such approaches will open the minds of people for the gospel message as they see the good news dressed in the local culture.[18]

The Balinese Church in Denpasar has, for example, incorporated local cultural themes in the architecture of its church building. Among key themes in the culture are water, light, and wind. As you enter the church, you pass over a basin of water. Isn't the water of baptism the entry to the church? Inside the huge structure with a high, steep roof there are no windows except at the very top of the roof. There a row of flat windows throw light down into the sanctuary so that one can almost see the rays of light. Isn't Christ the light of the world? There is no air conditioning in the building, but an opening under the roof and over the low walls permits a constant small breeze in the church, so that one can feel it almost everywhere. Isn't the Holy Spirit like a wind? Altogether, it is an interesting attempt at making church architecture intercultural.

As stated at the beginning of this chapter, contextualization is impossible without communication. We have looked at various aspects of this process, and ten dimensions have been proposed. These ten dimensions together form one approach. Such an approach will demand that communication insights will be shared among missionaries, pastors, and other leaders in the Christian community. Our resolve could, therefore, be:

(1) Pastors and new missionaries must be trained in basic communication theory and skills if they are to apply communication principles in contextual situations.

(2) Experienced missionaries and Christian leaders should be brought in to evaluate and plan their ministries in the context of applied communication principles.

NOTES

[1] This negative attitude to the topic of communication theory has been evident from personal experience, letters, and reports of various consultations.

[2] See William F. Fore, *Television and Religion, The Shaping of Faith, Values, and*

Culture (Minneapolis: Augsburg, 1987). Also Malcolm Muggeridge, *Christ and the Media* (London: Hodder and Stoughton, 1977).

[3] The background study to these dimensions is found in Viggo Sogaard, *Applying Christian Communication* (Ann Arbor, Mich.: University Microfilm, 1986).

[4] Chuck Fromm, "Who's Converting Whom?" *Charisma and Christian Life* 1987 (July): 42–48.

[5] Viggo Sogaard, *Applying Christian Communication*, 67ff.

[6] Edward R. Dayton and David A. Fraser, *Planning Strategies for World Evangelization* (Grand Rapids: Eerdmans, 1980).

[7] Charles H. Kraft, *Communication Theory for Christian Witness* (Nashville: Abingdon, 1983), 15–34.

[8] Viggo Sogaard, "A Star: Crystal or Stained Glass?" in *Worship Times* (Fall) 1987.

[9] Jeffrey K. Hadden and Charles E. Swann, *Prime Time Preachers* (Reading, Mass.: Addison-Wesley, 1981).

[10] Kraft, *Communication Theory*, 23.

[11] Ibid. 19.

[12] Viggo Sogaard, "A Star", 225–63.

[13] Ibid., 227ff., 247ff.

[14] Dayton and Fraser, *Planning Strategies*, p. 43.

[15] Project and accompanying research commissioned by World Vision International and World Vision India and conducted under the supervision of Viggo Sogaard. Author's files.

[16] Eagles Evangelism in a Christian organization, based in Singapore, whose president is Peter Chao.

[17] See, for example, Charles H. Kraft, *Christianity in Culture* (Maryknoll, N.Y.: Orbis, 1979), or Paul Hiebert, *Cultural Anthropology*. (Grand Rapids; Baker, 1983).

[18] Jeremy Tunstall, ed., *Media Sociology, A Reader* (Urbana, Ill.: University Press, 1970).

[19] The Thai dance-drama team is a part of the Christian Communication Institute of Payap University, Chiangmai, Thailand.

9

Crosscultural Use of Leadership Concepts

J. Robert Clinton

LEADERSHIP CONCEPTS WHICH HAVE ORIGINATED in the leadership concentration of the School of World Mission can usually be transferred to other cultures (and vice versa). Transfer of concepts depends upon careful adaptation or application as judged by:

(1) Several usefulness criteria.
(2) The specificity of the concepts being considered.
(3) In general, the cultural distance between the culture of the originating theoretical ideas and the culture to which they are being transferred.

This chapter is seeking to view that aspect of contextualization that is involved in the transfer of theories or theoretical ideas from one culture to another. It is concerned with the appropriateness of ideas as they move from without a culture to within that culture.

J. ROBERT CLINTON, B.E.E., M.E.E., M.A.B.E., D.Miss., Ph.D., associate professor of leadership at Fuller Theological Seminary, was associated with Worldteam for eleven years. As a missionary to Jamaica he was principal of the Jamaica Bible College and later, the director of the Learning Resource Center. He is author of *Spiritual Gifts* and *The Making of a Leader*.

A CONTEXTUALIZATION PROBLEM

Historically, missiological schools have taught their students various core missiological subjects.[1] These students, whether Western or non-Western, have returned to crosscultural ministries and have sought to apply these ideas to their local cultural settings. Most of these core missiological courses involve theories that are Western in their analytical frameworks and underlying assumptions. Does that mean that they are not useful in other cultures? No, obviously these ideas have been transferred by missionaries and nationals who have studied at Western missiological schools and who minister in many countries around the world. But problems have arisen from the attempt to use theories in one culture which have originated in another culture.

Practitioners have been forced to grapple with the appropriateness of given theories to specific cultures. The fact that some theories are useful, or fit a given culture, or must be adapted to it, or do not fit and have to be discarded, does point out a basic problem of contextualization. Theories or disciplines (or subdisciplines) originate in a culture; we will call it the "base culture." People study them and seek to transfer ideas from them to another culture, "the application culture." The process of adapting the ideas to fit the application culture reflects an important methodology of contextualization. Figure 18 relates the three elements involved in the problem: the base culture, the process of transfer of ideas, and the application culture.

The base culture could be Western or non-Western, as could be the application culture. Transfer of theoretical notions—whether anthropological, folk religion, theological, historical, church growth,

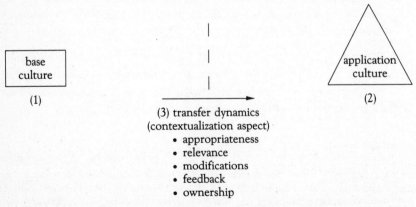

Figure 18   Three Elements in the Contextualization/Transfer Problem

leadership—must deal with the dynamics of transfer. That is, is the theory appropriate for the application culture? Is it relevant? Does it meet a need? What modifications are needed to make it appropriate and relevant? Can the theory be modified so as to focus on issues not touched on by the theory, but needed by the application culture? That is, how do ideas existing in the culture affect or feedback into the transferring theory? Will the theory be accepted by the application culture? What must be done to it in order to make it genuinely acceptable to the application culture as a theory that belongs in the culture?

Thus, one basic issue of contextualization is the possible transfer[2] and necessary modification of theoretical ideas from the base culture to the application culture.

Historically, the problem has involved the transfer of Western theories into non-Western situations. However, the transfer problem exists whether going from Western to non-Western or non-Western to Western or non-Western to another non-Western culture and, to a lesser degree, in going Western to Western. The rapid rise of Third World missions has pointed out the problem that contextualization is not just a Western missionary problem.[3]

Problematic questions concerning the basic issue and elements of contextualization come to mind.

To what extent can theories originating in a base culture be transferred in whole or part to an application culture? Or more specifically, to what extent can theories originating in Western cultures be contextualized in whole or part to non-Western cultures?

Can theories originating in non-Western cultures be contextualized in whole or part to Western cultures? Can theories be contextualized from one Western culture to another distinctly different Western culture? Can theories be contextualized from one non-Western culture to another distinctly different non-Western culture? What are some useful guidelines in approaching the contextualization of theoretical ideas from one culture to another? What has been the approach at the School of World Mission concerning contextualization of leadership theories or ideas?

Guideline 1

The dominant guideline that has been used historically by graduates with missiological training as they have gone around the world and applied church-growth theory, anthropological theory, folk-religion theory, historical theory, ideas from mission theology, or leadership theory has been a pragmatic one. I call it the *usability criterion.* That is, a theory and/or theoretical ideas are useful across cultures if the theory and/or ideas gives relevant answers to the following usability criteria questions:

1. Does it give categories and typologies that help one analyze the situation?
2. Does it help one predict tendencies or trends or recognize next stages in a situation?
3. Does it help explain past events so that causes can be inferred or patterns seen that may prove useful in the present or as one looks toward the future?
4. Does it give perspectives or insights for exercising better control over situations?

In other words, do the theoretical ideas operate like theories are supposed to operate by providing useful information as to categories, explanation, prediction, and control? In transferring notions learned at the School of World Mission, practitioners have been forced by differences between base and application cultures to modify theoretical notions in terms of the usability criteria.

Guideline 2

Apart from pragmatic concerns are there guidelines that can help one approach a theory prior to pragmatically using it? I can suggest two which, though inadequate at present, are starting points for further research. The two are interrelated.

The first is the *specificity guideline.* The higher the level of theory (that is, couched in abstract and less culturally specific terms) along a specific to generic continuum the more likely the theory will apply across cultures. The lower the level of theory (that is, couched in culturally specific terms) the less likely it will transfer to another culture (unless the application culture shares much in common with the base culture).

Two other implications follow from the specificity guideline. The more specific the level of theory along the specific-generic continuum, the easier it is to see applications and adapt it (provided it can be transferred). The more generic the level of theory, the more work that must be done to see its applicability.

Practitioners usually do not relate well to high-level abstract theories that speak in broad generalities. So then, counter forces are in opposition between the levels of specificity and generality. The more specific is a given theory the easier it is to see it in terms of application, but the more likely it is that the theory will not transfer across cultures. The more general is a theory the more likely it will apply across cultures, but the more difficult it is to apply it practically. More will be said of this when we consider the leadership framework used in the School of World Mission.

Guideline 3

Another guideline closely related to the specificity guideline is the *cultural-distance guideline*. The more closely related are two cultures in terms of Hofstede's four major cultural-distance factors[4] the more likely it is that theories emanating in one will apply in the other. And conversely, the more two cultures differ in terms of the four major factors the less likely will a theory be transferred; or, to state it another way, theories transferred (if they can be transferred) will undergo much modification.

Hofstede's four factors include the power-distance dimension, the uncertainty-avoidance dimension, the individualism-collectivism dimension, and the task-relationship behavior orientation.[5]

The power-distance dimension[6] refers to the extent to which leaders and followers accept hierarchical differences between leaders and followers. That is, power distance indicates the extent to which a society is willing to accept the fact that power in institutions and organizations is not distributed equally. This value is reflected by both leaders and followers. Power distance between a leader and a follower in a hierarchy is the difference between the extent to which the leader can determine the behavior of the follower and the extent to which the follower can determine the behavior of the leader.

Cultures with a high power-distance factor have leaders and followers who accept the appropriateness of hierarchical distinctions between leaders and followers. Figure 19 indicates relative power distance between six countries which are involved in mission activity today—some both as sending and receiving countries.

Power distance definitely affects the transfer of numerous leadership theories. For example, leadership-style theories that have originated in the U.S., such as Fiedler's contingency model[7] or Hersey and Blanchard's situational leadership,[8] contain assumptions that reflect democratic values associated with low power distance. To transfer these theories to high power-distance cultures will require serious

Austria		Australia	U.S.A.		Korea	Venezuela	Philippines
⊢—x——————————————x—x——————————————x———x————x—⊣							
Low Power Distance						High Power Distance	

Figure 19   Example of Power Distance Factor—Six Countries

modifications that take into account high power distance. The reverse would be true. To transfer theories originating in Korea to the U.S., one must consider whether the Korean theory carries underlying high power-distance assumptions. On the other hand, theories transferred between the U.S. and Australia that carry power-distance assumptions most likely can be adapted readily. U.S. church-growth theoretical ideas which depend upon "strong leadership" will face obstacles in moving toward countries with a small power-distance value like Austria.[9] Yet they will be readily acceptable in countries valuing high power distance, such as Venezuela and the Philippines.

The uncertainty-avoidance dimension[10] indicates the dynamics involved in a society's approach to uncertain and ambiguous situations. Societies that are threatened by uncertain and ambiguous situations try to avoid these situations by providing greater stability and by establishing more formal rules, not tolerating deviant ideas and behaviors, and believing in absolute truths. Societies with high uncertainty-avoidance will try to provide greater career stability. They will reflect higher levels of anxiety and aggressiveness that frequently works out in a strong inner urge to work hard. Figure 20 indicates relative distance for four countries for this factor.

Change-dynamics theories and leadership-training theories will be affected by this cultural factor. Countries with strong uncertainty-avoidance will most likely require careful change strategies and favor formal training models—or at least, only culturally accepted models. I have yet to ascertain fully the implications of this cultural factor. Partly this is due to the central location on the continuum of the United States with regards to this factor. The factor is not dominant one way or another among U.S. leadership practitioners.

The individualism-collectivism dimension[11] describes the relationship between the individual and the collectivity that prevails in a given society.

Individualism implies a loosely knit social framework in which people are supposed to take care of themselves and of their immediate families only. Collectivism is characterized by a tight social framework in which people distinguish between "in" groups and "out" groups; they expect their in-group (relatives, clan, organizations) to look after them, and in exchange for that they feel they owe absolute loyalty to it.

Denmark	Hong Kong		U.S.A.		Japan	Greece
├──────x──────x────────────────x────────────────x────────x──┤						

Weak Uncertainty-Avoidance   Strong Uncertainty-Avoidance

Figure 20   Example of Uncertainty-Avoidance Factor—Four Countries

Figure 21   Example of Individualism-Collectivism Factor

The individualism-collectivism cultural factor affects theories that are rooted in individualistic societal values (see Figure 21). For example, Maslow's motivational theory has heavy individualistic presuppositions. Cultures with high collectivism may not value the higher levels of his hierarchy. Collective societies may well place collective values in the culture—such as harmony—much higher than self-actualization.[12]

The task-related behavior versus relationship behavior describes a continuum along which a leader's bent toward a leadership style is dominated by task behaviors or relationship behaviors (see Figure 22). Values of task-related behavior include assertiveness, success orientation in material things, need for power and domination, high ambition, and performance. Values of relationship behavior include interdependence, empathy for people, need for nurturing roles, and service for others.[13]

For each of the four dimensions, plots can be made along a continuum for a given base culture and a given application culture. The closer the distance along the continuum between the two plots the closer in cultural distance are the two cultures for that cultural dimension.

In addition, two-dimensional plots can be made for various combinations of the cultural factors. For example, the power dimension could be plotted on a horizontal axis and the individualism dimension on the vertical axis as shown in Figure 23.[14]

In Figure 23, Australia and the United States are close in culture distance in terms of these two factors. Leadership theories based on values reflecting these cultural factors can most likely be transferred with minimum adaptation. Colombia and Venezuela are close in cultural distance; hence, leadership theories originating in one or the other will most likely transfer with a minimum of transfer dynamics. But leadership theories originating in the United States or Australia which depend heavily on democratic values (such as participation in

Figure 22   Example of Task- or Relational-Behavior Factor

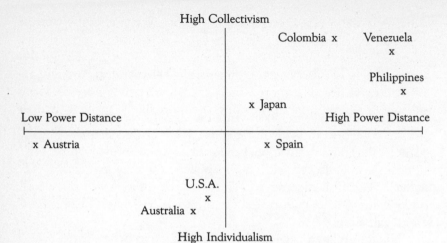

Figure 23   Example of Power versus Individualism Factors

decision making, etc.)[15] will most likely not transfer readily to countries like Colombia and Venezuela. In general, theories originating in a culture distant from another culture and which have underlying assumptions based on these factors will be difficult to transfer and be appropriately contextualized in the new culture.

Hofstede has done plots for about 67 countries.[16] Comparisons of the various combinations for base cultures and application cultures indicate cultural distances and the relative ease or difficulty of transferring ideas or theories between the two. Usually the underpinnings of a theory are rooted in cultural factors that relate to one or several of the cultural dimensions. A missiological student interested in transferring theoretical ideas must indeed know a theory well in terms of its underlying cultural factors. Though much more study needs to be done to assess Hofstede's notions on cultural distance,[17] it appears promising as an early indicator of the ease or difficulty of transferring culturally rooted theories from base cultures to application cultures.

Taken together, Guideline 2, dealing with specificity and generality, and Guideline 3, dealing with cultural distance, imply that a specific theory will most likely transfer between a base culture and application culture if the two are closely related in terms of Hofstede's four major factors (close in cultural distance) and will not transfer readily between cultures which differ greatly in the factors (far in cultural distance).

In summary then, Guideline 3 suggests the possibility of predictability concerning the contextualization of a given leadership idea or theory. We must assess the idea or theory in terms of the cultural dimensions from the base culture that are associated with the theory. Using Hofstede's or other plots, we then determine the cultural distances of the relevant cultural dimensions between the base and application cultures. The more closely related are two cultures in terms of the relevant cultural dimensions, the more likely it is that theories originating in one will apply in the other. Dissonance in cultural distance factors between two cultures will signal areas most likely high in terms of resistance to the theory. Dissonance will also suggest where modifications of the theory must be made if it is to be accepted—i.e., become contextualized to fit and be useful in the application culture.

In actual practice, theories or ideas are often transferred from a base culture to an application culture without regard to dissonance in cultural distance factors. This can occur very easily when base-culture proponents are insensitive to cultural-distance factors and have power—such as status, prestige, or economic control—in the application culture. The theories can be applied without needed adjustments (even though dissonance does exist). This abuse or lack of contextualization is much less when those in the application culture have equal power or prestige with the base-culture proponents of the theories. In such situations, cultural sensitivity and the need for "fit" or "relevance" become the motivation for contextualization.

In order to apply Guidelines 2 and 3, two things are helpful. Practitioners need to be thoroughly familiar with a theory so as to understand its implications for cultural-distance factors. That has been the import of Guideline 3 and the last several paragraphs on cultural distance. And they need to understand and use the general notion of "levels" of a theory. That is the import of Guideline 2, with its transfer implications. The notion of levels of a theory is perhaps best illustrated by using two examples.

In the leadership concentration at the School of World Mission, the following theories are prominent and have one or more courses which expound them: a General Leadership Framework, Leadership Development, Leadership Training, Organizational Theories, and Change Dynamics. Figure 24 lists these theories, indicates levels of complexity from generic to specific, and suggests a narrative description of the highest level (generic, most abstract) of the theory.

These theories are still evolving, so it is difficult to precisely identify levels from generic concepts to specific concepts.

In general, these theories all have originated from Western frameworks though ideas from other cultures have influenced their development. I will illustrate the notion of levels of generality using

Theory	Levels	Thrust of Highest Level
1. General Leadership Framework	Four	The understanding and evaluation of leadership at a given point in the history of a given leader is contingent upon complex factors including the basal elements of leadership (leader, follower, situation), the influence means (individual and/or corporate), and the values motivating the leadership.
2. Leadership Development Theory	Four	The evaluation of development of a given individual leader can be explained to a large degree by the use of and relationship among three sets of variables: processing, time, response.
3. Leadership Training Theory	Four	Leadership training necessitates a philosophy based on development, takes place over a lifetime, can be analyzed and evaluated by generic evaluation models, and always involves a mix of specific models categorized under three training modes: formal, nonformal, and informal.
4. Organizational Theory	Four	Christian organizations by and large resemble secular organizations in that they can be described by five organizational components that form the base from which organizational configurations can be derived for use in understanding and evaluating specific manifestations of Christian organizations.
5. Change Dynamics Theory	Three	Planned change can be implemented in Christian organizations with the least personal and organizational trauma by the use of bridging strategies.

Figure 24   Leadership Theories in the School of World Mission and Levels

the first two theories—the General Leadership Framework and Leadership Development. Both of these theories have emerged due to research in the School of World Mission.

The General Leadership Framework[18] provides a basis for analyzing leadership issues. It is a theory in process. The lower levels of the theory are continuing to evolve as more research is being focused on the specific lower-level elements. Its components are given in descending order, from most general to most specific in the Tree Diagram of Figure 25. The highest level of generality includes the basic components of leadership that must be assessed. Three are given: the basal components, the influence means, and the underlying values behind leadership. The three highest-level theoretical assertions include the following:

1. Contingency Assertion—leadership at a given point in the history of a given leader is contingent on a number of complex factors.
2. Complexity Assertion—The explanation, evaluation, and prediction of leadership of a given leader must take into account the diverse factors and interrelationships between them.

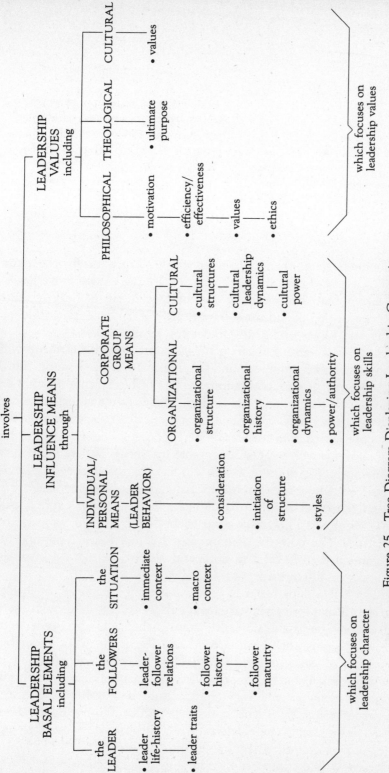

Figure 25 Tree Diagram Displaying Leadership Categories

3. Balanced Focus—Christian leadership involves leadership character, skills, and values interacting together in a dynamic process
which is rooted in the culture of the leaders and followers.

Four levels are identified with this general leadership framework:
Level 1—the three essentials: basal, influence means, value bases
Level 2—(1) the basal elements of leader, follower, and situation;
(2) the individual and corporate means of influence; (3) the
kinds of value bases
Level 3—the individual elements under the Level 2 headings,
such as leader life-history, leader traits, etc.
Level 4—the specific cultural manifestations of level three
elements.

Guideline 2 states that the higher the level, generically, the more
likely it is that the notions will transfer. In case of the above levels,
this means that the notion of the three essentials of Level 1 most
likely occur in all cultures. There are basal elements, influence
means, and values underlying leadership in all cultures.

Level 2, which is still very general, asserts that basal elements will
involve the leader, followers, and the dynamics of the situation. This,
too, is broadly true of most cultures. The notable exception would be
cultures with pure plurality of leaders. There are individual-influence
means in all cultures. Corporate means will differ depending on the
extent of modernity in cultures. Where modernity has impact, organizational means will dominate corporate influence. Where modernity
has less impact, corporate means will manifest itself in cultural networks. All cultures have motivational values underlying leadership
though the exact nature of *philosophy* versus *religious* versus *cultural* "oughts" will vary again depending on the impact of
modernity. The point being emphasized is that Level 2 notions are
less general than Level 1 notions and will be widespread but may
not apply in all cultures.

Level 3 notions begin to move to specific categories. Such elements as leader traits will vary from culture to culture though there
will usually be some similarity among them. Under leadership-
influence means, such Level 3 items as *styles*, or the major leadership
groupings of *consideration* (relationship behavior) or *initiation of
structure* (task behavior), or the various organizational or cultural-
dynamics elements will vary from culture to culture. And under
leadership value bases, the notions of ethics, motivational values,
efficiency or effectiveness, and ultimate purpose will most likely occur; but they will differ from culture to culture.

Level 4 refers to specific cultural manifestations.

For example, Fiedler's contingency theory is an approach to leadership style that has relevance in the U.S. But it may or may not have validity in a non-Western culture. The guideline asserts that at the higher generality, concepts are more likely to transfer across cultures; but their umbrella-like nature make them more difficult to understand in terms of application. At the lower levels, such as Fiedler's style theory, the application of the theory can be understood more readily, but it is less likely to apply to other cultures.

A second theory illustrates the notion of levels. Leadership Development Theory[19] asserts at the highest generic level that, symbolically:

$$L = f (P, T, R),$$

In narrative, the development of a given leader can be described by noting the effects of three variables: processing, time, and response. *Processing* describes those critical incidents in a Christian leader's life in which God shapes the leader. *Time* refers to the analysis of the processing in terms of development phases. *Response* refers to patterns that describe the leader's response to the processing as viewed over time. This theory has a high individualistic focus and assumes that God works (even in high-collectivism cultures to develop leaders specifically and individually). This highest level of the theory generally applies crossculturally.

The second level of this theory asserts that processing viewed over time in terms of its cumulative effect on a leader accomplishes three major goals. One goal of *processing*, viewed cumulatively, involves spiritual formation resulting ultimately in the goal of leadership character. A second goal of *overall processing* involves ministerial formation, resulting in leadership skills. The third goal of *cumulative processing* involves strategic formation resulting in leadership values and, finally, in a ministry philosophy. These three goals appear to fit the many cultures that have been represented at the School of World Mission.

The third level describes *processing definitions, time patterns,* and *response patterns*. These definitions are relatively more numerous and more specific in terms of language than are the Level 1 and Level 2 concepts just described.

The final level of this theory describes specific cultural incidents of the processing and patterns.

As the levels descend, the theoretical statements proliferate and become more culture-specific and easier to understand in terms of application; but they become less likely to transfer directly into other cultures.

To apply Guideline 2, a practitioner must be able to assess theories in terms of levels of generality. Most theories advocated in missiological schools are neither complete nor organized in terms of levels. This means that missiological students must be aware of this and do their own organizing of theoretical ideas into levels of generality.

Some Closing Suggestions

Leadership theories originating in one base culture cannot automatically be contextualized to any given application culture. They must be evaluated in terms of pragmatic concerns. Do they do what a theory is supposed to do in the application culture? They must be evaluated in terms of cultural-distance factors and modified accordingly.

Some final suggestions are given to guide the person who is seeking to introduce leadership ideas into another culture. These suggestions assume the background that I have been previously describing in this chapter. They provide an outline for the training of missiologists concerning theory construction within cultures and transfer across cultures.

1. Begin where you are. Use what resources and background you have as you develop your leadership theories or philosophy of ministry. Your theories and philosophy will most likely be filled with underlying cultural values and themes specific to the base culture.

2. Identify specific ideas or theoretical notions inherent in your leadership theories or philosophy. Recognize in these ideas the differing levels of specificity—within the base culture.

3. Raise the level of generality of the ideas in the base culture to increase the possible broader usage across cultures.

4. Analyze cultural-distance factors involved in the specific and general ideas of steps 2 and 3.

5. Compare cultural-distance factors in base and application cultures for possible harmonious transfer or dissonance problems.

6. Suggest the use of general theory in other application cultures. Illustrate its relevance in specific terms in the given culture in which it originated, that is, the base culture. Advise on potential problems arising from cultural-distance factors.

7. Leave the application of general theory in specific terms appropriate to the application culture to those who are aware of the application culture and the need for contextualization.

8. Recognize the underlying base-cultural factors influencing the general theory or specific theory so as to suggest contextualization issues.

9. Suggest research in individual application cultures to originate specific theories that are already contextualized to the culture.

NOTES

[1] At the School of World Mission, the subjects anthropology, folk religion, theology of mission, history of mission, church growth, and leadership are known as core courses and are required of every person majoring in a missiology program.

[2] When I use the word *transfer*, I am implying that the practitioner will use the theoretical framework as a perspective for viewing and interpreting reality in the application culture as well as propagate its ideas to others in that culture. Eventually then the perceptions thus influenced by the theoretical framework will have effect in decision making, a prime function of leadership.

[3] With the rapid rise of Third World missionaries we have seen a related increase of those missionaries after one or two terms who are coming to the School of World Mission recognizing that they, too, are repeating some of the earlier mistakes of Western missionaries as they propagate the gospel in crosscultural situations. They are imposing on others views originating in their base culture which do not fit the application culture. Several recent Ph.D. research projects are underway which are studying the transfer problem of non-Western to non-Western cultures.

[4] See Geert Hofstede, "Motivation, Leadership, and Organization: Do American Theories Apply Abroad?" in *Organizational Dynamics* (Summer 1980) and *Culture's Consequences—International Differences in Work Related Values*, abridged edition (Beverly Hills: Sage Publications, 1984), for a full explanation.

His crosscultural study involved managerial values. He is saying that international differences in work-related values of managers can be measured in terms of the four major cultural dimensions. I am suggesting that his four cultural dimensions in fact measure or at least are a start toward a measure of cultural distance which applies broadly to understanding contextualization of leadership ideas and theories from any base culture to any application culture. The notion of cultural distance affecting contextualization of theories most likely applies to theories other than just leadership theories. The four cultural dimensions may need other functional equivalents depending on the nature of the theories involved. I recognize that managers and leaders are not identical. Leadership goes beyond the art/science of management. Yet, I still see the relevance of his four cultural dimensions in determining contextualization issues for leadership theories.

[5] Hofstede actually uses the terminology masculine-femininity for his fourth factor. I have changed the name to one which, in my opinion, is functionally equivalent in terms of what is being measured. It is also more familiar to leadership-theory students and has no pejorative connotation to women students of leadership theory. My assessment of this functional equivalence has yet to be proven. At least at first glance many of the masculine attitudes or values seem to be task-behavior motivations, and many of the feminine values seem to be underlying factors in relationship behavior.

[6] Hofstede, *Culture's Consequences*, 45.

[7] See F. E. Fiedler, *A Theory of Leadership Effectiveness* (New York: McGraw-Hill, 1967).

[8] See P. Hersey and K. H. Blanchard, *Management of Organizational Behavior* (Englewood Cliffs, N.J.: Prentice-Hall, 1977).

[9] See C. Peter Wagner's *Leading Your Church to Growth* (Ventura, Calif.: Regal, 1984). Wagner advocates strong leadership values for effective church growth. See also Erich W. Baumgartner's doctoral tutorial, "Leadership Theory and Its Potential Contribution to the Understanding of Leadership for Church Growth," an unpublished paper in the School of World Mission of Fuller Theological Seminary, October 1988. Baumgartner is an Austrian pastor who recognizes the low power-distance value in Austrian culture and its impact on church-growth theory.

[10] Hofstede, *Organizational Dynamics*, 45.

[11] Ibid., 45–46.

[12] See M. Maccoby, *The Gamesman* (New York: Bantam Books, 1978). Maccoby (who is crosscultural in orientation) views McGregor and Maslow's motivational theories as suspect and highly culture-specific in terms of individualistic values. See also Douglas McGregor, *The Human Side of Enterprise* (New York: McGraw-Hill, 1960) and Abraham Maslow, *Motivation and Personality*, second edition (New York: Harper and Row, 1970).

[13] Hofstede, 1980, 46.

[14] Ibid., 52.

[15] Theories such as that of McGregor, *The Human Side*, or R. R. Blake and J. S. Mouton, *The Managerial Grid* (Houston: Gulf, 1964).

[16] Hofstede, *Culture's Consequences*, 15.

[17] Even if the four specific cultural factors that Hofstede has identified do not fit as universally as his research initially indicates, the notion of "cultural distance" as indicated by orientation of certain cultural factors is valid, and searches can be made for functional equivalents of Hofstede's cultural factors. The church-growth concepts of E1, E2, and E3 are less sophisticated concepts dealing with this same cultural distance notion.

[18] The Leadership Framework as a theoretical perspective for viewing leadership emerged out of a historical study of the development of leadership theory which identified five paradigmatic eras (major theoretical research traditions for viewing leadership): Great Man Era, Trait Era, Ohio State Behavioral Era, Contingency Era, and Complexity Era. See J. Robert Clinton, *A Short History of Leadership Theory—A Paradigmatic Overview of the Leadership Field From 1841–1986* (Altadena, Calif.: Barnabas Resources, 1985).

[19] See J. Robert Clinton, *Leadership Development Theory—Comparative Studies Among High Level Christian Leaders* (Ph.D. dissertation, Fuller Theological Seminary, School of World Mission, 1988).

10

Contextualized Christian Social Transformation

Edgar J. Elliston

DEVELOPING CONTEXTUALLY APPROPRIATE SOCIAL TRANSFORMA-
TION MINISTRIES is important for three key reasons. (1) To evangelize
with no intentional concern for the social or physical situation will
result in a truncated evangelism and disobedience to the command of
the Lord to love our neighbors. (2) To do development without an
intentional concern for discipling the nations will likely lead to a disobedience to the Lord's command in the Great Commission.
(3) And to disregard the context—social, physical, and spiritual—will
lead to dysfunctions with both the evangelistic and cultural mandates.

The context does not set the eternal priorities between evangelism and social ministries, but it does affect the present strategic balance. Context serves to condition what can and should be done in the
light of the clear commands of the Lord. Rural contexts in Kansas or
Kenya, or urban slums in São Paulo or Jakarta will each require a
different balance if we are to be obedient.

EDGAR J. ELLISTON, M.A., Ph.D., associate professor of leadership selection and
training at Fuller Theological Seminary, served in Ethiopia and Kenya for eighteen
years. Working with the Christian Missionary Fellowship, his ministries were in evangelism, leadership training, and relief and development. His most recent book is *Christian Relief and Development: Developing Workers for Effective Ministry*.

This chapter does not address the old debate of evangelism vs. social ministries. Rather, I assume God has mandated both with a view of bringing every person and people under the lordship of Christ and then working with them so they will be equipped and free to become fully Christlike in all he created them to be. Evangelism and social ministries are viewed as conceptually distinct, but symbiotically related in practice. In fact, some activities serve both. Each contributes to the motivation, processes, and goals of the other. Evangelism requires a theologically and logically based priority, but often the actual ministry requires actions of mercy and justice.[1] Compassionate ministries emerge from the people of God and may serve to draw other people to know and serve him. Both are expected in the kingdom. The dichotomies of the past are giving way to a recognition of a more wholistic approach now as we face the twenty-first century.

The following definitions aim to clarify the perspective of this chapter:

- *Social transformation* refers to what is popularly called "development" or "Christian wholistic development."
- *Christian social transformation* is the freeing of people from constraints to become all that God intends for them in their relations with him, with other people, and with their environment. Social transformation or social ministries are expected to be wholistic. This term, *wholistic*, serves to emphasize the integral relationships among the physical, social, spiritual, and environmental components of life for a person, a family, or a whole community. Dyrness places development squarely in the theological arena when he writes:

Development is really an extension of the rule of God in the affairs of men. It is essentially related to the kingdom Christ came to announce. Therefore, wherever genuine human devlopment is taking place it reflects God's own creative and recreative role in history.[2]

CHRISTIAN DISTINCTIVES

Christians have long served in many forms of social ministries which combine to serve the spiritual, social, and physical needs of people. These ministries have variously been called "development," "social ministries," "social transformation," "wholistic development," "community development," "rural development," "relief," or "compassionate ministries." However, the Peace Corps, World Bank, Canadian International Development Agency, and scores of both private and governmental agencies also claim to be doing the same things. Does a Christian approach differ from secular approaches?

Because many Christians are involved with secular development agencies and many Christian agencies are led by people whose training and experience come from the secular institutions, the lines of distinction are often blurred. While the vocabulary may often be similar and some of the initial issues addressed may be the same, Christian social transformation differs significantly from both traditional colonial and contemporary secular models in *motive*, *methods* and *goals*.

Motive

Government officials often promote development with a great deal of rhetoric, announcing its altruistic goals to help the "poor" and "underdeveloped" nations. However, at the governmental level development generally serves either to provide raw materials or to open new markets for the providing government. Often, it serves both objectives as well as providing a means to propagate the donor's ideology. In any case, the primary benefit is for the donor. President Richard Nixon made the purpose all too clear when he said, "Let us remember that the main purpose of American aid is not to help other nations, but to help ourselves."[3] In addition to the economic benefit, a potential military strategic advantage often is in view as well. The ethnocentric assumption that the donor's way is best— especially for the donor—appears clearly in the policies and practices of governmental agencies.

Christians working in compassionate ministries, however, differ from this approach in their driving motivation. Their motivation comes from significant differences in terms of *whose* they are, *who* they are, and their *view of the future*. Each of these distinctives serves to motivate Christians both to work toward a clear goal and to work with the people where they are.

Whose Disciples Are They?

Jesus said, "Anyone who gives a cup of water in my name because you belong to Christ will certainly not lose his reward" (Mk. 9:41; cf. Mt. 10:40-42). Jesus' focus is on the primary controlling allegiance of the person and how that allegiance motivates the person. The focus is not on the authority of Jesus, but the allegiance and motivation of the disciple.

Whose follower is the Christian? Under whose discipline is the Christian? The question of lordship arises in this context. Who is one's master—Jesus Christ or the state? The question of lordship determines the ultimate allegiance of the disciples and the direction they will go. Allegiance profoundly influences one's motivation.

Who Are They?

The Christian is a different person because of what Jesus Christ has done. The apostle Paul wrote that the believer is a "new creation." Jesus described the change in terms of a "new birth." A Christian is different from within and so has a different set of motives driving toward ministry.

Christians have experienced and continue to experience several developmental initiatives of the Holy Spirit which not only change them, but which drive them to ministry with others. Some of these are forgiveness of sin, reconciliation with God, adoption as heirs of God, being "called," receiving "spiritual gifts" for ministry with others, and the bearing of "spiritual fruit" which deeply affect relationships with other people.

View of the Future

Since the Christian's view of the future differs from the secular community's view, the motivation for working for the future differs. Both the capitalist and the Marxist see the future in material, technological, and economic terms. Government-based development can be counted on to focus on technological or economic issues. The bright future is defined in terms of a successful technological transfer, an improved GNP, high-level employment, the absence of debt, and a surplus in the budget.

While an active participant in the economic structures, the Christian sees both the immediate future and an eternity in terms of the kingdom of God. With a different view of the future, the present motives for both personal growth and working with others take on a very different character. With a different view of the future, the important issues of economics take a different priority. What is of eternal significance also comes into focus.

The motive for Christians, then, reflects who they are in their context as they have been changed by the Lord, called by him, and as they serve as his disciples. As believers experience conversion, every dimension of life is changed, giving them freedom to become all that God intended. The excitement of the good news of this conversion provides the motivation for incarnational witness wherever they are. A characteristic of their incarnational witness and ministry is that it is always focused on the benefit of the other.

The personal transformation through the renewing work of the Holy Spirit motivates a person to look outward and to participate in the converting, redeeming, reconciling transformation of what surrounds him or her. This motivation in a social ministry appears in interpersonal relationships before it surfaces in institutionalized forms. The motive comes from the good news of a changed life which now has hope and peace—a life which has experienced an undeserved justice and the lifting of oppression. The motive again is kingdom-based and focused on others for their good.

Methods

While many "surface level" methods parallel secular development, other "deeper level" process issues differ. Facing both the person in a purely secular setting as well as the Christian are many of these: needs assessment, planning, funding, staffing, training, managing, evaluating, making reports, relating to other agencies, and coping with cultural and communicational differences. However, in the midst of these issues comes a set of distinctive Christian processes.

The key concept which describes the Christian distinctive is *incarnation*. The Christian lives *among* the people, *within* the community *sharing* and *receiving* from the people being served. The incarnation of God's message requires two important attitudes which again often set the Christian apart from the secular development worker: respect and meekness.

Respect for the other person and the other person's culture characterizes the Christian's approach. Respect for the other person facilitates both learning from that person and the building of a relationship of trust. Trust, in turn, facilitates communication and change. The behaviors characterizing this respect include patience, kindness, gentleness, and goodness.

On the other hand, meekness is that restrained self-control that enables one to control one's pride and potential misuse of power. Paul said Jesus did not "grasp"; rather, he humbled himself (Phil. 2:5). Meekness is not the weak groveling of a slave, but voluntary, disciplined submission under the lordship of Christ to serve others.

The incarnational approach demonstrates the essence of a contextualized Christian approach in social ministries: (1) One lives *with* the people. (2) The focus is always on the people with whom one is working and their benefit, not one's own. (3) One addresses the people in their frame of reference. (4) The message is delivered prophetically. God's will is faithfully interpreted for that time and place, with redemptive implications for all of one's key relationships. (5) The messenger is one with the people and so learns and participates with them in their life processes. (6) Common "development issues," such as "needs," are experienced from "inside" and so are not insensitively projected.

An incarnational approach causes the server to avoid both an egocentric and an ethnocentric approach, to adopt a receptor-centered reciprocal approach. The level and quality of participation can be expected to improve as one moves in an incarnational mode. Both motive and process then change for the Christian.

Ward suggests five successive levels of participation: giving, helping, teaching, leading, and sharing.[4] The motive for each is honorable, but only a reciprocal sharing engages both parties in a nondominating, truly enduring developmental relationship. Each of the other levels results in some kind of inequality and risks oppressive behavior.

Christians take the context seriously in the process of development. By approaching the context incarnationally they affect both the issues to be addressed and the ways the issues are addressed.

Goals

The goal for Christian social transformation differs sharply from any secular goal. While Christians will see intermediate goals, such as improved economics, roads, water systems, social structures, and justice as deserving of their best efforts and support, they will also see the issue of reconciliation with God as having eternal significance. Three kinds of relational goals distinguish a Christian's perspective: relations with God, relations with others, and relations with the environment.

Christians seek to be "right" in each of these sets of relationships, recognizing that a failure in one affects the other two. A right relation with God begins from where the people are in terms of their faith commitment. Right relations with other people require attention to where people are culturally, socially, economically, politically, and spiritually. Right relations with the environment require attention to the broad ecological situation.

In every case the goals can only be achieved through a "contextualizing" process that begins with the context and moves toward the "ideal" as authoritatively revealed by God and interpreted in that context. A developmental goal for Christians, which relates both to the individual and to the community, is the establishment, reestablishment, and maintenance of right relations with others. Right relations with others facilitates not only one's own growth but the development of others as well. Much attention is given in the Scriptures to the matter of relations with others. Good relationships are not to be maintained at any cost, that is, at the cost of integrity or one's faith; but just, merciful, peaceful, and loving relationships are a key element in our own and others' development.

Whatever one's ministry or vocation, as a Christian the goal ought to be focused on the reconciliation of others with God (2 Cor. 5:18; Mt. 28:10–20). This goal includes right relations with others. Part of maintaining one's own right relationship with the Lord is obediently pursuing this goal with others. The interactive nature of these relationships further clarifies the goal of Christian wholistic development.

CONTEXTUALIZING CONSTRAINTS

Growth—whether biological, sociological, or spiritual—always results from internal changes. Growth always occurs in the context of a person's or community's environment. Development can never be fully understood without considering the relationships within the context. Whenever one intervenes in a situation to participate in the development of the people, these contextual relationships arise.

Development or growth does not occur unchecked or unconstrained. When Christians initiate intervening developmental activities, these developmental constraints should then be considered: relations with other people, relations with the environment, and relations with God.

Relations with Other People

Relationships with other people provide a primary set of constraints for development. To the degree that the interpersonal relations reflect trust, hope, and a commitment to the mutual good, they can be said to be developmental. However, when trust erodes, when hope fades, or when one's primary commitment is self-centered, the resulting relations soon deteriorate and the processes of "underdevelopment" begin.

Relations with the Environment

The shared/learned behavior of people, which is passed from one generation to another, happens in the context of the physical environment. The Turkana live in a desert west of Lake Turkana in northwest Kenya. With less than ten inches of rain per year, very poor soil, and daily temperatures that average one hundred degrees, development options are limited. The environment provides little support for permanent settlements. Within this "risky" situation the people have developed a way to distribute wealth without costly government overhead or delay. It functions simply as a begging system.

However, in western Kansas where I grew up, it was possible to raise a variety of crops or to successfully engage in a variety of businesses. A people's relationship to the physical environment conditions the development of complexity and specialization.

Relations with God

One's relations with God carry powerful influences either for the good or ill of the individual or community. When the relationship with God reflects separation, several constraining characteristics emerge. All of these constraints are linked to a Christian view of sin.

For example, covetousness results in greed on a personal level and unjust economic and political structures on community and societal levels. Covetousness has deeply affected Western societies, leading to enormous debt as well as to the forming of structures that are to the great disadvantage of the poor. This covetousness provides powerful bases for oppression and a distribution of resources that increasingly favors the wealthy. It also constrains wholistic contextually appropriate development.

From a Christian perspective, these three key relationships undergird and interact to serve successful development endeavors. Likewise, these same three sets of relationships may serve as the primary barriers or constraints to effective development. The nature of each and their mutual influence determines the effectiveness of intervening developmental efforts. These sets of relationships are complexly interrelated.

THEOLOGICAL BASES FOR CONTEXTUALIZED TRANSFORMATION

As with the other issues of evangelical contextualization, whether they relate to theology, leadership, or church growth, a consistent reliance on the authority of what God has revealed in his Word remains essential. The biblical text provides useful perspectives on both the causes of "underdevelopment," the motivation for addressing developmental concerns, and the broad outlines of the processes and goals for Christian social ministries.

This section will only briefly mention some biblical concepts that provide the revelational base on which Christian social ministries are to be designed so as to fit in the context. These basic biblical concepts include: the kingdom of God, sin, redemption, stewardship, neighbor, the poor, love, incarnation, reconciliation, and good works.

The Kingdom of God

The kingdom of God is the rule of God; and it may be seen in its power over nature and in the lives of people. The final consummation of God's kingdom is pending, but its power and active presence are evidenced now. The rule of God requires obedience of all in and under his domain. God's rule extends to all of our relationships: with himself, with other people, and with nature, or creation.

When one begins to reflect on some of the developmental issues raised by teachings about the kingdom of God, it is easy to see why Jesus spoke of the "good news" of the kingdom. Dyrness suggests at least six implications of the kingdom of God for development: (1) dignity of the person, (2) community goal-setting, (3) need for mutual sharing, (4) dissatisfaction with the existing situation, (5) ability to master the environment, and (6) hope.[5]

The good news of the kingdom remains good news today, both for the so-called "underdeveloped poor" and the "overdeveloped wealthy." The good news is that there are benefits for all, regardless of one's nationality, ethnicity, gender, or economic status. The citizenship that is offered is one of equality in a family under the rule of God, transcending national boundaries and political or economic differences. We can see how the Jew could embrace the Roman in the early church. Now the American can embrace his or her Chinese, Russian, or even Iranian brother or sister.

Relationships in the kingdom are enduring. The trauma of a coup or the stress of an election never arise. The king is eternal. Through his present reign we have experienced his initiatives in each of our key sets of relationships and with our becoming all he would have us be. His election, adoption, redemption, reconciliation, justification, and sanctification all serve to remove the constraints holding us back now. The promise of glorification provides hope in the midst of our present circumstances. The guidance of his sovereign presence in our situation allows us to walk through the valley of the shadow of death without fear. We know he is in control for our ultimate good. As his initiatives continue, empowerment in the kingdom emerges.

Outside the kingdom, or as one looks at the characteristics of "underdevelopment," the signs are clear—self-interest, lack of hope, fragmentation, powerlessness, alienation, oppression, and ever-increasing interpersonal and environmental risks. The kingdom provides hope beyond a bleak despair of uncertainty. Within the kingdom is a living hope, a sure inheritance, and a set of sure relationships based on a covenental commitment for our good. The good news is that the kingdom is not closed, but open to whoever would by faith accept God's rule by allowing Jesus, his Son, to be the one in charge.

Sin

An understanding of the biblical concept of sin and its consequences provides a base to understand "underdevelopment." Underdevelopment can be seen in the broken or inappropriate relations a person or a people may have with God, with others, or with the environment.

The alienating results of sin can certainly be observed in three key sets of relationships. Sin alienates people from their neighbors. Sin leads to an exploitative and alienating use of the environment. Sin alienates a person from God, leaving only rebelliousness and hopelessness where a preserving and nurturing relationship could have existed.

Redemption

Redemption results from God's initiative.

He paid the price for freeing all that was alienated because of sin—both people and the environment. The primary relationship affected was the relationship between people and himself. However, redemption carries other broader relational implications as well (e.g., one's accountability in the use of his or her own body [1 Cor. 6:20], the accountability of leaders for others [Acts 20:28], submissive relations with others [1 Cor. 7:23], and freedom from being under the curse of sin [Gal. 3:13]). Redemption will also affect our environment (cf. Col. 1:19–20; Eph. 1:9–10, 22ff; 4:10).

Stewardship

The primary stewardship perspective is that of ownership. God is *the* owner and sovereign. He owns the land (Exod. 19:5; Lev. 25:23). He is sovereign over all living things (Ps. 24:1; 50:10) including the souls of people (Rom. 14:8).

A second basic concept of stewardship is accountability. A steward is accountable for utilizing resources appropriately to accomplish the objectives of the owner (Matt. 25:14–30; Luke 16:2; 19:11–27), for enlarging the resources of the owner and for any waste.

A useful way to understand a concept is to look at its opposite or what it is not. Covetousness provides that contrast to stewardship. Covetousness is that personal desire to possess what belongs to someone else. Consumerism, which builds on covetousness, is the opposite of stewardship. Some synonyms of covetousness that also contrast with stewardship include: *greed*, which demonstrates a lack of restraint and discrimination in desire; *acquisitiveness*, which seeks to possess and keep; *grasping*, which suggests unfairness or ruthlessness; or obsessive acquisitiveness and stinginess.

Covetousness is both forbidden and condemned in the Bible (Exod. 20:17—do not covet; Luke 12:15—be on guard against covetousness; Gal. 5:19–21—idolaters will not inherit the kingdom; Col. 3–5—greed is idolatry). The fruits of covetousness read as a list of the traits of underdevelopment: oppression—Gen. 31:41; theft—Josh. 7:21; disobedience—1 Sam. 15:9; meanness—1 Kings 21; robbery—1 Kings 20:6; unscrupulousness—2 Kings 5:20; scoffing—Luke 16:14.

Neighbor

Christ revolutionized our concept of "neighbor" in the Parable of the Good Samaritan (Luke 10:25–37). Jesus' teaching raises the issue of how one becomes a neighbor. The parable does not address the question of physical proximity. The Jews and Samaritans were two different peoples. Certainly, their religious biases were strongly in conflict—the men in the parable had little in common. Apparently, the one was a well-to-do Jew and the other a poor Samaritan.

Jesus' concept of neighbor underscores the importance of *need*. The one who is in need provides the opportunity for one to become a neighbor. The one who related to the need was the neighbor. He broadened the Old Testament law for concern for neighbor outside of culture and across religious lines into the immediate context of the one in need.

Neighborliness as Jesus taught it was "crosscultural helping." Within this parable one who gives without concern for himself demonstrates neighborliness, and the love which Jesus affirmed is required (Mark 12:28–31; Rom. 13:10; 15:1–2; Gal. 5:14; Jas. 2:8).

The roots of Jesus' teaching reach into the Old Testament concerns for the alien/refugee (Exod. 22:21; Lev. 19:34; Deut. 10:18–19; 27:19), the widow and orphan (Exod. 22:22; Isa. 58:7; Zech. 7:10;

Matt. 25:35; Jas. 1:27), the enslaved (Luke 4:18–19), the oppressed and the poor.

The Poor

The Scriptures say much about the poor. Santa Ana points out that

> In the Old Testament poverty is considered as evil, as a constant and painful fact, whose consequences are the establishment of relationships of dependence and oppression which lead to the false elevation of the powerful (false because it is not in accord with the true will of God) and to the humiliation of the helpless.[6]

Within the Mosaic covenant, the poor were to be cared for as an expression of obedience to God. Conditions that led to poverty were denounced by the prophets (e.g., Amos and Isaiah).

However, wealth, as depicted in the Old Testament, provided the means of caring for the poor and the underprivileged rather than as personal possessions to be accumulated. The harvesting of crops, the tenure of land, and the paying of the tithe all illustrate the deep concern for the poor in the Old Testament (cf. Deut. 24:19–21; Lev. 19:9–10; 23:22). The sabbath had a social significance as it provided a day of rest for the slave and the alien (Exod. 23:12). The triennial tithe was not to be given to the temple; rather, it was for the alien, the orphan, and the widow (Deut. 14:28–29).

Jesus began his ministry by announcing that he was fulfilling the prophecy of Isaiah 61 "and the poor have good news preached to them" (Matt. 11:5; Luke 4:17–19). Early in his ministry he pronounced a blessing on the poor (Mt. 5:3) and he continued to show concern for the poor throughout his ministry. The concept of poverty in the Scriptures is not limited solely to economic poverty. It refers, rather, to the dependent and the needy whose lives are limited, and who, therefore, look to God to change their condition and bring justice. Poverty is not considered a virtue; it is the result of evil or injustice.[7]

Love

If we take the New Testament seriously, the most important developmental concept and relationship is *love*. Love is commanded both toward God and our neighbor (Mark 12:28–31; Luke 10:25–37).

Love is not only a commandment; it is a fruit of the Spirit (Gal. 5:22), and it is essential for the employment and functioning of spiritual gifts (1 Cor. 13). Love is a conscious, willful decision to act in a way that is for the good of the other person without regard to the cost to oneself.

Love requires a pairing of two important relationships—(1) to God, to be obedient, and (2) to do the best for our neighbor. One cannot express the first without the second, and one cannot be effective with the second without the first and a genuine commitment to relate the two. Love requires both a concern for one's eternal relationship with God through Christ *and* a commitment to the present justice, redistribution of wealth, and freedom of others.

Incarnation

Jesus demonstrated what the Incarnation meant. John tells us, "The Word became flesh and lived for a while among us. We have seen his glory . . . full of grace and truth" (Jn. 1:14 NIV). The apostle Paul further explains the Incarnation to the church in Philippi. Jesus did not "grasp" equality with God, but rather took on the very nature of a servant and was made in human likeness. He obediently humbled himself (cf. Phil. 2:5–11).

As one thinks about the development of other people and bringing them to obedience in the kingdom, some of the key concepts related to the Incarnation include: "living among," "serving," "not grasping," "likeness," "humility" and "obedience." The purpose for Jesus' incarnation models the purpose for today—"that at the Name of Christ every knee should bow in heaven and on earth."

Reconciliation

Reconciliation with God provides the basis for reconciliation with other people and for the ongoing improved relations with them through the emergence of the fruit of the Spirit (Gal. 5:22–23). The apostle Paul wrote,

> Therefore if any man is in Christ, he is a new creature; the old things passed away; behold, new things have come. Now all these things are from God, who reconciled us to himself through Christ, and gave us the ministry of reconciliation, namely, that God was in Christ reconciling the world to himself, not counting their trespasses against them, and he has committed to us the word of reconciliation. Therefore, we are ambassadors for Christ, as though God were entreating through us; we beg you on behalf of Christ, be reconciled to God. He made him who knew no sin to be sin in our behalf, that we might become the righteousness of God in him (2 Cor. 5:17–21 NASB).

From this passage, we can see the apostle's relating of reconciliation with God and reconciliation with other people. The fruits of the Spirit further demonstrate the working of the Spirit in an individual to result in reconciliation. One's relations with others demonstrates his or her relationship with God.

Good Works

Good works result from conversion and confirm the Christian's testimony to God's grace. Jesus said to do good works so people would glorify God (Matt. 5:16). James suggested that good works demonstrate one's faith (Jas. 2:14-26). Paul writes that we are not saved by but for good works, which God has prepared for us to do (Eph. 2:8-10).

Jesus taught that the ethical criteria for judgment are the acts of concern (cf. Matt. 25:31-46). These same criteria apply to both the "nations" and to believers. The response of the righteous (Matt. 25:37) was not the response of those who were doing those things "deliberately" or "strategically." Rather, they were transformed people responding out of their new nature without being deliberately conscious of "doing it for Jesus." They were doing it because it was the natural expression of their transformed nature as "Christ's ones."

This passage gives a glimpse of the heart of God who shows a concern not for the motive or the decorations or rationale, but for the involvement, even without preoccupation about doing it for Jesus. The emphasis in Matthew 25 is not on a deliberate strategy of development, but rather on a changed nature and the outworking of that nature. Similarly, when Jesus spoke of giving a cup of cold water (Matt. 10:40-42; Mark 9:41), the focus was on the giver.

People who approach development as though it is only a key to gaining access to people to deliver the verbal message of the gospel are perverting the Word of God. One's concern for his or her neighbor should not be manipulative, but rather for both the present and eternal good of the other person.

Any one of these biblical concepts will lead into all the others. The issues of relationships are primary—with God, with other people, and with the environment. In each case, the beginning point is God's reigning in the context where people live. God's goals for both the present and future are inextricably woven into a person's relationships in his or her context.

NEEDS

The statement, "they need . . ." often provides the beginning point for development and frequently sets the patterns for relationships for the beginning of development and evangelistic activities. While it is crucial to consider needs in any development project, an inappropriate view of needs often clouds the issues of relationships and inhibits both effective development and evangelism. As with the other concerns in relating the church and development, a primary question that must be addressed as we think of needs is, again, that of *relationships*. Ward warns of a danger in reducing the concept of development to simply meeting needs. This reductionist approach poses a grave danger because it tends to facilitate the design of projects which have very short-term purposes and little sense of accountability for the longer-term development of a people.[8]

Three assumptions about needs set the stage for understanding them: (1) Everyone has needs. (2) Needs always look different to the needy than to observers. (3) Common needs may allow for many alternative solutions.

Several different kinds of noncontextualized developmental approaches based on needs serve to confuse and frustrate development. The first brings change without concern for the needs of the people, as if local needs do not matter. This approach rarely produces satisfying results.

A second brings change based on the outsider's views of the needs of the people. Missions often fall into this inappropriate view. There certainly is a need in every person to come to God through Christ. However, projecting needs beyond the deep spiritual reconciliation with God leaves one on shaky ground. To project a need and then to follow it with "development" programs to change this or that social custom may well be more disruptive both to evangelism and to development in the long run than doing nothing.

The only sure ground for assessing a need in people is the ground of relationship to God. Beyond that relationship many things follow. But they should all be a process of cooperative, participative involvement, not just of the outsider as the decision maker, but of the outsider in the prophetic role—and of the insider in terms of identifying the application of truth in that society. This is the single most important principle in contextualization.

Looking at some contrasts again will help us understand the concept of needs. Needs differ from wants. Certainly not every *want* is a *need*, although that is what contemporary advertising would have us believe. A *need* refers to some psychological, emotional, physical or spiritual condition which, if not fulfilled or changed, will in some way be detrimental to the person, community or society.

Needs may be classified as innate or acquired. Innate needs are those that come from human nature. Acquired needs come from one's lifestyle. Acquired needs often have their base in covetousness and emerge from within the society.

Another contrast exists between functional needs and felt needs. Outsiders project "functional needs" as essential for the insider to function in the given context. A "felt need" is simply a need an insider feels. The problem with this pair of views about needs is that outsiders are often *perceived* to have an expertise or informational power that can become oppressive. To project one's own view of needs on people at best inhibits relationships and may seriously frustrate insiders, because the outsiders do not understand their needs.

It may be wise to begin with "felt needs" to facilitate the local people's growth in their understanding of needs. However, due to a history of oppression, a lack of hope, a heightened sense of risk or a lack of confidence, "felt needs" or "expressed needs" are often very limited and will not, if satisfied, go very far in the development of the people. Felt needs are generally expressed in the context and only to the limit of one's view of hope and risk. What can be hoped for with the listener? What are the risks involved in the treatment of the need? Without hope—or if the risks are too high—the felt needs and projected functional needs will differ widely. Felt needs, however, must be considered.

> Regardless of how the conflict of wants is resolved, it is essential for development agents to know what the client community's wants actually are and to take them fully into account. . . . Neglecting to take account of clients' wants is a major cause of failure in development programs.[9]

Abraham Maslow's view of needs has dominated much of Western thinking on the subject for more than twenty years. His taxonomy of needs suggests a five-stage sequence:

1. Physiological
2. Safety and security
3. Love and belonging
4. Self-esteem
5. Self-actualization[10]

Maslow argues that when any of the lower-level needs are threatened they will emerge as the dominant set. If, for example, some adults are threatened in their security needs, all other needs are subordinated because that one is going unmet.

This taxonomy provides a useful theory when considering needs in a Western context. However, when this taxonomy is considered crossculturally, it lacks the power to explain as it does in the West because of the Western individualistic presuppositions on which it is built. In many cultures of the world, one's identity, self-esteem, and sense of belonging and security are much more group-oriented than in the West. Even the category of "self-actualization" may be inappropriate. The view of needs then ought to be contextually appropriate.

DEVELOPING LEADERS

The development of leaders for social ministries is essential if the ministries are to effectively serve and fulfill their purposes. Leadership development is broader than leadership training, and is certainly an important component; but it may not always be the most important factor in developing leaders.

Contextual concerns set the priorities for leadership development in social ministries. To consider leadership development, attention must be given to functions, motivation, goals, resources, and local world-views. In every case, however, the focus is on the *context* to be served and the people—both leaders and followers in that context. No leadership development can reasonably take place without a firm ongoing commitment to contextualization.

ETHICAL CONCERNS

Because of their ethics, Christians do take the situations where they live and work seriously. Goulet suggests that developmental goals and processes require serious ethical evaluation. He goes on to suggest that a development ethicist must also give attention to the strategies and theoretical frameworks that guide development-related work.[11] Not only are the goals, processes, strategies and theoretical frameworks to be contextually appropriate, but Christian workers must also recognize their accountability for the outcomes. Goulet writes:

> Ethics has a special interest in the consequences of choices. Responsibility and freedom—the twin components of ethics—are indissolubly linked to consequences. The burden of freedom resides in precisely this, that one is accountable for the consequences of his actions.[12]

Other contextual ethical issues appear in the ways one views other people. Adeney suggests three ways which others may be seen as (1) scenery, (2) machinery and other useful things, and (3) people.[13] When people are seen as scenery or simply as a means, the potential for meaningful and enduring development is seriously threatened.

Another ethical issue Christians face is the use of development as a means to manipulate. Social ministries certainly can facilitate a wide range of growth, including growth in the Christian faith. However, when they are used to reduce the choices of a person or community so as to manipulate or influence people into doing what they would not freely choose, that is simply wrong. It flies in the face of Christian ethics and the principles of sound contextualization.

CONTEXTUALIZED DEVELOPMENT:
A TURKANA CASE STUDY

Randy and Edie Nelson began their ministry in the Turkana District of Kenya by moving to Lakori and building a thatched house. There they remained in the center of the community for about a year, learning the language and culture. Their home became a community center for visiting late into the warm evenings, for finding transportation if someone became ill, and for protection when bandits would raid the village.

After learning the language, they moved to Kaputir to work primarily in evangelism and church planting. In Kaputir the people expected this new missionary couple to do what missionaries "always" do, that is, to build a clinic or school or to help with other kinds of development projects. Kaputir is a small trading center located on the Turkwell River in northwest Kenya. Just across the river, some two miles away, a clinic, sponsored by the Roman Catholic Church, served the people for eight or nine months a year when the river was low enough to cross. However, during the rainy season, when more people were ill, the river's flow prevented the people's crossing it. Expecting Randy to simply build, stock, and operate a clinic, the village elders approached him about it. Without refusing them, he made it clear that he did not represent a funding agency, but that he was genuinely interested in their shared community problems.

As time went on Randy recognized that the appropriate forum for the discussion of community issues was at the occasional goat roast, which brought the elders of the community and the surrounding countryside together. As the "felt need" for a clinic became increasingly apparent to Randy and Edie, Randy agreed to bring in an outsider to discuss the options at a goat roast.

Men came to the roast from as far as a day's walk away—twenty to twenty-five miles—and several goats were ritually slaughtered, roasted, and shared. By now, Randy and Edie had entered into the humor and daily life of the community. They knew the people by name and shared in such common tasks as getting water at the community well, along with everyone else.

The discussions that followed examined the options, the mission limits on funding, and potential community support. Some weeks later, a decision was made to establish a community clinic. Randy served as a "process helper," but not as the donor. Every segment of the community, including the Muslim Somalis, participated by giving and working. Randy also served along with some of the community elders as an advocate to the district government offices. Within a few months the community saw the clinic stocked and staffed. They saw it as *their* clinic, and the government officials, upon assuming responsibility for its continued operation, cited it as an outstanding community project. Within only a few months this community built its first new church building with the same kind of ownership and pride. While the Muslim traders were not yet members of the church, they were now working with the Christians and seeing the Christian commitment to them as well.

To begin contextualized development or social ministries, one may take a cue from Jesus. His incarnational approach provides the principles and values for both our message and method. He was committed for life to be with the people. He lived among them as an insider. He spoke the language. He accepted no special status, rank or privilege. He demonstrated accountability both to God for his mission and to his followers for their present and eternal good. He was compassionate in the present with an eternal perspective. His use of power was disciplined by meekness and humility and always focused on the good of others. He lived according to the name given to him by the prophet Isaiah—Immanuel—God with us. We begin the contextualization process when we follow in his steps.

NOTES

[1] Social action raises another set of concerns that are beyond the scope of this article. In social action, the societal structures are addressed and often confronted with a view toward bringing change. To fully treat the issue of social action would require a critique of liberation theologies, which have a large commitment to social action. The commitment to social action from these points of view often has a somewhat different goal than does the evangelical Christian working with

an evangelical agency or church. Not only would the goal differ, but the process as well.

[2] William A. Dyrness, "The Kingdom is Our Goal," *Together* (October–December 1983):1.

[3] Wayne G. Bragg, "From Development to Transformation," in Vinay Samuel and Chistopher Sugden, eds., *The Church in Response to Human Need* (Grand Rapids: Eerdmans), 25.

[4] Ted Ward, "The Church and Development," a series of lectures given at Daystar University College, Nairobi, 1979.

[5] Dyrness, "The Kingdom" 39–40.

[6] Julio Santa Ana, *Good News to the Poor: The Challenge of the Poor in the History of the Church* (Grand Rapids: Eerdmans, 1974), 2.

[7] Ibid., 95.

[8] Ward, ibid.

[9] Ward Hunt Goodenough, *Cooperation in Change* (New York: John Wiley, 1966), 37–38.

[10] Abraham Maslow, *Motivation and Personality* (New York: Harper and Row, 1954).

[11] Denis Goulet, *The Cruel Choice* (New York: Atheneum, 1978), 12.

[12] Ibid.

[13] Miriam Adeney, *God's Foreign Policy* (Grand Rapids: Eerdmans, 1984), 3.

11

Contextualizing Theology in the American Social Mosaic
C. Peter Wagner

THE CHALLENGE OF THE CONTEXTUALIZATION OF THEOLOGY is just as great within the borders of the United States as it is internationally. In one sense it is even greater because of the common assumption that all Americans would or should buy into some sort of a generic American version of theology. Few would disagree that theological adjustments might have to be made in Japan or Guatemala or Sri Lanka or Indonesia. But are similar adjustments needed for Japanese or Guatemalans or Sri Lankans or Indonesians who now happen to be American citizens? Many fail to see that if our evangelization and church-planting efforts among ethnic Americans are to attain their full potential, skillful contextualization needs to take place. Some of them do not see the need because they fail to recognize how ethnically diverse the real America is today.

C. PETER WAGNER, M.A., M.Div., Th.M., Ph.D., Donald A. McGavran Professor of Church Growth, served as a missionary to Bolivia for sixteen years before joining the Fuller faculty in 1971. Among the most recent of his books are *How to Have a Healing Ministry Without Making Your Church Sick* and *Strategies for Church Growth*.

AMERICA IS NOT A MELTING POT

I should think that when historians of the twenty-first century look back on the United States of the twentieth century, they will judge that the most significant decade was that of the 1960s. The two world wars, the Great Depression, the advent of space travel, and the cybernetic revolution will certainly be important. But I believe that even more important has been the civil rights movement of the sixties.

This movement, stimulated largely by black Christian leaders, has permanently changed America's self-image from that of an assimilationist to a pluralistic society. Most of us learned in school that America was a melting pot. We were led to believe that when people come across our borders from other nations, they quickly forget about their past and become so-called Americans. The American way was to abandon all claims to Frenchness or Polishness or Irishness or Chineseness or Mexicanness, and to adopt the so-called more civilized Anglo-American cultural values. This attitude also applied to the peoples who were here before the Anglos, such as the Mohawks or the Sioux or the Comanches or any of hundreds of other Indian tribes. It was fully expected that they would inevitably recognize the superiority of Anglo culture and melt into the melting pot.

Up to the decade of the 1960s, most Americans actually thought the melting pot had worked. With only a few exceptions, ethnics were socially and legally invisible. Sociologists studied Americans only as individuals, and did little work on analyzing their group loyalties, which were not even supposed to exist. Mild doses of non-American behavior were tolerated and even regarded as somewhat colorful. St. Patrick's Day, French restaurants, and Polish jokes were a part of American life. But at levels that might affect government, law, or economics, ethnic behavior was frowned upon. At worst, ethnicity was a serious threat to society; at best it was a nuisance that hopefully would disappear in a generation or two.

Ethnicity did not disappear in a generation or two, nor will it. The real America is not a melting pot; it never was. The real America is a stewpot. While some prefer using analogies of salad bowl, mosaic, tapestry, or rainbow, I prefer the stewpot. Here each ingredient is changed and flavored by the others. The changes are for the better. The carrots, potatoes, meat, and onions all taste better after they come in contact with each other in the stewpot. While they enrich each other, each ingredient nevertheless maintains its own identity and integrity. If the stew is overcooked, the ingredients lose their identity and the contents become unpalatable mush.

In the new American society that emerged from the civil rights movement of the 1960s, each ethnic ingredient now has the potential to be enriched through intercultural contact with the others. But ideally they are no longer under social pressure to become culturally Anglo-American in order to "make it" in our country. It is true that we have not always lived up to the ideal, but the sweep of social history over the last two or three decades is encouraging.

American blacks, in particular, have taken giant steps toward the ideal, with mayors in four of the six largest cities in the nation, two black Miss Americas, a black Tournament of Roses queen, and a presidential candidate who accentuated his blackness instead of pretending to ignore it. Other ethnic minorities are advancing as well. We need to recognize that this could not be happening under the melting-pot ideal.

What does this stewpot look like?

Time magazine called the Los Angeles area, with which I am most familiar, "The New Ellis Island." Waves of immigrants flood in. Parts of the city change almost overnight from one ethnic group to another. Blacks in south-central Los Angeles are complaining that Mexicans are "spoiling the neighborhood." In Hollywood a fast-food stand, operated by Koreans, sells "Kosher tacos." Students in the Los Angeles Unified School District speak 104 languages, with over one thousand students speaking each of these languages: Spanish, Korean, Vietnamese, Cantonese, and Armenian.

The Los Angeles metropolitan area has the greatest population of Koreans outside the Orient, with estimates as high as 270,000. Despite the fact that Korean immigration started only in the seventies, there are now 4 daily Korean-language newspapers, a Korean telephone directory, 3 banks, a savings and loan, 130 Korean schools, 5 art galleries, 2 symphony orchestras, 300 voluntary associations, and 430 Korean churches.

For the past few years I have been collecting and updating facts concerning the ethnic* makeup of the Los Angeles area. Here are the known groups and their estimated population: Hispanics (4 million), blacks (972,000), Germans (450,000), Italians (350,000), Koreans (270,000), Armenians (225,000), Iranians (200,000), Japanese

---

*Unless otherwise noted, I am using "ethnic" to describe groups residing in the U.S. which are not Anglo-American. In my definition, "Anglo-American" is a cultural rather than a racial or national-origin category, including, for example, those who trace their ancestry to Germany or Sweden or Italy but who have assimilated into the Anglo-American culture. To illustrate, the 450,000 Germans in the above list live in the U.S. but still choose to maintain their primary self-identification as Germans rather than Anglo-Americans.

(175,000), Arabs (160,000), Yugoslavs (150,000 divided sharply between Serbians and Croatians), Chinese (150,000), Filipinos (150,000), Vietnamese (100,000), American Indians (95,000), Russians (90,000), Israelis (90,000), Dutch (75,000), Hungarians (60,000), Samoans (60,000), French (55,000), Thai (50,000), Greeks (50,000), British (50,000), Asian Indians (30,000), Dutch Indonesians (30,000), Egyptian Copts (10,000), Romanians (10,000), Turks (5,000), and Gypsies (5,000). I expect information on other groups to surface as time goes by. One television station has programs in English, Spanish, Arabic, Farsi, Armenian, Vietnamese, Korean, Japanese, Cantonese, and Mandarin.

Los Angeles is not an exception to the rule. Most metropolitan areas in the United States are seeing the development of a similar situation. A recent study has shown the following percentages of ethnics, excluding black Americans: San Antonio (90 percent); Los Angeles (78 percent); New York (70 percent); San Francisco (63 percent); Chicago (61 percent); San Diego (59 percent); Houston (56 percent); New Orleans (53 percent); Milwaukee (52 percent); Phoenix (50 percent); Sacramento (50 percent). These are not melting-pot statistics. Our land is a nation of ethnics blended into an urban stewpot.

The Statue of Liberty has long expressed America's invitation to the world: "Give me your tired, your poor, your huddled masses, yearning to breathe free." The recent extensive renovation of the statue itself is indication enough that America intends to keep the doors open. I like the way a brochure from the Southern Baptist Language Missions Department expresses this sentiment:

> It is unlikely any other nation in the world is so *intentionally* pluralistic: the people of the United States have chosen to come to these shores: men, women and children giving up home and family, status and stability, human beings drawn by things more powerful than might or wealth; for here triumphs the concept of freedom and hope, here promises a fresh start, an equal chance: the opportunity to be *somebody*.

PLURALISM BRINGS CHANGES

The consequences of an era of newly recognized pluralism in America are far reaching. More and more Americans are celebrating their ethnicity without the embarrassments or inferiority complexes of the past. The hyphen in the names of hyphenated-American groups is now being read more as an equal sign than a mark of discrimination. American society is becoming proud of the nation's ability to handle demographic diversity. The intellectual climate has changed so much that now a sociologist can ask, "'Is there any large multi-national, multi-racial society that the world has ever known that has been so successful at coping with diversity and so willing to face the injustices that it has done to some of the diverse components that constitute it?'"[1]

The American legal system is being affected by the new pluralism. Bills dealing with the desires for national sovereignty of some American Indian groups may find their way to congressional agendas before long. Voting instructions, ballots, and other public documents are being issued in a variety of languages. Hispanic-Americans are reminding the State of California that Spanish was the official language before English was spoken there. Demands for bilingual education affect many American school districts and are bringing school board members to difficult new policy decisions.

America's churches are also affected by the new pluralism. Now that black is beautiful, are black churches beautiful? If they are, how about Korean churches or Sioux churches or Armenian churches or Cuban churches? How about Anglo-American churches, or more specifically, upper middle class Anglo-American churches? During the time that assimilationist models for interpreting American society were predominant, ethical arguments reinforcing assimilation were common. However, now that pluralist models are becoming respectable among American intellectuals, alternative theological arguments are emerging. One visible manifestation of such a change was noted on the part of black theologians, such as Joseph Washington, who switched from an assimilationist position to one advocating "equal partnership in a pluralistic society."[2]

The new climate for accepting a diversity of peoples as proper in American society favors the development of Christian churches along cultural lines. The great majority of America's 330,000 churches are, of course, already culturally homogeneous. The same could be said about Christian churches worldwide. But many of them have been made to feel guilty about their homogeneity by the theological attitude that condemned eleven o'clock on Sunday morning as being the most segregated hour in America. It is time now to explore new theological options. Perhaps a respectable theological case can be made for a society that celebrates pluralism and for churches that develop freely within just one piece of the sociological mosaic if they so desire. That churches naturally develop along cultural unit lines nobody denies. Whether such development is right or wrong constitutes an ethical problem for some.

AMERICAN ETHNIC THEOLOGY

A prime question raised by a volume on contextualization such as this is whether, as Christian churches multiply within the different components of the American cultural stewpot, these churches will be expected to adopt Anglo-American theology in order to be considered orthodox. Notice that this question was not dealt with seriously, if at all, over the first three centuries of the history of American churches. So long as the melting-pot ideal was assumed, ethnic theologies were not recognized as a need. The civil rights movement of the 1960s changed this picture permanently. Many ethnic leaders began to see the imposition of a standardized Anglo-American theology as just one more tool of the social oppression of ethnic groups.

The paramount theme in the development of a theology which adequately deals with pluralism is liberation. For some time now, liberation has been a major theological topic, first in Latin America and then in other areas of the Third World. Liberation theology consistently advocates social justice for groups of people who are being oppressed by existing social structures. The poor, the outcast, and the objects of prejudice and discrimination are assured by liberation theologians that God is on their side. This assurance may be given to minorities within a nation, to a nation itself, or even to a continent, such as South America, which is often perceived to be under the neocolonial dominance of the Anglo-Saxon world and thus also in need of liberation.[3]

While it is important to discuss liberation theology when dealing with contextualization in American ethnic groups, I do not wish to be misunderstood. Many contemporary theologies of liberation are nothing more than thinly veneered humanism and Marxism. They have little touch with the biblical theology of redemption and as such have become hindrances, rather than helps, to world evangelization. Because of this, many perceive any mention of liberation theology as capitulation to liberalism. For the most part I agree, and I myself oppose any theological development that would be a hindrance to the spread of the kingdom of God and the multiplication of Christian churches.

It is a fact of life, however, that at this particular moment, when American society is working out the implications of moving from a melting-pot ideal to a stewpot ideal, the more theologically sophisticated leaders of ethnic churches are very much interested in the theology of liberation because to them it represents the liberation of theology. It is an excellent example of the process of contextualization.

During the sixties, the black community in America took the lead in protesting its position as an oppressed group and developed a variation of liberation theology. James Cone's *Black Theology and Black Power* was one of the pioneer attempts. More recently the theme of liberation has been applied to other American ethnic groups. *God is Red* declares Sioux Indian Vine Deloria, Jr. Japanese-American Roy Sano writes on "Ethnic Liberation Theology." Irish-American Andrew Greeley is the author of "Notes on a Theology of Pluralism." And, inevitably, Anglo-American theologians are beginning to add their word. Donald Shockley, in *Free, White, and Christian*, develops, among other themes, "Ethnic Theology and White Liberation." Benjamin Reist is another. His *Theology in Red, White, and Black*, while certainly not the last word, is nevertheless an interesting starting point for developing the process of what could be called "theological conscientization," to borrow a good liberationist term.[4]

Benjamin Reist points out that theology is always intermixed with culture. There is no such thing as a gospel in abstract form. Because the very essence of the gospel is a word communicated by God to human beings, that word is always filtered through each recipient's particular cultural domain of relevances. As Reist says, the major problem in our understanding the gospel is "Christ and cultures."[5] Note the plural "cultures." Too much theologizing has been done as if culture were a singular, and the dangers of this nearsighted view have not always been evident to theologians. Reist argues:

> Leave the phrase in the singular, and inexorably the dominance of prior cultural arrangements remains unchallenged and intact, with the result that the proclamation of the gospel deteriorates into the ideological propagation of some prior understanding of how the uniqueness of the Christ is to be known and understood.[6]

Once we recognize that a supracultural gospel must be contextualized anew each time it is applied to a different culture, new horizons for theological development emerge. Reist argues that most American theology has been an importation of ideas originating in Europe. "What dominates American theological reflection," he says, "is not *white* theology, but European-American theology, 'North Atlantic Theology.'" He argues for liberation from such alien theological bondage, while at the same time acknowledging the valuable contributions that European theology has made. He urges the development of a truly white theology in America, along with black and red theologies. "Liberation for white brothers and sisters," he reasons, "is precisely analogous to liberation for *all* the brothers and sisters—for them it means becoming white, not as the epitome of humanity in general, but as one component of the full mosaic."[7]

The heart of the Christian gospel is that God, because he loved all human beings, sent his son Jesus to free, to save, to liberate. The very name *Jesus* means *savior*. "And you shall call his name Jesus, for he will save his people from their sins" (Mt. 1:21). The New Testament describes many kinds of bondage from which people need liberation through the grace of God. Men and women are said to be in bondage to sin (Rom. 6:17), to death (Rom. 6:23), to the law (Rom. 8:2), to rulers and powers and world forces (Eph. 6:12), and to culture (Gal. 4:3). From all of these and from anything else that might enslave, Christ promises liberation. He said, "The Spirit of the Lord is upon me, because he has anointed me to . . . proclaim release to the captives . . . to set at liberty those who are oppressed . . . ." (Lk. 4:18).

As the liberation theme of theological reflection is developed in each concrete situation, different emphases emerge. Victims of oppression who are in need of liberation are identified in different ways, under different social circumstances. The predominant interpretation of America's current social structures by theologians and ethicists representing ethnic groups is that the dominant group, namely the Anglo-Americans, has for generations been guilty of oppressing blacks, Hispanic-Americans, American Indians, Asian-Americans, Appalachian whites, and other minority groups.

This oppression has taken the forms of racism, economic exploitation, social discrimination, and cultural chauvinism. At the root of this oppression is the policy of cultural assimilation implicit in the melting-pot ideal. Perhaps the most blatant attempts on the part of American whites to force integration on a minority group have been the persistent efforts to coerce American Indians to abandon their tribal cultures and become red white men, but most minorities have been the object of such efforts in one degree or another. Few American ideals are as consistently denounced by ethnic theologians as the "myth of the melting pot." Their major ethical concerns derive from the question: Did Jesus not come to liberate us from the cultural oppression of Anglo-Americans and thus allow us the freedom to be ourselves and to serve and worship him in our own way? As one exasperated Native-American worker said, "Do Indians *really* have to love the organ?"[8]

THE DANGER OF RELIGIOUS CHAUVINISM

The annals of crosscultural missionary work are replete with examples of missionaries confusing the Christian gospel with the cultural values through which they themselves had come to understand Christianity. Preaching the gospel has too often meant "become a Christian like me and my people." Becoming an adherent of Christianity implied in many cases undergoing a "cultural circumcision" or, in extreme circumstances, committing ethnocide. Ethnic theology of liberation is now determined to make Americans of all groups recognize such religious cultural chauvinism for what it is, not only on the remote mission fields of the world, but specifically right here in America.

One of the stronger voices for contextualized ethnic theology is that of Japanese-American Roy Sano. He elaborates on the "two-category" analysis of American society made by Harry Kitano, dividing the nation into the "colorless" upper category of privileged and powerful people and the "colorful" lower category of less privileged and only partially enfranchised peoples. Sano chides white theologians for not coming to terms with this structure, charging that "the espousal of the universal gospel and crusading social pronouncements blind them to the realities of these persisting categories."[9] He lumps together both Protestant liberalism and neo-orthodoxy as having fallen victim to the melting-pot theory, a theory which he sees operating on two levels, not to be confused with Kitano's two categories. The first and explicit level "promised unity and acceptance of all peoples and their distinctive contributions," while the second and hidden level "promoted a monochrome, or colorless, culture and society dominated by whites."[10]

Sano's point is extremely important for understanding the contradiction inherent in the pre-1960s pronouncements of theologians and ethicists on the matter of culturally homogeneous churches. They were critical of churches that were made up of only one kind of people, and they implied that the most authentic Christian churches were those that took whatever steps were necessary to mix people of different cultural units in their membership. At that time, few of these theologians realized that the long-range implication of what they were advocating was the virtual destruction of American ethnic groups and their assimilation into the Anglo-American culture.

In developing the theme of the legitimacy of contextualizing theology in America, James Cone reacts negatively to the insistence of many white theologians that there is but one universal standard of hermeneutical methodology and theological reflection which merits intellectual respectability in the academic community. Cone argues that such thinking is inherently wrong because it springs from a white perspective. He hears such theologians saying, "Unless you black people learn to think like us white folks, using our rules, then we will not listen to you."[11] Cone charges that "white ethicists, from Reinhold Niebuhr to James Gustafson, reflect the racism current in the society as a whole." He is incensed, for example, that Niebuhr could speak of the "'cultural backwardness'" of blacks and go on to argue that "'we must not consider the Founding Fathers immoral just because they were slaveholders.'" Asks Cone, "What else can this ethical judgment mean than that Niebuhr derived his ethics from white culture and not biblical revelation?"[12] Roy Sano says, "A rereading of Reinhold Niebuhr will reveal how much of his writings sought to convince fellow whites that they were in a position of power and could influence the course of history."[13]

THE RISK OF THEOLOGICAL RELATIVISM

In accepting a theology of liberation, each people group must also accept the right and responsibility to contextualize Christian theology, that is, to bring the supracultural principles of God's revelation to bear on its own concrete situation. An awareness of contextualization questions the propriety of speaking of theology in the singular, as if there were some universal Christian theology which could apply to all peoples at all times. Black theologian Reuben Sheares suggests, for example, that blacks attempt to move beyond white theology. "That choice," he argues, "relates to the awareness that white theology is not necessarily normative. It is not the standard by which matters of faith and life must be judged."[14]

Freed from theological as well as other kinds of oppression, liberated peoples become released to develop their own kinds of Christian witness, worship, theology, and ethical code. These developments take place within the unique frame of reference through which they interpret the lordship of Jesus Christ and God's revelation in his Word. Of course, liberated people are also free to abandon their culture and become part of a different group if they wish. But the choice must always be their own, not something overtly or covertly superimposed from outside.

When theology is changed from singular to plural, the possibility arises for a certain amount of theological relativism. Some people may object to this stance unless they realize that Christianity has always been relative. Ernst Troeltsch's The Social Teaching of the Christian Churches documents the changes that Christian social ethics has undergone through the centuries within the Western tradition alone.[15] A vast body of international missiological research provides example after example of the contextualization of Christianity in cultures of the world.

It needs to be recognized, furthermore, that cultures themselves are dynamic, not static. That is why many Christians have discovered that creedal statements should always be subject to review lest they fail to convey a true statement of Christian belief for the next generation.

While theological relativism is not new or unusual, the test of theological validity in any context remains its faithfulness to the supracultural dimensions of the Word of God and to the will of God as applied to each particular life situation. A recognition of the validity of theological relativism does not mean there is no longer such a thing as heresy. Of course there is. The danger of demonic influence in the handling of sacred truth will always be present. But it must be understood that whereas heresy is difficult enough to uncover within one's own cultural milieu, it is doubly difficult to uncover in someone else's. It is much better to live as a Christian in an open environment where the integrity of different expressions is honored than to live in a society characterized by the theological chauvinism of a dominant group. The risk involved in choosing tolerance may not be so great when accompanied by a high level of trust in the work of the Holy Spirit to "guide [God's people] into all the truth" (Jn. 16:13).

THE BASIC PROBLEM: HERMENEUTICS

The methodology of theological contextualization needs to be clearly understood. God is absolute, and he communicates absolute, or supracultural, truth to his people. However, none of the recipients of God's revelation has understood God's truth apart from concrete historical situations. They, as we, were always people-in-culture. God's revelation to the Hebrew prophets, for example, represented the contextualization of absolute truth in Semitic cultural forms. If God had chosen to reveal himself to the world through the Egyptians or the Chinese or the Incas instead of through the descendants of Abraham, the resulting Scriptures would have been vastly different but just as true.

Consequently, the basic methodological problem for the contextualization of theology does not revolve around the doctrinal concepts of biblical authority, inspiration, or inerrancy, as some theologians perceive it. The problem is, rather, hermeneutical. It is possible to subscribe, as I do, to a doctrine of biblical inerrancy, and go on from there to recognize that those who received God's inerrant word and wrote the Jewish and Christian Scriptures did so, not as people who were somehow magically detached from their own cultural environment, but as people who had individual personalities and group identities, both of which were respected by God as he communicated with them. God said the right thing and made no mistakes in saying it, but he said it to a people who existed in a specific historical situation and interpreted what they received through a specific cultural frame of reference.

The Bible is inerrant in the sense that what it describes was actually said and actually happened, because God made sure that those who inscribed his revelation did so accurately. This is not the area in which relativity is an issue in the evangelical view of contextualization. However, those who wrote the Scriptures used language, thought forms, proverbs, idioms, and cultural assumptions which made what they wrote perfectly intelligible *at face value* in only one cultural setting at one point in history. Attempts to understand Scripture by people of any other culture at any other time need a special effort of interpretation that the original receptors took for granted.

This is why the basic problem must be seen as hermeneutical. A full understanding of the absolute principles in the Bible cannot come, apart from an understanding of the precise historical situations in which they were given. As the context is more adequately understood, the supracultural content of revelation becomes clearer.

Supracultural Truth

What is the supracultural content of Scripture? A great deal of caution must be exercised in answering this important question. All attempts to reduce the supracultural content of revelation to a creed will naturally be colored by the cultural context in which the creed is formulated. Even the phrase "I believe in the resurrection of the body" from the Apostles' Creed (which may come as close as any to summarizing supracultural truths) does not have a directly transferrable meaning for some cultures in Africa or the South Pacific, for example, where the understanding of death is quite different from that of the Greco-Roman culture of the first century. The "resurrection of the body" is such a common occurrence for some of those peoples that it would seem strange to them that it could be a concept important enough to be mentioned in a religious creedal statement.

I myself hesitate to draw up a catalog of supracultural truths lest they be successfully challenged by someone who knows something about some of the world's cultures that I do not and shows that I have guessed wrong. Nevertheless, there are certain concepts that emerge from Scripture which probably would be universally recognized as supracultural principles of Christianity: truth, justice, love, sin, the existence of God, faith, forgiveness, prayer, honesty, marriage, the historicity of Jesus. These and other concepts could be safely listed as supracultural Christian truths. But as words, they are so abstract that they have very little intrinsic meaning. The practical meaning of each of these concepts can only emerge in a historical and cultural context. Here is where a degree of relativity is introduced, and I know of no way around it. I believe, for example, that the supracultural essence of the gospel is a personal relationship with Jesus Christ. But how a person comes into and expresses that relationship is a highly sensitive cultural issue. Among equally committed Christians there might be a wide divergence of explanations of how it happens, all of which might be equally valid.

This may well be why Paul writes that "now we see in a mirror dimly. . . . Now I know in part; then I shall understand fully . . ." (1 Cor. 13:12). Such an approach to theological reflection requires a measure of humility that some people might not be able to accept. However, it clears the way for theology to become theologies, reduces the possibility of a dominant group of Christians becoming theologically chauvinistic, and allows for a full and free working of the Spirit of God among diverse peoples in a pluralistic society.

Dynamic Equivalence

Charles Kraft, who has contributed a chapter to this volume, uses "dynamic equivalence" to describe the way in which Christian theology should be contextualized in different cultures. He borrows his approach from linguistics and Bible translation theory.

The "formal correspondence" concept of cultural and linguistic diversity is now giving way among linguists to the more current idea of what Eugene Nida calls "dynamic equivalence translation" explained as "the closest natural equivalent to the source-language message."[16] Kraft suggests that theologians should regard cultures much as Bible translators regard language. If we adopt such a starting point, we will not tend to evaluate a Christian community in another culture on the basis of how well their theology or worship or ethical system might attain a formal correspondence to "our kind of Christianity." Kraft argues that:

> A church that is merely a "literal" rendering of the forms of one church, be it American or first century Greco-Roman, is not according to the dynamic equivalence model, since it is not structured in such a way that it can perform the functions and convey the meanings

that a Christian church is intended to manifest in a culturally appropriate way.[17]

Perhaps one rather fascinating illustration of dynamic equivalence will clarify the methodology. This example involves church leadership. Some theologians have assumed, rather uncritically, that the bishop-elder-deacon hierarchy displayed in first-century churches should be applied to all Christian churches in all cultures on the formal correspondence rather than on the dynamic equivalence model. Kraft, however, sees in the New Testament

> not a single leadership pattern set down for all time, but a series of experiments with cultural appropriateness ranging from a communal approach (Acts 2:42–47) to, apparently, a leadership council of "apostles and elders" (Acts 15:4, 6, 22), to the more highly structured patterns alluded to in the Pastoral Epistles.[18]

A list of leadership qualifications is given in the later epistles for those who would be selected to govern the churches (see 1 Timothy 3 and Titus 1). Among them are requirements that the candidate be married to a wife and have his household under subjection to his authority, that he not be a novice, and that he have a good reputation in the wider community outside the church.

Apparently, contemporary, white American churches have long since contextualized the marital requirement on the dynamic equivalence model. Youth is much more highly regarded in white America than it was in first-century churches, and in order to make way for youthful leadership in the church, ordination of unmarried young people is not uncommon, even though the Bible suggests otherwise. This example is not intended to criticize these developments but to point out that contextualization has in fact taken place in white American churches, as it has wherever Christianity has become historically authentic.

White American Christians should recognize that some non-Anglo cultures in the U.S. could be closer to the first-century model than their own in their views of how church leadership should be selected. This means, for example, that to set up just one academic standard for ordination, as some American denominations have done, may cripple the process of leadership development in American Indian or other such ethnic churches affiliated with that denomination.

Even somewhat more complex is the application of the dynamic equivalence model to the leadership patterns of a culture like the Higi of West Africa. Kraft makes the interesting observation that in order for a church leader in the Higi culture "to effectively function in a way equivalent to that intended for the first century leaders, he would not only have to manage his household well but would have at least two wives in that household."[19] Kraft quotes a proverb of the Kru in Liberia: "You cannot trust a man with only one wife."[20]

Such an apparent violation of the Christian ethical norm of monogamy common among Westerners may be difficult for some people to accept. However, a dramatic change in attitude toward polygamy has been taking place among the current generation of missionaries who are introducing Christianity into polygamous cultures. A generation ago, few missionaries would even baptize a man married to more than one wife, much less ordain him as a church leader. But a fresh reading of the Scriptures with an openness to contextualization has questioned whether monogamy was ever intended to be a universally applied normative ethical marriage form.

For one thing, the biblical levirate marriage pattern of the Hebrews where a man was to marry his brother's wife even though he already had a wife was clearly ordained of God (Dt. 25:5). Divorce seems to be much more clearly and strongly condemned by Scripture than polygamy. Nevertheless, many missionaries did not realize that, when a man was required to put away three of his four wives in order to be baptized into the Christian community, the action was interpreted by members of the polygamous culture as requiring three divorces to qualify as a good Christian. Furthermore, three divorcees who were left behind often had no social option but to become prostitutes.

CONTEXTUALIZING IN AMERICA

Much work remains to be done on the contextualization of theology and ethics in America's minority groups. Authentic contextualization, of course, must be done by insiders, not by beneficent outsiders. Understandably, most of the theological energy of ethnic leaders has been spent on liberation, for unless liberation takes place, contextualization is academic. James Cone is among those who have begun the contextualization process. He forthrightly states that ethics must be grounded in the black community, and that "the oppressor cannot decide what is Christian behavior."[21]

To illustrate, Cone analyzes the moral code of black Christian slaves. "Black slaves," he says, "did not discuss the logic of ethical theory but created ethical structures for behavior in the struggle for survival." For example, how were slaves to relate the commandment "Thou shalt not steal," he asks, to a people who stole them from Africa and enslaved them in America? Black slaves responded by making an ethical distinction between "stealing" and "taking." Cone observes that "Stealing meant taking from a fellow slave, and slave ethics did not condone that. But to take from white folks was not wrong, because they were merely appropriating what was in fact rightfully theirs."[22] Cone and others can be expected to contextualize theology and ethics among the contemporary descendants of the slaves; and the results may be surprising to many white theologians.

In the light of this discussion, a Christian must read Vine Deloria's writings with a degree of remorse. Here is a competent American Indian figure whose father and grandfather were Christian leaders, who was trained in a theological seminary, but who now rejects Christianity as a viable religious option for American Indians. One feels that Deloria's statement, "One of the major problems of the Indian people is the missionary," is another way of saying that Christianity was never properly contextualized among Native Americans. Deloria argues that "while the thrust of Christian missions was to save the individual Indian, its result was to shatter Indian societies and destroy the cohesiveness of the Indian communities."[23]

No wonder rejection is the result when the Indian religious dynamic of receiving revelations through visions and dreams was opposed despite numerous biblical precedents. No wonder, when missionaries insisted that such a trivial thing as cutting men's hair short was a religious duty. No wonder, when land sacred to the Indians was treated as a commodity. No wonder, when many denominations refused to ordain Indian ministers because they openly feared that doctrine might become impure if entrusted to them. Even in the rare cases in which sincere efforts were made to contextualize Christianity, such as among the Sioux of the Dakotas where the Sun Dance was reinterpreted as the annual convocation of the missions, success was minimal. The reason, as Deloria sees it, was that "Christianity was presented in such a dogmatic form to the Sioux that it became frozen in a rigid structure" and was not able to change with the times.[24]

Christianity does not have to be presented in such a rigid form, however. An openness toward contextualization will contribute greatly to overcoming what Reist calls "its myopic imperialism, rooted in the absolutizing of its own history."[25] The unanswered question now is, can a change be made before it is too late?

CANONIZING THE MELTING POT

A significant theological incident occurred during the heat of the civil rights struggles when white liberals were feeling very guilty about their racism and were doing all kinds of things to make tangible amends. The event was the development of a United Presbyterian statement of faith called "The Confession of 1967." Predictably structured around the theme of reconciliation, the Confession states:

> God's reconciling work in Jesus Christ and the mission of reconciliation to which he has called his church are the heart of the gospel in any age. Our generation stands in peculiar need of reconciliation in Christ. Accordingly this Confession of 1967 is built upon that theme.[26]

Reconciliation in The Confession of 1967 was not balanced with liberation. The statement obviously was not framed by ethnic theologians, but is a creed of its own particular cultural unit, described by John Fry as "upper-middle class, largely white, economically conservative. . . ."[27] Ironically, the Confession's opinion of culturally homogeneous churches is clear:

> Congregations, individuals, or groups of Christians who exclude, dominate, or patronize their fellowmen, however subtly, resist the Spirit of God and bring contempt on the faith which they profess.[28]

The Confession of 1967 comes as close as an ecclesiastical document can to canonizing the melting pot. The peoples of the earth are called "one universal family," and much is said of personal rights while nothing is mentioned concerning group rights. In fact, the very desire to belong to a specific cultural group is called by Edward Dowey, in his commentary on the Confession, "demonic and a blasphemy when it controls the life of the church."[29] The Confession implies that an assertion of ethnicity inexorably leads to discrimination, racism, and patronage. The document does not recognize at all the positive side of group identity in society. Statements such as "Jesus is a black Messiah" or "God is black" or "God is red" would probably be pronounced as heresy by the framers of the Confession.

In my opinion, the best way to bring about the ultimate reconciliation of group to group in America and elsewhere is to recognize the right of each cultural unit to be Christian and to do theology in its own way—in other words, to be liberated from the ecclesiastical oppression of a dominant group. John V. Taylor sees such recognition already taking place in the World Council of Churches. He notes that "the old inter-denominational ecumenism" is being overtaken by an "inter-cultural ecumenism," which he labels simply "cultural ecumenism." Warning against a takeover by any dominant culture, he cautions:

> We do not want the westernisation of the universal Church. On the other hand we don't want the ecumenical cooks to throw all the

cultural traditions on which they can lay their hands into one bowl and stir them to a hash of indeterminate colour.[30]

Taylor's reference to the cooks recalls Greeley's "stewpot." Stew is not "hash of indeterminate colour." Each ingredient in stew contributes to the savor of the others, while retaining an identity and an integrity of its own. Cultural ecumenism, whether on a denominational, a regional, a national, or an international basis, should create conditions that allow Christian churches—each healthy and thriving within a particular culture richness—to establish a creative interrelatedness with each other. None of the cultures represented will dominate any of the others.

Unity remains an ideal for the Christian church, but authentic unity is always unity in diversity. Augustine himself, as an African within a Roman church, recognized the need for a full respect of the integrity of group expression within universal Christianity. He said:

> This heavenly city, then, while it sojourns on earth, calls citizens out of all nations, and gathers together a society of pilgrims of all languages, not scrupling about diversities in the manners, laws, and institutions whereby earthly peace is secured and maintained, but recognising that, however various these are, they all tend to one and the same end of earthly peace. It therefore is so far from rescinding and abolishing these diversities, that it even preserves and adapts them, so long only as no hindrance to the worship of the one supreme and true God is thus introduced.[31]

Conclusion

For over thirty years now the Church Growth Movement, which I represent, has advocated, among many other things, what is termed the homogeneous unit principle. This is rooted in the observation of its founder, Donald A. McGavran, that "men like to become Christians without crossing racial, linguistic, or class barriers."[32] Far from being a racist statement, as some have construed it, this principle is aimed at liberating cultural groups to serve God in ways appropriate to their own frames of reference. It will readily be seen that what has been discussed concerning contextualization assumes the validity of the homogeneous unit principle.

Ethnic theologians, both in America and in the Third World, are recognizing that what has passed as "Christian" theology for centuries is only one particular form of contextualized Western or, more accurately, North Atlantic theology. These theologians are making a sincere attempt to liberate themselves from traditional theological molds and to contextualize theology anew in their cultures. They realize that when a theology is uncritically extracted from one culture and imposed upon another it will invariably lose some authenticity and, to that degree, become less Christian.

To preserve its integrity, theology must be the product of a Christian community. Valid contextualized theologies will emerge from communities that accept their cultural identity and integrity. This kind of a community—one that has all the potential for creating the positive cultural environment for an "ethnotheology"—is what is meant by a homogeneous unit church.

Pressures on Christians of different cultural groups to assimilate into and conform to Anglo-American Christian communities in the United States tend to stifle the creativity within those different groups to develop their own culturally relevant theological expressions. If Christian people are denied their natural right and inclination to form their primary fellowship groups with other Christians who share the same world-view, creative contextualization of theology will not be possible.

Unfortunately, homogeneous unit churches that would encourage theological pluralism are still seen as a threat by many who argue that what we need is not an African theology or an Asian-American theology or an American Indian theology, but a biblical theology. I hope that this chapter has shown that such a view is precisely opposite to the theme of ethnic theologians of liberation who reason that it is necessary for Christians of all groups to enjoy the freedom in the Holy Spirit to apply the Bible to their own problems within their own frame of reference and without pressures from the outside to work on someone else's theological and ethical agenda. I believe that if this approach were taken seriously, we would see more effective churches, more illuminating theology, and more harmony and mutual understanding among Christian communities of differing cultural identities in American society.

NOTES

For further reference, the material in this chapter can be found in greatly expanded form in my *Our Kind of People*, which was in print under the John Knox Press label, 1979–1985. See also my "A Vision for Evangelizing the Real America," *International Bulletin of Missionary Research* (April 1986), 59–64.

[1] Andrew M. Greeley, "Letters from Readers," *Commentary* 54 (October 1972), 20.

[2] Cf. Joseph R. Washington, Jr., *Black Religion: The Negro and Christianity in the United States* (Boston: Beacon Press, 1964), 289, and idem, *Black and White Power Subreption* (Boston: Beacon Press, 1969), 8.

[3] See Jose Miguez Bonino, *Doing Theology in a Revolutionary Situation* (Philadelphia: Fortress, 1975).

[4] James H. Cone, *Black Theology and Black Power* (New York: Seabury Press, 1973); Vine Deloria, Jr., *God is Red* (New York: Grosset and Dunlap, 1973); Roy I. Sano, "Ethnic Liberation Theology: Neo-Orthodoxy Reshaped—or Replaced?" *Christianity and Crisis* (10 November, 1975):258-64; Andrew M. Greeley, "Notes on a Theology of Pluralism," *Christian Century* (3 July 1974):696-700; Donald G. Shockley, *Free, White, and Christian* (Nashville: Abingdon, 1975); Benjamin A. Reist, *Theology in Red, White, and Black* (Philadelphia: Westminster, 1975).

[5] Reist, *Theology*, 23.

[6] Ibid.

[7] Ibid., 26-27.

[8] Hunter Keen, "Must Indians Love the Organ?" *Eternity* (October 1975), 74.

[9] Sano, "Ethnic Liberation Theology," 259.

[10] Ibid., 261.

[11] James H. Cone, *God of the Oppressed* (New York: Seabury Press, A Crossroad Book, 1975), 8.

[12] Cone, *God of the Oppressed*, 201.

[13] Sano, "Ethnic Liberation Theology," 262.

[14] Reuben A. Sheares II, "Beyond White Theology," *Christianity and Crisis* (2 and 16 November 1970):233.

[15] Ernst Troeltsch, *The Social Teaching of the Christian Churches*, tr. Olive Wyon (New York: Macmillan, 1931).

[16] Charles H. Kraft, "Dynamic Equivalence Churches," *Missiology: An International Review* (1 January 1973):43.

[17] Ibid., 48.

[18] Ibid., 51.

[19] Ibid., 53-54.

[20] Ibid., 54.

[21] Cone, *God of the Oppressed*, 208.

[22] Ibid., 209.

[23] Vine Deloria, Jr., *Custer Died for Your Sins: An Indian Manifesto* (New York: Macmillan, Avon Books, 1969), 105-06.

[24] Ibid., 111.

[25] Reist, *Theology*, 164.

[26] United Presbyterian Church in the U.S.A., *The Book of Confessions* (Philadelphia: General Assembly of the United Presbyterian Church in the U.S.A., 1966, 1967), Sec. 9.06.

[27] John R. Fry, *The Trivialization of the United Presbyterian Church* (New York: Harper and Row, 1975), 10.

[28] United Presbyterian Church, *Book of Confessions*, Sec. 9.44.

[29] Edward A. Dowey, Jr., *A Commentary on the Confession of 1967 and an Introduction to "The Book of Confessions"* (Philadelphia: Westminster, 1968), 129.

[30] John V. Taylor, "Cultural Ecumenism," *Church Missionary Society Newsletter* (November 1974):3.

[31] Saint Augustine, *The City of God* (New York: Modern Library, 1950), 696.

[32] Donald A. McGavran, *Understanding Church Growth*, rev. ed. (Grand Rapids: Eerdmans, 1980), 223.

12

Contextual Considerations in Responding to Nominality
Eddie Gibbs

AS "NOMINALITY" IS A BROADLY DEFINED TERM—the specifics depending on the context in which it is being used—we must begin this chapter by offering a definition of nominality as it relates to the Christian commitment of individuals and communities. To avoid confusion, it is better to speak of "nominality" rather than "nominalism," for the latter properly refers to a philosophical position that arose in the eleventh to the fourteenth century in opposition to Platonism.[1] Nominality, on the other hand, refers to *the extent of deviation between the identity claimed by persons and their actual commitment to that identity.* Etymologically, it signifies "existing or being something in name or form only"—that is, making claims which lack substance.

TOWARD A DEFINITION OF NOMINAL CHRISTIANITY

People who claim to be Christian but do not attend church are popularly referred to as "nominal Christians." However, this

EDDIE GIBBS, B.D., D.Min., associate professor of evangelism and church renewal at Fuller Theological Seminary, served with the South American Missionary Society in Chile and with the British and Foreign Bible Society in England. The national training director for the Billy Graham Association in its Mission England, he is author of *I Believe in Church Growth* and *Followed or Pushed?*

perception of nominality is as simplistic as it is unsatisfactory, for a commitment to a Christian lifestyle embraces other activities besides churchgoing. Yet, the popular definition prevails because it is the most easily quantifiable, and places the regular churchgoer outside of the problem!

Furthermore, a more comprehensive definition of "nominal Christian" cannot be attempted without first securing agreement as to what being a "normative Christian" entails. Confronted as we are with the wide range of theological positions, ecclesiastical disciplines, and models of piety, it soon becomes evident that "nominality" will be variously described depending on the Christian tradition by which it is judged. For the purpose of this chapter, I will be describing nominality in terms of a broad-based evangelical Christianity, which represents the position of the author as well as that of the intended readership. Clearly, some aspects will be relevant beyond that tradition, while other traditions will have their own distinctives.

The clearest, most comprehensive definition and description of nominality within the evangelical tradition has been formulated by the Lausanne Movement in its Thailand Report, *Christian Witness to Nominal Christians among Protestant Christians*. That report defines a nominal Protestant Christian in the following terms:

> A nominal Protestant Christian is one who, within the Protestant tradition, would call himself a Christian, or be so regarded by others, but who has no authentic commitment to Christ based on personal faith. Such commitment involves a transforming personal relationship with Christ, characterized by such qualities as love, joy, peace, a desire to study the Bible, prayer, fellowship with other Christians, a determination to witness faithfully, a deep concern for God's will to be done on earth, and a living hope of heaven to come.[2]

This definition has merit in that it recognizes that nominality relates to a number of dimensions rather than being viewed in terms of neglect of churchgoing. The emphasis is not placed on the individual or community's relationship to the institutional church, but on whether or not there is a prior commitment to Jesus Christ. The cumulative evidence of such a commitment embraces character traits, as well as incorporation into a body of fellow believers in a range of activities that express their commitment to Christ, and a shared, assured hope regarding a future to be consummated in Christ.

Various attempts have been made by sociologists of religion to define the core elements of religiosity. The most famous of these attempts is that of C. Y. Glock and C. R. Stark, who identified five core elements.[3] The first of these is the *knowledge dimension*, that people possess some minimum information about the basic tenets of their faith and its rites, Scriptures, and traditions. The second is the *belief dimension*, which relates to theological outlook and the acknowledgment of the truth of the tenets of the religion. The third is their *religious practice*, which relates to their acts of worship and devotion, corporate rituals, and solitary prayer. The fourth is the *experience dimension*, which refers to their expectations which achieve a direct, subjective knowledge of ultimate reality. And the fifth is the *consequence dimension*, how people's religious belief, practice, experience, and knowledge affect their day-to-day lives. This description of the elements of religiosity has been criticized for its usefulness both as a sociological measuring tool and its conceptual validity.[4] But for the purposes of this chapter, these elements provide avenues along which nominality can be explored.

From the above it is evident that nominality is a problem that lurks within the ranks of the faithful churchgoers as well as those who no longer occupy a church pew. Indeed, to be strong in one area of religiosity does not guarantee that a person will be strong in the other areas. Inconsistency may be evident in any one of a number of points.

THE EXTENT OF THE NOMINALITY PROBLEM

If nominality is difficult to define, it is even more difficult to quantify. When it is measured exclusively in terms of churchgoing, it is evident that the problem is endemic throughout the Western world. In Scandinavia and the Protestant regions of West Germany, over 95 percent of the population are baptized in the Lutheran Church, between 60 and 85 percent are later confirmed, but church attendance has slumped to between 3 to 5 percent of the population.[5] Sören Kierkegaard once remarked of the people of his own country of Denmark, "We are all Christians without having as much as a suspicion what Christianity is!"

The situation is little better in the United Kingdom. Church attendances per Sunday account for 9 to 11 percent of the population. It is impossible to give a meaningful overall statistic of church membership because membership is variously defined in the three main traditions which make up the churchgoing population. For Roman Catholics, every baptized person is a member, while Anglicans generally speak in terms of electoral role figures which represent those who have taken the trouble to have their names included. The Free Churches define membership in more restricted terms.

According to data collected by Peter Brierley of MARC Europe,

17 percent of the population are "active members" (8 percent are in church on a given week, with the other 9 percent absent). A further 3 percent who are in church are not yet members. A further 47 percent want to be identified as Christians but do not attend church. Twenty-six percent of the population are either atheist or agnostic and the remaining 7 percent belong to other religions or cults.[6] Projecting present trends forward to the year 2015, he observes that far fewer people will claim church membership (although they are nonattending) or identify themselves as Christian.

A similar story is evident in Australia and New Zealand. According to the 1981 Australian Census, 76.4 percent of the population claimed to be Christian[7] as against a percentage of 88.2 in 1966, while church attendance has dropped from 44 percent in 1950 to an all-time low of 24 percent in 1983-4.[8] When the percentage of affiliates is compared with the monthly attenders of the two largest denominations, the growing nominality problem becomes evident. Twenty-six percent of the population identify themselves as Anglican, but only 4 percent are monthly attenders, and while 13 percent are Uniting Church members, only 3 percent are monthly attenders.[9] Church attendance in New Zealand is around 9 percent as against 73 percent who describe themselves as Christian.[10]

In the United States, the religious situation seems to be more stable in terms of overall church membership and attendance figures. At the present time, 68 percent of the population claim church membership, with a high of 76 percent in 1947. And 40 percent of the population claim to have attended church during the previous seven days. This last figure represents a decline from a high of 49 percent in 1955 and 1958.[11] The significant shift has been a migration of members of the mainline denominations to the more theologically conservative, charismatic, and independent churches, which trend began in the mid-1960s and continues to the present time.

In the foregoing we have concentrated on nominality in terms of commitment to churchgoing by Western Christians. While nominality is endemic in Western Europe it is also a growing problem in other areas of the world. Dr. Ralph Winter, of the U.S. Center for World Mission, estimates that the proportion of nominals to active Christians is 6.4 to 1 in Western Europe, Latin America, Australia, and New Zealand; for the U.S.A. and Canada it is 2.1 to 1; while in Africa it is 2.8 to 1.[12]

Our concern at this stage is to describe nominality more comprehensively and then to investigate the causes, with special reference to the contextual factors and with some suggestions as to ways in which churches might begin to address the issues. In this discussion we will confine ourselves to nominality as it affects the Protestant churches in the Western world where nominality is a more chronic condition. Their experience provides warnings to churches in the Two-Thirds World which may be in danger of losing their spiritual vitality as they move from being composed of predominantly first-generation, to second- and third-generation Christians.

Nominality Described

The Lausanne study paper previously cited describes five types of nominal Christian:

1. One who attends regularly and worships devoutly, but who has no personal relationship with Jesus Christ.
2. One who attends regularly, but for cultural reasons only.
3. One who attends church only for major church festivals (Christmas, Easter, etc.) and ceremonies (weddings, baptisms, funerals).
4. One who hardly ever attends church but maintains a church relationship for reasons of security, emotional or family ties, or tradition.
5. One who has no relationship to any specific church and who never attends but yet considers himself a believer in God in a traditional Christian sense.[13]

According to this description, the decisive factor which lifts a person out of the category of "nominal" is a personal relationship to Christ. Happily, the criteria is not simply that one has at some time in the past turned to Christ to receive him as Savior and Lord, but one who is abiding in an existential relationship on the basis of continuing faith and obedience.

Factors Contributing to Nominality

If the task of defining nominality is fraught with difficulties, the investigation of the contributing causes is equally complex. At a national symposium in 1978 on Church Growth and Decline: Implications for Evangelism, sponsored by the Hartford Seminary Foundation, a framework was suggested by which influences affecting church attendance could be classified.

The first distinction is between contextual factors and institutional factors. Contextual factors are external to the church. They are in the community, the society, and the culture in which a church exists. A church has little control over them. Institutional factors are internal to the church and are aspects of its life and functioning over which it has some control. The second distinction is between national and

local factors. National factors are those affecting all churches regardless of the local setting, while local factors are those specific to a given
locale.[14]

These different categories provide four segments: the national
and local contextual factors, and the national and local institutional
factors. Since the focus of this chapter is on contextualization, we
will mainly be concerned with the contextual factors that contribute
to the nominality problem. However, the institutional aspects cannot be ignored entirely, because the boundary between institutional
and contextual is a porous one. The one influences the other: Renewal in the church can bring about a revival of religion in society,
and secularization in society can permeate the church in terms of
both its belief and behavior. In the course of this chapter we will
first examine some of the ways contextual factors have contributed
toward nominality. Then we will focus attention on ways the church
might make a more significant impact on society by establishing its
credibility in terms of a consistent lifestyle, and by addressing more
clearly those issues which have emaciated the life of the church as
well as driven society at large on a different course.

While the church succeeded in exerting a profound impact
on Western societies until the early eighteenth century, since the
Enlightenment society has had the most widespread and lasting impact upon the church. After analyzing patterns of churchgoing in
the British Isles since 1700, Robert Currie, Alan Gilbert, and Lee
Horsley conclude that "whatever efforts are expended by a church,
increased recruitment cannot be obtained in unfavourable exoge-
nous (i.e., contextual) conditions."[15] The power of contextual factors
is further emphasized by the authors in the following observation.

> There are two further indications of the primacy of exogenous factors
> in causing membership growth to assume a cyclical pattern. Almost all
> available evidence suggests that this pattern tends to be common to
> all churches, a phenomenon difficult to explain except on the hypoth-
> esis that the activation phase of each cycle is often synchronized in
> different churches by exogenous factors operating upon every church.
> Moreover, since 1900 exogenous events have had a very obvious effect
> upon the increase and decrease of church membership: above all, both
> world wars have coincided with severe falls in membership which
> were at least partly made up at the end of the war period, an associa-
> tion in which it is difficult not to see a casual connection.[16]

Nominality represents a process of disengagement from the institutional church accompanied by an erosion of belief. First, the regular
worship-attenders become occasional in attendance and marginal to

church life. They then become lapsed or dormant, only returning to church at major festivals such as Easter or family events—baptisms, weddings, and funerals. The next generation is nominal in the sense of continuing to identify with a local church or denomination despite the fact that they seldom, if ever, attend, while subsequent generations become increasingly notional, defining themselves still as Christian, but without necessarily identifying with any specific church or denomination.

In some parts of the West, as in Scandinavia, the association of church and culture is so close that the people, almost entirely, still identify with the church and avail themselves of its occasional ministries. This is true even though many have abandoned some of the basic tenets of the Christian faith and uphold an ethical agenda shaped by secular humanism rather than Christian values.

Churches, in the way they incorporate members, are of two types: There are Christian communities into which one is born (*gemeineschaft*) and there are those one chooses to join (*gesellschaft*). Clearly, the Lutheran model in Europe is of the former. But the same social dynamic is at work in some parts of the U.S.A., where the population is still fairly homogeneous in small-town communities. If young people are brought up in a Lutheran community in the Midwest or a Southern Baptist or Methodist community in the South, many will join the church and be faithful torchbearers of the tradition—that is, until they move into a new and different environment, which causes them to loosen their former associations and question their world-views. The membership losses sustained by this mobility and resultant pluralism is particularly injurious to the mainline denominations in the U.S.A. which have been established through colonization rather than conversion. Such churches tend to have a more static mindset, which says that our doors are open for people to come to us rather than our going out to find the lost sheep.

Another aspect of the contextualization problem is the fact that mainline Protestantism has largely been shaped by a small-town mentality, which is reflected in its parochial mindset. Churches that think "neighborhood" rather than "city" have a fixation on "roosting areas"—where people sleep at night—and mistakenly imagine that the neighborhood represents community. Consequently, the sociological fragmentation of the neighborhood and population turnover mean that the neighborhood can no longer survive in the city. Their only recourse is to sell out and follow their clientele into suburbia.

Religious sociologists have offered a variety of explanations as to why church attendance on the West Coast is lower than in the remainder of the United States. Gallup Poll surveys indicate that it is not because people are less religious in California, Oregon, and Washington. The explanation must lie elsewhere.

The most likely reason is that the West Coast is without a long Caucasian history, and the majority of the population consists of recent arrivals or pilgrims passing through. Its transient nature is further emphasized now that the region has become one side of the Pacific rim, as Asia assumes the role of world economic leader. Those churches are making an impact which have abandoned the parochial mindset and reliance on a denominational label, to draw a following, replacing them with a clearly articulated philosophy of ministry that reflects the needs and aspirations of the culture. These factors help explain why the region of the U.S.A. with the smallest percentage of church attendance also has many of the country's largest and fastest-growing congregations. These churches are growing at the expense of the tradition-bound mainline churches, both Protestant and Catholic. Young families moving into new areas are looking for churches that have a range of ministries to meet the varied needs of different members of the family, irrespective of the "brand label."

There are grave dangers, however, in identifying too closely with culture. As has been shown by other contributors to this symposium, the gospel cannot be submerged beneath culture. The gospel acts redemptively on all cultures, affirming some aspects while passing judgment on other elements. When contextualization goes to the extent of complete identification, it becomes enculturation. The plea of the contributors of this volume is for "critical contextualization." This principle is as appropriate to the nominality issue of a post-Christian society, as it is to the pioneering phase in evangelizing a pre-Christian society.

The Impact of Urbanization

The impact of urbanization on the church has taken a different course in the U.S.A. than in Europe. In the former, the industrial revolution took the church, unprepared for the massive shift of population, from the rural to the burgeoning urban centers which sprang into being in the later part of the eighteenth and nineteenth centuries. In Europe it was not a case of the churches losing the urban proletariat; they never had them to lose in the first place. In England, from the time of the Reformation to the end of the seventeenth century, it was a punishable offense to be absent from worship, which no doubt helped to swell the number of churchgoers. But this law was unenforceable in the cities, where large numbers of people were pouring in from all parts of the country. Not only was the Established Church unable to apply sanctions, it failed to provide churches for the swelling numbers of migrants to the cities. John Gay concludes that "in the areas where population and industry were growing most rapidly the Anglican Church had failed to expand its parochial system and hence failed to gain the allegiance of the people."[17]

The one and only national census to include church attendance was conducted in 1851 which revealed that 39 percent of the population were in church on census Sunday. Most of the absent millions were to be found in the towns. Horace Mann, the government appointee to compile the census, drew up a separate table for the seventy-three large towns in England and Wales which had populations of over ten thousand. Taking these towns collectively it was discovered that only about 25 percent were in church on the Sunday in question.[18]

E. R. Wickham, in his significant study, *Church and People in an Industrial City*, observes that the urban areas became "missionary territory" in which the preliminary work of Christianization and even religious socialization had to start virtually from the beginning.[19] The response of the Church of England, as with the Free Churches, was a case of too little too late. Currie et al. provide an example from one northern industrial town:

> The parish of Sheffield, for example, served 2,000 people in 1615 and 10,000 in 1736. By 1851, when Sheffield had grown to be a town of 135,000 persons, it contained sixteen churches and chapels of the Church of England and forty-three buildings belonging to other bodies, which provided in all 43,000 seats, or one for every three citizens.[20]

Other northern towns, such as Blackburn, Bolton, Bradford, Halifax, Huddersfield, and Oldham, which grew from an average population of 12,000 inhabitants in 1801 to 109,000 in 1881, experienced a rapid decline in church-membership density.[21]

Unfortunately, there is no more recent evidence available of a comprehensive nature. Estimates offered by those working in inner-city areas today put the percentage in church at around 2 percent, which may rise to 14 percent in the suburbs and small towns. Rural depopulation has made it difficult to assess churchgoing, especially as many rural churches have been closed or services reduced from weekly to monthly.

In Australia, where more reliable and extensive data are available from census questionnaires, it is evident that Protestant churches are stronger in stable dormitory suburbs where people are of higher socio-economic status. Attendance rates are much lower in the more diverse, multicultural, or blue-collar communities. Utilizing a multiple regression analysis on the survey data, it has been shown that where a person lives can have an impact on levels of church attendance over and above individual characteristics.[22]

In the United States the urbanization factor does not seem to be so significant. Reviewing the findings of several studies in the 1970s, Dean Hoge and David Roozen conclude that the bulk of the research has found no relationships at all.[23]

Among the 215 metropolitan areas defined by the U.S. census, Pittsburgh, with a church membership of 71.1 percent, occupies 24th position, Chicago 67.9 percent (32nd), Milwaukee 65.6 percent (40th), Philadelphia 62.3 percent (54th), New York 61 percent (67th). Of the bottom twenty-five cities for percentage of church members all but four are in the far West; the lowest places are occupied by Los Angeles/Long Beach 34.3 percent, Seattle 28.8 percent, and Eugene-Springfield, Oregon, 26.2 percent.[24] Unfortunately, the only data available is for church membership rather than for church attendance, which would have provided a more precise measure.

The difference between Europe and the United States in regard to the impact of urbanization on church affiliation may be due to a number of causes. Urbanization has come more recently to the United States, and with less social disruption, due to the fact that many immigrants to the United States came as a group and established themselves within a transplanted social network rather than arriving as isolated individuals to make their way in an alien world.

Second, there was no state church monopoly to cause social intimidation, so people took the initiative to establish new churches after the patterns of their homelands. The period of population migrations westward coincided with the Second Great Awakening, which occurred in the early 1800s. Martin Marty writes that "the evangelizers started a Soul Rush that soon outpaced the Gold Rush. This Second Great Awakening churched the West. Here was a textbook example of free enterprise in the marketplace of religion, a competition in which the fittest survived."[25] The Methodist and Baptist circuit riders were in fierce competition for the souls of the new townships. In order to reach them they developed the "campmeeting," where thousands gathered in prolonged outdoor gatherings.

Such revivalism found a fresh impetus after the Civil War with the citywide campaigns of Chicago-based Moody and Sankey. Moody's appeal was primarily to the urban middle class. "He apparently drew chiefly the previously converted or the half-converted, displaced church people who reaffirmed their faith when he reclaimed them and sent them back to supportive churches."[26]

Third, the strength of the black churches in the inner city has no counterpart in Europe or Australasia. True, in England the black churches represent the fastest-growing segment of the Christian church, but the percentage of blacks in the population of the United Kingdom is much less than in the United States.[27]

The changing urban context in the United States means that the churches will have to continue to think through their urban policies. Presently the movement out into the suburbs continues, but there is also a move back into the city-center districts with the "gentrification" of rundown areas plus development projects to build townhouses and apartment complexes. If this inflow of population assumes significant proportions, a new problem will have to be faced, that of reestablishing churches in areas where only ethnic churches presently exist and where land for construction is prohibitively high.

The Challenge of Urbanization

How are the churches to face the challenge of urbanization if they are to win back their nominal adherents? This is a huge topic, and within the space of this chapter we can only suggest a few pointers.

1. *Protestant churches must shed their parochial mindset derived from their small-town origins and begin to think in terms of the city as a whole.* City dwellers do not necessarily regard their residential neighborhood as the primary locus of their social identity. The old style of community has broken down, to be replaced by "lifestyle enclaves." Robert Bellah helpfully distinguishes between "community" and "lifestyle enclave."

> Whereas a community attempts to be an inclusive whole, celebrating the interdependence of public and private life and of the different callings of all, lifestyle is fundamentally segmental and celebrates the narcissism of similarity. It usually explicitly involves a contrast with others who "do not share one's lifestyle." For this reason, we speak not of lifestyle communities, though they are often called such in contemporary usage, but of lifestyle enclaves. Such enclaves are segmental in two senses. They involve only a segment of each individual, for they concern only private life, especially leisure and consumption. And they are segmental socially in that they include only those with a common lifestyle.[28]

A postindustrial city is very different from its preindustrial counterpart. In the former, work was largely based in the home, so that communities were established in various sections of the city dependent on a common trade. Thus, even in large cities, people lived for much of their time in face-to-face communities. Industrialization removed work from the home to the factory, which was often located in a different part of the city. So people began to travel, make wider networks of relationships, finding themselves living in different and unconnected worlds: the neighborhood where they lived, the place where they worked, and, eventually, the location of their leisure pursuits.

Many clergypersons continued to live close to their churches; the parochial *system* in Europe and the parochial *mindset* in America prevented the majority of ministers, especially in the traditional denominations, from adjusting to the social reality of the city. Those churches which have generated a vision for the city, throwing off parochial restraints, are the ones that have begun to make a significant impact.

2. *Churches will develop long-term urban strategies, ensuring that population movements and ethnic changes are being noted.* Each metroplex requires a center for research and ministerial training. Its task would be to train church leaders, ordained and lay, with courses tailor-made to fit the social reality, evangelistic opportunities, and ministry needs of the area. The curriculum would be developed in conjunction with the churches, and the usefulness of the courses evaluated by the churches which were encouraging their leaders to attend. The majority of the courses offered would be in the form of two-week intensives or night classes, so that the leaders could improve their schools without having to leave either their employment or leadership positions in the church. Classroom learning would go side-by-side with continuing ministry experience.

3. *A grass-roots ecumenism needs to be developed so that churches can pool their resources.* Many inner-city churches are small and over-stretched. Small churches have to recognize that they cannot meet every need, so each must identify its particular strengths and build on its God-given resources. They must be content to do a few things well, rather than attempt to do everything.

No one church can minister to everyone, so those persons who come with problems that require specialized ministry and an appropriate support group may need to be introduced to another church which has the resources to respond. Furthermore, urban churches need to band together to make a combined approach to city groups to voice matters of concern or to offer resources to tackle a particular issue, such as the plight of latch-key children, homelessness, gang violence, ethnic-minority concerns.

4. *Local church renewal needs to be combined with church-planting projects, in order to reach out to the new people moving into urban areas.* These new residents are most receptive during the first six months. They need, therefore, to be identified promptly, befriended by Christian groups, and welcomed and incorporated into churches which are flexible enough to involve people who do not belong to their ecclesiastical tradition and may not remain in the neighborhood for more than a few years.

These suggestions are in line with some of the needs identified by pastors questioned by urban missiologist Ray Bakke. Whether they were laboring in Copenhagen in the First World, or Cairo and Mexico City in the Two-Thirds World, or, as in the example below, from Belgrade in the Second World, they mentioned such things as:

1. There is not enough organized prayer in a city of 1.4 million people.
2. We have too few properly trained leaders, both pastors and lay.
3. Most evangelicals lack vision, motivation, and a burden for the lost.
4. Churches and pastors have a rural mentality.
5. We fail to use the opportunities for witness that we are given.
6. The Christian community lives as though it is in a ghetto, and Christians lose their non-Christian friends.
7. The churches do not cooperate.
8. Christians live busy lives and have many church meetings.
9. There is a generation gap between the existing leaders who are mostly over 55, and the emerging leaders who are under 30. There are few leaders in the churches between 30 and 45.
10. We lack suitable buildings and facilities.[29]

The Influence of Secularization

While urbanization contributed to the social climate which helped foster nominality, secularization provided the cultural context. Os Guinness helpfully distinguishes *secularization*, the process, from *secularism*, the philosophy which undergirds that process.[30] While the philosophy has a limited following, the process exerts an all-embracing influence. Secularization has shaped a world-view, which people have not consciously chosen but which permeates their thinking in every area of life. Secularism, the philosophy, is built on empiricism and positivism, maintaining that the only real world is the world experienced through the five senses. It is also a by-product of the Enlightenment, which beginning 250 years ago has paralleled the rapid urbanization associated with the Industrial Revolution. The latter provided the social context in which people were free to develop revolutionary lines of thinking without the restraining peer pressure of small face-to-face communities. The Enlightenment represented a shift from viewing the world and creation in terms of purpose to the search to explain all things in terms of the operation of natural laws of cause and effect. The belief that one does not have to look outside of anything to explain the causes that produced it obviously has a profound bearing on the nature of religious belief.[31]

Many Christians, living their daily lives in a secular context, found that they were living in two antithetical conceptual worlds, the one being the world experienced by the five senses, and the other, a more ethereal world of faith.[32] This philosophical bifurcation was reinforced by a social marginalizing of the church, for the process of secularization removed the "sacred canopy" which unified the pre-Enlightenment world-view by progressively marginalizing Christian influence, both in terms of religious values and institutions.

The secularization process has produced two separate spheres: the one consisting of the public sphere and the other regarded as the private sphere. The former embraces the world of big business, politics, education, military, mass media, etc., while the latter is the world of the family, personal preferences, and leisure pursuits. Religion has become increasingly identified with the private world, and its influence either excluded completely from the principal power centers of the public sphere, or only allowed in to further the purposes of the public sphere. In the European context religion appears in the public sphere in terms of ceremonial religion, whereas in the U.S.A. it takes the form of a deistic, civil religion. Os Guiness observes that in "the central sectors of modern society: the worlds of science, technology, bureaucracy, most business, most politics, most education and so on—the 'real world' as it is referred—here is where you will find faith most irreverent and secularization closest to being universal and uniform, even though thousands of religious people may service these areas."[33]

Such a context provides an ideal breeding ground for nominality. People in the public sphere find that they have to leave those beliefs in abeyance while, at the same time, they accept non-Christian philosophical positions and anti-Christian ethical values. It is those individuals who live their lives outside of these spheres of power, who are best able to integrate their world-views. Evidence to support this view is suggested by the fact that women have outnumbered men by about three to two in most churches in the West. This female overrepresentation may not have occurred because females are inherently more religious, but because their world, until recent times, centered on the home and family; they were, consequently, protected from many of the hard choices facing their spouses. But since women have figured much more prominently in the work force in the period since the Second World War, studies suggest that women in the business world are just as likely as their male counterparts to be absent from church.[34]

In discussing the influence of secularization in society, its impact can be both underestimated and exaggerated. It is underestimated because the boundary between the public and private spheres is porous. The fact that many Christians are operating in the public sphere assures that salt and light are having some influence, providing preservation from some consequences of thoroughgoing secularism and injecting values that arise out of the Judeo-Christian ethic. Yet, the source is often ignored. However, when this influence is withdrawn because believers feel compromised or unable to take the heat, or is excluded by the power structure because someone fears the operation will be jeopardized, then ethical restraints are lost, with dire consequences for conduct in public life.[35] The problem arises from the fact that values and ethics have traditionally been rooted in religion.

The overestimation of the impact of secularization arises from the fact that secularists persistently underplay the strength of religion in the private sphere. A decline in church attendance may be due as much to the decline in influence of the church in the public sphere as to an erosion of people's faith. Such is evident when one contrasts attitudes toward church attendance in Europe and in the United States. In the former, church attendance brings little or no social benefits, whereas in parts of the U.S. church attendance may still bring economic and social advantages. Reduced church attendance should not immediately be taken as evidence that people are becoming less religious. Religious surveys consistently point to the continuing strength of personal religion in the private sphere. The majority of people still believe in the existence of God, that Jesus was a "special person," and the reality of the afterlife; and they also pray on a fairly regular basis. Outside of Christianity, there is further evidence for a continuing and widespread search for the transcendent, as demonstrated by the popularity of Eastern religions, the occult, and the rapid spread of New Age ideas. This religious quest survives despite predictions to the contrary in those countries where atheism is actively promoted in education and reinforced by social and economic sanctions against those who persist in their religious beliefs.

In the United States, the approach is one of avoidance, in the interest of affirming a religious pluralism that is both unavoidable and valued in such an ethnically diverse population. Joanmarie Kalter, writing in the *TV Guide* (November 16, 1985), highlights this conspiracy of silence in commenting on the reporting, or rather nonreporting, of religious news on the major network channels.

> It sometimes seems that the networks' evening news broadcasts take religion as seriously as they take old Saint Nick. Clergy, scholars and even newspeople agree it is one of the media's most neglected subjects. No wonder Americans are so unaware of the religious depth of their fellow citizens, as studies show. A TV viewer would be hard put to know that more than 90 percent of Americans say they believe in God; that three-quarters pray at least once a day; that about 41 percent attend religious services weekly. A Gallup poll found the United States to be more religious than any other industrialized country in the world. In fact, more Americans go to church or a synagogue on any given weekend than attend professional sports events all year— yet not a single network has a full-time religious reporter. Executive producer of the CBS Evening News with Dan Rather, says, "Religion has been ignored. But an awful lot of people care about it. An awful lot. And it affects the way they think and feel about other issues we take for granted are important."

In the educational arena, Europe has taken a different route than the United States. In those countries of Europe where it is required by law to teach religion in schools, the contradiction between religious and secular values lies within the school curriculum.

In Britain, Clifford Longley, the religious correspondent for the *London Times* observes that the confusion over the place of religious education is "the reflection of a religiously confused society, which does not know what it wants its children to believe, and is, therefore, prepared to settle for the kind of RE [Religious Education] which ducks that very question." The kind of religious education to which he refers is the comparative-religion approach which is indifferent to the truth or untruth of the claims of any religion. He expresses the disadvantage and dilemma faced by any Christian teachers of religious education in the state school system who, unlike their colleagues in mathematics, physics, or geography, cannot teach Christianity as true:

> An RE teacher in a secular school in the state sector cannot call upon the ordinary authority of his status in the classroom in order to teach Christianity as true. For he has no mandate. Neither society in general, nor parents, in particular, would back him up. Or if they would, they have not yet said so.[36]

Religion in the United States, however, is excluded from the classroom even to the extent of the outlawing of periods of silent prayer. The elimination of religion from the curriculum according to the American system does not entirely solve the problem, because religious consideration and values impinge on the total curriculum. It has been argued that the exclusion of religion has, in fact, meant that secular humanism has been given a monopolistic position as the philosophy undergirding so much of public education.

Despite the public sphere's invasion of the private sphere through education and the mass media, religion retains its strength in the context of the private lives of individuals and families in crisis situations. Peter Berger, who has been a principal exponent of secularization since his influential book *The Sacred Canopy* appeared in 1969, has, himself, come to doubt his thoroughgoing secularization model. He realized that he may have overstated its power and irreversibility in view of the religious revival in the United States which represents a counter-secularization process, as, indeed, does the growing influence of the New Age Movement.[37] The same affirmative position is taken by Andrew M. Greeley in his book *The Persistence of Religion*, published in 1973, where he argues that the functions of religion persists because the *gemeinschaft* infrastructure of society also persists.

Although a persistent core of religious belief remains, it is evident that the specifically Christian content of that core has been seriously eroded over the years. The fabric of the "sacred canopy" has developed some large holes and the social significance of religious thinking, practice, and institutions has been significantly down graded.[38] Although 80 to 90 percent of the population claim that they believe in God, the nature of the God in whom they believe may have undergone a significant change from a traditional Trinitarian belief to that of a cosmic "life force"; which shift explains the receptive ground for New Age thinking.

The church may be able to thrive institutionally, for a time at least, by inculcating the values of the society in which it is set. But, as Dean Inge perceptively commented, "If you marry the spirit of the age you are likely to soon find yourself widowed." Liberalism did this in terms of its philosophic framework, and significant sections of evangelicalism have done the same thing in terms of embracing the materialistic values of this age. With regard to the latter, a nationwide economic downturn could precipitate a cooling of religious commitment on the part of evangelicals who have bought into the prosperity message.

In responding to secularization, the church must seek to work out the implications of a Christian lifestyle in a secular society. It cannot continue to address the world around it in the same terms it used in previous centuries. The wandering sheep of rebellion and nominality are rapidly being replaced by the goats of secular human- ism. The old methods of restoring the lapsed are becoming less and less effective. Wandering sheep can be invited back into the fold with comparative ease, because they still remember what life was like in the sheepfold; they know the language of the flock and recall the voice of the Shepherd. None of those assumptions holds truth for a large segment of the baby boomers (those people born between 1945 and 1965).

We need Christian spokespersons in the local church who will challenge our generation as effectively as the early Christian apolo- gists addressed the Roman world. Some present-day philosophers be- lieve that we are now witnessing the end of the Age of Enlightenment with the crumbling of the Newtonian world-view. We now under- stand the world to be far less tidy and predictable than Newton envis- aged. Modern math and physics is endeavoring to come to terms with indeterminacy and to see patterns within chaos.[39]

Lesslie Newbigin suggests that instead of looking at Christianity from the point of view of this scientific world, we look at the scien- tific world from the point of view of Christian revelation.[40] The same can be said for the political, and the business world. There needs to be a counter-offensive, not of Christian institutional power blocs in the form of universities, religious radio and TV stations, and Christian political parties, but rather groups of Christians in these spheres of influence who are thinking through the implications of Christian faith in terms of their academic disciplines, media mes- sages, and business practices. If we are rapidly drawing to the close of the Enlightenment era, we need to be alert to the kinds of influ- ences which are competing to replace that world-view which has dominated the scene for the past 250 years.

THE CHALLENGE OF PLURALISM

Religious pluralism constitutes a relatively recent challenge to the Protestant churches of the West. Since the Reformation, Protestantism has been preoccupied in defining itself either as against Roman Catholicism or in terms of the relationship between one section of Protestantism and another. Until the beginning of the modern missionary era in the nineteenth century, it existed in almost total isolation from the rest of the world, due to the sur- rounding wall of Islam to the East and South, and the vastness of the Atlantic Ocean to the West. Only in this century, and more especially since the Second World War, has there been extensive immigration into Europe and North America by people with faiths other than Christianity. The churches then began to discover that the mission field had come to their own doorstep. Experiencing people of other faiths firsthand brought mixed reactions. Those ethnocentric persons who felt threatened by the "invasion" retreated into social stereotypes, resulting in mounting racial prejudice. For others, who made the effort to break through the cultural barriers, there came a new appreciation of non-Westerners whose values challenged the materialism and selfish individualism of the West. "Heathen darkness" no longer seemed as dark as many missionaries had painted it.

Furthermore, as Asians and Africans experienced life in the "Christianized West" they came to realize that there were aspects of their own cultures which they wanted to affirm as superior to what they found in the host culture.

Many laypersons have a much wider exposure to people of other religions than do the pastors of the churches to which they belong. This is especially true of those in education, medicine, and the social services, and of managers in industries which employ immigrant laborers. How are people of different faiths to relate to each other, especially when each believes that he or she is a recipient of a divinely revealed religion and each has a duty to try to convert the other?

The cultural pressure toward the relativizing of religious beliefs has prepared the ground for a loss of nerve among Western Christians who have received no training in how to relate the gospel to other faiths. Ernst Troeltsch rejected Christianity's claim to absoluteness on the grounds that it was a historical religion and, therefore, relative. Historian Arnold Toynbee argued that the criteria for comparison of religions was not to be found in their dogmas and religious practices, but rather in the attitude or "spirit" of a religion. Sincerity and not truth became the all-important criteria. Christians are drawn toward nominality as they water down the distinctives of the Christian position, and compare the residual Christianity of the West (which they had previously regarded as normative) with, say, the religious commitment of Hindus or Moslems.

On the theological level, focus of attention shifts from a christocentric or trinitarian emphasis to a more general theistic approach. As a part of this refocusing, the seemingly exclusivist claims made by Christ himself—as being the Way, the Truth, and the Life, and the only Way to the Father—are relativized. They came to mean that while Christ fulfills this exclusive role for Christians, those of other faiths will have their own legitimate messiahs. Such is the position adopted by Protestant theologians John MacQuarrie and John Hick, and Roman Catholic missiologist Paul Knitter, who argues that:

> Jesus need not be proclaimed as the absolutely *final* prophet, or as the *only center* of history; and still he can be affirmed as a universally meaningful savior who gives both promise and power to work for an eschatological future, for a kingdom that will be the transformation of the world as we know it now.[41]

He refers to the doctrinal language of the New Testament as "survival language." "In talking about Jesus, the New Testament authors use the language not of analytic philosophies but of enthusiastic believers, not of scientists but of lovers," he claims. He explains away the Acts 4:12 that "there is no other name . . . by which we must be saved," as not intended to rule out the possibility of other saviors, but to proclaim that this Lord Jesus was still alive and that it was he, not they, who was working such wonders in the community." On this basis he argues that the text "is abused when used as a starting point for evaluating other religions."[42]

How is Christianity to be regarded in relation to other faiths? A number of responses have been argued.

One regards Christianity as the *fulfillment* of the unmet aspirations of other religions; another places Christianity in an *antithetical* position to all other religions, regarding them as either demonic distortions or the result of futile human efforts to establish a relationship with God or gods. Still others regard the relationship as one of *paradox*; God's grace is active throughout all humankind. Therefore, there are elements of genuine revelation in most if not all religions. But there is no parallel in other religions of the person and saving work of Jesus Christ.

If the nominality produced in a climate of religious pluralism is to be effectively challenged, Christian churches in the West must take seriously the need for their own renewal in order to more adequately represent the values of the gospel of redeeming and reconciling love. And more training must be given in seminary education to prepare pastors to minister in a multicultural and multifaith milieu. Western churches may need to call upon the insights of Christians from the Two-Thirds World, who have lived in confrontation and dialogue with people of other faiths, as a persecuted or barely tolerated minority. It may be that it will require Christian missionaries from the Two-Thirds World to bring about the revitalization of nominal Western Christians as they demonstrate the radical claims of the gospel and exemplify a loving and enthusiastic spirit.

Throughout this chapter, our principal emphasis has been on

nominality in the Western churches. This approach was deliberately taken because the great majority of those who now call themselves Christian are part of an unbroken Christian tradition that has existed for centuries. Clearly, the churches of the Two-Thirds World are exposed to the same nominality-producing factors of urbanization, secularization, and religious pluralism. The full impact has not yet been felt, however, because the majority of these churches still is comprised of first- or second-generation believers.

The problem suddenly arises with the emergence of the third generation, which has not experienced a radical conversion from the world, and is losing touch with the firsthand testimony of those who had such an experience. Israel experienced such a radical erosion of commitment after the conquest of the land. "Israel served the Lord throughout the lifetime of Joshua and of the elders who outlived him and who had experienced everything the Lord had done for Israel" (Jos. 24:31 NIV; see also Jgs. 2:7). . . . "After that whole generation had been gathered to their fathers, another generation grew up, who knew neither the Lord nor what he had done for Israel. Then the Israelites did evil in the eyes of the Lord . . ." (Jgs. 2:10, 11a NIV). The test of any movement is its ability to survive its third generation. This is the challenge facing the Soviet Union and the Eastern bloc countries at the present time, now that they are into their third generation after the revolution.

The Christian church has demonstrated throughout history its ability to survive in the face of overwhelming odds. The church has the advantage of possessing the Spirit of Christ while embracing a rich diversity of cultures, each making a distinct contribution to the body of Christ here on earth. Christians have the assurance provided by the declared intention of the Lord to build his church with a view to the gathering of countless multitudes around his throne from every nation, tribe, and language (Rv. 7:9ff).

NOTES

[1] *The Oxford Dictionary of the Christian Church*, ed. F. L. Cross (London: Oxford University Press, 1958) defines "nominalism" as "a theory of knowledge which denies reality to universal concepts," 978-79.

[2] Lausanne Occasional Papers No. 23 Thailand Report, *Christian Witness to Nominal Christians Among Protestant Christians*, (Wheaton, Ill.: Lausanne Committee for World Evangelization, 1980), 5.

[3] C. Y. Glock and C. R. Stark, *American Piety: The Nature of Religious Commitment* (Berkeley: University of California Press, 1968).

[4] See Robin Gill, *The Social Context of Theology* (London and Oxford: Mowbrays, 1975) and Roland Robertson, *The Social Interpretation of Religion* (London: Blackwell, 1969), 53.

[5] For data relating to each country see David B. Barrett, *World Christian Encyclopedia* (Nairobi: Oxford University Press, 1982).

[6] Peter Brierley, *Towards 2000—Current Trends in European Church Life* (Bromley, Kent, U.K.: MARC Europe, Monograph, 1984), 14, and *Nominality—The Plague of the Twentieth Century* (Bromley, Kent, U.K.: MARC Europe, Monograph, 1985).

[7] Bruce Wilson, *Can God Survive in Australia?* (Southerland, N.S.W.: Albatross Press, 1983), 25.

[8] Peter Kaldor, *Who Goes Where? Who Doesn't Care?* (N.S.W. Australia: Lancer Books, 1987), 25.

[9] Ibid., 2.

[10] Patrick Johnstone, *Operation World* (Pasadena: STL Books, William Carey Library, 1986), 317.

[11] George Gallup, *Religion in America, 50 Years 1935–85* (Princeton: The Gallup Report, 1985).

[12] The data is summarized on the *Unreached Peoples of the World 1985* chart published by the U.S. Center for World Mission, Pasadena, Calif.

[13] Lausanne, No. 23, 5.

[14] Dean R. Hoge and David A. Roozen, eds., *Understanding Church Growth and Decline* (New York: The Pilgrim Press, 1979), 39.

[15] Robert Currie, Alan Gilbert and Lee Horsley, *Churches and Church-goers* (Oxford: Clarendon Press, 1977), 98.

[16] Ibid., 98.

[17] John D. Gay, *The Geography of Religion in England* (London: Duckworth, 1971), 74.

[18] Ibid., 58.

[19] E. R. Wickham, *Church and People in an Industrial City* (London: Lutterworth, 1957), 34, 41, 281.

[20] Currie et al., *Churches* 85.

[21] B. R. Mitchell and Phyllis Deans, *Abstract of British Historical Statistics* (Cambridge, 1971), 19, 24–27, cited in Currie et al., p. 104.

[22] Kaldor, *Who Goes Where?* ch. 6.

[23] Hoge and Roozen, *Understanding Church Growth*, 47.

[24] Rodney Stark and William Sims Bainbridge, *The Future of Religion: Secularization and Renewal and Cult Formation* (Berkeley: University of California Press, 1985), 71.

[25] Martin E. Marty, *Pilgrims in Their Own Land* (Boston: Little, Brown and Company, 1984), 169.

[26] Ibid., 315.

[27] See *UK Christian Handbook 1987/88* (Bromley, Kent, U.K.: MARC Europe), 135, where it is stated that 959 African/West Indian congregations have 65,184 members.

[28] Robert N. Bellah, *Habits of the Heart* (New York: Harper and Row, 1985), 72.

[29] Raymond Bakke, *The Urban Christian* (Bromley, Kent, U.K.: MARC Europe, 1987), 60.

[30] Os Guinness, *The Gravedigger File* (Downers Grove: InterVarsity Press, 1983), 52–53.

[31] Lesslie Newbigin provides a perceptive description of the impact of secularization on religion in *Foolishness to the Greeks: The Gospel and Western Culture* (Grand Rapids: Eerdmans, 1986).

[32] Harry Blamire, *The Christian Mind* (London: SPCK, 1963).

[33] Guinness, *Gravedigger*, 64–65.

[34] The Australian Values Study Survey, conducted in 1983, showed that church-attendance rates of men and women who work full-time reveals little difference (18 percent female; 23 percent male), which is in marked contrast to the overall gender difference (29 percent and 21 percent). Reported in Kaldor, *Who Goes Where?* 115, 109.

[35] The cover story of the May 23, 1987 issue of *Time* magazine, "Whatever Happened to Ethics?" is significant in this regard.

[36] *The Times*, London, Nov. 19, 1988.

[37] Foreword to *Zur Dialektik von Religion und Gesellschaft*, German ed. of S. Rischer, *Social Reality* Verlag, 1973.

[38] See David A. Martin, "Towards Eliminating the Concept of Secularization" in Julius Gould (ed.), *Penguin Survey of the Social Sciences* (New York: Viking, Penguin Books, 1965), 169ff.

[39] James Gleick, *Chaos: Making a New Science* (New York: Viking, Penguin Books, 1987).

[40] Newbigin, *Foolishness* 14, 23.

[41] Paul F. Knitter, *No Other Name?* (Maryknoll, N.Y.: Orbis, 1986), 184.

[42] Ibid., 185.

13

Ethical Particularism as a Chinese Contextual Issue

Tan Che-Bin

SINCE THE ARRIVAL OF THE JESUITS in China, efforts in "bridge building"[1] between Christianity and Chinese culture have been characterized, in general, by a comparison of or dialogue between, Christian faith and classical Confucianism. This exercise has always been interpreted along the lines of neo-Confucianism, or Buddhist doctrines. The weaknesses in this approach are twofold. Firstly, classic Confucian or Buddhist followers have always been in the minority. The dominant religion and world-view of the majority of the Chinese is a mixture of Confucianism, Buddhism, and Taoism.[2]

Furthermore, in the twentieth century both Confucianism and Buddhism have been rapidly losing ground, if not already rejected outright by the Chinese people. As a result, even earlier when Confucianism was still official orthodoxy, the resultant "bridge" may not have been meaningful to the majority of the people. At best, it represents something that addressed those in the high culture.

TAN CHE-BIN, B.D., Th.M., Ph.D., associate professor and director of Chinese studies and evangelism at Fuller Theological Seminary, was born in Japan and has had a teaching ministry in Singapore, Taiwan, and Hong Kong. Tan did his doctorate under F.F. Bruce and is the author of numerous articles and books, mostly in Chinese, including *An Introduction to New Testament Theology* and *Discussion on New Testament Ethics*.

The introduction of social sciences into the study of Chinese history and the development of sociological and anthropological research on Chinese society and culture gave important insights into the nature, characteristics, and underlying values of Chinese culture. Such studies also have provided us with a better understanding of Chinese culture because they take full account of the folk culture as well as the rapid cultural change since the turn of the century.

Chinese culture, however, unlike tribal culture, is not homogeneous. It is a complex system, consisting of various traits and themes. This present discussion, therefore, is not meant to be exhaustive, nor do we intend to offer a comprehensive contextualized theology. Our purpose is to examine an important cultural trait, which is present in both high and folk cultures, in the light of biblical teaching, with a view to pointing to certain directions in a contextualized Chinese theology. We begin by tracing the roots and formulation of a Chinese cultural characteristic, in this case, ethical particularism. Then we will discuss this cultural characteristic in action. Thirdly, we will attempt to examine what the Bible has to say of parallel concerns underlying this particular cultural trait. And finally, we will point out some practical implications for an "incarnation model"[3] of a contextualized Chinese theology.

ETHICAL PARTICULARISM AS A CHINESE CULTURAL CHARACTERISTIC

One of the characteristics of Chinese culture is usually described as particularistic, because, in contrast to the "universalistic" love in the Christian tradition, no general rule(s) applies in interpersonal relationship in every case for everyone. Yet, at the same time, it is called *ethical* particularism because such a relationship is built on an ethical base.

In order to achieve a proper understanding of the issue, it is important for us to trace the historical development of ethical particularism. So far as evidence goes, we can be sure that ancestral worship can be traced back to the Shang dynasty (1750–1100 B.C.), which is believed by all historians to be the earliest dynasty in China. Both written records as well as archaeological findings show that while the Chinese in this period believed in a personal high god along with other nature gods, it is obvious that the center of Chinese religion at that time was ancestral worship. The famous oracle bones all bear witness that the will of god was sought through deceased ancestors in all aspects of life, whether military, agricultural, or daily life.

With the establishment of the so-called feudal system in the Chou Dynasty (1100–222 B.C.), the family basis was extended to cover the whole socio-political structure. A characteristic of the Chinese feudal system, according to Cho-yun Hsu, is that it is built upon blood relationship or marriage, in contrast to the European contract system.[4] This system does not mean an occupation of eastern territories by the Chou conquerors, but rather a reorganization of the population, with each of the feudal lords leading different groups of people or heading an assigned territory. In terms of structure, it was "a case of 'superstratification' in which a conquering federalism puts itself over an already stratified society."[5]

By integrating familial relations with the feudal system, the Chou kings identified political leaders with family heads. The terms of address used by the king to his dukes and vice versa were those of the family. "Dukes possessing the same surname as the royal house were addressed by the king as paternal uncle; dukes with other surnames were addressed as maternal uncles."[6] This means that the political system in China became an extension of the family. The Chinese social structure in terms of stratification can be best expressed in terms of a pyramid-shape structure with the king at the top, followed by the dukes, *Tai-fu* (great official) and *Ching* (baron), Shih, and the majority of the populace at the bottom.

Such structure was enforced by *li*, commonly translated as "propriety," a code of conduct that regulated every aspect of life for the society of the ruling class.

Two historical incidents may be related to demonstrate the relationship of *li* and social order. At the time of spring and autumn, the duke of Lu, Chao Kung (541–510 B.C.), met with the duke of Chi, Ching Kung. Ching Kung greeted Chao Kung with the rite of *kow-tow*, but the latter returned the greeting only by making a bow with hands folded in front because, as the Lu officials later explained, a duke only performs the rite of *kow-tow* to the king.[7]

Later on, a messenger of the state of Chin, the strongest state, was sent to report a victory to the royal court, which was no more than a puppet at the time. But he was refused reception because his rank and mission were considered improper in the light of propriety.[8]

Thus far, what we have demonstrated is that the Chinese culture, with family as its base and enforced by the concept of *li*, is relationally oriented and particularistic. With Confucius, ethical particularism came in place. Studying from the perspective of social change, Confucius is credited with "the overthrowing of the feudal system by undermining its cornerstone, the belief of the inborn superiority of the noble."[9] Yet he was definitely no revolutionary seeking a total break with the past. He was concerned with the establishment of a new socio-political order which had continuity with the past.[10] And he did it by giving the concept of *li* an ethical base.

That Confucius continues to emphasize the role of *li* as the foundation of social order is well supported. The following sayings are sufficient to demonstrate our point.

> Yen Hui asked about Goodness [*Jen*]. The Master said, "He who can himself submit to ritual is Good." If [a ruler] could for one day "himself submit to ritual [*li*]," everyone under Heaven would respond to his Goodness. For Goodness is something that must have its source in the ruler himself; it cannot be gotten from others. Yen Hui said, "I beg to ask for the more detailed items of this [submission to ritual]." The Master said, "To look at nothing in defiance of ritual, to listen to nothing in defiance of ritual, to speak of nothing in defiance of ritual, never to stir hand or foot in defiance of ritual." Yen Hui said, "I know that I am not clever; but this is a saying that, with your permission, I shall try to put into practice."[11]

> The Master said, "Courtesy not bounded by the prescriptions of ritual becomes tiresome. Caution not bounded by the prescriptions of ritual becomes timidity, daring becomes turbulence, inflexibility becomes harshness." The Master said, "When gentlemen deal generously with their own kin, the common people are incited to Goodness. When old dependents are not discarded, the common people will not be fickle."[12]

Speaking on the idea, Schwartz says, "If the word *tao* seems to refer to an all-encompassing state of affairs embracing the 'outer' sociopolitical order and the 'inner' moral life of the individual, the word *li* on the most concrete level refers to all those 'objective' prescriptions of behavior, whether involving rite, ceremony, manners, or general deportment."[13]

He goes on to point out that "what makes *li* the cement of the entire normative sociopolitical order is that it largely involves the behavior of persons related to each other in terms of role, status, and position within a structured society," and that "the system of *li* within the Analects presupposes and reinforces the proper networks of hierarchy and authority."[14]

On the other hand, the innovation of Confucius, it seems, is that he linked the concept of *jen* with *li*. As we quoted earlier, a definition of *jen* is that it is in submission to *li*. But according to Confucius, *jen* is actually the basis of *li*. "If a man is without *jen*, what can he have to do with *li*? If a man is without *jen*, what can he have to do with music?"[15]

In the outworking of *li*, it is also important for us to observe that the basis of *li* is *yi*, or righteousness, which carries the idea of what is proper and right; and that which is proper and right is relationally based. As a result, what is right and conformed to *li* may vary in different situations. Illustrative of this principle is the following saying:

> The "Duke" of She addressed Master K'ung saying, In my country there was a man called Upright Kung. His father appropriated a sheep, and Keep bore witness against him. Master K'ung said, In my country the upright men are of quite another sort. A father will screen his son, and a son his father—which incidentally does involve a sort of uprightness.[16]

The correct understanding of this saying, as Ying-shih Yu points out, is to be sought through the perspective of *li*. "'Law' (*fa*) is not the highest authority in the Chinese value system; therefore it should be coordinated with another basic value: filial piety. . . . 'A father will screen his son, and a son his father,' expresses the kind of 'justice' in the Chinese value system."[17]

In another context, he says: "the Confucians are seeking a higher 'justice' and a more reasonable 'order.' Such high 'justice' and 'order' are derived from the person who is endowed with self consciousness of value. 'A father will screen his son, and a son his father' is to arouse the feeling of shame in the thief. 'Law' in itself is negative; it can only prevent things after they happened; *li* is positive, it can prevent things from happening. . . . This is the basic stand of Confucius."[18]

With Mencius (372–289 B.C.?), who is regarded as the second sage after Confucius, ethical particularism is further developed. Most important is his theory of the inherent moral intentionality of human beings. To quote Schwartz: "As Confucius, Mencius also believes in the 'objective' prescriptions of *li*. He even seems to believe that they must be learned. Yet he has a burning faith that what is learned is really ours to begin with because *li* are ultimately the external expressions of a capacity for 'humanity' [*jen*] and righteousness [*yi*] as intrinsic to the human organism as is his whole physical organization."[19]

For Mencius, the outworking of *li* can be categorized in terms of five human relations:

> "The Sage [Shun] worried about this and appointed Hsieh minister of education to teach the people the human relationships: between father and son there was affection; between sovereign and minister, yi; between husband and wife, distinction of functions; between old and young, a proper order of precedence; and between friends, sincerity."[20]

To practice these relations is equivalent to the practice *jen* and *yi*.

"The substance of jen is to serve one's parents; the substance of yi is to obey one's older brother. The essence of wisdom is to know these two things and not to depart from them; the essence of li is to perform these two things according to ritual orders; the essence of music is to rejoice in these two things. When joy is found in them, [filial piety and fraternal affection] arise; if so, how can they be repressed? When they cannot be repressed, unconsciously one's feet will dance and one's hands will flutter."[21]

He believes, on the one hand, that a good government must assume the responsibility of promoting, besides others, these ethical characters in the people:

If Your Majesty will indeed practice "jen government," abating severe punishment, lightening taxes and levies, causing the farms to be attended with care and industry, and enabling the strong-bodied in their leisure days to cultivate their filial piety, fraternal love, loyalty, and sincerity, so that at home they will serve their fathers and elder brothers and abroad their elders and superiors [under conditions such as these], your people can be employed with wooden staffs to oppose the strong nail and sharp weapons of the troops of Ch'in and Ch'u. For those rulers [of Ch'in and Ch'u] encroach upon their people's time, so that they cannot attend to the farming to support their parents. As a consequence, their parents suffer from cold and hunger; brothers, wives, and children are separated and scattered abroad. Those rulers drive their people into distress and suffering. If Your Majesty go to punish them, who will resist you? Here is the saying: "The jen-hearted man has no enemies." I beg your Majesty not to doubt my words.[22]

On the other, in practice, the practice of human relations begins with oneself and one's family:

Of the services of men, which is the greatest? The service to parents is the greatest. Of the duties of men, which is the greatest? The duty of self-preservation is the greatest. I have heard of being able to serve one's parents by preserving oneself. I have never heard of being able to serve one's parents by not preserving oneself. There are many services, but service to one's parents is the root of all services.[23]

This does not mean, of course, that there was no social change in the history of China. The feudal system, by the time of Confucius, was already breaking down. And we have quoted instances that show such a process. Later on, Chinese society was dominated not by feudal families, but gentry families. With the disappearance of feudal lords and later introduction of an examination system, a new social class, the gentry, emerged. Even the exact prescription of *li* changed with time.

Nor is Confucianism the only factor in Chinese culture. Legalists, Taoists, and followers of the Ying-yang School all contributed to the development of Chinese culture, added to, later on, by Buddhists. Yet it must also be emphasized that the influence of Confucian ethical particularism in the Chinese culture is also pervasive. The five human relations propounded by Mencius were later accepted not only by the Confucian orthodoxy but by the Taoists and Buddhists, who believe in monastery life. In 1670, Kang Hsi (A.D. 1662–1722), an emperor of the Ching Dynasty who posed himself in the tradition of a Confucian sage-king, issued an edict which became the moral standard throughout the dynasty. In this edict ethical particularism permeates the sixteen maxims.

Chinese subjects were exhorted in the first place "to esteem most highly filial piety and brotherly submission, in order to give due importance to social relations," and also to "elucidate propriety and yielding courtesy, in order to make manners and customs good."[24] In another popular religious tract, still being circulated and possibly dating back to the Ming Dynasty, believers of folk religion are also exhorted to practice the following virtues: "Do not tread evil paths; do not take advantage of dark rooms [so as to do evil]. Treasure virtues and compile merits; be merciful to everything. Be loyal to the ruler, practise filial piety and friendship, and serve also your elder brothers; correct yourself and edify others. Be kind to orphans and have compassion on widows; respect the elders and nurture the young."[25]

As a result, one finds in the Chinese social system what the Chinese anthropologist Fei Xiaotong called, "differentiation structure (Chaxu Geju)." The configuration of Chinese society is "like the rings of successive ripples that are propelled outward on the surface when you throw a stone into water. Each individual is the center of the rings emanating from his social influence. Wherever the ripples reach, affiliation occurs. The rings used by each person at any given time or place are not necessarily the same."[26]

ETHICAL PARTICULARISM IN ACTION IN CONTEMPORARY CHINESE CULTURE

Ethical particularism as a cultural trait in action can be seen in the political, social, and family life and structures. In this section we shall attempt to study how it works in a contemporary life setting and to see what are the problems that come with it.

Since the family is a basic social structure in Chinese culture, we shall begin with observations on Chinese family. Again we can start with the remarks of Fei Xiaotong:

The most important kinship relations in our society have the characteristics of these ripples of concentric circles formed by throwing a
stone. Kinship relations are social relationships based on the facts of
birth and marriage. The network formed by birth and marriage can
emanate outward to include an infinite number of persons, past,
present, and future. . . . This network, like a spider's web, has a center, which is oneself. Every one of us has such a web of kinship relations, but no web covers the same people as another. The people (in
a society of this kind) can use the same system to identify their kin
relations, but they share only this system. A system is an abstract configuration, a conceptual category. When we apply this system to identify actual relatives, those recognized by each person are different.
. . . It is impossible for any two people in the world to have the exact
same relatives. Brothers of course have the same parents, but each has
his own wife and children. Consequently, the network of social relations formed by the affiliations of kinship relations is particularistic.
Every network has a "self" as center, and the center of each and every
network is different.[27]

In such a network, the sphere of one's closest loyalties is highly
elastic. As Fei observed,[28] family in China is not so well defined as
it is in the West. When it is said in an invitation that "your entire
family is invited," few people could say exactly how many are included. A wealthy, powerful person may include anyone who is related in some way, whereas a poor family may include only a few.

Furthermore, Fei points out that the nature of one's obligations
to another in Chinese society depends on the precise nature of
one's relationships to the other. The further the ripples of one's
social relations are propelled, the fainter they become. One's obligation to immediate family members are more intense than that to
distant kin.[29]

In practice, this kind of thinking carries with it several consequences. Firstly, one's social responsibility and social behavior differ
from person to person. A scholar-official like Fan Chung-yen
(A.D. 989–1052) may claim that a true *chun-tzu* should "worry for
the world before it worries for itself and rejoice for the world after
it rejoices." As far as the ideal for the folk people is concerned, one
should also realize that "all men are brothers" and, therefore, should
practice *jen* and *yi* even to strangers.

A leader may also sacrifice the narrow private interests of his
immediate family and closest neighbors for the good of a larger
group. But considerations based on ethical particularism may also
work exactly the other way: sacrifice of the large group to the
smaller family interest. And this seems to be most prevalent in
most cases.

Sacrificing the family for oneself, sacrificing one's lineage for one's family—this formula is an actual fact. Under such a formula what would someone say if you called him self-centered? He would not be able to see it that way, because when he sacrificed his clan, he might have done it for his family, and the way he looks at it, his family is the common interest. When he sacrificed the nation for the benefit of his small group in the struggle for power, he was also doing it for the common interest—for the common interest of his small group. . . . Common interest (gong, also translatable as "public interest") and selfishness (si, also translatable as "private interest") are relative terms; anything within the circle in which one is standing can be called common.[30]

Secondly, ethical particularism also underlies the social dynamics in Chinese social exchange. In recent years, several anthropological and sociological studies have demonstrated that in social exchange, the concepts of face, *pao*, *jen-ching*, and *kuan-shi* all relate to the concept of *li*, and are still operative in Chinese society.

Kwang-kuo Hwang, in an article that was first published in Chinese in 1985 and later in English, provides us with a conceptual framework.[31] He points out that there are three kinds of interpersonal ties, based on the particularistic cultural trait, which govern the rules of Chinese social conduct: the *expressive*, the *instrumental*, and the *mixed*. The expressive ties occur "mostly among members of such primary groups as family, close friends, and other congenial groups.

Aside from the satisfaction of affective feelings, one can, of course, utilize this tie as an instrument to promise some desirable material resource. But its expressive component always claims precedence over its instrumental components.[32] The process in this tie is governed by the rule of need.

The instrumental tie is established with people outside of the family and the relationships serve only as a means or an instrument to attain other goals. The rule is equity.

As to the mixed tie, it is a relationship in which an individual seeks to influence other people by means of *jen-ching* and face. It occurs chiefly among relatives, neighbors, classmates, colleagues, teachers and students, people sharing a natal area, and so forth. "Both sides know each other and keep a certain expressive component in their relationship, but it is never so strong that all participants in this tie could express their authentic behavior as freely as can the members in the expressive tie."[33] In practice, *jen-ching* as a social norm means, proverbially, "if you have received a drop of beneficence from other people, you should return to them a fountain of beneficence."[34] Hwang also points out that:

In order to maintain the affective component in the mixed tie, the participants have to remember the principle that "etiquette requires reciprocity" and follow the rule that "if one gives you a peach, you should requite his favor with a plum." Whenever a participant in this tie is struck by poverty, disease, or some other difficulty that demands timely help from the other tie member, who has a desired resource at his disposal, the latter, taking into consideration the possible reciprocation that the former may give in the future, will help the distressed on to a certain degree.[35]

As this is the most common tie in a society, it is the key for gaining advantage over others in many situations, especially in the securing of scarce resources.

Thus, for example, in a Taiwanese society, this particularistic tie was employed as the way in which votes were mobilized in rural elections.[36] The widespread use of strategies of "going through the back door" and "pulling" and "working" connections to solicit favors from organizational authorities controlling scarce resources is also to be understood against such cultural background. By using all kinds of connections through the mixed tie, people in China can obtain scarce materials on ration, buy tickets for trains or theatre, and gain special consideration in all kinds of applications, whether it is a job, a passport, affidavit, certificate or school. "Units with connections" has been a special term. And the importance of establishing mixed ties can be illustrated by the following report:

> To build a factory in a *Hsien*, it is not enough simply to work on connection with the *Hsien* officials and *Hsien* office. One has to work on connections with every other unit which has certain power on things, such as the chief accountant, chief economic officer, commercial office, transportation office, education office, health office, building office and all the companies, even production teams nearby. One cannot afford to hurt any of them. If they come to ask for things ten times and are turned down only once, they will immediately create problems for you. For example, if the people in electric office ask for a car and do not get it, they will stop your electric supply on certain unfounded reasons.[37]

R. Madsen, in his study of a Chinese village, also describes a local village cadre who, while attempting to maintain a strict impartiality in village affairs, had to resort to "pull" relations with a powerful outsider who had the say on the distribution of materials.[38] And he also mentions the fact that in communist rural China, *jen-ching* is a decisive factor.[39]

In the political realm, ethical particularism is the cause of much discussion and debate. Since the beginning of the imperial period, the relations of emperors and officials have been seen in terms of a father-son analogy and given the same weight theoretically.[40] The ruling officials are called "parent-official" (fu-mu-kuan). As such, the government is expected to practice what is called ethocracy, government by the principle of jen; and the people are expected to be obedient.

Some Chinese scholars, however, had observed a long time ago that there is no real basis for thinking that the relation between the ruler and the subjects is as natural as that between parents and children. With the collapse of the Ching dynasty, the five basic human relations of Confucianism as a basis for the state also came to an end. Present-day Confucian scholar/philosophers all agree that democracy should be the ideal political system.[41] The debate right now is whether the state/citizen relation can be used as a substitute for the original ruler/official relation, and whether some other relations— between self and group, for example—should be added to the traditional five.[42]

Despite the consensus of the rejection of the imperial system as the form of government for modern China, politically and socially we can still see traces of ethical particularism in political and social structures. A recent study on the Chinese communist society, for example, has shown that China was united as a nation on the family model, and that communist evolution, instead of destroying the family as a social unit, actually reinforces the tradition of patriarchy.[43]

In his study of power on the village level, R. Madsen also shows that the village often functions like an extended big family.[44] Studies on the Chinese society in Hong Kong and Taiwan confirm that the operating model in these two localities is also that of the family. Siu-kai Lau, in a study of the political stability in Hong Kong, argues that utilitarianistic familism is the key. For Lau, utilitarianistic familism is defined as "a normative and behavioural tendency of an individual to place his familial interests above the interests of society or any of its component individuals and groups, and to structure his relationships with other individuals and groups in such a fashion that the furtherance of his familial interest is the primary consideration."[45] It is an adaptation of traditional familism to the industrial, urban, and colonial society of Hong Kong. "Utilitarianistic familism, typical of the cultural ethos of the ordinary Chinese . . . does not value very much the non-material rewards which society can proffer, rather, society is considered to be largely insignificant, and the family is to 'exploit' society for its own utilitarian purposes."[46]

Two separate studies of the factories in Hong Kong and Taiwan also have shown that Chinese factories are basically run on the family model.[47] Therefore, preferences in managerial positions are definitely biased for the close relatives, and there is a general tendency to pay more attention to the accumulation of wealth than to the improvement of benefits of employees. As a consequence, the continuity of the enterprise is threatened because employees are tempted to give priority to individual family interest over company interest and establish their own businesses. As a result, Chinese factories and businesses are, as a whole, small in size.

BIBLICAL TEACHING AND ETHICAL PARTICULARISM

People of God as Covenant Community

Having overviewed the idea of ethical particularism and its function in Chinese culture, it is appropriate to ask what the Bible has to say on the themes and concerns of this particular trait of Chinese culture.

The obvious starting point is the idea of covenant. This is definitely not the place to argue over the problem of unity and diversity in biblical theology nor its related question, i.e., whether the idea of covenant is the unifying theme of the Old Testament. I am in no doubt that the idea of covenant is an important one.

Israel as God's chosen, covenanted people is obviously a recurrent theme in the Old Testament. As it stands in the present textual form, it seems clear that the Exodus event is the focal point of history in the Pentateuch. In the account of God's epiphany to Abraham in Genesis 15, the author obviously has the Exodus in mind. If the story of the patriarchs points forward to Exodus, the Book of Deuteronomy harks back to the same event as the foundation of Israel's existence in Canaan. The prophets also refer to it often. Hosea tells us that in the Exodus God carried the infant Israel as a little child (Hos. 11:1) and, together with Jeremiah, he uses the language of marriage to describe the relationship between God and Israel (Hos. 2; Jer. 2:2–3).

These references also remind us of the idea of covenant in Sinai, which is the culminating point in the Exodus account (Ex. 19–24).[48] Summarizing the basic tenets of God in this covenantal relationship, John Bright points out that the faith of Israel consists in three aspects: that it was a monotheism, that it was aniconic (God could not be depicted or imagined in any form), and that the God of Israel both could and did control the events of history, through which he reveals his righteousness, judgment, and saving power.[49] Under the covenant, Israel's uniqueness is also delineated: it is a special possession, a kingdom of priests, and a holy nation.

> Israel is God's own people, set apart from the rest of the nations. Israel as a people is also dedicated to God's service among the nations as priests function within a society. Finally, the life of Israel shall be commensurate with the holiness of the covenant God.[50]

If the setting of the covenant in Sinai provides us with Israel's relation to God, to the nation, and to herself as a people, the Ten Commandments—especially the last half—will also help us glimpse what it means to live a life of holiness in relation to one's parents, spouse, and neighbors, which is based on one's relation to God. Here a "persistent attention to the structures that affect everyday life" can be observed.[51] As the case laws that follow in Exodus 21:1–22:16 pay special attention to the protection of the enclaved, the poor, and the bereaved, "we have the explicit meaning of a concept central to the nation of community structure in early Israel, divine *compassions*".[52] Yet the context of such manifestation, as P.D. Hanson points out, is significant: it is through the stipulation of the law—in other words, righteousness, as a response of God's people in worship—that the compassion is manifested. In his words,

> *Torah* originated a response to Gospel. Righteousness was not directed inward in the manner of the "introspective consciousness of the West," but was directed outward in dedication to the construction of a healthy community, that is, a community in which a compassionate openness to those falling outside of its orbit of protection would be preserved. Moreover, righteousness oriented outward toward the *šālôm* of the whole community was not construed in terms of human achievement—which inevitably leads to the pride and exclusivism of work righteousness—but in terms of the ongoing manifestations of God's creative, redemptive activity."[53]

Family and Human Relations

In his sociological exegesis of 1 Peter, John H. Elliott points out that in the Greco-Roman world and the Hebraic tradition, family is an important motif. Elliott documented that in Egypt, the state was equated with the family and provided a centralizing concept of political, economic, social, and national life.

> The *oikos* thereby provided the mode, the terminology and the ideological framework for the organization of the state as a whole, its smaller parts (e.g., *epoikia*, "villages"), its various types of subjects (e.g., *metoikoi*,

paroikoi, "resident aliens"; *katoikoi*, "military colonists"), and its administrative officials (e.g., *dioiketes*, chief financial officer; *hypoiketes*, his subordinate supervisor of several nomes; and *oikonomos*, the financial administrator of a *nome*).[54]

Moreover, the household is the basis and model for Greek social, economic, and political life from Homeric times through the advent of the Roman rule. In Roman time, the Caesars actually used dependents for their authority in the patronage of the republican aristocracy. And the emperors exploited these personal forms of alignment by seeking personal oaths of allegiance from all segments of the population. Moreover, to administer the affairs of the state, including the keeping of imperial records, the supervision of coinage, and the oversight of the fiscal estate, the early emperors employed a personal, familial mode of bureaucratic administration known as the "household of Caesar," comprising of personal servants, imperial freedmen, and slaves.

In the Old Testament, Elliott notes that "it is hardly possible or necessary here to elaborate on the sundry social, economic, political, ethnic or religious connotations of 'house' in the Old Testament. Suffice it to note that *oikos* (and its Hebrew equivalent *bayith*) throughout the strata of the Old Testament tradition serves as a prime expression of communal identity and organization and of social, political and religious solidarity. In religious terms it is this form of Israelite community as 'house' with which Yahweh has entered into special relationship. It was to the chosen patriarch Abraham and his *oikos* (Gen. 18:19), called from their father's house (Gen. 12:1) into *paroikia* (Gen. 12:10; 15:13; 17:8, etc.), to whom the promises of divine blessing were given (Gen. 12:1-3; 18:19).[55]

For Elliott, the household or family is "the basis of all definition" of Israelite community, implying historical, psychic, social, as well as religious cohesion.

In the New Testament, one aspect of Jesus' uniqueness is his popularization, if not innovation, of the father-image in addressing God, by calling him "Abba, Father."[56] In the Pauline Epistles, we find Paul includes all believers as children of God (Gal. 4:6, Rom. 8:15), using the language of adoption, and also continues the Old Testament tradition by naming the church as the family of God (Eph. 2:19-20). In recent years, scholars have also called our attention to the fact that there were even "house-churches" in the New Testament period, and conversion by family as a unit.[57]

There are at least three aspects of this household language that are significant for our understanding of the image. Firstly, if the children of God are primarily defined ethnically or by blood relationship in the Old Testament, the teaching of Jesus definitely clashed with the popular Jewish perception of the time and opened the way for the inclusion of gentiles among the children of God (e.g., Acts 12:9-21, 15:7-11) in the early church. When this is taken into consideration together with our previous observation that there were household churches and conversion by the family as a unit, it means that the family model is retained and expanded, at the same time, to transcend the blood relationship.

This leads to our second observation. In recent New Testament studies from a sociological perspective, attention has been called to the recurrent motif of *Haustafel*, or household code. Scholars seem to agree that basically the three basic household relations—husband-wife, father-son, and master-slave—are exactly what one finds in the Greco-Roman world. Yet it also seems certain that the content has been modified into what is called "love-patriarchalism," described as follows:

> This love-patriarchalism takes social differences for granted but ameliorates them through an obligation of respect and love, an obligation imposed upon those who are socially stronger. From the weaker are required subordination, fidelity, and esteem. Whatever the intellectual sources feeding into this ethos, with it the great part of Hellenistic primitive Christianity mastered the task of shaping social relations with a community which, on the one hand, demanded of its members a high degree of solidarity and brotherliness and, on the other, encompassed various social strata.[58]

At the same time, the ultimate motive of such household codes is also provided. The concern of the New Testament writers is not only to stabilize internal communal relations, but possibly also to stabilize relations with outsiders with a view to the easing of tensions with them and to pave the way for evangelization.[59]

Lastly, the difference between the biblical image of the family and that of Egypt and Greco-Roman world lies in the view of the king/leader. A study of the Old Testament texts on kingship (Deut. 17:14-20, 1 Sam. 5:1-2) seems to show that "the king would remain aware both of his human status as a man among his brethren, and also of his status in relation to the kingships of God."[60] This is in line with the earlier structure in the time of the judges when "the covenant league was a brotherhood . . . ruled only by the law of the covenant God."[61]

Later, we find in the New Testament that the apostles see themselves as brothers and co-workers along with other Christians and elders/bishops (e.g., Phil. 2:25, 1 Pet. 5:1). Jesus Christ, despite his title as Lord and Savior, is also the elder brother (e.g., Rom. 8:29,

Heb. 2:10-11). The underlying motif is that the ultimate goal of Jesus' lordship is the sharing of his glory and power with all believers. Moreover, in the New Testament, the most important principle of leadership and exercise of power is that of suffering servant. Effective exercise of authority is not suppression from the top, but uplifting from under (Mark 10:45, 2 Cor. 10:8) and personal modeling of suffering and love (1 Pet. 5:2-3, 1 Cor. 11:1).

The Practice of Universal Love

Although the biblical ideal of community consists of worship, righteousness, and compassion, the history of the people of God demonstrates that they are always in danger of departing from it.

In the Old Testament, we find case after case of leaders, especially kings, becoming despotic. The story of Ahab's taking away of Naboth's vineyard, for example, is a classic example of violating the principle of compassion, and manipulation of the law to the advantage of a despotic ruler (1 Kings 21:1ff).

In the New Testament, the Pharisees are also presented as making the people of God the slaves of Torah (Mark 2:1ff, 7:1ff). Overemphasis of grace to the total neglect of law, on the other hand, would lead to antinomianism, a position Paul refused to accept (Rom. 6:1ff). For both Jesus and Paul it seems, grace and love transcends law but do not abolish justice; and such a life can only be achieved by reconciliation with God (e.g., Matt. 18:21-35, 2 Cor. 5:14-21). In other words, the existence of sin and need of repentance are factors to be taken account of in the real-life situations of the people of God.

Such observation also implies that, in the application of the Biblical principle of compassion and righteousness, the starting point would be the individual. It seems, moreover, that priority may even be given to members of the family in certain situations. This seems to be confirmed by the Old Testament *go'el*, or redeemer, system (Lv. 25:23-28, Ruth 4) and the New Testament demand of taking care of one's own poor (1 Tim. 5:3).

In saying that one cannot love God without first loving one's Christian brother (1 Jn. 4:20), John seems to imply, too, that the practice of love begins within the fellowship of believers. Having said this, it must also be observed that in all these instances, religious affiliation rather than blood relation is the primary reason, and that the boundary between believers and nonbelievers is not as hard and fast as the one that is based on blood relation. The story of the Good Samaritan in Luke 10 seems to indicate, moreover, that geographical proximity is another factor that one should take seriously in the practice of love.

In this sense, we may say that while particularism based on the blood-relation tie is not totally negated in the Bible, it is again extended in the larger family of God.

Implications for Contextualization

Ethical particularism in the Chinese culture involves a socio-political order, an underlying structure of interpersonal dynamics, and a philosophical presupposition. To begin with, it indicates to us a basic understanding of reality in the Chinese culture. Humankind in the Chinese culture can be defined as social-oriented,[62] other oriented,[63] or situation centered.[64] While the Bible would like to add a vertical dimension of humankind in relation to God to such a horizontal dimension, the Chinese view is definitely not further away from truth than is American individualism.

In terms of the horizontal dimension, an important feature in Chinese ethical particularism is that it is elastic. Its scope encompasses, at least to some, the whole world. The ethical system covers not only the individual, but is extended to one's family, nation, and the whole world. The strength of such a system, as some modern Confucian scholars put it, lies in that it is applicable at all times. In a favorable environment, one can apply the system on a national scale; and in a time when the *tao* is rejected by the ruler, one can still apply the same principle oneself and serve as a model to the society. This implies that a good contextualized theology should, on the one hand, emphasize personal integrity and morality and, on the other hand, provide a theological framework on the national level. As the weakness of the Chinese ethical particularism is most obvious on the national level, any alternative that is offered as a solution to the Chinese problem must include options for a new political system.

Theologically speaking, the church is both witness to and manifestation of the kingdom of God. Historically, it is also traditions. It seems, therefore, a good beginning can be made by formulating a doctrine of the church that takes the Chinese family tradition seriously. In the formulation of a doctrine of salvation, a system which pays attention to the corporate and cosmic aspects of redemption is obviously needed. In other words, a fundamentalistic approach to salvation emphasizing the individual, which is American, is not sufficient to meet the needs in the Chinese context, nor does it take the basic Chinese understanding of humankind seriously enough.

Besides the form, there is also a particularistic interpersonal dynamic. The Chinese concepts of face, *jen-ching*, and *pao*, again, do contribute positively to the society. The Chinese may not be characterized as emotional; but certainly there is no lack of affection. Nor are concepts like equality, justice, or human dignity totally absent in the Chinese culture. The difference between biblical and Chinese interpersonal relationships may possibly be stated this way: *In the biblical ideal, the elements of righteousness/justice and compassion/love must pervade and undergird all relationships, whereas the Chinese is particularistic in the sense that different elements are given priority and prominence in different relationships.* In the ruler and ruled relation, the biblical brotherhood and servanthood relation is also different from the Chinese parent/children relation. Possibly love-patriarchalism can also be an intermediate step in the transition.

Yet, after all that is said, we must always bear in mind the eschatological tension of the present and not yet, the presence of both Holy Spirit and sin in this age. The experiences of the people of God in both Old and New Testaments all point to the importance of the vertical, divine human relationship, or the element of worship in human relation. Without it, there is always the danger of distortion, despite clear biblical teaching. A contextualized theological system without the regeneration and renewal of the Holy Spirit will not be a reality experienced in life.

NOTES

[1] D. Hesselgrave, *Today's Choices for Tomorrow's Mission* (Grand Rapids: Academia Books, 1988), 147ff.

[2] The transliteration system followed is that of Wade-Giles, except the names of the authors in China and their works.

[3] Charles H. Kraft, *Christianity in Culture* (Maryknoll: Orbis, 1979), 113ff.

[4] Cho-yun Hsu, *History of Western Chou Dynasty* (Taipei: Lien Chin, 1984), 173.

[5] W. Ebehard, *A History of China* (Berkeley: University of California Press, 1977), 24.

[6] Cho-yun Hsu, *Ancient China in Transition* (Stanford: University Press, 1965) 3.

[7] Cheng-tung Wei, *History of Chinese Thought* (Taipei: Ta Ling Press, 1974), Vol. 1:42–43.

[8] Cho-yun Hsu, *Ancient China*, 22.

[9] Ibid., 178.

[10] B. I. Schwartz, *The World of Thought in Ancient China* (Cambridge, Mass.: Harvard University Press, 1985), 65.

[11] *Analect* XII, 1, A. Waley, 162.

[12] *Analect* XIII, 2, A. Waley, 132.

[13] B. I. Schwartz, *The World of Thought*, 67.

[14] Ibid., 68.

[15] *Analect* III, 3, A. Waley, 94.

[16] *Analect* XIII, 18, A. Waley, 175–76.

[17] Ying-shih Yu, "Chinese Culture Seen From the Perspective of Value System," *A Contemporary Interpretation of Traditional Chinese Thinking* (Taipei: Lien Chin, 1987), 29.

[18] Ibid., 32.

[19] B. I. Schwartz, *The World of Thought*, 264.

[20] *Mencius*, III. A. 4, see C. Chai and W. Chai, eds. and trs., *Books of Confucius and Other Confucian Classics* (New Hyde Park: University Books, 1965), 193–94.

[21] *Mencius* IV. A. 27, Chai, 157.

[22] *Mencius* I. A. 5, Chai, 109–10.

[23] *Mencius* IV. A. 19, Chai, 156.

[24] V. H. Mair, "Language and Ideology in the Written Popularization of the Sacred Edict," *Popular Culture in Late Imperial China*, N. A. Johnson and E. Rawski, eds. (Berkeley: University of California Press, 1985), 325–26.

[25] Cheng-chih Li, "Popular Chinese Moral Thinking," Appendix to Chi-ching Cheng, *Chinese Society and Religion* (Taipei: Student Press, 1986), 364.

[26] Fei Xiaotong, "Chinese Social Structure and its Values," in *Changing China: Readings in the History of China from the Opium War to the Present*, J. Mason Gentzler, ed. (New York: Praeger, 1977), 211.

[27] Ibid., 211–12.

[28] Ibid.

[29] Ibid., 213.

[30] Ibid.

[31] Kwang-kuo Hwang, "Face and Favour: The Chinese Power Game," *American Journal of Sociology*, 92 (1987):944–74.

[32] Ibid., 949.

[33] Ibid., 952.

[34] Ibid., 954.

[35] Ibid., 957.

[36] Bruce J. Jacobs, "A Preliminary Model of Particularistic Ties in Chinese Political Alliances: Kan-ching and Kuan-hsi in a Rural Taiwanese Township," *China Quarterly*, 78 (1979):237–73.

[37] *Peoples' Daily* (Nov. 15, 1980), p. 3, quoted in Chien Chiao, "A Preliminary Study on Kuan-hsi," *The Sinicization of Social and Behavioral Science Research in China*, K. S. Yang and C. Y. Wen, eds. (Taipei: Academia Sinica, 1982), 353.

[38] R. Madsen, *Morality and Power in Chinese Village* (Berkeley: University of California Press, 1984), 91–101.

[39] Ibid., 61–62.

[40] Ying-shih Yu, "Anti-Intellectualism and Chinese Political Tradition," *History and Thought* (Taipei: Lien Chin, 1984), 1–46. Yu sees this as the influence of legalists on Confucianism.

[41] For example, Chun-yi Tang, *The Spiritual Value of Chinese Culture*, rev. ed. (Taipei: Cheng Chung, 1979), 504ff.

[42] Jen-ho Tsai, "Reconsideration of Confucian Ethics," and Yun-yuan Yang, "Sixth Human Relation, or *Kung, Shu* and Contemporary Spirit," both in *The Unfolding of Chinese Culture*, Tunghai University, eds. (Taipei: Department of Education, Taiwan Provincial Government, 1982), 4:121–35, 460–66.

[43] J. Stacey, *Patriarchy and Socialist Revolution in China* (Berkeley: University of California Press, 1983), esp. 108–57.

[44] R. Madsen, *Morality*, 79.

[45] Siu-kai Lau, "Utilitarian Familism," *Social Life and Development in Hong Kong*, A. Y. C. King and R. P. C. Lee, eds. (Hong Kong: The Chinese University Press, 1981), 201.

[46] Ibid., 202.

[47] C. N. Chen, "Traditional Chinese Familism and Organization in Chinese Enterprise," *Chinese Management*, K. S. Yang and S. C. Cheng, eds. (Taipei: Kuei-Kuan Press, 1988), 213-36. And G. Redding and G. Y. Y. Wong, "Chinese Organizational Behavior," *The Psychology of the Chinese People*, M. H. Bond, ed. (Hong Kong: Oxford University Press, 1986), 267-95.

[48] B. S. Childs, *The Book of Exodus* (Philadelphia: Westminster, 1974), 347ff, 366.

[49] John Bright, *The Kingdom of God* (Nashville: Abingdon, 1981), 24-25.

[50] Childs, *Exodus*, 367.

[51] Paul D. Hanson, *The People Called* (San Francisco: Harper and Row, 1986), 42.

[52] Ibid., 49.

[53] Ibid., 80.

[54] J. H. Elliott, *Home for the Homeless* (Philadelphia: Fortress, 1981), 172.

[55] Ibid., 182-83.

[56] J. Jeremias, *New Testament Theology*, (London: SCM, 1971), 1:61-68.

[57] Wayne A. Meeks, *The First Urban Christians* (New Haven: Yale University Press, 1983), 75-77.

[58] G. Theissen, "Social Stratification in the Christian Community," *The Social Setting of Pauline Christianity* (Philadelphia: Fortress, 1982), 107-08.

[59] Margaret Y. MacDonald, *The Pauline Churches* (Cambridge: Cambridge University Press, 1988), esp. 121-22, 237.

[60] P. C. Craigie, *The Book of Deuteronomy*, NICOT (Grand Rapids: Eerdmans, 1976), 253.

[61] John Bright, *Kingdom*, 31.

[62] K. S. Yang, "Social Orientation and Individual Modernity Among Chinese Students in Taiwan," *Journal of Social Psychology* 113 (1981):159-70.

[63] Lung-chi Sun, *The Deep Structure of Chinese Culture* (Hong Kong: Yi-shang Press, 1983), 11-20.

[64] F. L. K. Hsu, *American and Chinese*, third ed. (Honolulu: University Press of Hawaii, 1980), 137.

14

Contextualization among Muslims: Reusing Common Pillars

J. Dudley Woodberry

RECENTLY I STOOD IN THE GREAT MOSQUE in Qairawan in present-day Tunisia and looked at the collection of pillars from various sources that had been assembled together into one harmonious whole. As was also done elsewhere in the Empire, the early Muslim builders of Qairawan had freely incorporated pillars from previous Christian churches—and modified and whitewashed them—to make them blend into their new "home."[1]

These pillars illustrate what also took place in early Muslim religious observance, for what have come to be known as the "pillars" of Islam are all adaptations of previous Jewish and Christian forms. If this fact were better understood, some of the current Muslim and Christian reaction to contextualization would be alleviated, for it would not seem artificial.

The present study notes some current plans that have been drawn up for reusing these pillars of faith, and the reaction that

J. DUDLEY WOODBERRY, M.Div., M.A., Ph.D., associate professor of Islamic studies at Fuller Theological Seminary, was a Presbyterian (USA) missionary/fraternal worker in Pakistan and a pastor in Kabul, Afghanistan, and Riyadh, Saudi Arabia. Currently he is the director of program and publication of the Muslim track of the Lausanne Committee for World Evangelization. He has edited *Muslims and Christians on the Emmaus Road*.

these have elicited from Muslims and Christians. Then, an attempt is made to add to this material in two ways. First, we look more closely at the previous use of these pillars by Jews and Christians, to see the extent to which we can reutilize what was originally our own. Second, we evaluate a contemporary people movement to Christ among Muslims where the believers are adapting the pillars of their previous faith to bear the weight of their new faith in Christ.

VARIOUS PERSPECTIVES ON REUSING THE PILLARS

The need for contextualization has been expressed by Muslim converts and inquirers. Last year I received a letter from a West African country which described some new believers who objected to attending the local church for the following reasons:

> Their customs are too different from ours. They keep their shoes on, sit on benches (and close to women at that), and they beat drums in church. We are used to worshipping God by taking our shoes off, sitting and kneeling on mats, and chanting prayers in the Arabic and _____ languages. Also we teach our women at home. If we go to the _____ church, we will feel very uncomfortable. What's more, our other Muslim friends will not join us. If we worship God the way we are used to, other Muslims will be interested. But we will pray in the name of Jesus and teach from the Arabic and _____ Bibles.[2]

Not only have the worship forms been irrelevant or offensive to the person of Muslim background, but the Bibles used have often shrouded the gospel in foreign terms. The traditional Bengali Bible, for example, often used a Hindu rather than a Muslim vocabulary. Even the most commonly used Arabic translation of the Bible, by Eli Smith and Cornelius Van Dyck (first published in 1865), adopted some Syriac religious and ecclesiastical terms not seen in Muslim Arabic. Likewise it utilized some Syriac names of Bible characters that are different from those adopted by the Quran (Koran)—for example, *Yuhanna* rather than *Yahya* for John and *Yasu'* rather than *Isa* for Jesus. The translators consciously avoided using the wording and style of the Quran.[3] An Omani sheikh lamented:

> I have the Gospel, too. One of your missionaries gave me a copy twenty years ago. I frequently get it down and try to read it but its Arabic is so strange that I understand nothing.[4]

Such problems have led to a number of recent studies applying contextualization theory to Muslims,[5] monographs on specific topics,[6] and contextualized materials for Muslims.[7]

Despite the need for contextualization, Christian communities in the Muslim world have often opposed it. The opposition echoes a comparable tension in the early church between the Hebrew Christians who used Jewish forms and the new gentile Christians who felt free to use other forms. Gabriel Habib, the Greek Orthodox director of the Middle East Christian Council, in a letter to many evangelical leaders in North America, asserted:

> Unfortunately, we have all too frequently attempted to "contextualize" our sharing of the gospel—at the risk of diminishing the value of the churches' spiritual heritage. The loss of such a precious spiritual heritage in our efforts to communicate the message of Christ diminishes the real potential of accumulated spiritual experience.[8]

In a questionnaire for Arab Christians in Jordan and Bahrain, Bruce Heckman asked, "How do you feel about Muslim believers using Islamic styles of worship when they meet together?" The negative answers included, "The use of Islamic styles of worship is wrong. We cannot accept expressions of worship that relate to idolatry or strange rituals." Another affirmed, "I personally believe Islamic worship is devised by the devil. The worship structure of Muslim believers should therefore be different and not attached to the past."[9]

Heckman then asked, "What could be the effects of using Islamic styles of worship?" The negative answers included, "Those using Islamic style of worship would deviate from true Christianity." Another believed, "Using old forms of worship would take them back to the life from which they were delivered." Still another affirmed, "Continuity with the past will tie the Muslim believer to darkness."[10]

Not only resident Christians but Muslims too have objected to Christian contextualization. Ata'ullah Siddiqi in *Arabia: Islamic World Review* (July, 1987) charged:

> Christian missionaries are now adopting a new, underhanded style in their outreach to Muslims. Known as the *Contextualized Approach*, it means they now speak in the context of the people and the culture of the country where they are operating, and are less honest in their dealings with simple, often illiterate, peasants. They no longer call themselves openly Christians in a Muslim area, but "Followers of Isa." The church is no longer a "church," but a *"Masjid Isa."* Missionaries assiduously avoid calling Jesus the "Son of God" to Muslims, who no matter how ignorant will be alarmed by the term. He is called to them *"Ruhullah"* (the Spirit of God).[11]

The Malaysian *New Straits Times* (Kuala Lampur, March 24, 1988) reported on a government white paper on Christian attempts at contextualization in which the church "would emulate the Muslim practice of reading the Quran when reading the Bible, sitting on the floor, using the *rehal* (wooden stand) to prop up the Bible," and wearing clothing traditionally worn by Muslims. Such practices are seen as deceptive, confusing, and causing "suspicion between Malays and Christians."

Considerable debate was caused in Malaysia when *The Star* (Kuala Lampur, April 5, 1988) reported on a bill passed by the Selangor state government forbidding non-Islamic religions from using the following words: Allah (God), *Rasul* (Apostle), *Fatwa* (legal opinion), *Wahyu* (from *Wahy*—revelation), *Iman* (faith), Imam (leader of mosque prayer or the Muslim community), *Ulama* (religious scholars), *Dakwah* (from *Da'wa*—lit. "call," mission), *Nabi* (prophet), *Hadith* (prophetic tradition), *Syariah* (from *Shari'a*—religious law), *Injil* (gospel), *Ibadah* (religious duties such as prayer), *Qiblat* (from *Qibla*, direction of prayer), *Salat* (ritual prayer), *Kaabah* (cubical building in the Meccan mosque), *Haj* (from *Hajj*—pilgrimage), *Kadi* (from Qadi—religious judge), and *Mufti* (giver of legal opinions; today, sometimes the religious leader).

To these prohibited words were added such exclamations as *Subhanallah* (Praise be to God!), *Alhamdulillah* (Praise be to God!), *Lailahaillallah* (There is no god but God!), and *Allahu Akbar* (God is greater!). A similar bill was passed in Malacca (*The Star*, April 7, 1988) as had previously been done in Kelantan, Trengganu, Negri, Sembilan, and Penang.[12]

Whatever the final outcome, it is significant that the Muslim community felt these words and exclamations were exclusively their own. Their opposition to such contextualization as well as the similar opposition of many Christians might be alleviated if it were shown how many of the religious terms and worship forms are the common heritage of both communities.

Previous Use of the Pillars by Jews and Christians

Islam may be viewed as originally a contextualization for the Arabs of the monotheism inherited directly[13] from Jews[14] and Christians,[15] or indirectly through Arab monotheists.[16] This interpretation of the earlier preaching would be supported by references to the Quran as an Arabic book, confirming the earlier revelation (e.g., sura [chapter] 46:12, Egyptian ed./11, Fluegel ed.).[17] Ultimately, of course, the message was seen to be for all humans (sura

34:28/27).* All that is necessary for our purposes, however, is to show that the pillars of faith along with associated vocabulary were largely the previous possessions of Jews and Christians. Any reusing of them then is but the repossession of what originally belonged to these communities.

The earliest Muslim exegetes showed no hesitation in recognizing the Jewish and Christian origin of many religious terms in the Quran. Later the orthodox doctrine was elaborated so that the Quran was a unique production of the Arabic language.[18] Arthur Jeffery argued that Syriac was the major source of borrowed vocabulary.[19] This borrowing is of special interest because a number of the words banned to non-Muslims in parts of Malaysia can be shown to have been used by Jews or Christians before the advent of Muhammad (A.D. 570–632). They are treated here because of the relevance of a number of them to the "pillars" of Muslim faith and practice.

Since our purpose here is limited to showing the origin of these "Islamic" terms, we shall not do the detailed "componential analysis" that a Bible translator would to see the use and meaning of these terms in Muslim sources as compared to the use and meaning of these and other terms in Christian sources.[20] Nor shall we consider the emotions their use by Christians may arouse nor the primary associations they may now have with one religious community and the new meanings it may have given to the terms. Again, our purpose here is only to show that Jews and Christians were already using many of these terms when Muhammad began his preaching; so they have been held in common. Subsequently, when we look at the pillars of religious observance themselves, we will investigate their meaning and function as well as their source.

The terms banned in Malaysia include the following:

- Allah is of Christian Syriac origin and was in use long before Muhammad's time.[21]
- Wahy (revelation) is at least etymologically related to Jewish-Aramaic and Christian Ethiopic words and is used by the pre-Islamic poets.[22]
- Nabi (prophet) is probably from Jewish Aramaic rather than Syriac and was apparently known to the Arabs long before Muhammad.[23]
- Injil (gospel) is based on the Greek euaggelion and probably came through the Ethiopic of Christian Abyssinia.[24]

---

*Standard scholarly practice today lists the verses of the Egyptian edition of the Quran first and then the Fluegel edition, if different. The Egyptian edition frequently gives a lower verse number.

- The *Qiblat* (direction of prayer) obviously predates Muhammad. We find allusion to it in 1 Kings 8:44 and clear reference to it in Daniel 6:10. Syriac Christians faced the east; and Jews faced Jerusalem—the direction from which it was changed in sura 2:142/136-152/147. One tradition, reported by al-Tabari, even ascribes the change to remarks by Jews concerning Muhammad's dependence on Judaism.[25]
- *Salat* (ritual prayer) may be from Jewish Aramaic but is more probably from Syriac and was familiar in pre-Islamic times.[26]
- *Haj* (pilgrimage) is from the Hebrew *hag*, meaning "festival," in Exodus 23:18 and Psalm 81:3.

Similar Jewish or Christian pre-Islamic usage can also be found for exclamations banned in parts of Malaysia—for example, *Subhanallah* (Praise be to God!). Allah has already been traced to the Syriac before Muhammad, as can *subhan*.[27] Likewise, the Semitic scholar Eugen Mittwoch finds *Allahu Akbar* (God is greater!) similar to the benedictions of the Jewish *tefillah* prayers performed three times a day.[28] There were, of course, alterations of meaning as words and practices moved from Jewish and Christian systems of thought to a Muslim one; but, as will be seen, the systems were similar enough that the core meanings remained.

Pillar I: Confession of Faith (*shahada*)

The first part of the Muslim confession of faith (*shahada*—"I bear witness that there is no god but God") is based on verses like suras 37:35/34 ("There is no god but God") and 112:1-2 ("Say, 'He [is] God, One [*ahad*]. God the Alone'"). The wording, as Hartwig Herschfeld[29] indicates, is apparently based on the *shema* in Deuteronomy 6:4 ("Hear O Israel, the Lord our God is One [*ahad*] Lord"). Both emphasize the same word *ahad*. The Talmud of Jerusalem cites certain rabbis as counseling the faithful to put emphasis on this word.[30]

Not only is the form of the *shahada* similar to the *shema* and apparently is based on it; the functions of the two are the same. They not only introduce every formal service of worship but are the basic confessions for both faiths. Those confessions separate the Hebrews and the Muslims from the surrounding polytheists. Both also linked the affirmation of who God is with the obligations due him. The *shema*, especially in its longer form in Numbers 15:37-41, introduces commandments. The relationship is pointed out in Mishna *Berakoth* 2:213 where it says that one takes on "the yoke of the kingdom of heaven" by reciting the first sentence and "the yoke of the commandments" by reciting the subsequent part.[31] Furthermore, that which is affirmed in the first sentence of the *shemaʿ*—the unity of God—forms the basis for the first commandment of the Decalogue: "Thou shalt have no other gods before me." The same relationship between confession and obligation is seen in the *shahada*, for this first pillar affirming what God is is followed by four pillars concerning obligations to him. The same linkage is found in the Quran 20:14: "In truth, I am God. There is no god but I; therefore serve me, and perform the prayer of my remembrance."

That which has been said about the *shemaʿ* in the Old Testament can also be said about it in the New, for Jesus gives it as the most important commandment in Mark 12:29–30.

In looking for the meaning of these confessions to the devotees, we must note their simplicity and clarity. Further, both *shahada* and *shemaʿ* require more than intellectual assent. The *shahada* is prefaced by "I bear witness" and the *shemaʿ* is introduced by "Hear O Israel": both require confession. This is more than James speaks of in 2:19: "You believe that God is one; you do well. Even the demons believe—and shudder."

As it involves rejection of polytheism, it also involves the rejection of intermediaries and associates with God in popular beliefs. In Sufi mysticism it involves the rejection of all earthly gods like wealth. It means seeing his signs in all things. "Wherever you turn, there is the face of God" (sura 2:115/109).[32]

Many traditions mention only the uniqueness or unity of God as the essential article of belief.[33] The traditional confession goes on, however, to declare, "Muhammad is the Apostle of God" based on quranic passages like sura 4:134/135. We shall not deal with this part here because it is obviously an addition to Jewish and Christian faith.

When Christians look for a substitute affirmation, it is noteworthy that Islam's most celebrated theologian Abu Hamid al-Ghazali (d. 1111) twice gives a confession that Muslims as well as Christians should be able to accept—the *shahada* with the name of Jesus substituted for Muhammad: "There is no god but God and Jesus is the Apostle of God."[34] Alternatively the Christian might substitute one of the early Christian confessions reflected in the New Testament, such as "Jesus is Lord" (Romans 10:9).

Pillar II: Ritual Prayer (*salat*)

In the Asian case study we shall be analyzing below, Muslims watched Christian relief workers come and selflessly serve them. They said that they should be called angels because they were so good, kind, and honest, "but they do not say their prayers." It was not until they were seen praying publicly at regular times that they were finally accepted as godly.

One of the first definitions of a Muslim was one who "pronounces the name of the Lord and prays" (sura 87:15). Yet the term chosen (verb *salla*—"to bow"; noun *salat*) had long been used for institutionalized prayer in synagogues and churches. *'Aqama 'l-salat* (to perform the prayer) was apparently borrowed from the Syrian church while Muhammad was still in Mecca, but the roots of the prayer service are also seen in Judaism as will be shown in the terminology, postures, and content.

Although the Old Testament mentions morning and evening prayer (Exod. 29:39; Num. 28:4), Judaism developed three prayers a day on the pattern of Psalm 55:17 (cf. Dan. 6:10) as is seen in the Talmud of Jerusalem.[35] Christian monks prayed seven times a day on the pattern of Psalm 119:164. The Quran does not mention the five prayers but gives a variety of prayer times (suras 2:238/239; 17:78/80; 20:130; 24:58/57). The traditions, however, clearly list five;[36] so Islam took a middle position.[37] Of significance for Muslim converts is the fact that the early Jewish Christians maintained their former institutionalized prayer times and places (Acts 3:1; 10:9; 16:13).

Preparations

The removal of sandals in places of prayer (sura 20:12) follows the Hebrew pattern (Exod. 3:5) also practiced by many Eastern churches. The ablutions also reflect the earlier faiths. The minor ritual ablution (*wudu'*) is used to get rid of "minor" ritual impurity (*hadath*). The Jewish influence here is evident by the latter part of Muhammad's life: "You, who believe, when you prepare for the prayer, wash your faces and your hands up to the elbows and rub your heads and your feet up to the ankles" (5:6/8; cf. 4:43/46). The Old Testament Tabernacle had a basin for washing the hands and feet of the priests before they entered the presence of the Lord (Exod. 30:17-21; 40:30-32), and others also were to consecrate themselves when coming into his presence (1 Sam. 16:5). Muslims follow the same order in their ablutions as the Jews do—the face, then the hands, then the feet. The name of God is pronounced, and the right side is done before the left. Each part is washed three times.[38]

"Major" ritual impurity (*janaba* or major *hadath*) requires washing of the total body (*ghusl*) before prayer. This is necessitated by such occurrences as seminal discharge or menstruation.[39] It is also common practice before Friday noon prayers and the two major annual feast days (*Id al-Fitr* and *Id al-Adha*). The quranic distinction is based on sura 5:6/8-9 which adds to a prior description of the minor ablutions "if you are in a state of pollution, purify yourself."

Again, similar details are found in Judaism where occurrences such as seminal discharge and menstruation require bathing the body (Lev. 12:1-5; 14:8; 15; 17:15; Num. 19:19). The Friday bath in Islam corresponds with the sabbath bath in Judaism. Likewise, the bathing of the convert to Islam corresponds with proselyte baptism in Judaism, which, of course, was the precursor of Christian baptism.[40] In the light of the fact that both Christian baptism and Muslim proselyte *ghusl* are reinterpretations of Jewish proselyte baptism, it might be possible to interpret Christian baptism as proselyte *ghusl* without causing as much furor as arose earlier when a Christian author temporarily raised the question of a possible alternative initiation rite for baptism.[41]

Another parallel is rubbing the hands and face with sand (*tayammum*) if water cannot be found, which is permitted by both the Quran (suras 4:43/46 and 5:6/9-9) and the Talmud.[42] Christian baptism too has been performed in the desert with sand.[43]

The function of the ablutions is purity from defilement (4:43/46; 5:6/8-9; 87:14-15), and water from heaven is also "to put away . . . the defilement of Satan" (8:11). The intention is inward purity which is seen as both an act of God (5:6/9; 24:21) and of the worshipers themselves (9:108/109) resulting in Paradise (20:76/78). Therefore, the purification obviously involves the forgiveness of sin.

The Bible likewise associated ablutions with purity of heart (Ps. 24:3-4; Is. 1:16-18; Ezek. 36:25-26; Jn. 3:4-5; Heb. 10:22). Jesus went further in shifting the emphasis from the ablutions to purity of heart (Matt. 15:1-20; Mark 7:1-23). The writer of the Epistle to the Hebrews makes ablutions merely a foreshadowing of inner purity provided through Christ (Heb. 6:1-2; 9:10-14). Church fathers like Tertullian and Chrysostom emphasized that such rituals were deprived of value unless accompanied by purity of heart.

Christ and the church, however, made the ablution of proselyte baptism more prominent than the other two faiths did and emphasized the symbolism of being dead to sin and buried with Christ and being resurrected with him to newness of life. The other two faiths, as has been seen, practiced a proselyte baptism; but circumcision has been a more central confession of faith for Judaism, as has the *shahada* for Islam.

Along with ablutions, another preliminary essential in Muslim prayer is the proper orientation (*qibla*). It comes from '*aqbala 'ala* (direction toward a point) and, as has been noted, has ancient roots.

The Garden of Eden was toward the east (Gen. 2:8), as was the door of the tabernacle (Exod. 27:13), and the temple entrance in Ezekiel's vision (47:1). It was the direction from which the glory of God came.

Zechariah compared Christ to the rising sun (Luke 1:78), thereby associating him with Malachi's prophecy of the sun of righteousness that would come with healing (Mal. 4:2). Thus Christians in the early centuries prayed toward the east,[44] even though Jesus had made plain to the woman of Samaria that places and orientation were not important in the worship of God (Jn. 4:19-24).

The Jews prayed toward Jerusalem (1 Kings 8:33; Dan. 6:10), a practice regulated in the Talmud.[45] Muslims for a time prayed toward Jerusalem (sixteen or seventeen months according to al-Bukhari).[46] It remained a center of devotion because of the temple area (now the Dome of the Rock and the Aqsa Mosque) where Muhammad is reported to have gone in his night journey (sura 17). The direction of prayer, however, was changed to Mecca in sura 2:142/136-152/147. As Jerusalem had been the center of the world for Jews (Ezek. 5:5), Mecca became the center of the world for Muslims. Mosques came to include a mihrab (a niche indicating the direction of Mecca) as some synagogues had a mizrah (indicating the direction of Jerusalem).

In noting the prescribed direction of prayer, the Quran (sura 2:115/109), like the Talmud, recognizes that God is everywhere.[47] The Quran, however, notes that true piety consists not in the direction you face; it teaches that piety consists in belief in God, the Last Day, the angels, the Book, and the Prophets, and to give of one's substance to the needy, to perform the prayer and pay alms, to fulfill one's covenant, and endure adversity (2:177/172).

The worshipers also must pronounce their intention (niya) to perform the salat, specifying the number of times they plan to repeat the ritual. Although the term does not appear in the Quran, it probably developed under Jewish influence to become analogous to the Hebrew kawwana and the Latin Christian intentio. The value of any religious duty depends on the intention of the devotee.[48] As thus developed, the meaning gets somewhat closer to that of Jesus in the Sermon on the Mount where he moves the focus from the external act to the heart condition (Matt. 5:17-28).

Praying

The Muslim postures of prayers also replicate those of Jews and Christians. First, there is the posture of standing (sura 22:26/27). In the Old and New Testaments, worshipers stood to pray (1 Kings 8:14,22; Neh. 9:2; Mark 11:25). The Jewish tefilla prayers were called

'amida (standing), indicating the posture when they were performed.[49]
The second posture is bowing (ruku; sura 22:26/27, 77/76), which has
an equivalent in Jewish piety and communicates the sense of humble
servitude that the genuflection does in the Roman Catholic mass.

The third posture is prostration with the forehead on the ground
(sura 22:26/27, 77/76). Again, this form is found in both the Old and
New Testaments (Num. 16:22; 1 Sam. 24:8; Neh. 8:6; Matt. 26:39). It is
the equivalent of the Jewish hishtahawah and a similar Eastern Christian form.[50] On Yom Kippur rabbis and cantors still prostrate themselves in this way, and I have observed Coptic Orthodox monks and
worshipers do this in worship. Prostration with the body fully extended is practiced in Roman Catholic ordination and consecration
and on Friday and Saturday of Holy Week.

The fourth posture is half kneeling and half sitting. Kneeling is
a biblical form; sometimes the hands are lifted up as in biblical times
(Ps. 28:2; 134:2; 1 Tim. 2:8).

The content of the prayers also have stylistic agreement with
Jewish and Christian prayers.[51] The repetition of "God is greater"
(Allahu akbar) corresponds with benedictions like "God is blessed"
in the Jewish tefilla. The recitation of the Fatiha, the first chapter of
the Quran, includes materials that would be common in Jewish and
Christian prayers. In fact, the missionary statesman Samuel Zwemer
recited it in a public gathering in Calcutta in 1928 and then concluded with the words "in Jesus' name, Amen." The use of "Praise
be to God" in the beginning of the Fatiha corresponds to a similar
blessing in Syriac liturgy.

Blessings upon Muhammad come after the basic prayer ritual
(rak'a) and are, of course, an addition to Jewish and Christian worship. The prayer concludes with the worshiper turning to the left
and the right and saying, "Peace be upon you." This form also concludes the main Jewish prayer[52] as the "passing of the peace" is often
included in the celebration of the Christian eucharist.

The Friday prayer is mentioned in sura 62:9 where the day is
called "the day of Assembly" (yawm al-Jum'a). the same meaning as
the Hebrew name yom hakkenisa for the sabbath.[53] The development
of these prayers during the Umayyad Period (A.D. 661–750) may have
been under Christian influence.[54] The choice of a day each week was
a result of Jewish and Christian contacts according to a Tradition:

> The Jews have every seventh day a day when they get together [for
> prayer], and so do the Christians; therefore, let us do the same.[55]

Goitein argues that Friday was chosen because it was a market
day in Medina when people could more readily come to prayer.[56]

Unlike the Jewish sabbath and the Christian Sunday, it was not a day of rest. Sura 62:9 suggests they leave their trafficking to come to prayers. Unlike the biblical account of creation where God rested the seventh day and the children of Israel were to do likewise (Gen. 2:2–3; Exod. 20:8), the Quran makes a point of noting that God was not tired after the six days of creation (sura 50:38–37)—a topic also noted by Jewish scholars.

The supererogatory night vigil (salat al-lail; tahajjud meaning "waking" in 17:79/81) reflects the Syriac Christian ascetic practice of keeping awake (shahra).[57] Its function included merit (especially during Ramadan, the month of fasting, and before the two major annual festivals),[58] and it loosens one of the knots that Satan ties in the hair of a sleeper.[59]

The imam who leads the prayers corresponds to the sheliah hassibbur of Jewish worship. Both can be done by any qualified person in the community.

Meaning and Function

When we turn to the meaning and function of prayer in Islam to see how adaptable aspects of it are for Christian worship, we encounter formidable misunderstandings between the two communities. Constance E. Padwick, who has done so much to lead us into the heart of Muslim prayer,[60] said of several excellent books on Christian prayer in Arabic:

> When put into the hands of Moslems (unless those educated in Christian schools) these books have proved to be nearly unintelligible. Not only are the fundamental thoughts of Moslem readers about God and about prayer very different from those of the Christian writers, but through the centuries the Church has developed her own Arabic Christian vocabulary, and even when she uses the same word as the Moslem, she may read into it a Christian meaning of which he knows nothing. The first and most obvious example of this is the very word "salat," which for the Moslem means the prescribed prayers of the five hours, and for the Christian is full of many rich and delicate meanings.[61]

We have, however, seen sufficient overlapping of forms and shall see an overlapping of meanings and functions, so that understanding and adaptation of prayers between the two communities is possible.

First, it is necessary to make the distinction between corporate liturgical worship (salat) and personal invocation (du'a)[62]—a distinction found in both traditions (e.g., sura 14:40/42; Matt. 6:6–13; Acts 4:24–31). Islam and liturgical Christians focus on the former, and nonliturgical Protestants emphasize the latter. Here we shall direct our attention to orthodox/orthoprax meanings and functions rather than those of the mystical Sufis and folk Muslims.

The concept of acquiring merit through prayer is strong in Islamic thought—both in the traditions[63] and in contemporary practice. Recently, a nine-month pregnant Syrian woman explained, "In my condition the merit is multiplied 70 times."

Judaism developed a strong legalism (e.g., Tobit 12:9) as did the postapostolic church, which led to Alexander of Hales (d. 1245) advancing the doctrine of the Treasury of Merit. Protestants, however, although seeing the rewards of prayer (Matt. 6:5-6) and that good can lead to life and divine acceptance (Rom. 2:6-7; Acts 10:35), do not see it as merit but the fruit of faith. Salvation is not seen as a result of merit (Tit. 3:5); therefore, Protestants would want to eliminate this function of prayer.

Muslims have viewed the *salat* as a duty;[64] yet it is more. Muhammad is reported to have said, "the *salat* is the comfort of my eyes."[65] Likewise he is quoted as saying, "If one of you performs the *salat*, he is in confidential conversation with God."[66] It functions to intensify belief: "between man and polytheism and unbelief lies the neglect of *salat*."[67]

The prayer has been described as providing cleansing: "the *salat* is like a stream of sweet water which flows past the door of each one of you; into it he plunges five times a day; do you think that anything remains of his uncleanness after that?"[68] Likewise we read, "an obligatory *salat* is a cleansing for the sins which are committed between it and the following one."[69] Since the *salat* proper does not include penitence, the anticipated forgiveness is apparently based on human merit and divine mercy. However, it is common practice to insert before the final pronouncement of peace: "O God, forgive me my former and my latter [sins], my open and my secret [sins] and my extravagances and what Thou dost know."[70] Furthermore, as has been seen, the ablutions include a sense of inner cleansing.

The ritual prayer includes many themes that Christians share:

1. Witness ("I bear witness that there is no god but God" in the call to prayer which, however, also witnesses to Muhammad's apostleship; cf. Deut. 6:4).
2. God's mercy ("In the name of God, the Compassionate, the Merciful" in the Fatiha; cf. Ps. 86:5 and pre-Islamic use of these introductory words in south and central Arabia and in early Arabic manuscripts of the Bible after Muhammad).[71]

3. Praise to God ("Praise be to God" in the Fatiha; cf. Heb. *Haleliu Yah* and Latin Christian *Alleluia*).
4. God's sovereignty ("Lord of the worlds" in the Fatiha; cf. Talmudic *Melek ha 'olam* —king of the universe.)
5. Judgment ("King of the Day of Reckoning" in the Fatiha; cf. Rom. 2:2-3; John 5:22; Matt. 25:34; 1 Cor. 15:24).
6. Worship ("Thee do we worship" in the Fatiha; cf. Ex. 24:1. The Heb. *hishtahawah* and Greek *proskyneo* indicate prostration.)
7. Refuge ("To Thee we cry for help" in the Fatiha; cf. Ps. 46:1).
8. Guidance ("Guide us in the right path" in the Fatiha; cf. Ps. 31:3; 119:1).
9. God's glory ("Glory to my Lord" in the *ruku*; the nominal form of *sabbaha* is used, borrowed from the Hebrew and Aramaic *shabeah* of Jewish worship).
10. God's greatness ("the Great" in the *ruku*; cf. Ps. 48:1).
11. God's exaltation ("the Most High" in the *sujud*; cf. Ps. 83:18).
12. Petition and intercession (possible in the *du'a*; cf. 1 Tim. 2:1).

Obviously there is considerable overlapping of the themes of Muslim and Christian prayer.[72] Christian prayer can include most of Muslim prayer except the references to Muhammad and, for most Protestants, prayer for the dead. This has been evident in the study of the *salat* with its inclusion of the Fatiha.[73]

Muslim prayer cannot include quite as much of Christian prayer because of the references to God as Father, Jesus as Lord, the Trinity, and the crucifixion of Christ. Although Muslims may misunderstand parts of the Lord's Prayer, its themes resonate in Muslim devotion; and a tradition even says that Muhammad proposed a prayer which is obviously a free rendering of the Lord's Prayer without the initial words "Our Father."[74]

The Mosque

Some Muslim followers of Christ stay for at least a time in the mosque as the early Jewish followers of Christ remained in the temple and synagogue. Where whole villages have turned to Christ, they have reutilized the mosque for a church. Others have continued mosque-like worship. To evaluate the appropriateness of these approaches, we shall seek to determine the extent to which the mosque has been influenced by synagogues and churches and what its meanings and functions are.

The word for a mosque, *masjid*, is from the Aramaic and has the root meaning "to worship" or "prostrate oneself," found also in the Ethiopic *mesgad* used of a temple or church.[75] In the Quran it is a general word that is used not only of Muslim sanctuaries but also of the Christian sanctuary associated with the Seven Sleepers of Ephesus (sura 18:21/20) and the Jewish temple in Jerusalem (if we adopt the traditional interpretation of sura 17:1). Ibn Khaldun (d. 1406) still used the word in a general sense to include the temple of Solomon.[76] The underlying meaning of "synagogue" and "church" (*ekklesia*) is "gathering" as is *jami'*, a word that increasingly came to be used for mosques.

Muhammad certainly knew about synagogues and churches or chapels, for they are mentioned in the Quran (sura 20:40/41). As Islam spread, various arrangements with Christian and Jewish sanctuaries developed. In Damascus, tradition says that the church of St. John was divided, half for Muslims and half for Christians. In any event, the two centers of worship were beside each other until the mosque incorporated the church.

In Hims in Syria and Dabil in Armenia, Muslims and Christians shared the same buildings. Umar, the second caliph, built a mosque on the site of the temple in Jerusalem where later the Dome of the Rock was built. Many churches and synagogues were transformed into mosques. Muslims were told, "Perform your *salat* in them [churches and synagogues]; it will not harm you." The transfer of buildings was further facilitated whenever they were associated with biblical people who were also recognized by Islam. On the other hand, the second caliph Umar is reported to have declined to perform the *salat* in the Church of the Holy Sepulcher to guard against its being made into a mosque.[77]

The mosque performed many functions. Primarily for worship, it also was a place for public political assembly or even for strangers who needed a place to sleep and eat. Worship included not only prayer but might include the repetition of the names and praises of God, a practice cultivated by the Sufis.[78]

Mosque worship also included the recitation of the Quran. Here the influence of the previous monotheistic faiths is evident. *Quran* is from the Syriac *qeryana* used to denote the "reading" or "reciting" of the Scripture lesson by Christians,[79] as the Muslim *qira'a* (the recitation itself) is the equivalent of *Qeri'a* of the synagogue.[80] Sermons, too, were included, especially at Friday noon. Evidence of Jewish and Christian influence would seem to include the requirement of two sermons, with the preacher standing but pausing to sit down in between. This would correspond with the practice of the rabbi sitting while the law was rolled up, between the reading of the Torah and the prophets.[81]

The earliest mosques were open spaces with arbors or booths, but they soon developed under Christian influence. Pillars and other materials were taken from churches and the booths were replaced with pillared halls. The caliph Abd al-Malik (646–705) had Byzantine builders erect the Dome of the Rock in Jerusalem, consciously copying the dome of the Church of the Holy Sepulcher. His son al-Walid (d. 715) not only had Byzantine architects transform the basilica of St. John the Baptist in Damascus into the Umayyad Mosque, but used Christian architects to direct the building of the mosques of Mecca and Medina. When he was inspecting the work in Medina, an old man said, "We used to build in the style of mosques; you build in the style of churches."[82]

The minaret may have been influenced in a number of ways. It was not part of the earliest mosques, but was included when churches such as the basilica of St. John in Damascus became mosques. The church had a watchtower—the meaning of *manara*, its common Muslim name. It may also have been influenced by the dwelling-towers of Christian ascetics in North Africa where it had the name *sawma'a* (a saint's cell) and was used as such in Egypt and Syria.

The *mihrab* (a niche indicating the direction of prayer) was not in the earliest mosques. In churches it was a principal niche that might contain the bishop's throne or an image or picture of a saint. Muslim literature attests that it was taken over from churches. It was even opposed because it was inherited from churches and was compared with altars as the holiest place. It is the place where the imam stands. Churches that became mosques, such as the Hagia Sophia in Istanbul, often had to alter the inside to indicate the *mihrab*. A Roman Catholic orphanage in Kabul, Afghanistan, supervised by the Islamicist S. de Beaurecueil, had two orientations so that Christians and Muslims could worship in the same room.

The *minbar* is probably a loan word from Ethiopic and means "seat, chair." Traditions indicate that the original maker was a Byzantine or Coptic Christian. 'Amr, the companion of Muhammad who conquered Egypt, had one made in his mosque, and it was said to be of Christian origin. Obviously it was analogous to a Christian pulpit.

A platform (*dakka*) from which the *mu'adhdhin* gives the call to prayer is found in larger mosques. There is also a *kursi* (a wooden stand with a seat and a desk to hold a Quran). The seat is for the reader (*qari*, *qass*). Water for ablutions is often provided in a basin (*fisqiya* or *piscina*, which in the Mishna and Syriac is *piskin*). Unlike churches, in mosques the hanging of pictures and images is banned. The use of carpets is traced back to Muhammad, who used a mat woven of palm leaves.[83]

Of interest here is that Rabbi Abraham, who inherited the position of "leader of the Jews" upon the death of his father Maimonides in 1237, demanded that pillows be removed from synagogues and carpets and prayer mats be used. He believed that Islam (and especially the Sufis) had preserved many practices of the former Jewish sages, such as the use of these along with prostration and kneeling, ritual immersions, and nightly prayers.

Since Islam expresses a total way of life, and traditionally "religion" and "politics" were not separated, the functions of the mosque were, and to a lesser extent still are, broader than most churches today. Originally the caliph was appointed the leader of the *salat* and the preacher (*khatib*) for the community and was installed on the *minbar*. In the provinces, governors served a similarly broad function, administering "justice among the people" and the *salat*. The mosque also served as a court of justice. Some early judges sat in judgment beside the *minbar* or in the square beside the mosque—practices that were also associated with churches.[84]

To determine the extent to which Muslim followers of Christ may still worship in a mosque or mosque-like context, we need to determine the function of both mosques and churches. Contemporary mosques are more like Christian chapels (where people only worship) than local churches (where people are also members), although many mosques in the United States have also assumed the latter function. The early Christian community applied themselves to teaching, fellowship, breaking of bread, prayer, performing signs and miracles, sharing, and praising God. They continued to go regularly to the temple, but broke bread in their homes (Acts 2:42–47). Here we at least have a precedent for continuing the previous incomplete worship even as the new believers remembered Christ's death (the completion of the worship) in their homes. Paul continued to go to the synagogue and temple until put out (e.g., Acts 19:8–9; 21:26–30). James, too, still worshipped in the synagogue, or a place called a synagogue (James 2:2).

Pillar III: Almsgiving (*zakat*)

Zakat is obligatory almsgiving of a prescribed percentage of different kinds of property (2½ percent for most) and distributed to the needy. The Quran specifies the recipients of various kinds of alms as parents, relatives, orphans, the poor, the needy, travelers, those who work on [collecting] them, those whose hearts are to be conciliated, slaves, debtors, and for God's purposes (2:115/211; 9:60). *Zakat* is an Aramaic loan word which originally was a general term for virtue but came to be used by the rabbis for charitable gifts, an understandable shift when almsgiving was considered as particularly virtuous. The same shift in meaning can also be traced in the Quran from virtue in general (suras 87:14; 92:18) to almsgiving (sura 7:156/155; 21:73).

Sadaqa is another quranic word for almsgiving. It, too, is a loan word from the Hebrew sedaqa or sedeq, meaning "honesty" or "righteousness," but was used by the rabbis of "almsgiving." The relationship between upright actions (sedeq) and caring for the poor is already seen in Daniel 4:27. The word sadaqa is used in two ways in the Quran and the traditions. First, it is a synonym of zakat (obligatory alms) in the Quran (sura 9:58-60, 103/104-104/105) and the traditions (where al-Bukhari talks about sadaqa in sections on zakat). Secondly, sadaqa is used of voluntary almsgiving (e.g., 2:263/265-264/266), sometimes called sadaqat al-tatawwu' (alms of spontaneity).

'Ushr is a tithe on produce levied for public assistance. It was similar to the tithes on the land of the Mosaic law (Lev. 27:30-33; Num. 18:21-26). In places, half went to the poor and half went to the ruler.

Almsgiving had great importance in all three monotheistic faiths. The Quran makes a clear distinction between believers, who give alms (suras 8:2-4; 23:1-4), and disbelievers, who do not (sura 41:7/6). There is considerable concern that alms be given to the poor (sura 9:60)—a concern shared with the Old Testament (Deut. 15:11; Prov. 19:17) and the New Testament (Matt. 6:1-4; 25:35-46).

There are numbers of parallels between the Quran and the Bible. One has to do with not giving to be seen by people. The Quran indicates that God does not love those who dispense their goods ostensibly to be seen by people (sura 4:38/42) in a context that suggests almsgiving. Likewise Jesus said, "When you give alms, sound no trumpet before you as the hypocrites do . . . that they may be praised by men" (Mt. 6:1-4). In the Quran, however, public giving is all right: "Say to my servants who believe, that they . . . expend of that we have provided them, secretly and in public" (sura 14:31/36). It says, "If you publish your freewill offering, it is good; but, if you conceal them and give to the poor, that is better" (sura 2:271/273). Islam's most celebrated theologian, Abu Hamid al-Ghazali (d. 1111) even argued in the Ihya that much can be said for both open and secret alms, depending on the circumstances and the motive.[85]

Another parallel between the Quran and the Bible has to do with the attitude and conduct that accompanies almsgiving. Sura 2:262/263 says, "Those who expend their wealth in the way of God then follow not up what they have expended with reproach and injury, their wage is with their Lord." Paul speaks of the importance of attitude in 2 Corinthians 9:7: "Each man should give . . . not reluctantly or under compulsion, for God loves a cheerful giver" (NIV).

Still another parallel between the two Scriptures has to do with God's recompense. Although the Quran warns not to give in order to gain more (74:6), rewards are promised: "What you give in alms desiring God's face . . . they receive recompense manifold" (sura 30:39/38). The reward is compared to the multiplication of corn when it is planted (sura 2:261/263).

Proverbs 19:17 likewise promises, "He who is kind to the poor lends to the Lord, and he will repay him for his deeds." Jesus also said, "Give and it will be given to you" (Luke 6:38). The rich young ruler whose focus on wealth kept him from following Jesus was told, "Go, sell your possessions and give to the poor, and you will have treasure in heaven. Then come, follow me" (Matt. 19:21 NIV). Jesus knew "wherever your treasure is, there will your heart be also" (Matt. 6:21).

There is an area in which alms accomplish a function with which Protestants would take issue. The Quran affirms:

> whosoever forgoes it [legal retribution] as a freewill offering (sadaqa), that shall be to him an expiation (kaffara) [for his own sins] . . . the expiation [for breaking oaths] is to feed ten poor persons . . . or to clothe them, or to set free a slave . . . expiation [for slaying game during pilgrimage is] food for poor persons (Sura 5:45/49, 89/91, 95/96).

The Roman Catholic canon in the apocrypha has a similar teaching: "almsgiving atones for sin" (Ecclus. 3:30), and "almsgiving delivers from death and saves people from passing down to darkness" (Tobit 4:7).

Some of the church fathers also associated almsgiving with the forgiveness of sins. The second epistle attributed to Clement of Rome claims: "Almsgiving is excellent as penitence for sin; fasting is better than prayer, but almsgiving is better than either. . . . almsgiving alleviates sin" (16:4). Cyprian, Athanasius, Jerome, and Augustine also associated almsgiving with the forgiveness of sins.[86]

Much more could be said on the function of zakat in contemporary Muslim economics.[87] But, from a Christian perspective, we need to note that Jesus expected it to be a regular part of the believer's practice (Matt. 6:3); and James classified attention to orphans and widows in their affliction to be part of religion that is pure and undefiled before God (1:27). Yet underlying all Christian giving should be the response of gratitude for God's "inexpressible gift" (2 Cor. 9:11-15).

Pillar IV: Fasting (*sawm*)

Fasting is listed as a characteristic of those who submit to God—that is, true Muslims (sura 33:35). Many Christians, however, believe it is wrong, or at least unwise, to keep the fast of Ramadan.[88] To evaluate this, as with the other pillars, we need to look at the roots, meaning, and function of Muslim and Christian fasting.

The words which Muslims use, *sawm* and *siyam*, originally had a different meaning in Arabic, "to be at rest." In Judeo-Aramaic usage, however, they already meant "fasting," which suggests this was the source of Muslim use. This connection is supported by the Quran which makes the prescription to fast a continuation of the prescription to previous recipients of revelation (sura 2:183/179). The traditions are even more specific:

> The Prophet came to Medina and saw the Jews fasting on the day of 'Ashura. He asked them, "What is this?" They told him, "This . . . is the day on which God rescued the children of Israel from their enemy. So Moses fasted this day." The Prophet said, "We have more claim to Moses than you." So the Prophet fasted on that day and ordered Muslims to fast on it.[89]

The first year in Medina, the fast was "a few days," apparently the ten days of penance leading up to the Jewish Day of Atonement— 'Ashura (the "tenth" in Hebrew-Aramaic), the word Muslims use. It was also a time of seclusion for the pious in the place of worship—a practice that later was incorporated by Muslims into the last ten days of Ramadan and called *i'tikaf*, when that month was made the required fast.

Other practices are also similar to Judaism. Abstaining from eating and drinking in the day but not at night was Jewish.[90] Even in biblical times this was sometimes practiced (Judg. 20:26; 2 Sam. 1:12; 3:35). Likewise, the Quran says, "Eat and drink until the white thread becomes distinct to you from the black thread at dawn" (sura 2:187/183). The source is the Jewish *Mishnah*.[91]

Fasting has played a significant role in Judaism and Christianity—including those of extended periods like the month of Ramadan. Moses, Elijah, and Jesus all fasted forty days and nights (Deut. 9:9, 18; 1 Kings 19:8; Luke 4:1–2). Jesus expected people to fast (Matt. 6:16–18), and Paul fasted frequently (Acts 13:2; 2 Cor. 6:5; 11:27). Fasting was emphasized by the church fathers, and the forty-day fast or self-denial of Lent is even mentioned at the Council of Nicea in 325.

When we look at the meanings and functions of Muslim and Christian fasting, we see many parallels and some differences. For the

Muslim, fasting is above all an act of obedience, for it is prescribed for them (sura 2:183/179). Secondly, it is an act of commemoration of the "descent" of the first verses of the Quran on the twenty-seventh of Ramadan (sura 44:1–5/4). Thirdly, in the traditions it has developed the meaning of contrition and forgiveness that is more prominent in the Judeo-Christian tradition. One says, "All sins are forgiven to one who keeps Ramadan out of sincere faith and hoping for a reward from God." Another affirms, "When the month of Ramadan starts, the gates of heaven are open and the gates of hell closed." The reference to the gates of heaven being open seems to be based on the old Jewish practice of praying when the temple gates were open since that was a propitious time.[92] This same sense of pardon is found in the fasts for expiation (suras 2:196/192; 15:89/90, 95/96). The concept is very prominent in the biblical examples (Deut. 9:25–29; Exod. 32:30; Neh. 1:4–6; 9:1–2; Matt. 12:41), as it is in the Torah.[93] Likewise, the Roman Catholic Church has used the fast as penitence and preparation before the Mass and leading into Holy Week.

The nights of Ramadan are times of joy and celebration, and decorations are often put in the streets during the month. Although fasting was used to express sorrow in biblical times (e.g., 2 Sam. 1:11–12), it could also be a time of joy (Zech. 8:19).

Christians are given warnings against the misuse of fasting (Matt. 6:16–18; Luke 18:10–14), but Jesus expected his disciples to fast (Mark 2:18–20). It is interesting that Paul includes his going hungry as one of the deprivations he endured so that he would "put no obstacle in any one's way" (2 Cor. 6:3). Lack of fasting is seen by Muslims as being irreligious. God asked the Israelites, "Was it really for me that you fasted?" (Zech. 7:5 NIV). We need to ask ourselves the same question.

Pillar V: Pilgrimage (Hajj)

Not too much attention will be given to the pilgrimage, since it was an adoption and reinterpretation of pagan rituals. The traditions make this clear. Muhammad's wife Aisha, for example, told how the pagans used to enter a consecrated state (ihram) in the name of the idol Manat. Out of honor for that idol, they did not perform the pilgrimage ritual between the hills of al-Safa and al-Marwa at the Kaaba until the Quran explained that they were now symbols of God (sura 2:158/153).[94]

Despite its pagan origin, many of its elements were those that God adopted for use in the schoolhouse of his children Israel. The word hajj is the Hebrew hag used in Psalm 81:4 (v. 3 in English) for a sacrifice when the Israelites were gathered in Jerusalem. Likewise, the word *qurban*, frequently used to describe the festival of sacrifice during the pilgrimage, is used for "offering" or "consecrated" in Leviticus and Numbers.

Muslims are required to perform the pilgrimage once in their lifetime if possible, as the Israelites were to go to Jerusalem three times a year. One of these, the feast of tabernacles, has a number of similarities to the *Hajj*—for example, going around the sanctuary (Ps. 26:6) as Muslims do around the Kaaba and standing before God as an act of worship.

The concept of the mosque of Mecca being *haram* (a sacred place restricted to Muslims—sura 9:28) has its counterpart in the court of the gentiles for gentiles, who could not enter the temple. Mecca is seen as the place of the Last Judgment, as Jerusalem is. Abraham is associated with the Kaaba as Jews associate him with Mount Moria under the temple area. The Kaaba has a covering (*kiswa*) which is replaced every year like that of the tabernacle. The direction of prayer for Muslims and Jews has been toward their respective sanctuaries. As the temple had a place for ablutions, the Meccan mosque has *zam zam* water, later supplemented. As Muslim pilgrims put on white clothing when in a consecrated state, so the high priest put on holy garments (Lev. 16:4). Likewise the hair is not cut when one is in a consecrated state as was the case with the biblical Nazarite vow (Num. 6:5).

If all these elements were used by God in his schoolhouse for his people, can they not serve again for lessons as he gathers a new people for himself? The lessons will no longer be in Mecca. As Jesus told the woman of Samaria, worship will not be restricted to specific locations (Jn. 4:20-24). God, however, used pilgrimages to teach the people lessons concerning his holiness and their unity as a people. We shall need to find ways to do the same.

CURRENT REUSING OF THE PILLARS

The case study we are considering is in a Muslim country that has had missionaries and churches for many years. Very few conversions have come from the Muslim community; almost all the Christians were from another religious group.

Five years ago the church responded to a natural catastrophe by sending twenty Christian couples to serve there, only one of whom was from a Muslim background. Their work was appreciated, but their Muslim neighbors would not eat the food they gave them. It was assumed that the Christians were "unclean" when they prepared it because they did not bathe (*ghusl*) in the morning when they may have had sexual relations the night before. When they changed their bathing habits, their Muslim neighbors ate their food. The Christians were called angels because of their service, but were still considered "irreligious" because they did not perform ritual prayers (*salat*). Even when God answered their prayers miraculously, their neighbors did not follow Christ until the Christians were seen to perform ritual prayers.

Less than three years ago a more contextual approach was adopted with help from some who had studied with Fuller School of World Mission personnel. Only Muslim converts were employed in the villages, and many thousands have since responded. God has used a number of factors along with the contextualization. The New Testament had been translated, using Muslim vocabulary rather than words from the other religion, and copies had been sold throughout the villages. Natural catastrophes had occurred which were interpreted as divine judgment, and the Christian couples had responded with a wholistic ministry. These Christians had prayed for the sick, the natural catastrophes, and for personal relationships, and God had answered with amazing power. Muslims who opposed the conversions were even stricken with ailments.

An important factor was that some of the Christian leaders knew the Quran well. The Muslims believed that Muhammad would be an intercessor on the Last Day.[95] The Christians challenged this, asking if they could show him mentioned by name in the Quran in this role. The Christians showed that only one whom God approves may intercede (suras 19:87/90; 20:109/108; 53:26/27). The *Injil* (Gospel), which the Quran affirms, says that God approved of Jesus (Matt. 3:17; Mark 1:11; Luke 2:22) and states that he is the only mediator between God and humanity (1 Tim. 2:5). This would fit in with the common Muslim belief that Jesus will return as a sign of the Hour of Judgment—a belief they base on sura 43:61.

When asked about their attitude toward the Quran, the Christians answered that it was meant for the people of Mecca and neighboring villages according to sura 6:92: "This is the Book that we have revealed, a blessing and a confirmation to those who were before it, and that the Mother of Cities [Mecca] may be warned and those who are around her." Sometimes other verses were used to show that the Quran was for Mecca[96] and the Arabs.[97] When they were asked about their attitude toward Muhammad, they said that he was a prophet to the Arabs according to the same verse and others.[98] Historically, this is a valid interpretation of part of the Quran; but ultimately Muhammad saw his mission as universal (sura 34:28/27).[99]

Although the old practice of debating has normally been viewed as counterproductive today, in at least one union of villages the chairman called on the followers of Jesus to defend their position against four religious scholars. A Muslim spokesperson started, "We the people of this area are Muslims. . . . We heard that you came here to make us Christians, which is a foreign religion, a religion of infidels." Here "Christian" is being defined as "foreign" and a state of "disbelief"; so the convert refused to be called one and said that he had nothing to do with the Christians in the country (who originally were from a different religious community).

The follower of Jesus claimed to be a "Muslim." This led to a discussion between "brothers" of what a Muslim was. The follower of Jesus said that according to the Quran a "Muslim" is one "who has completely surrendered himself to the will of Allah." He could point to this meaning of the term in the Quran (2:112/106; 3:64/57), where it is also used to describe Jesus' disciples (5:111, 112). Thus, he was technically right in the sense that he had completed his submission to God through Christ, though historically, of course, the word has come to be restricted to those who follow the message delivered by Muhammad. The followers of Jesus have come to be called "believers"—a term more in keeping with the original followers of "the Way" before they were called "Christians" in Antioch.

After being assured that the follower of Jesus believed in the final judgment, the Muslim spokesperson asked, "Do you believe that Muhammad is the mediator on the day of final judgment?" The follower of Jesus responded, "Does the Quran say so?" When the four scholars could not show a verse that clearly did, the news spread, and many decided to follow Jesus.

Decisions are normally made in groups. The chairman announced that another meeting would be held the following month. If the scholars won, the followers of Jesus should return to Islam. On the other hand, if they lost, he and his relatives would follow Jesus. In another situation, a Sufi mystic leader learned in a Good Friday message that the veil of the Holy of Holies was torn from top to bottom. He cried, "Why should I bother with the law any more if Jesus has opened up the Holy of Holies?" He is leading his disciples to follow Jesus. Attempts are made to keep social units together by baptizing people only if the head of the family is also being baptized.

Conversions are following the web pattern along family, friendship, and occupational lines. When whole villages come, the mosque remains the center of worship. Teachers of their new faith are supported locally in the pattern of the imams of the mosque.

Muslim convert couples developed a prayer ritual which follows the Muslim pattern but expresses their new allegiance to God through Jesus. Morning prayer starts with the normal "intention" (*niya*) to pray but adds "in the name of my Lord and Savior Jesus Christ" before the traditional exclamation "God is greater" (*Allahu akbar*). In the first *rak'a* (the basic ritual which is repeated), Psalm 23 or any other biblical passage is recited. The rest of the *rak'a* follows the traditional postures and praises to God, although "All praise to Jesus Christ" may be substituted for the first.

The Lord's Prayer is recited in the second *rak'a* plus another passage if desired. After two *rak'as*, the worshiper adds to the thanksgiving, "Please give me favor to worship you this way until your [Christ's] second coming." Then the regular greeting and blessing are given to the ones on the right and left of the worshiper. A time for *du'a* (spontaneous prayer) is suggested for intercession and petition. The *iqama* (which normally includes an affirmation of Muhammad's apostleship) is altered to:

> God is love. God is love.
> And all praises belong to God.
> Present. Present before God.
> Present. Present in the name of Jesus Christ.

The remaining four daily prayers, plus any additional *rak'as* at these times, follow the same pattern with different Scripture passages indicated for each.[100] After the night prayer a special prayer of three *rak'as* is suggested. In the first, John 1:12 is recited followed by:

> O Almighty God, the experience that you have given me to be your child through placing my faith in Jesus Christ and accepting him as my personal Savior, give the same experience to the lives of the _____ million Muslims of _____.

In the second *rak'a* John 3:16 is recited with the prayer:

> O God, the experience that you have given to me to have eternal life through your gift of grace in the Lord Jesus Christ, I claim the same experience in the name of Jesus Christ for the lives of _____ million Muslims of _____. Please acknowledge this.

Psalm 117:1–2 is recited in the final *rak'a*. At the conclusion, time is spent in intercession for the country, government officials, believers and their leaders, neighbors, relatives, and oneself.

* * *

We have seen that the so-called "pillars of Islam" have for the most part been used before by Jews and Christians and, with some adjustments, are being used again. Their forms, meanings, and functions have been sufficiently similar to allow this to happen. Yet, many factors could weaken or topple them and what they support. One is the problem of training leadership for such a creative and rapidly growing movement. A second is how to build bridges to other segments of the church without inhibiting growth. The demise of the Nestorian Church gives mute witness to the results of being isolated.

A third problem is how to reuse Muslim forms without retaining Muslim meanings, such as merit. A fourth is how to avoid an ossified contextualization that inhibits maturity—an apparent problem of the Jewish believers to whom the Epistle to the Hebrews was written. Despite the dangers, we are seeing God blessing the refurbishing of these pillars in our day as they bear the weight of new allegiances to God in Christ.

What is happening can be visualized in the Hagia Sophia, a fourth-century church that was close to its Jewish and Eastern foundations. Its pillars held up a dome on which was painted the face of Christ. Muslims made the church into a mosque—altering the direction of prayer, adding the names of Muslim heroes, and painting over some of the Christian mosaics. Over the face of Christ in the dome they painted the quranic words "God is the Light of the heavens and earth" (sura 24:35). The same pillars continued to hold up this witness. Should the artisans painstakingly remove its paint as they have from some of the other Christian pictures, they could once again see "the light of the knowledge of the glory of God in the face of Christ" (2 Cor. 4:6). And the same pillars would continue to hold it up.

NOTES

[1] J. Pedersen, "Masdjid," *Shorter Encyclopaedia of Islam*, ed. H. A. R. Gibb and J. H. Kramers (Leiden: E. J. Brill, 1961), 339B–340A.

[2] Letter dated March 1, 1987.

[3] For a broader discussion of the anti-Quranic bias of Arabic Bible translation, see Samuel P. Schlorff, "The Missionary Use of the Quran: An Historical and Theological Study of the Contextualization of the Gospel" (Th.M. thesis; Philadelphia: Westminster Theological Seminary, 1984), 61–71.

[4] Paul W. Harrison, "The Arabs of Oman," *The Moslem World* 24 (1934): 269.

[5] John Wilder, "Some Reflections on Possibilities for People Movements Among Muslims." *Missiology* 5 (1977): 301–20; chapters by P. Hiebert, D. Larson, B. A. Massih, H. Conn, C. Kraft, and C. Tabor in Don M. McCurry, ed., *The Gospel and Islam* (Monrovia, Calif.: MARC, 1979); Phil Parshall, *New Paths in Muslim Evangelism* (Grand Rapids: Baker, 1980), and *Beyond the Mosque* (Grand Rapids: Baker, 1985); chapters by P. Parshall, R. Uddin, F. Antablin, and D. Green in J. Dudley Woodberry, ed., *Muslims and Christians on the Emmaus Road* (Monrovia, Calif.: MARC, 1989).

[6] E.g., Larry G. Lenning, *Blessing in Mosque and Mission* (Pasadena: William Carey Library, 1980); Evertt W. Huffard, *Thematic Dissonance in the Muslim-Christian Encounter: A Contextualized Theology of Honor* (Ph.D. dissertation, Pasadena: Fuller Theological Seminary, 1985), and "Culturally Relevant Themes about Christ in *Muslims and Christians on the Emmaus Road*, ed. Woodberry, 177–92; doctrines of God and Christ in Muslim context in Michael Nazir-Ali, *Frontiers in Muslim-Christian Encounter* (Oxford: Regnum Books, 1987), 15–37.

[7] E.g., for Sufi mystics, Lilias Trotter, *The Way of the Sevenfold Secret* (Cairo: Nile Mission Press, 1926); [Fouad Accad], *Seven Muslim-Christian Principles* (Ar-Rabitah, P.O. Box 1433, Limassol, Cyprus); Bible passages in *The Pillars of Religion in the Light of the Tawrat, Zabur and Injil* (Beirut: The Bible Society, 1984); Sobhi W. Malek, "Allah-u Akbar Bible Lessons: Aspects of Their Effectiveness in Evangelizing Muslims" (D. Miss. dissertation, Pasadena: Fuller Theological Seminary, 1986); Life of Christ in quranic style in *Sirat al-Masih bi-Lisan Arabi Fasih* (Larnaca, Cyprus: Izdihar Ltd., 1987). For a comparison of this style with existing Arabic Bible translations, see: David Owen, "A Classification System for Styles of Arabic Bible Translations," *Seedbed* (P.O. Box 96, Upper Darby, PA 19082) 3 (1988), 8–10. For reactions to it, see Schlorff, "Feedback on Project Sunrise (Sira): A Look at 'Dynamic Equivalence' in an Islamic Context," ibid., no. 2, 22–32. Phil Goble and Salim Munayer, *New Creation Book for Muslims* (Pasadena: Mandate [William Carey Library]).

[8] Dated July 3, 1987.

[9] Bruce Heckman, "Arab Christian Reaction to Contextualization in the Middle East" (M.A. thesis, Pasadena, Fuller Theological Seminary, 1988), 73–75.

[10] Ibid., 80–81.

[11] Ata'ullah Siddiqi, "Islam and Missions: Mohammad or Christ?" *Arabia-Islamic World Review* 6 (July, 1987): no. 71, p. 30.

[12] *Berita NECF: A Bimonthly Publication of the National Evangelical Christian Fellowship of Malaysia* (Petaling Jaya, Selangor) I:no. 1 (April/May 1988), 5.

[13] Suggested by sura [chapter] 16:103/105.

[14] See, e.g., Abraham Geiger, *Judaism and Islam*, trans. F. M. Young (New York: KTAV, 1970; originally publ. as *Was hat Mohammed aus dem Judentum aufgenommen?* 1898); Charles Torrey, *The Jewish Foundation of Islam* (New York: Jewish Institute of Religion Press, 1933); Alfred Guillaume, "The Influence of Judaism on Islam," *The Legacy of Israel*, ed. Edwyn R. Bevan and Charles Singer (Oxford: Clarendon Press, 1928), 129–71; W. Montgomery Watt, *Muhammad at Medina* (Oxford: Clarendon Press, 1956), 192–220.

On the possible influence of unorthodox variants affected by Christian monastic piety, see S. D. Goitein, *Jews and Arabs: Their Contact through the Ages* (Third rev. ed., New York: Schocken Books, 1974), 57–58. On the possible influence of a late offshoot of the Qumran community, see Chaim Rabin, *Qumran Studies* (London: Oxford University Press, 1957), 112–30.

[15] See, e.g., Tor Andrae, *Les Origines de l'Islam et le Christianisme*, trans. Jules Roch (Paris: Adrien-Maisonneuve, 1955); Richard Bell, *The Origin of Islam in its Christian Environment* (London: Macmillan, 1926); J. Spencer Trimingham, *Christianity among the Arabs in Pre-Islamic Times* (London: Longman, 1979); Watt, *Medina*, 315–20.

[16] See, e.g., Hamilton A. R. Gibb, "Pre-Islamic Monotheism in Arabia," *Harvard Theological Review* 60 (1962):269–80; J. Fueck, "The Originality of the Arabian Prophet," *Studies on Islam*, trans. and ed. Merlin Swartz (New York: Oxford University Press, 1981), 86–98; Watt, *Muhammad at Mecca* (Oxford: Clarendon Press, 1960), 158–61.

[17] Cf. Watt's view, based partly on sura 19:16–33/34 that Muhammad originally thought that the monotheism he preached was identical to that of the Jews and Christians (*Medina*, 315 and n.).

[18] Arthur Jeffery, *The Foreign Vocabulary of the Quran* (Baroda: Oriental Institute, 1938), vii–viii.

[19] Jeffery, *Foreign Vocabulary*, 19.

[20] For the method, see Eugene A. Nida, *Componential Analysis of Meaning: Approaches to Semantics* (The Hague: Mouton, 1975).

[21] Jeffery, *Foreign Vocabulary*, 66, and Bell, *Origin of Islam*, 54.

[22] A. J. Wensinck, "Wahy," *Shorter Encyclopaedia of Islam*, 622A.

[23] Jeffery, *Foreign Vocabulary*, 276.

[24] Ibid., 71–72.

[25] Wensinck, "Kibla" in *Encyclopaedia of Islam* (new ed.), ed. H. A. R. Gibb et al. (Leiden: E. J. Brill, 1960—) 5, 82; Mahmoud M. Ayoub, *The Qur'an and Its Interpreters*, I (Albany: State University of New York Press, 1984), 167–75; Abu-i 'Abbas al-Baladhuri, *Kitab Futuh al-Buldan*, p. 2, trans. Philip K. Hitti as *The Origins of the Islamic State*, 1 (New York: Columbia University, 1916), 15.

[26] Jeffery, *Foreign Vocabulary*, 198–99; Wensinck, "Salat," in *Shorter Encyclopaedia of Islam*, 491B.

[27] Jeffery, *Foreign Vocabulary*, 161–62.

[28] "Zur Entstehungsgeschichte des islamischen Gebets und Kultus" in *Abhandlungen der koeniglich preussischen Akademie der Wissenschaften* (Berlin: Koeniglich der Wissenschaften, 1913), Philosophisch-Historische Classe, no. 2, p. 16; Guillaume, "Influence of Judaism on Islam," 156.

[29] *New Researches into the Composition and Exegesis of the Qoran* (London: Royal Asiatic Society, 1902), 35.

[30] *The Talmud of Jerusalem*, Eng. trans. Moses Schwab (London: Williams and Norgate, 1886), I, chap. 2, no. 3 (pp. 34–35); D. Masson, *Le Coran et la révélation judéo-chrétienne* (2 vols.; Paris: Adrien-Maisonneuve, 1958), I: 32.

[31] Torrey, *Jewish Foundation*, 133–34. On the *shema'* as a confession of faith, see Mishna *Berakoth* 2:2 in *The Mishna*, trans. Herbert Danby (London: Oxford University Press, 1949), 3; George Foot Moore, *Judaism in the First Centuries of the Christian Era* (Cambridge, Mass.: Harvard University Press, 1950), I: 465; Vernon H. Neufeld, *The Earliest Christian Confessions* (Grand Rapids: Eerdmans, 1963), 34–41.

[32] For the meaning of the *shahada* see: Wensinck, *The Muslim Creed* (Cambridge: Cambridge University Press, 1932), 17–35; Wilfred Cantwell Smith, *The Faith of Other Men* (New York: New American, 1965), 50–62. For the meaning of God's unity to a Sufi mystic, see Seyyed Hossein Nasr, ed., *Islamic Spirituality* (New York: Crossroad, 1987), 312–15.

[33] See Wensinck, *A Handbook of Early Muhammadan Tradition* (Leiden: E. J. Brill, 1960), s.v. "unity."

[34] *Al-Qustas al-Mustaqim*, ed. V. Chelhot, 68, in Chelhot, "La Balance Juste," *Bulletin d'Etudes Orientales*, 15 (1958); 62; *al-Munqidh min al-dalal* (*The Deliverer from Error*), ed. Jamil Saliba and Kamal 'Ayyad (3d ed.; Damascus, 1358/1939), 101; trans. in W. Montgomery Watt, *The Faith and Practice of al-Ghazali* (London: Allen and Unwin, 1953), 39.

[35] (Berakoth) 4: 1 (p. 73).

[36] Al-Bukhari, *Sahih al-Bukhari* (Arabic-English), trans. M. Muhsin Khan (9 vols.; Beirut: Dar al-Arabia, n.d.), vol. I, Bk. 8 (*Salat*), chap. 1 (pp. 213–14).

[37] For the argument that Islam chose a middle position as noted in a slightly different context in sura 2:143/137, see S. D. Goitein, *Studies in Islamic History and Institutions* (Leiden: E. J. Brill, 1968), 84–85.

[38] Guillaume, "Influence of Judaism," 162–63.

[39] Al-Bukhari, *Sahih*, I, Bk. 5 (*Ghusl*) (pp. 156–76); G. H. Bousquet, "Ghusl," *Encyclopaedia of Islam* (new ed.), s.v.

[40] Al-Bukhari, *Sahih*, I, Bk. 8 (*Salat*), chap. 76 (pp. 268–69); Guillaume, "Influence of Judaism," 162.

[41] On the controversy, see Parshall, "Lessons Learned in Contextualization," *Muslims and Christians*, ed. Woodberry, 279.

[42] *The Talmud of Babylonia, I: Tractate Berakhot*, trans. Jacob Neusner (Chico, CA: Scholars Press, 1984), fol. 15A (chap. 2, sec. 22, p. 116); Wensinck, "Tayammum," *Shorter Encyclopaedia of Islam*, 589A.

[43] Cedrenus, *Annales*, ed. Hylander (Basle, 1566), 206 in Wensinck, "Tayammum," 589A.

[44] Masson, *Le Coran* I: 531.

[45] *The Talmud of Jerusalem*, trans. Schwab, I (Berakoth), chap. 4, nos. 6–7 (pp. 91–93).

[46] Vol. 4, Bk. 60, chap. 20 (p. 18).

[47] *Baba Bathra*, fol. 25A, in *The Babylonian Talmud: Seder Nezikin*, ed. I. Epstein, trans. Maurice Simon and Israel A. Slotki (London: The Soncino Press, 1935), 124–25.

[48] Abu Hamid al-Ghazali, *Ihya Ulum-id-Din*, trans. Fazal-ul-Karim (Lahore: Islamic Book Foundation, 1981), Bk. 4, chap. 7 (389–407); Guillaume, "Influence of Judaism on Islam," 156; Wensinck, "Niya," *Shorter Encyclopaedia of Islam*, s.v.

[49] Eugen Mittwoch, "Entstehungsgeschichte," 16; Wensinck, "Salat," 493B.

[50] Mittwoch, "Entstehungsgeschichte," 17; Wensinck, *Mohammed en de Joden te Medina* (2nd ed., 1928), 104 in his "Salat," 494A.

[51] For Christian parallels, see A. Baumstark, "Juedischer und Christlicher Gebetstypus im Koran," *Der Islam*, XVI (1927), 229.

[52] *Yoma*, 53B, in *The Babylonian Talmud: Seder Mo'ed*, v. 2/5, ed. I. Epstein, trans. Leo Jung (London: The Soncino Press, 1938), 250.

[53] Goitein, *Studies*, 117–18.

[54] C. H. Becker, "Zur Geschichte des Islamischen Kultus," *Der Islam*, 3 (1912): 374–99; Hava Lazarus-Yafeh, *Some Religious Aspects of Islam* (Leiden: E. J. Brill, 1981), 40.

[55] Al-Qastallani 2: 176 in Goitein, *Studies*, 112.

[56] Goitein, *Studies*, 113–14.

[57] Bell, *Origin of Islam*, 143; Wensinck, "Salat," 495A.

[58] Ibn Maja, *Siyam*, bab. 68 in Wensinck, "Tahadjdjud," *Shorter Encyclopaedia of Islam*, 559.

[59] Abu Da'ud, *Tatawwu'*, bab. 18 in Wensinck, "Tahadjdjud," 559.

[60] Constance E. Padwick, *Muslim Devotions: A Study of Prayer Manuals in Common Use* (London: SPCK, 1961), and "The Language of Muslim Devotion," *The Muslim World*, 47 (1957): 5–21, 98–110, 194–209.

[61] Quoted in Samuel M. Zwemer, *Studies in Popular Islam* (London: Sheldon Press, 1939), 15.

[62] See Louis Gardet, "Du'a," *Encyclopaedia of Islam* (new ed.), 617–18.

[63] E.g., prayer in the mosque is considered twenty-five times more meritorious than elsewhere in al-Bukhari, *Sahih*, I, Bk. 8 (*Salat*), chap. 87 (p. 277).

[64] Al-Bukhari, *Sahih*, I, Bk. 8 (*Salat*), chap. 1 (p. 211).

[65] Ahmad b. Hanbal, *Musnad*, 3: 128, 285 in Wensinck, "Salat," 498A.

[66] Al-Bukhari, *Sahih*, I, Bk. 8 (*Salat*), chap. 38 (p. 244).

[67] Muslim b. al-Hajjaj, *Sahih Muslim*, trans. Abdul Hamid Saddiqi (Lahore: Ashraf, n.d.), I (*Iman*), trad. 146 (p. 48).

[68] Malik b. Anas, *Muwatta'*, 9 (*Qasr al-salat fi 'l-safar*), trad. 91 in Wensinck, "Salat," 498A.

[69] Ahmad b. Hanbal, *Musnad*, 2: 229 in Wensinck, "Salat," 498A.

[70] Tradition from Muslim, *Adhkaru 'n-Nawawi*, 33 in Padwick, *Muslim Devotions*, 173.

[71] Regis Blachere, *Introduction au Coran* (2nd ed.; Paris: G. P. Maisonneuve, 1959), 142-44; Y. Moubarac, "Les etudes d'epigraphie sud-semitique et la naissance de l'Islam," *Revue des Etudes Islamique* 25 (1957), 58-61; B. Carra de Vaux and L. Gardet, "Basmala," *Encyclopaedia of Islam* (new ed.), 1084-1085; *Mt. Sinai Arabic Codex 151*, ed. Harvie Stahl, 2 vols. (Leuven: Peepers, 1985).

[72] See, e.g., Padwick above n.60; Kenneth Cragg, ed., *Alive Unto God: Muslim and Christian Prayer* (London: Oxford University Press, 1970); Marston Speight, "Muslim and Christian Prayer," *Newsletter of the Task Force on Christian-Muslim Relations* (Hartford: National Council of Churches and Duncan Black MacDonald Center), no. 12 (Mar. 1980):1-3.

[73] See Cragg, "A Study in the Fatiha," *Operation Reach* ([Beirut and Jerusalem]: Near East Christian Council, Sept.-Oct., 1957), 9-18.

[74] Ignaz Goldziher, *Muhammedanische Studien* (2 vols.; Halle: Max Niemeyer, 1889-1890), 2: 386; trans. S. M. Stern, *Muslim Studies* (London: Allen and Unwin, 1971), 350.

[75] Jeffery, *Foreign Vocabulary*, 263-64; Pedersen, "Masdjid," 330A.

[76] *The Muqaddimah*, trans. Franz Rosenthal (3 vols.; New York: Pantheon Books, 1958), II, 249.

[77] Pedersen, "Masdjid," 330-37.

[78] Gardet, "Dhikr," *Encyclopaedia of Islam* (New ed.), s.v.

[79] J. Horovitz, "Quran," *Der Islam*, XIII (1923), 66-69.

[80] Guillaume, 156; Theodor Noeldeke, *Geschichte des Qorans* (Hildesheim: Georg Olms Verlagsbuchhandlung, 1961; reprint of 2nd ed.; Leipzig, 1909), III, 116-248; R. Paret, "Kira'a," *Encyclopaedia of Islam* (New ed.), s.v.

[81] Mittwoch "Entstehungsgeschichte"; Becker, "Geschichte" 374-419, and "Die Kanzel im Kultus des alten Islam," *Orientalische Studien Theodor Noeldeke zum siebzigsten Geburtstag*, ed. Carl Bezold (2 vols.; Giessen: Alfred Toepelmann, 1906), 2:331-52; al-Bukhari *Sahih*, 2 (*Jum'a*): chap. 28 (p. 24); Wensinck, "Khutba," *Encyclopaedia of Islam* (New ed.), s.v.

[82] F. Wuestenfeld, *Geschichte der Stadt Medina* (Goettingen, 1860), 74 in Pedersen, "Masdjid," 339B-340A.

[83] Pedersen, "Masdjid," 343-46; al-Bukhari, *Sahih* I, Bk. 8 (*Salat*), chaps. 20-21, 54 (pp. 231-32, 254-55).

[84] Al-Bukhari, *Sahih*, 9, Bk. 89 (*Ahkan*), chaps. 18-19 (pp. 209-11); Pedersen, "Masdjid," 347-48; Adam Mez, *The Renaissance of Islam*, trans. S. Khuda Bakhsh and D. S. Margoliouth (London: Luzac, 1937), 233.

[85] Abu Hamid al-Ghazali, *Ihya 'Ulum al-Din*, Bk. I, chap. 5, sect. 4 (pp. 219-21).

[86] Masson, *Le Coran*, 608 and n.3.

[87] See, e.g., John Thomas Cummings, Hossein Askari, and Ahmad Mustafa, "Islam and Modern Economic Change," *Islam and Development: Religion and Sociopolitical Change*, ed. John L. Esposito (Syracuse: Syracuse University Press, 1980), 25-47.

[88] Donald R. Richards, "A Great Missiological Error of Our Time: Keeping the Fast of Ramadan—Why We Shouldn't," *Seedbed* 3 (1988): 38–45.

[89] Bukhari, *Sahih*, 3, Bk. 31 (*sawm*), chap. 70 (p. 124).

[90] W. O. E. Oesterly and G. H. Box, *The Religion and Worship of the Synagogue* (London: Pitman and Sons, 1907), 326, 404.

[91] *The Talmud of Jerusalem*, I (Berakhoth), chap. 1, par. 5 (p. 15).

[92] Al-Bukhari, *Sahih*, 3, Bk. 3 (*sawm*), chaps, 5–6 (pp. 69–70); Goitein, *Studies*, 100.

[93] *The Torah, A New Translation of the Holy Scriptures* (Philadelphia: Jewish Publication Society, 1902), 212.

[94] Al-Bukhari *Sahih*, 6, Bk. 60 (*tafsir*), chap. 284 (pp. 362–63).

[95] This could be based on 20:109/108; 34:23/22 and 43:86, but Muhammad is not mentioned by name.

[96] Suras 43:7/5 and 43:44/43 (which say this clearly) and 27:91/93; 28:85; 37:149 and 43:31/30 (which may refer to Mecca but are not as clear).

[97] Suras 12:2; 13:37; 16:103/105; 20:113/112; 26:195; 39:28/29; 41:3/2, 44; 42:7/5; 43:3/2; 44:58 and 46:12/11. The Christians also pointed out that the Quran was for a people who had not had a previous warner (32:3/2; 34:44/43; 36:6/5) nor a previous Book (34:44/43; 43:21/20).

[98] To the pagans or gentiles (62:2) and to one people or "my people" (13:30/29; 25:30/32; 38:4/3 and 43:44/43).

[99] Suras 4:79/81 and 7:158/157 may also be taken in a universal sense but do not have to be.

[100] Ps. 24:1–6; 25:1–7, 8–14, 15–22; 26:1–8; 34:1–8; 91:1–7; 92:1–8; 134:1–3; 136:1–9; 139:1–6; 141:1–5; 145:1–5; Isa. 61:1–3; Mt. 5:3–12; Jn. 1:1–5; 2 Cor. 5:18–19; Gal. 3:26–29; Eph. 1:3–8, 11–14; Phil. 2:5–11; Col. 1:15–20; Tit. 2:11–14; Heb. 2:1–4, 10–12; 2 Pet. 1:5–9 and Rev. 5:9–10, 12–13.

Appendix

CONTEXTUALIZATION MODELS

In the last five to eight years we have seen various approaches to contextualization taking shape. In some ways, these reflect the variety of ways that theologians have always gone about their task. The constructing of models of theology shows the way to arrange ideas or to map, so to speak, what the end result will be and how it will be attained. A theological model can only suggest how thinking about God and the Christian faith is to be done. But it is essential to know what tools are used in constructing the model as well as the biases of the proponents of the given model. It is accurate, therefore, to speak of an orthodox model of theology or a liberal model or a neo-orthodox model since each has certain assumptions, sources, and objectives. The process by which all these components are arranged and interact defines what the model is.

Models of contextualization all have their differences, and some of the differences are extremely important. Still, all of them have several things in common. They all have a commitment to relevance and a focus on real situations in which people live. They all have the purpose in mind to make Christianity a vital, needs-oriented experience and to give ownership of the church to specific communities of believers. However, the assumptions and methodology of certain of these models make them unacceptable for an evangelical approach to missiology. Contextualization must give the highest place to God's Word and must be guided by the call of Christ to evangelize and to build believers into strong communities of faith, while keeping a respectful creative role for culture.

The formation of models in the last decade has opened up a variety of ways to approach contextualization.

The Anthropological Model: Culture is absolutely essential if we are to know the way a people see their world and what they consider to be real. Culture shows where values are and what kinds of needs a people have. Culture also helps us understand where changes are taking place. All of this corresponds to the human dimension involved in the Incarnation. When the Word became flesh, it was God taking unto himself a completely human form. The keys to communication and pathways to the human heart and spirit lie in the culture. People can speak about and reflect upon their own realities without training. The symbols of the life of a people reveal their assumptions and needs. This is the information we must have if the gospel is to speak with authority. Since this must be understood as completely as possible, the anthropological method puts primary importance on the culture.

It is easy to view culture as a completely trustworthy vehicle of truth. To suppose that culture is an adequate guide to all truth is erroneous. Often those who study cultures, especially outsiders to the culture, are unprepared to see contradictory elements which the gospel must judge and transform. No culture is above the highest revelation of God which we have in Christ and in the Scriptures. Unless discernment about a culture is brought to the Word for affirmation or judgment, the initial forms of Christianity can be distorted, and all that follows will be crippled. On the other hand, if unsuitable (Western) forms are introduced with the intention of putting right what is wrong in the culture, the result will be a more subtle, but equally damaging, consequence. So, the specific culture must be the matrix in which the theology takes root and grows; but, equally, it must be brought under the scrutiny and judgment of the Word of God.

The Translation Model: The source of this term is the field of linguistics. Here, great care is taken to ensure that the nearest possible meaning intended in the source document is transferred to the receiving culture. Form and meaning is a dimension of translation that has a long history. The ideal is that equivalent meanings will be expressed in the receptor culture, even though the form that expresses the meaning may be something different. In the translation model, therefore, the attempt is made to separate the absolute or "supracultural elements" of the gospel from what is secondary. This is often referred to as distinguishing the "kernel" from the "husk." There must be "dynamically equivalent" terms and forms in the receptor culture to achieve maximum meaning and understanding.

The gospel is not relative. It is absolute and revelational in nature and, therefore, is constant regardless of the place or people. This is the gospel of the Word of Christ. It is equally binding on and equally salvific for all peoples. It is the *kerygma* of Peter and Paul, calling both Jew and gentile to repentance and faith. But the idiom of delivery, the symbols used to convey the message, the type of response it elicits, all must conform to the uniqueness of the receptor audience. Further, the church that results must authentically reflect the context in worship and witness. This approach provides the tools for committed Christian leaders to deal with problems raised in their own cultures. Still, criticisms have been raised by some who feel the Bible is not taken seriously enough. The fear is that in the name of an "ill-defined and infinitely plastic 'dynamic equivalence' almost any translational aberration may be justified" (Carson) for the sake of cultural relevance. On the other hand, Schreiter thinks it would be quite impossible to identify what the "kernel" of the gospel is and apply this to all cultures.

The Praxis Model: The dominating assumption in the praxis approach to contextualization is that truth can only be realized when people actually participate in the events of their own history. The goal of theology must be to produce change. Change does not come by the knowledge of doctrines or the recitation of creeds. As for culture, it is not simply forms, symbols, and customs, but includes the assumptions of history that have locked people into a dehumanized society. To change this demands involvement. Praxis is not simply "doing something about it." It is reflection on the social realities with the Bible and Christian tradition in the background. The reflection then takes one into the situation to effect change, whereupon analysis of the action is taken up again. The change dimension of theology is badly needed in today's hurting world. No one will argue with the fact that evangelicals have been very good at insisting on orthodoxy and have tended to look away from sinful systems that control people's daily lives.

But there is justifiable criticism of the praxis model even though there is considerable variety in application. The classic form is preoccupied with the human situation; its agenda is drawn up, almost exclusively, from the socio-political context. This error fails to give adequate place to the Bible generally, so that the whole of the biblical record is not taken seriously. The dominating motif is secular liberation rather than the changed life in Christ or the cultivation of the Holy Spirit's presence in the individual and community. The method is widely associated with justification for violence and has been under considerable criticism for this. The basis of truth is not revelation but knowledge transmitted through participation in history. A basically Marxist view of knowledge such as this is unacceptable as a model for incarnational contextualization.

The Adaptation Model: The principle behind the adaptation model is to make, as much as possible, the historical foci of systematic theology fit into particular cultural situations. It is assumed that the well-known philosophical categories can be rearranged or adapted to themes arising from the culture. But the background of theologizing for each particular situation is what is contained in historical theology. How this works out from place to place is the work of the local theologian, who obviously must first be trained in Western theology. Here the Christian traditions or creeds are brought to the local culture; what is irrelevant is set aside, what can be modified is changed, and what fits in the new locus from the original is not changed. This approach takes seriously the fact that some sort of Christian tradition is already known. The framework in which theology is done is more universal, so there is continuity with the wider church and with history.

But, again, the assumption that there is one philosophical framework within which all cultures can talk to each other is faulty. Other forms of knowledge are just as legitimate and are rich in the expression of religious truths. The hope in adaptation theology is to keep thirteenth-century European thinking alive! The university, where theology integrates with other forms of epistomology, is not the church. It is tragic when leaders leave dynamic cultural churches to be trained. They learn philosophical theology well and then cannot help their own people. Theology has to touch the body of believers and build them up in the faith in ways that are authentic to their own lives. Any adapting also must take into account that no culture is completely uninfluenced by other cultures, and some form of church tradition has already been established in most places. All this will affect the adaptation results.

The Synthetic Model: The synthesis is in the bringing together of four basic elements—the gospel, Christian tradition, culture, and social change. The product comes from the dialogue between these, using the insights of the people themselves. There is a recognition that no culture exists in a vacuum but is influenced by other cultures and contexts; so it is important to recognize the elements that are shared with others. No cultural setting is complete in itself but needs the complementary features of other contexts. The advantage of the synthetic model is that it is through the dialogical process that a real appreciation for truth arises. Third World Christians can bring their own insights and cultural gifts to the exercise of theologizing. Each Christian group has distinctives. Yet these distinctives must be understood as a part of the universal Christian faith, which, in turn, is applicable to every culture.

This model has to be orchestrated very carefully if it is not to become an exercise in universalism. It appears to have all the data necessary—it brings together the trained Western expert and the untrained local Christian as a broad symbol of the church. Yet the temptation would be to keep this openness, this belongingness, so in the foreground that a truly Christian theology with conviction and solid principles for the local group would not emerge. Generalities serve little good in building up a new Christian community. What spiritual disciplines are required as the Christian group looks at their own lives against the church as a whole? What role will the Holy Spirit have in illuminating the principles of the Word? The result could be too artificial, too Western, and the openness would lead to ambiguity.

The Semiotic Model: The term "semiotic" has to do with "signs" and symbols. The idea is to "read" a culture through the signs it offers to the discerning researcher. Here again, as with the anthropological model, truth is primarily revealed from within the culture. This method is dealt with at great length in Schreiter's book (*Constructing Local Theologies*) where he speaks of contextual theologies as "local theologies." A whole matrix of data has to be reckoned with, including whatever previous theologies have already influenced the place and people. Semiotics, popularized by C. Geertz, is felt by many anthropologists to be the best way to analyze a culture, in addition to which there is a close watch on where changes are taking place in society. Areas of change will show where the gospel needs to impinge upon the lives of the people.

The method of semiotics is difficult to work with, except for the Western-trained person. The model is developed in such a way that it would be rare if the person who is able to use it has remained a legitimate, intimate member of the popular society. Or, even worse, it would have to be done by outsiders. When contextualization is taken out of the hands of local Christians and becomes an exercise for the elite only, there is a denial of the very thing we claim to be doing. Contextualization is to simplify, clarify, and give ownership of the Bible and the whole gospel to the community of faith in a given place. When the system for doing this can only be understood by an outsider, we have closed off the channels for incarnation of the Word. It is a contradiction of what contextualization sets out to do when truth for the people is hidden in a maze of scientific terminology that only the highly trained expert can unscramble. The intentions of semiotics are laudable, but not within reach of ordinary people.

The Critical Model: Each model has its strength and particular function. A comprehensive approach to contextualization calls for integration and borrowing from several approaches, depending on the particular emphasis and demand of the situation. The School of World Mission has made use of both the linguistic and anthropological models because of the facility of these models for such issues as form and meaning and dynamic equivalence. The Critical Model (Hiebert) has the advantage of taking both the culture and the Scriptures seriously and asks the church as a body to participate in the hermeneutical task. Critical contextualization confronts the double-edged risk of too much permissiveness in the role of culture on the one hand, and the outright rejection or denial of traditional belief and practice on the other. The first risk is uncritical contextualization which leads to syncretism, while the second is a refusal to contextualize which results in foreign forms and/or a supression of old forms which then go underground.

Critical contextualization is carried out through an exegesis of the culture as one exercise and a fresh study of corresponding biblical themes as another. With the cultural and biblical information in hand, these two sources are critically reviewed with the objective of making a new response, which is culturally authentic and biblically appropriate. As culture passes through the biblical filters, some existing forms will be brought across the bridge, so to speak, while others can be used in the Christian context with modification. Others must be rejected. The goal of the critical method is to arrive at contextualized practices which have the consensus of the redeemed community. Critical contextualization must take responsibility for the wider sociopolitical issues or it is in danger of being a narrow cultural exercise. Further, it must be balanced by insights from historical theology and checked against theologies developed outside the particular locale if it is to be a responsible discipline.

Dean S. Gilliland, Editor

Bibliography

[Accad, Foud]. n.d. *Seven Muslim-Christian Principles*. Limassol, Cyprus: Ar-Rabitah.

Adeney, Miriam. 1984. *God's Foreign Policy*. Grand Rapids: Eerdmans.

Al-Baladhuri, Abu-l Abbas. 1916. *Kitab Futuh al-Buldan*. Trans. Philip K. Hitti as *The Origins of the Islamic State*. New York: Columbia University.

Al-Ghazali, Abu Hamid. 1981. *Ihya Ulum-id-Din*. Trans. Fazal-ul-Karim. Lahore: Islamic Book Foundation.

Allen, Roland. 1972. *Missionary Methods: St. Paul's or Ours?* Grand Rapids: Eerdmans.

American Bible Society. 1976. *Good News Bible: The Bible in Today's English Version*. New York: American Bible Society.

Anderson, Gerald H. 1988. "American Protestants in Pursuit of Mission: 1886–1986." *International Bulletin of Missionary Research* 12 no. 3 (July).

Andrae, Tor. 1955. *Les Origines de l'Islam et le Christianisme*. Trans. Jules Roch. Paris: Adrien-Maisonneuve.

Archer, Gleason. 1964. *A Survey of Old Testament Introduction*. Chicago: Moody Press.

Armerding, Carl E., ed. 1977. *Evangelicals and Liberation*. Nutley, N.J.: Presbyterian and Reformed Publishing Co.

Arrupe, Pedro. 1977. "Letter to the Whole Society on Inculturation." *Studies in the International Apostolate of the Jesuits* 7.

Augustine, Saint. 1950. *The City of God*. New York: The Modern Library.

Ayoub, Mahmoud M. 1984. *The Qur'an and Its Interpreters*. Albany: State University of New York Press.

Bakke, Raymond. 1987. *The Urban Christian*. Bromley, Kent, U.K.: MARC Europe.

Barbour, Ian G. 1974. *Myths, Models and Paradigms*. New York: Harper and Row.

Barclay, William. 1975. *The Mind of St. Paul*. New York: Harper and Row.

Barr, O. Sydney. 1964. *From the Apostles' Faith to the Apostles' Creed*. New York: Oxford University Press.

Barrett, C. K. 1955. *The Gospel According to St. John*. Philadelphia: Westminster.

Barrett, David B., ed. 1982. *World Christian Encyclopedia*. Nairobi: Oxford University Press.

Barth, Karl. 1933. *The Epistle to the Romans*. 6th ed. Trans. E. C. Hoskyns. London: Oxford University Press.

———. 1957. *Church Dogmatics*. vols. I, 2; II, 1; IV, 1; IV, 3. Edinburgh: T & T Clark.

Baumgartner, Erich W. 1988. "Leadership Theory and Its Potential Contribution to the Understanding of Leadership for Church Growth," an unpublished paper in the School of World Mission, Fuller Theological Seminary.

Baumstark, A. 1927. "Juedischer and Christlicher Gebetstypus im Koran." *Der Islam* 16.

Baur, F. C. 1876. *Paul the Apostle of Jesus Christ*. 2d ed. London: Williams and Norgate.

Bavinck, Herman. 1956. *Our Reasonable Faith: A Survey of Christian Doctrine*. Grand Rapids: Eerdmans.

Becker, C. H. 1906. "Die Kanzel im Kultus des alten Islam." *Orientalische Studien Theodor Noeldeke zum siebzigsten Geburtstag*. Ed. Carl Bezold. 2 vols. Giessen: Alfred Toepelmann.

———. 1912. "Zur Geschichte des Islamischen Kultus." *Der Islam* 3.

Beeby, H. D. 1987. "Comments on Mark Spindler's Visa for Witness." *Mission Studies* 4, no. 1.

Beekman, John and John Callow. 1974. *Translating the Word of God*. Grand Rapids: Zondervan.

Beekman, John, John Callow, and Michael Kopesec. 1981. *The Semantic Structure of Written Communication*. Dallas: The Summer Institute of Linguistics.

Beker, J. Christiaan. 1980. *Paul the Apostle: The Triumph of God in Life and Thought*. Philadelphia: Fortress Press.

———. 1986. "The Method of Recasting Pauline Theology." *Society of Biblical Literature* (Seminar Papers).

Bell, Richard. 1926. *The Origin of Islam in its Christian Environment*. London: Macmillan.

Bellah, Robert N. 1985. *Habits of the Heart*. New York: Harper and Row.

Berger, Peter L. 1967. *The Sacred Canopy*. Garden City, N.Y.: Doubleday.

Berita NECF: A Bimonthly Publication of the National Evangelical Christian. 1988. Fellowship of Malaysia. Petaling Jaya, Selangor 1, no. 1. (April/May).

Berkhof, Hendrikus. 1979. *Christian Faith*. Grand Rapids: Eerdmans.

Berkhof, Louis. 1932. *Reformed Dogmatics*. Grand Rapids: Eerdmans.

———. 1955. *General Revelation*. Grand Rapids: Eerdmans.

Berlin, Brent and Paul Kay. 1969. *Basic Color Terms: Their Universality and Evolution*. Berkeley: University of California Press.

Berlo, David K. 1960. *The Process of Communication*. New York: Holt, Rinehart and Winston.

Bertsche, James E. 1966. "Kimbanguism: A Challenge to Missionary Statesmanship," *Practical Anthropology* 13. Reprinted in Smalley, 1978.

Bettenson, H. 1970. *The Latter Christian Fathers*. London: Oxford University Press.

Bevans, Stephen. 1985. "Models of Contextual Theology." *Missiology* 13, no. 2 (April).

Blachere, Regis. 1959. *Introduction au Coran*. 2d ed. Paris: G. P. Maisonneuve.

Blake, R. R. and J. S. Mouton. 1964. *The Managerial Grid*. Houston: Gulf.

Blamire, Harry. 1963. *The Christian Mind*. London: SPCK.

Boer, Harry R. 1961. *Pentecost and Missions*. Grand Rapids: Eerdmans.

Bond, Michael H., ed. 1986. *The Psychology of the Chinese People*. Hong Kong: Oxford University Press.

Bonino, José Miguez. 1975. *Doing Theology in a Revolutionary Situation*. Philadelphia: Fortress.

Bosch, David. 1980. *Witness to the World*. London: Marshall, Morgan and Scott.

————. 1983. "An Emerging Paradigm for Mission." *Missiology* 11, no. 4 (October).

Bradley, James E. and Richard A. Muller, eds. 1987. *Church, Word, and Spirit*. Grand Rapids: Eerdmans.

Bragg, Wayne G. 1987. "From Development to Transformation," in Vinay Samuel and Christopher Sugden, eds., *The Church in Response to Human Need*. Grand Rapids: Eerdmans.

Breytenbach, Cillers. 1986. "Reconciliation: Shifts in Christian Soteriology." *Reconciliation and Reconstruction*. Praetoria: University of South Africa.

Brierley, Peter. 1984. *Towards 2000—Current Trends in European Church Life*. Monograph. Bromley, Kent, U.K.: MARC Europe.

————. 1985. *Nominality—The Plague of the Twentieth Century*. Monograph. Bromley, Kent, U.K.: MARC Europe.

Brierley, Peter, ed. 1986. *UK Christian Handbook 1987/88*. Bromley, Kent, U.K.: MARC Europe.

Bright, John. 1959. *A History of Israel*. Philadelphia: Westminster.

————. 1976. *Covenant and Promise*. Philadelphia: Westminster.

————. 1981. *The Kingdom of God*. Nashville: Abingdon Press.

Brown, Schuyler. 1984. *The Origins of Christianity: A Historical Introduction to the New Testament*. New York: Oxford University Press.

Bruce, A. B. 1898. *The Training of the Twelve*. 5th ed. Edinburgh: T & T Clark.

Bruce, F. F. 1974. *Paul and Jesus*. Grand Rapids: Baker.

————. 1977. *Paul: Apostle of the Heart Set Free*. Devon: Paternoster.

Brunner, Emil. 1946. *Revelation and Reason: The Christian Doctrine of Faith and Knowledge*. Trans. Olive Myon. Philadelphia: Westminster.

————. 1949. *The Christian Doctrine of God*. Philadelphia: Westminster.

Bukhari, al-, *Sahih al-Bukhari* (Arabic-English), Trans. M. Muhsin Khan. 9 vols. Beirut: Dar al-Arabia, n.d.

Carnap, R. 1950. *Meaning and Necessity*. Chicago: University of Chicago Press.

Carriker, Timothy. 1987. "A Review of J. Christiaan Beker's Thesis in Light of 1 Thessalonians 4:13–5:11 and 1 Corinthians 15:20–28." Unpublished Ph.D. seminar paper. Pasadena: Fuller Theological Seminary.

Carson, D. A., ed. 1984. *Biblical Interpretation and the Church: The Problem of Contextualization.* Nashville: Thomas Nelson.

Casagrande, Joseph and Kenneth Hale. 1967. "Semantic Relationships in Papago Folk Definitions." *Studies in Southwestern Ethnolinguistics.* Eds. D. Hymes and W. E. Bittle. The Hague: Mouton.

Cerfaux, Lucien. 1959. *The Church in the Theology of St. Paul.* New York: Herder and Herder.

Chai, Chu and W. Chai, eds. and trans. 1965. *The Sacred Books of Confucius and Other Confucian Classics.* New Hyde Park: University Books.

Chartier, Myron R. 1981. *Preaching as Communication.* Nashville: Abingdon.

Chelhot, V. 1958. "La Balance Juste." *Bulletin d'Etudes Orientales* 15.

Chen, Chi-nan. 1988. "Traditional Chinese Familism and Organization in Chinese Enterprise." *Chinese Management.* Eds. K. S. Yang and S. C. Cheng. Taipei: Kuei-kuan Press.

Chiao, Chien. 1982. "A Preliminary Study on Kuan-hsi." *The Sinicization of Social and Behavioral Science Research in China,* Eds. K. S. Yang and C. Y. Wen. Taipei: Academic Sinica (in Chinese).

Childs, B. S. 1974. *The Book of Exodus.* Philadelphia: Westminster.

Christian Witness to Nominal Christians Among Protestant Christians. 1980. Lausanne 1980 Occasional Papers, No. 23, Thailand Report.

Clinton, J. Robert. 1977. *Interpreting the Scriptures: Figures and Idioms.* Pasadena: Barnabas Resources.

———. 1988. *Leadership Development Theory—Comparative Studies Among High Level Christian Leaders.* Pasadena: School of World Mission, Fuller Theological Seminary. Ph.D. dissertation.

Cloete, G. D. and D. J. Smit, eds. 1984. *A Moment of Truth.* Grand Rapids: Eerdmans.

Coe, Shoki. 1976. "Contextualizing Theology." Eds. Anderson and Stransky, *Mission Trends No. 3.* Grand Rapids: Eerdmans.

Condon, John C. 1975. *Semantics and Communication.* 2nd ed. New York: Macmillan.

Cone, James. 1969. *Black Theology and Black Power.* New York: Seabury Press.

———. 1975. *God of the Oppressed.* New York: Seabury Press, A Crossroad Book.

Conn, Harvie. 1978. "Contextualization: A New Dimension for Cross-Cultural Hermeneutic." *Evangelical Missions Quarterly* 14, no. 1 (January).

———. 1984. *Eternal World and Changing Worlds.* Grand Rapids: Zondervan.

Coote, Robert T. and John R. W. Stott, eds. 1980. *Down to Earth: Studies in Christianity and Culture.* Grand Rapids: Eerdmans.

Cragg, Kenneth, ed. 1970. *Alive Unto God: Muslim and Christian Prayer.* London: Oxford University Press.

Cragg, Kenneth. 1957. "A Study in the Fatiha." *Operation Reach.* Beirut and Jerusalem: Near East Christian Council, Sept.–Oct.

Craigie, Peter C. 1976. *The Book of Deuteronomy.* NICOT. Grand Rapids: Eerdmans.

Cullmann, Oscar. 1949. *The Earliest Christian Confessions*. Trans. J. K. S. Reid. London: Lutterworth Press.

Cummings, John Thomas, Hossein Askari, and Ahmad Mustafa. 1980. "Islam and Modern Economic Change." *Islam and Development: Religion and Sociopolitical Change*. Ed. John L. Esposito. Syracuse: Syracuse University Press.

Currie, Robert, Alan Gilbert, and Lee Horsley. 1977. *Churches and Church-goers*. Oxford: Clarendon Press.

Dahl, Nils A. 1978. "Review of Sanders' Paul and Palestinian Judaism." *Religious Studies Review* 4.

Danby, Herbert, trans. 1949. *The Mishna*. London: Oxford University Press.

de Ridder, Richard. 1971. *Discipling the Nations*. Grand Rapids: Eerdmans.

Deissmann, Adolf. 1926. *Paul: A Study in Social and Religious History*. 2d ed. London: Hodder and Stoughton.

Dekker, James. 1985. "The 8th Reformed Missions Consultation: Covenant in Search of Mission." *RES Mission Bulletin* 5, no. 1 (March).

Deloria, Vine, Jr. 1969. *Custer Died for Your Sins: An Indian Manifesto*. New York: Macmillan, Avon Books.

———. 1973. *God is Red*. New York: Grosset and Dunlap.

Dewick, Edward C. 1953. *The Christian Attitude to Other Religions*. Cambridge: Cambridge University Press.

Dodd, C. H. 1953. *The Interpretation of the Fourth Gospel*. Cambridge: Cambridge University Press.

Dolgin, Janet L., David S. Kemnitzer, and David Schneider, eds. 1977. *Symbolic Anthropology*. New York: Columbia University Press.

Donfried, K. D. 1985. "The Cults of Thessalonica and the Thessalonian Correspondence." *New Testament Studies* 31.

Douglas, J. D., ed. 1975. *Let the Earth Hear His Voice*. Minneapolis: Worldwide Publications.

Douglas, Mary. 1966. *Purity and Danger: An Analysis of Concepts of Pollution and Taboo*. London: Routledge and Kegan Paul.

———. 1973. *Natural Symbols*. New York: Vintage Books.

Dowey, Edward A., Jr. 1968. *A Commentary on the Confession of 1967 and an Introduction to "The Book of Confessions."* Philadelphia: Westminster.

Dyrness, William A. 1983. "The Kingdom Is Our Goal." *Together* 1 (October-December).

Ebehard, Wolfham. 1977. *A History of China*, rev. ed. Berkeley: University of California Press.

Eichrodt, Walther. 1967. *Theology of the Old Testament*. London: SCM Press.

Eliade, Mircea. 1958. *Rites and Symbols of Initiation: The Mysteries of Birth and Rebirth*. New York: Harper and Row.

————. 1959. *The Sacred and the Profane: The Nature of Religion.* New York: Harcourt, Brace, Jovanovich.

Elliott, John H. 1981. *Home for the Homeless.* Philadelphia: Fortress.

Ellis, E. Earle. 1978. *Prophecy and Hermeneutics in Early Christianity.* Grand Rapids: Eerdmans.

Engel, James F. 1977. *How Can I Get Them to Listen?* Grand Rapids: Zondervan.

————. 1979. *Contemporary Christian Communications: Its Theory and Practice.* Nashville: Nelson.

Engel, James F., and Wilbert Norton. 1975. *What's Gone Wrong with the Harvest?: A Communication Strategy for the Church and World Evangelism.* Grand Rapids: Academie Books.

Epstein, I., ed. 1935. *The Babylonian Talmud: Seder Nezikin.* Trans. Maurice Simon and Israel A. Slotki. London: The Soncino Press.

————. 1938. *The Babylonian Talmud: Seder Mo'ed.* Trans. Leo Jung. London: The Soncino Press.

Evans-Prichard, E. E. 1962. *Essays in Social Anthropology.* London: Faber.

Fei Xiaotung. 1977. "Chinese Social Structure and Its Values." *Changing China: Readings in the History of China from the Opium War to the Present.* Ed. J. Mason Gentzler. New York: Praeper. "Xiangtu Zhongguo."

Feinberg, John S. 1988. *Continuity and Discontinuity: Perspectives on the Relationship Between the Old and New Testaments.* Westchester: Crossway Books.

Fielder, F. E. 1967. *A Theory of Leadership Effectiveness.* New York: McGraw-Hill.

Firth, Raymond. 1973. *Symbols: Public and Private.* Ithaca: Cornell University Press.

Fleming, Bruce. 1980. *Contextualization of Theology.* Pasadena: William Carey Library.

Fore, William F. 1987. *Television and Religion: The Shaping of Faith, Values, and Culture.* Minneapolis: Augsburg Publishing House.

Frank, Bernhard. 1988. "Reculturing, or the Kimono Won't Go in Oshkosh." *Translation Review* 26.

Fry, Evan. 1979. "An Oral Approach to Translation." *The Bible Translator* 30.

Fry, John R. 1975. *The Trivialization of the United Presbyterian Church.* New York: Harper and Row.

Fueck, J. 1981. "The Originality of the Arabian Prophet." *Studies on Islam,* Trans., ed., Merlin Swartz. New York: Oxford University Press.

Gallup, George. 1985. *Religion in America, 50 Years 1935–85.* Princeton: The Gallup Report.

Gay, John D. 1971. *The Geography of Religion in England.* London: Duckworth.

Geertz, Clifford, ed. 1971. *Myth, Symbol and Culture.* New York: W. W. Norton and Company.

Geertz, Clifford. 1973. *The Interpretation of Culture: Selected Essays.* New York: Basic Books.

———. 1983. *Local Knowledge.* New York: Basic Books.

———. 1984. "Distinguished lecture: anti anti-relativism." *American Anthropologist* 86 (June).

Geiger, Abraham. 1970. *Judaism and Islam.* Trans. F. M. Young. New York: KTAV Publishing House.

Gibb, H. A. R. 1962. "Pre-Islamic Monotheism in Arabia." *Harvard Theological Review* 60.

Gibb, H. A. R. and J. J. Kramers, eds. 1961. *Shorter Encyclopaedia of Islam.* Leiden: E. J. Brill.

Gibb, H. A. R., et al., eds. 1960. *Encyclopaedia of Islam* (New Ed.). Leiden: E. J. Brill.

Gill, Robin. 1975. *The Social Context of Theology.* London and Oxford: Mowbrays.

Gilliland, Dean S. 1983. *Pauline Theology and Mission Practice.* Grand Rapids: Baker Books.

Gilliland, Dean S. and Evertt W. Huffard. n.d. *"The Word Became Flesh":* A Reader in Contextualization. Unpublished reader. Pasadena: Fuller Theological Seminary.

Gillman, J. 1985. "Signals of Transformation in 1 Thessalonians 4:13–18." *Catholic Biblical Quarterly* 47.

Glasser, Arthur. 1979. "Help from an Unexpected Quarter, or the Old Testament and Contextualization." *Missiology* 7, no. 4 (October).

Gleick, James. 1987. *Chaos: Making a New Science.* New York: Viking, Penguin Books Ltd.

Glock, C. Y. and C. R. Stark. 1968. *American Piety: The Nature of Religious Commitment.* Berkeley: University of California Press.

Goble, Phil and Salim Munayer. *New Creation Book for Muslims.* Pasadena: Mandate, William Carey Library, 1989.

Goitein, S. D. 1968. *Studies in Islamic History and Institutions.* Leiden: E. J. Brill.

———. 1974. *Jews and Arabs: Their Contact Through the Ages.* 3d rev. ed. New York: Schocken Books.

Goldziher, Ignaz. 1889. *Muhammedanische Studien.* 2 vols. Halle: Max Niemeyer. Trans. S. M. Stern. *Muslim Studies.* London: George Allen and Unwin, 1971.

Goodenough, Ward H. 1966. *Cooperation in Change.* New York: John Wiley and Sons.

Goody, Jack. 1968. *Literacy in Traditional Societies.* London: Cambridge University Press.

Gottwald, Norman K. 1959. *A Light to the Nations.* New York: Harper.

———. 1979. *The Tribes of Yahweh: A Sociology of the Religion of Liberated Israel. 1250–1050 B.C.* Maryknoll: Orbis Books.

Goulet, Denis. 1978. *The Cruel Choice.* New York: Atheneum.

Greeley, Andrew M. 1972. "Letters from Readers." *Commentary* 54 (October).

———. 1974. "Notes on a Theology of Pluralism." *Christian Century* (3 July).

Griffin, Emory A. 1976. *The Mind Changers*. Wheaton: Tyndale House.

Guillaume, Alfred. 1928. "The Influence of Judaism on Islam." *The Legacy of Israel*. Eds. Edwyn R. Bevan and Charles Singer. Oxford: Clarendon.

Guinness, Os. 1983. *The Gravedigger File*. Downers Grove: InterVarsity.

Guthrie, Donald. 1968. *New Testament Introduction: Gospel and Acts*. London: Tyndale.

Guttiérez, Gustavo. 1972. *Teologia de la Liberacion: Perspectivas*. Salamanca: Ediciones Sigueme.

Haddad, Yvonne. 1983. "The Impact of the Islamic Revival in Iran on the Syrian Muslims of Montreal." *The Muslim Community of North America*. Edmonton: University of Alberta Press.

Haight, Roger. 1985. *An Alternative Vision: An Interpretation of Liberation Theology*. New York: Paulist.

Haleblian, Krikor. 1982. *Contextualization and French Structuralism: A Method to Delineate the Deep Structure of the Gospel*. Unpublished Ph.D. Thesis. Pasadena: School of World Mission, Fuller Theological Seminary.

————. 1982. "Evaluation of Existing Models of Contextualization," in K. Haleblian, *Contextualization and French Structuralism*.

————. 1983. "The Problem of Contextualization." *Missiology* 11, no. 1 (January).

Hall, Edward T. 1959. *The Silent Language*. New York: Doubleday.

————. 1976. *Beyond Culture*. Garden City: Doubleday.

————. 1976. *Beyond Culture*. Garden City: Anchor.

Hallpike, C. R. 1969. "Social Hair." *Man* 4.

Hansen, Paul D. 1986. *The People Called: The Growth of Community in the Bible*. San Francisco: Harper and Row.

Harrison, Paul W. 1934. "The Arabs of Oman." *The Moslem World* 24.

Harrison, Roland K. 1969. *Introduction to the Old Testament*. Grand Rapids: Eerdmans.

Hasselgrave, David. 1988. *Today's Choices for Tomorrow's Mission*. Grand Rapids: Academic Books.

Hayes, John H. 1979. *An Introduction to Old Testament Study*. Nashville: Abingdon.

Heckman, Bruce. 1988. "Arab Christian Reaction to Contextualization in the Middle East." Unpublished M.A. thesis. Pasadena: School of World Mission, Fuller Theological Seminary.

Heitmuller, W. 1912. "Zum Problem Paulus und Jesus." *Zeitschrift fur die Neutestamentliche Wissenschaft* 13.

Herschfeld, Hartwig. 1902. *New Researches into the Composition and Exegesis of the Qoran*. London: Royal Asiatic Society.

Hersey, P. and K. H. Blanchard. 1977. *Management of Organizational Behavior*. Englewood Cliffs: Prentice-Hall.

Hesselgrave, David J. 1978. *Communicating Christ Cross-Culturally*. Grand Rapids: Zondervan.

————. 1979. *New Horizons in World Mission: Evangelicals and the Christian Mission in the 1980s*. Grand Rapids: Baker.

————. 1984. "Contextualization and Revelational Epistemology." Eds., Earl D. Radmacher and Robert D. Preus. *Hermeneutics, Inerrancy, and the Bible.* Grand Rapids: Zondervan.

————. 1988. *Today's Choices for Tomorrow's Mission: An Evangelical Perspective on Trends and Issues in Missions.* Grand Rapids: Zondervan.

Hesselgrave, David J., ed. 1978. *Theology and Mission.* Grand Rapids: Baker.

Hick, John and Paul Knitter, eds. 1987. *The Myth of Christian Uniqueness: Toward a Pluralistic Theology of Religions.* Maryknoll: Orbis Books.

Hiebert, Paul G. 1976. *Cultural Anthropology.* Philadelphia: Lippincott.

————. 1978. "Conversion, Culture and Cognative Categories." *Gospel in Context* 1, no. 3 (July).

————. 1978. "The Gospel and Culture." Ed. Don McCurry. *The Gospel and Islam: A 1978 Compendium.* Monrovia: MARC.

————. 1985. *Anthropological Insights for Missionaries.* Grand Rapids: Baker.

————. 1985. "Epistemological Foundations for Science and Theology." *TSF Bulletin* 8, no. 4 (March-April).

————. 1985. "The Missiological Implications of an Epistemological Shift." *TSF Bulletin* 8, no. 5 (May-June).

————. 1987. "Critical Contextualization," *International Bulletin of Missionary Research* 11, no. 3 (July).

Hofestede, Geert. 1984. "Motivation, Leadership, and Organization: Do American Theories Apply Abroad?" *Culture's Consequences — International Differences in Work Related Values,* abridged ed. Beverly Hills: Sage Publications.

Hoge, Dean R. and David A. Roozen, eds. 1979. *Understanding Church Growth and Decline.* New York: Pilgrim.

Hohensee, Donald. 1980. "Models of Contextualization." *Rundi World View and Contextualization of the Gospel.* Unpublished D. Miss. Dissertation. Pasadena: School of World Mission, Fuller Theological Seminary.

Horovitz, J. 1923. "Quran." *Der Islam* 13.

Hsu, Cho-yun. 1965. *Ancient China in Transition: An Analysis of Social Mobility, 722-222 B.C.* Stanford: University Press.

————. 1984. *History of Western Chou Dynasty.* Taipei: Lien-chin (in Chinese).

Huffard, Evertt W. 1985. *Thematic Dissonance in the Muslim-Christian Encounter: A Contextualized Theology of Honor.* Unpublished Ph.D. dissertation. Pasadena: School of World Mission, Fuller Theological Seminary.

Hunn, Gene. 1982. "Utilitarian Factor in Folk Biological Classification." *American Anthropologist* 84.

Hwang, Kwang-kuo. 1987. "Face and Favor: The Chinese Power Game." *American Journal of Sociology* 92.

Inch, Morris. 1982. *Doing Theology Across Cultures.* Grand Rapids: Baker.

Jeffery, Arthur. 1938. *The Foreign Vocabulary of the Quran.* Baroda: Oriental Institute.

Jen-ho, Tsai. 1982. "Reconsideration of Confucian Ethics." *The Unfolding of Chinese Culture,* ed. Tunghai University. Taipei: Department of Education, Taiwan Provincial Government (in Chinese).

Jeremias, Joachim. 1971. *New Testament Theology*, vol. 1. London: SCM.

Jewett, Robert. 1986. *The Thessalonian Correspondence, Pauline Rhetoric and Millenarian Piety*. Philadelphia: Fortress.

Jocz, Jakob. 1968. *The Covenant*. Grand Rapids: Eerdmans.

Johnstone, Patrick. 1986. *Operation World*. Pasadena: William Carey Library (STL Books).

Jorgensen, Knud. 1986. *The Role and Function of the Media in the Mission of the Church*. Ann Arbor: University Microfilms.

Kaldor, Peter. 1987. *Who Goes Where? Who Doesn't Care?* NSW Australia: Lancer Books.

Käsemann, Ernst. 1969. *New Testament Questions of Today*. Philadelphia: Fortress.

Kaufman, Yehezkel. 1960. *The Religion of Israel*. Trans. and abridged by Moshe Greenberg. Chicago: University of Chicago Press.

Keck, Leander. 1979. *Paul and His Letters* (Proclamation Commentaries). Philadelphia: Fortress.

Keen, Hunter. 1975. "Must Indians Love the Organ?" *Eternity* 26, no. 10 (October).

Kelsey, D. H. 1975. *The Use of Scripture in Recent Theology*. Philadelphia: Fortress.

Keyes, Lawrence E. 1983. *The Last Age of Missions: A Study of Third World Missionary Societies*. Pasadena: William Carey Library.

Khan, M. Muhsin, trans. n.d. *Sahih al-Bukhari*. 9 vols. Beirut: Dar al-Arabia.

King, Roberta. 1982. *Readings in Christian Music Communication*. Unpublished M.A. thesis. Pasadena: School of World Mission, Fuller Theological Seminary.

———. 1987. "Say It with a Song." *Impact* 44, no. 1.

Kitchen, Kenneth A. 1968. *Ancient Orient and Old Testament*. Chicago: InterVarsity.

Kittel, Gerhard and Gerhard Friedrich, eds. 1985. *Theological Dictionary of the New Testament*. Trans. and abridged by Geoffrey Bromiley, vols. 2, 3, 4. Grand Rapids: Eerdmans.

Klem, Herbert V. 1982. *Oral Communication of the Scripture: Insights from African Oral Art*. Pasadena: William Carey Library.

Knight, Douglas A., ed. 1977. *Tradition and Theology in the Old Testament*. Philadelphia: Fortress.

Knitter, Paul F. 1986. *No Other Name?* Maryknoll: Orbis Books.

Koch, Klaus. 1972. "The Rediscovery of the Apocalyptic." *Studies in Biblical Theology*. London: SCM Press.

Kraft, Charles H. 1973. "Dynamic Equivalence Churches." *Missiology* 1, no. 1 (January).

———. 1979. *Christianity in Culture: A Study in Dynamic Biblical Theologizing in Cross-Cultural Perspective*. Maryknoll: Orbis Books.

———. 1979. *Communicating the Gospel God's Way*. Pasadena: William Carey Library.

———. 1983. *Communication Theory for Christian Witness*. Nashville: Abingdon.

————. 1989. *Christianity with Power*. Ann Arbor: Vine (Servant Publications).

Kraft, Charles and Tom Wisely, eds. 1979. *Readings in Dynamic Indigeneity*. Pasadena: William Carey Library.

Larson, Mildred. 1969. "Making Explicit Information Implicit in Translation." *Notes on Translation* 33.

————. 1984. *Meaning-Based Translation: A Guide to Cross-Language Equivalence*. Lanham: University of America Press.

Lau, Sin-kai. 1981. "Utilitarianistic Familism; The Basis of Political Stability." Eds. Ambrose Y. C. King and Rance P. L. Lee. *Social Life and Development in Hong Kong*. Hong Kong: The Chinese University Press.

Laudan, Larry. 1977. *Progress and Its Problems: Towards a Theory of Scientific Growth*. Berkeley: University of California Press.

Lausanne Occasional Papers No. 23. 1980. Thailand Report—*Christian Witness to Nominal Christians Among Protestant Christians*.

Lazarus-Yafeh, Hava. 1981. *Some Religious Aspects of Islam*. Leiden: E. J. Brill.

Lenning, Larry G. 1980. *Blessing in Mosque and Mission*. Pasadena: William Carey Library.

Leplin, Jarrett, ed. 1984. *Scientific Realism*. Berkeley: University of California Press.

Levi-Strauss, Claude. 1969. *The Raw and the Cooked*. New York: Harper and Row.

Levy-Bruhl, Lucien. 1926. *How Natives Think*. London: Allen and Unwin.

Li, Cheng-chih. 1986. "Popular Chinese Moral Thinking–An Exploration." *Appendix* to Cheng, Chih-ming. *Chinese Society and Religion*. Taipei: Student Press (in Chinese).

Lind, Millard. 1982. "Refocusing Theological Education to Mission: The Old Testament and Contextualization." *Missiology* 10, no. 2 (April).

Loewen, Jacob. 1975. *Culture and Human Values*. Pasadena: William Carey Library.

————. 1986. "Which God Do Missionaries Preach?" *Missiology* 14, no. 1 (January).

Luzbetak, Louis. 1963. *The Church and Cultures*. (Reprinted 1975) Pasadena: William Carey Library.

————. 1981. "Signs of Progress in Contextual Methodology." *Verbum* 22.

Maccoby, M. 1978. *The Gamesman*. New York: Bantam Books.

MacDonald, Margaret Y. 1988. *The Pauline Churches*. Cambridge: Cambridge University Press.

Madsen, Richard. 1984. *Morality and Power in a Chinese Village*. Berkeley: University of California Press. *Chen Village study*.

Madsen, William. 1957. *Christo-Paganism: A Study of Mexican Religious Syncretism*. New Orleans: Middle American Research Institute.

Mair, Victor H. 1985. "Language and Ideology in the Written Popularization of the *Sacred Edict*." Eds. Nathan Andrew Johnson and E. Rawski. *Popular Culture in Late Imperial China*. Berkeley: University of California Press.

Malek, Sobhi W. 1986. "Allah-u Akbar Bible Lessons: Aspects of Their Effectiveness in Evangelizing Muslims." Unpublished D.Miss. dissertation. Pasadena: School of World Mission, Fuller Theological Seminary.

Martin, David A. 1965. "Towards Eliminating the Concept of Secularization." Ed. Julius Gould, *Penguin Survey of the Social Sciences*. London: Penguin Books Ltd.

Martin, Ralph P. 1977. "Approaches to New Testament Exegesis." Ed. Howard Marshall. *New Testament Interpretation*. Exeter: Paternoster Press.

———. 1981. *Reconciliation: A Study of Paul's Theology*. Atlanta: John Knox Press.

Marty, Martin E. 1984. *Pilgrims in Their Own Land*. Boston: Little, Brown and Co.

Maslow, Abraham. 1970. *Motivation and Personality*. 2d. ed. New York: Harper and Row.

Massignon, Louis. 1968. *Essai sur les origines du lexique technique de la mystique musulmane*. Paris: Vrin.

Masson, D. 1958. *Le Coran et la revelation judeo-chretienne*. Paris: Adrien-Maisonneuve.

Mauss, Marcel. 1925. "Essai sur le Don, Forme Archaique de l'Echange." *L'Annee Sociologique*. Trans. Ian Cunnison. *The Gift*. London: Cohen and West (1954).

Mayers, Marvin K. 1987. *Christianity Confronts Culture*. Rev. ed. Grand Rapids: Academic Books.

Mays, James Luther. 1969. *Hosea, A Commentary*. Philadelphia: Westminster.

———. 1969. *Amos, A Commentary*. Philadelphia: Westminster.

McCurry, Don M. 1976. "Cross-Cultural Models of Muslim Evangelism." *Missiology* 4, no. 3 (July).

McCurry, Don M., ed. 1978. *The Gospel and Islam: A 1978 Compendium*. Monrovia: MARC.

McGavran, Donald A. 1980. *Understanding Church Growth*. Rev. ed. Grand Rapids: Eerdmans.

McGregor, Douglas. 1960. *The Human Side of Enterprise*. New York: McGraw-Hill.

McLuhan, Marshall. 1964. *Understanding Media: The Extensions of Man*. New York: McGraw-Hill.

Meeks, Wayne A. 1983. *The First Urban Christians: The Social World of the Apostle Paul*. New Haven: Yale University Press.

Mez, Adam. 1937. *The Renaissance of Islam*. Trans. S. Khuda Bakhsh and D. S. Margoliouth. London: Luzac.

Miguez Bonino, José. 1975. *Doing Theology in a Revolutionary Situation*. Philadelphia, Fortress.

Miller, Jay. 1982. "Matters of the (Thoughtful) Heart: Focality or Overlap." *Journal of Anthropological Research* 38.

Mitchell, B. R. and Phyllis Deans. 1971. *Abstract of British Historical Statistics*. Cambridge: Cambridge University Press.

Mittwoch, Eugen. 1913. *Zur Entstehungsgeschichte des islamischen Gebets und Kultus* in *Abhandlungen der koeniglich preussischen*. Berlin: Koeniglich Akademie der Wissenschaften.

Moore, George Foot. 1950. *Judaism in the First Centuries of the Christian Era.* Cambridge: Harvard University Press.

Morris, Leon. 1979. "First Epistle to the Corinthians." *ISBE*, vol. 1. Ed. G. W. Bromiley. Grand Rapids: Eerdmans.

Moubarac, Y. 1957. "Les etudes d'epigraphie sud-semitique et la naissance de l'Islam." *Revue des Etudes Islamique 25.*

Muggeridge, Malcolm. 1977. *Christ and the Media.* Grand Rapids: Eerdmans.

Muslim b. al-Hajja, *Sahih Muslim.* Trans. Abdul Hamid Saddiqi. Lahore: Ashraf, n.d.

Nasr, Seyyed Hossein, ed. 1987. *Islamic Spirituality.* New York: Crossroad.

Nazir-Ali, Michael. 1987. *Frontiers in Muslim-Christian Encounter.* Oxford: Regnum Books.

Neill, Stephen. 1964. *A History of Christian Missions.* New York: Penguin.

Netland, Harold. 1988. "Toward Contextualized Apologetics." *Missiology 16*, no. 3 (July).

Neufeld, Vernon H. 1963. *The Earliest Christian Confessions.* Grand Rapids: Eerdmans.

Neusner, Jacob, trans. 1984. *The Talmud of Babylonia, I: Tractate Barkhot.* Chico: Scholars Press.

New International Version Study Bible. 1985. Grand Rapids: Zondervan.

New Testament Commentary. 1954. vol. 2. Grand Rapids: Baker.

Newbigin, Lesslie. 1986. *Foolishness to the Greeks: The Gospel and Western Culture.* Grand Rapids: Eerdmans.

Nida, Eugene A. 1954. *Customs and Cultures.* Pasadena: William Carey Library.

———. 1960. *Message and Mission.* New York: Harper and Row (reprinted 1972, William Carey Library).

———. 1975. *Componential Analysis of Meaning: Approaches to Semantics.* The Hague: Mouton.

Nida, Eugene A. and Charles R. Taber. 1969. *The Theory and Practice of Bible Translation.* Leiden: Brill.

Nida, Eugene A. and William D. Reyburn. 1981. *Meaning Across Cultures: A Study on Bible Translating.* Maryknoll: Orbis.

Niebuhr, H. Richard. 1951. *Christ and Culture.* New York: Harper.

Noble, Lowell. 1987. *Socio-Theology.* Michigan: self-published.

Noeldeke, Theodor. 1909. *Geschichte des Qorans.* Hildesheim: Georg Olms Verlagsbuchhandlung, 1961; photocopy of 2nd ed. of 1909.

Noth, Martin. 1985. *The History of Israel.* Trans. Stanley Godman. New York: Harper and Row.

Oesterly, W. O. E., and G. H. Box. 1907. *The Religion and Worship of the Synagogue.* London: Pitman and Sons.

Owen, David. 1988. "A Classification System for Styles of Arabic Bible Translations." *Seedbed* 3, no. 1.

Oxford Dictionary of the Christian Church. 1974. 2d. ed. London: Oxford University Press.

Padilla, C. René. 1976. *The New Face of Evangelicalism.* Downers Grove: InterVarsity.

———. 1983. "Biblical Foundations: A Latin American Study." *Evangelical Review of Theology* 7, no. 1 (April).

———. 1985. *Mission Between the Times.* Grand Rapids: Eerdmans.

Padilla, René and Mark Lau Branson. 1986. *Conflict and Context: Hermeneutics in the Americas.* Grand Rapids: Eerdmans.

Padwick, Constance E. 1957. "The Language of Muslim Devotion." *The Muslim World* 47.

———. 1961. *Muslim Devotions: A Study of Prayer Manuals in Common Use.* London: SPCK.

Parshall, Phil. 1980. *New Paths in Muslim Evangelism.* Grand Rapids: Baker.

———. 1985. *Beyond the Mosque.* Grand Rapids: Baker.

Pelikan, J. 1971. *The Christian Tradition.* vol. 1. Chicago: University of Chicago Press.

Phillips, J. B. 1954. *Plain Christianity.* London: Epworth.

———. 1954. *When God Was Man.* London: Lutterworth.

———. 1960. *God Our Contemporary.* London: Hodder and Stoughton.

———. 1972. *The New Testament in Modern English* Rev. ed. New York: Macmillan.

Pike, Eunice and Florence Cowan. 1959. "Mushroom Ritual Versus Christianity." *Practical Anthropology* 6. Reprinted in Smalley, 1974.

Pike, Kenneth. 1967. *Language in Relation to a Unified Theory of the Structure of Human Behavior.* The Hague: Mouton.

Rabin, Chaim. 1957. *Quran Studies.* London: Oxford University Press.

Radmacher, Earl D. and Robert D. Preus. 1984. *Hermeneutics, Inerrancy, and the Bible.* Grand Rapids: Zondervan.

Reid, Gavin. 1969. *The Gagging of God.* London: Hodder and Stoughton.

Reist, Benjamin A. 1975. *Theology in Red, White, and Black.* Philadelphia: Westminster.

Reyburn, William D. 1960. "Identification in the Missionary Task." *Practical Anthropology* 7. Reprinted in Smalley 1978.

Richards, Donald R. 1988. "A Great Missiological Error of Our Time: Keeping the Fast of Ramadan—Why We Shouldn't." *Seedbed* 3.

Richardson, Alan. 1961. *The Bible in the Age of Science.* London: SCM Press.

Richardson, Don. 1974. *Peace Child.* Glendale: Regal.

———. 1981. *Eternity in Their Hearts.* Ventura: Regal/Gospel Light.

Ridderbos, Herman. 1958. *Paul and Jesus.* Grand Rapids: Baker.

Rischer, S. 1973. *Zur Dialektik von Religion und Gesellschaft,* German ed. of *Social Reality.* S. Fischer: Verlag.

Ro, Bong Rin and Ruth Eshenaur, eds. 1984. *The Bible and Theology in Asian Contexts.* Taiwan: ATA.

Robertson, Roland. 1969. *The Social Interpretation of Religion.* London: Blackwell.

Robinson, Wheeler. 1980. *Corporate Personality in Ancient Israel.* Philadelphia: Fortress.

Rosenthal, Franz, trans. 1958. *The Muqaddimah.* 3 vols. New York: Pantheon.

Rossi, Ino. 1983. *From the Sociology of Symbols to the Sociology of Signs.* New York: Columbia University Press.

Roth, Wolfgang and Rosemary Reuther. 1978. *The Liberating Bond.* New York: Friendship.

Ryan, Dawn. 1969. "Christianity, Cargo Cults, and Politics Among the Toaripi of Papua." *Oceania* 40.

Saddiqi, Ata'ullah, "Islam and Missions: Mohammed or Christ?" *Arabia: Islamic World Review* 6, no. 71 (July 1987).

Sanders, E. P. 1977. *Paul and Palestinian Judaism.* Philadelphia: Fortress.

Sano, Roy I. 1975. "Ethnic Liberation Theology: Neo-Orthodoxy Reshaped—or Replaced?" *Christianity and Crisis.* 10 (November).

Santa Ana, Julio. 1979. *Good News to the Poor: The Challenge of the Poor in the History of the Church.* Grand Rapids: Eerdmans.

Sapir, Edward. 1949. *Selected Writings of Edward Sapir in Language, Culture and Personality.* Berkeley: University of California Press.

Schaff, P. 1974. *Nicene and Post-Nicene Fathers.* vol. 1. Grand Rapids: Eerdmans.

Scherer, James. 1987. *Gospel, Church and Kingdom: Comparative Studies in World Mission Theology.* Minneapolis: Augsburg.

Schlette, Heinz Robert. 1966. *Towards a Theology of Religions.* New York: Herder and Herder.

Schlorff, Samuel P. 1984. "The Missionary Use of the Quran: An Historical and Theological Study of the Contextualization of the Gospel." Unpublished Th.M. thesis. Philadelphia: Westminster Theological Seminary.

———. 1988. "Feedback on Project Sunrise (Sira): A Look at 'Dynamic Equivalence' in an Islamic Context." *Seedbed* 3, no. 2.

Schreiter, Robert J. 1985. *Constructing Local Theologies.* Maryknoll: Orbis.

Schreiter, Robert J., ed. 1987. *Edward Schillebeeckx: The Schillebeeckx Reader.* New York: Crossroad.

Schwab, Moses, trans. 1886. *The Talmud of Jerusalem.* London: Williams and Norgate.

Schwartz, Bengamin I. 1985. *The World of Thought in Ancient China.* Cambridge: Belknap Press.

Schweitzer, Albert. 1931. *The Mysticism of Paul.* New York: H. Holt and Co.

Segundo, Juan Luis. 1976. *The Liberation of Theology.* Maryknoll: Orbis.

Senior, Donald and Carroll Stuhlmueller. 1983. *The Biblical Foundations of Mission.* Maryknoll: Orbis.

Shaw, R. Daniel. 1972. "The Structure of Myth and Bible Translation." *Practical Anthropology* 19.

———. 1987. "The Translation Context." *Translation Review* 23: Special Theory Issue.

———. 1988. *Transculturation: The Cultural Factor in Translation and Other Communication Tasks.* Pasadena: William Carey Library.

Sheares, Reuben A., II. 1970. "Beyond White Theology." *Christianity and Crisis* 30 (2 and 16 November).

Shockley, Donald G. 1975. *Free, White, and Christian.* Nashville: Abingdon.

Siddiqi, Ata'ullah. 1987. "Islam and Missions: Mohammed or Christ?" *Arabia: Islamic World Review* 6 (July).

Sirat al-Masih bi-Lisan Arabi Fasih. 1987. Larnaca, Cyprus: Izdihar Ltd.

Skorupski, John. 1976. *Symbol and Theory: A Philosophical Study of Theories of Religion in Social Anthropology.* Cambridge: Cambridge University Press.

Smalley, William A., ed. 1974. *Readings in Missionary Anthropology.* Pasadena: William Carey Library.

———. 1978. *Readings in Missionary Anthropology II.* Pasadena: William Carey Library.

Smith, Wilfred Cantwell. 1965. *The Faith of Other Men.* New York: New American.

Sogaard, Viggo B. 1975. *Everything You Need to Know for a Cassette Ministry.* Minneapolis: Bethany Fellowship.

———. 1986. *Applying Christian Communication.* Ann Arbor: University Microfilms.

———. 1988. *Audio Scriptures.* New York: United Bible Societies.

Speight, Marston. 1980. "Muslim and Christian Prayer." *Newsletter of the Task Force on Muslim Christian Relations* (Hartford, Conn.: National Council of Churches and Duncan Black Macdonald Center). no. 12 (March).

Sperber, Dan and Dierdre Wilson. 1986. *Relevance: Communication and Cognition.* Cambridge: Harvard University Press.

Spindler, Marc A. 1987. Comments on "Visa for Witness: A New Focus on the Theology of Mission and Ecumenism," Section 6. "Witness under Cross-Examination." *Mission Studies* 4-2.

Stacey, Judith. 1983. *Patriarchy and Socialist, Revolution in China.* Berkeley: University of California Press.

Stahl, Harvie, ed. 1985. *Mt. Sinai Arabic Codex 151.* 2 vols. Leuven: Peepers.

Stark, Rodney, and William Sims Bainbridge. 1985. *The Future of Religion: Secularization and Renewal and Cult Formation.* Rev. ed. Berkeley: University of California Press.

Stendahl, Kristor. 1976. *Paul Among Jews and Gentiles.* Philadelphia: Fortress.

Stocking, G. W., Jr. 1982. "Afterword: A View From the Center." *Ethnos* 47.

Stott, John R. W. and Robert T. Coote, eds. 1979. *Gospel and Culture.* Lausanne Committee on Theology and Education. Pasadena: William Carey Library.

Strong, Augustus H. 1907. *Systematic Theology: A Compendium.* London: Pickering and Inglis.

Sun, Lung-chi. 1983. *The Deep Structure of Chinese Culture.* Hong Kong: Yi-Shan Press (in Chinese).

Sundkler, Bengt. 1965. *The World of Mission.* Grand Rapids: Eerdmans.

Taber, Charles. 1978. "Is There More than One Way to Do Theology?" *Gospel in Context* 1, no. 1 (January).

————. 1979. "The Limits of Indigenization in Theology," in Charles Kraft and Tom Wisely, *Readings in Dynamic Indigeneity*. Pasadena: William Carey Library.

Tang, Chun-yi. 1979. *The Spiritual Value of Chinese Culture*. Rev. ed. Taipei: Cheng Chung (in Chinese).

Taylor, John V. 1963. *The Primal Vision: Christian Experience and African Religion*. London: SCM.

————. 1974. "Cultural Ecumenism." *Church Missionary Society Newsletter* (November).

Thannickal, John. 1975. *Ashram: A Communicating Community*. Ann Arbor: University Microfilms.

The Pillars of Religion in the Light of the Tawrat, Zabur and Injil 1984. Beirut: The Bible Society.

The Torah, A New Translation of the Holy Scriptures. 1902. Philadelphia: Jewish Publication Society.

Theissen, Gerd. 1982. *The Social Setting of Pauline Christianity*. Philadelphia: Fortress.

Tienou, Tite. 1983. "Biblical Foundations: An African Study." *Evangelical Review of Theology*. 7, no. 1 (April).

Time. 1987. "Whatever Happened to Ethics?" (May 23).

Times, The 1988. London (Saturday, November 19).

Torrey, Charles. 1933. *The Jewish Foundation of Islam*. New York: Jewish Institute of Religion Press.

Tracy, David. 1979. *Blessed Rage for Order*. New York: Seabury.

Trimingham, J. Spencer. 1979. *Christianity Among the Arabs in Pre-Islamic Times*. London: Longman.

Troeltsch, Ernst. 1931. *The Social Teaching of the Christian Churches*. Trans. Olive Wyon. New York: Macmillan.

Trotter, Lilias. 1926. *The Way of the Sevenfold Secret*. Cairo: Nile Mission Press.

United Presbyterian Church in the U.S.A. 1966, 1967. *The Book of Confessions*. Philadelphia: General Assembly of the United Presbyterian Church in the U.S.A.

U.S. Center for World Mission. 1985. *Unreached Peoples of the World 1985* Pasadena: U. S. Center for World Mission.

Van Engen, Charles. 1981. *The Growth of the True Church*. Amsterdam: Rodopi.

————. 1985. *Hijos del Pacto: Perdon, Conversion y Mision en el Bautismo*. Grand Rapids: TELL.

van Ruler, A. A. 1971. *The Christian Church and the Old Testament*. Grand Rapids: Eerdmans.

Verkuyl, J. 1986. "Contra de Twee Kernthesen van Knitter's Theologia Religionum." *Wereld en Zending*.

Vielhaur, Phillip. 1963–65. "Introduction to Apocalypses and Related Subjects." *New Testament Apocrypha*. 2 vols. Ed. W. Schneemelcher. Philadelphia: Westminster.

Visser T'Hooft, W. A. 1963. *No Other Name.* London: SCM.

von Allman, D. 1975. "The Birth of Theology." *International Review of Missions.* 64, no. 253 (January 25).

von Rad, Gerhard. 1962. *Old Testament Theology.* vol. 1. New York: Harper and Row.

———. 1972. *Wisdom in Israel.* Nashville: Abingdon.

Vos, Geerhardus. 1948. *Biblical Theology: Old and New Testaments.* Grand Rapids: Eerdmans.

Wagner, C. Peter. 1984. *Leading Your Church to Growth.* Ventura: Regal.

———. 1985. *Our Kind of People.* Atlanta: John Knox.

———. 1986. "A Vision for Evangelizing the Real America." *International Bulletin of Missionary Research* 10, no. 2 (April).

———. 1988. *How to Have a Healing Ministry Without Making Your Church Sick.* Ventura: Regal.

Wahlstrom, Eric. 1940. *The New Life in Christ.* Philadelphia: Muhlenberg.

Waleyu, Arthur, trans. 1938. *The Analects of Confucius.* London: Allen and Unwin.

Walls, Andrew. "The Gospel as the Prisoner and Liberator of Culture." *Faith and Thought* 108; no. 102.

Walter, Nikolaus. 1979. "Christusglaube und Heidnische Religiositat in Paulinishen Gemeinden." *New Testament Studies* 25.

Ward, Ted. 1979. "The Church and Development," a series of lectures given July 1979 at Daystar University College, Nairobi.

Washington, Joseph R., Jr. 1964. *Black Religion: The Negro and Christianity in the United States.* Boston: Beacon.

———. 1969. *Black and White Power Subreption.* Boston: Beacon.

Watt, W. Montgomery. 1953. *The Faith and Practice of al-Ghazali.* London: Allen and Unwin.

———. 1956. *Muhammad at Medina.* Oxford: Clarendon.

Webber, Robert E. 1980. *God Still Speaks: A Biblical View of Christian Communication.* Nashville: Nelson.

Weber, Hans-Rudi. 1957. *The Communication of the Gospel to Illiterates.* London: SCM Press.

Webster's Ninth New Collegiate Dictionary. 1984. Springfield: Merriam-Webster, Inc.

Wei, Cheng-tung. 1974. *A History of Chinese Thought.* 2 vols. Taipei: Ta Lim Press (in Chinese).

Wensinck, A. J. 1932. *The Muslim Creed.* Cambridge: Cambridge University Press.

———. 1960. *A Handbook of Early Muhammadan Tradition.* Leiden: E. J. Brill.

Westermann, Claus, ed. 1960. *Essays on Old Testament Hermeneutics.* Richmond: John Knox.

Whiteley, Denys H. 1964. *The Theology of St. Paul.* Philadelphia: Fortress.

Whorf, Benjamin. 1956. *Language, Thought, and Reality.* New York: John Wiley and Sons.

Wickham, E. R. 1957. *Church and People in an Industrial City*. London: Lutterworth.

Wilder, John. 1977. "Some Reflections on Possibilities for People Movements Among Muslims." *Missiology* 5.

Williams, Donald. 1989. *Signs, Wonders and the Kingdom of God*. Ann Arbor: Vine (Servant Publications).

Willis, Wendell, ed. 1987. *The Kingdom of God in 20th-Century Interpretation*. Peabody: Hendrickson.

Wilson, Bruce. 1983. *Can God Survive in Australia?* Southerland, NSW: Albatross Press.

Wimber, John. 1986. *Power Evangelism*. New York: Harper and Row.

———. 1987. *Power Healing*. New York: Harper and Row.

Wolff, Hans Walter. 1981. *Anthropology of the New Testament*. Philadelphia: Fortress.

Wonderly, William L. 1958. "Pagan and Indian Concepts in a Mexican Indian Culture." *Practical Anthropology* 5. Reprinted in Smalley, 1974.

Woodberry, J. Dudley, ed. 1989. *Muslims and Christians on the Emmaus Road*. Monrovia: MARC.

Wright, Cliff. n.d. *Melanesian Culture and Christian Faith*. Honiara, Solomon Is: The Association.

Wright, G. Ernest. 1968. *The Old Testament Against Its Environment*. London: SCM Press.

Yamamori, Tetsunao and Charles R. Taber, eds. 1975. *Christopaganism or Indigenous Christianity?* Pasadena: William Carey Library.

Yang, Kuo-shu. 1981. "Social Orientation and Individual Modernity Among Chinese Students in Taiwan." *Journal of Social Psychology* 113.

Yang, Yun-yuan. 1982. "Sixth Human Relation, or Kung, Shu and Contemporary Spirit." *The Unfolding of Chinese Culture*. vol. 4. Ed. Tunghai University. Taipei: Department of Education (in Chinese).

Yu, Ying-shih. 1984. "Anti-Intellectualism and Chinese Political Tradition." *History and Thought*. Taipei: Lien-chin (in Chinese).

———. 1987. "Chinese Value Seen From the Perspective of Value System." *A Contemporary Interpretation of Traditional Chinese Thinking*. Taipei: Lien-chin (in Chinese).

Zimmerman, Frank, trans. and ed. 1958. *The Book of Tobit*. New York: Harper and Bros.

Zwemer, Samuel M. 1939. *Studies in Popular Islam*. London: Sheldon Press.

Index